Thomas Hobbes of Malmesbury

LEVIATHAN

1651

LEVIATHAN OR THE
MATTER,
FORM, AND POWER OF
A COMMONWEALTH
ECCLESIASTICAL AND
CIVIL

HOBBES

The
Essential
LEVIATHAN

A Modernized Edition

Edited, with Introduction and Notes, by

Nancy A. Stanlick

with Daniel P. Collette, Associate Editor

Hackett Publishing Company, Inc.
Indianapolis/Cambridge

Copyright © 2016 by Hackett Publishing Company, Inc.

19 18 17 16   1 2 3 4 5 6 7

For further information, please address
   Hackett Publishing Company, Inc.
   P.O. Box 44937
   Indianapolis, Indiana 46244-0937

   www.hackettpublishing.com

Cover design by Deborah Wilkes
Composition by Aptara, Inc.

Library of Congress Cataloging-in-Publication Data is on file with the LOC.
ISBN-13: 978-1-62466-520-2 (pbk.)
ISBN-13: 978-1-62466-521-9 (cl.)

Dedication

To the memory of my mother and father,
with gratitude and honor,
with love and respect. —NS

For JDC, forever my brother, my hero, my friend. —DC

About the Editors

Nancy A. Stanlick is professor of philosophy and assistant dean in the College of Arts and Humanities at the University of Central Florida in Orlando, Florida. She received her Ph.D. in philosophy from the University of South Florida in 1995 and is the author of articles on Thomas Hobbes, ethics, and social philosophy; coauthor with Bruce Silver of *Philosophy in America: Volumes I and II* (Prentice Hall, 2004); coauthor with Michael Strawser of *Asking Good Questions: Case Studies in Ethics and Critical Thinking* (Hackett, 2015); and author of *American Philosophy: The Basics* (Routledge, 2012).

Daniel P. Collette received the Ph.D. in philosophy from the University of South Florida in 2016. His primary research interests include early modern philosophy (especially Descartes, Pascal, and Hobbes), ethics, and the philosophy of religion. He defended his dissertation, "Stoicism in Descartes, Pascal, and Spinoza: Examining Neostoicism's Influence in the Seventeenth Century," in March 2016.

CONTENTS

PART III: OF A CHRISTIAN COMMONWEALTH

PART IV: OF THE KINGDOM OF DARKNESS

PREFACE

This edition of Thomas Hobbes' *Leviathan* is intended to update Hobbes' style and language from early modern English to more contemporary twenty-first-century English and to clarify some important elements of the work that are problematic to beginning and casual readers of Hobbes. In fact, updating the style and language is one of the ways in which it may be possible to make Hobbes' most famous work more accessible both inside and outside the academy. In an article in the *Chronicle of Higher Education*, Carlin Romano noted that one sure way to shut down interest in classic works of literature or philosophy is to give students of today original works written in complicated prose that have little or no apparent reference or application to their lives.[1] Referring to the crisis in the humanities usually understood as "decline of institutional support for their disciplines" and "shunning of their majors," Romano writes that it may be that "the real crisis lies in ossified canons and syllabi that ignore globalization and the engagement with everyday life expected by today's undergraduate. Force her to read Chaucer, or sentence her to *gobs of Hobbes and his archaic diction*, and you've got a pretty good recipe for self-inflicted extinction."[2] While I started "translating" Hobbes from early modern English to contemporary English long before Romano's piece in the *Chronicle*, I am heartened by the publication of this sentiment that I have felt for a long time when teaching, and especially when teaching works such as those of Hobbes, David Hume, Baruch Spinoza, and Immanuel Kant, whose sentences sometimes seem never-ending; whose prose, while stylish and beautiful in its own way, is daunting for many readers, especially those wishing to introduce themselves to classic works of philosophy; and whose ideas are, for the contemporary reader—and I suspect for many of their own contemporaries—often obscured.

In this edition of *Leviathan*, therefore, Daniel Collette and I have, where practical and useful, shortened sentences or broken down very long, complicated sentences into two or more. In most editions of *Leviathan*, Hobbes' original paragraph title or marginal notes precede the main text or appear in the margins. For this edition, these marginal notes have been removed or, where retaining them is useful to clarify a section, they have become part of the paragraph to which they apply. I have also rearranged the presentation of ideas and terms in individual sentences, updated much of the punctuation and grammar, and did so with the intent to retain the meaning and as much of the flavor of Hobbes' style and work as possible. Perhaps some will claim that the beauty of Hobbes' language has been lost in this edition, and this I humbly admit. While I appreciate Hobbes' diction and style, I also appreciate the difficulties that many students and general readers have with the original

---

1. Carlin Romano, "The Toxic History of Philosophy's Racism," *Chronicle of Higher Education*, September 8, 2014, http://chronicle.com/article/The-Toxic-History-of/148603.
2. Ibid., emphasis added.

text, and my respect for the work of Hobbes is expressed in my desire to make this edition of *Leviathan* more accessible and pleasant to read.

To achieve the goals of accessibility and readability in this version of Hobbes' *Leviathan*, I have used two editions of the work. One is the Pelican edition of 1911[3] and the other is the standard Molesworth edition of 1839.[4] Hobbes wrote the first version of *Leviathan* in English, translating it himself into Latin only later. In using the Pelican and Molesworth editions, we have compared content and style, cross-checking editions for accuracy and completeness in and for this edition. Further, I have often consulted other editions of *Leviathan*, such as that of Edwin Curley;[5] the Norton Critical Edition edited by Richard Flathman and David Johnston;[6] and Michael Oakeshott's edition[7] among others.

It is important also to note that I have treated this edition as a "translation" as well as an edited version of *Leviathan*. Because of this, I have occasionally substituted equivalent words or phrases where it seemed useful or advantageous to do so. Further, and in order to retain with as much facility as possible the easy readability of the text, I have occasionally placed such changes in square brackets, but in most cases have simply made the changes. However, where sections of a significant size have been removed (more than one sentence in most cases, and always when an entire paragraph has been omitted), I have placed ellipses to indicate it. Even though I have tried to update the language to make it more accessible, I am hopeful that Hobbes' important, nuanced, and difficult arguments have not lost their strength and implications through that attempt.

I am indebted to many people who made this work possible. I am most appreciative of the time given to me to undertake research and writing for this edition of *Leviathan* by José B. Fernández, dean of the College of Arts and Humanities at the University of Central Florida. Finding time in a faculty administrator's schedule for research and writing is difficult. He made all the difference in providing me with research time every week to ensure that it would be finished. On the homestretch in producing this edition, Mr. Daniel Collette, an advanced graduate student in the Department of Philosophy at the University of South Florida who has since defended his dissertation and been granted the Ph.D., agreed to take on the task of proofreading and making suggestions for additions and deletions as well as providing his expertise on Hobbes' views about religion. After beginning to work with Mr. Collette, I asked him to share in the work of this book as associate editor. He has contributed significant commentary on Parts I and II of *Leviathan*

---

3. Thomas Hobbes, *Leviathan, or, The matter, forme, and power of a common wealth, eccleasiasticall and civil* (Green Dragon at the St. Paul's Church-yard, 1651), reprinted in The Pelican classics series, ed. C. B. Macpherson (New York: Penguin, 1968).

4. Thomas Hobbes, *Leviathan. The English Works of Thomas Hobbes, Vol. III*, ed. William Molesworth (London: John Bohn, 1839–1845).

5. Thomas Hobbes, *Leviathan: With Selected Variants from the Latin Edition of 1668*, ed. Edwin Curley (Indianapolis, IN: Hackett, 1994).

6. Thomas Hobbes, *Leviathan*, ed. Richard E. Flathman and David Johnston (New York: W. W. Norton, 1997).

7. Thomas Hobbes, *Leviathan*, ed. Michael Oakeshott (London: Basil Blackwell, 1950).

and substantial content in the online companion site to this edition of *Leviathan* concerning Parts III and IV. My confidence in his abilities and the fact that he shares with me an uncommon respect for the work of Hobbes make me very proud to work with him.

Thanks go also to the anonymous reader(s) of the text.

Finally, to my family, who makes everything I do and everything I am matter, I say "thank you" for always believing in me. We are an impressive "little commonwealth."

Nancy Stanlick
Orlando, Florida
December 2015

EDITORS' INTRODUCTION

In this edition of *Leviathan*, Parts I and II are presented largely in their entirety. Parts III and IV, however, appear in significantly truncated form while retaining some significant sections applying clearly to the moral, social, and political content that appears in Parts I and II. There are two reasons for this. First, there are limitations on the density of text and information that can be presented in a quarter- or semester-based college or university course, and including the entirety of Parts III and IV would have made this edition less useful for that purpose. Second, our intention is to provide a "translation" or "modernization" of Hobbes' *Leviathan* with notes and commentary that will serve to guide students and the general reader through Hobbes' moral, social, and political thought in a more easily readable manner than that in which it is usually published. Accompanying this "translation" of *Leviathan* are some clarifying footnotes, which are kept to the barest minimum in the main text in the interest of readability and to address some of the historical and theoretical implications and associations of Hobbes' philosophy. The intent of this edition is not in any way to "dumb down" Hobbes' work. Far from it. The intention is to provide a more accessible edition that will, we hope, serve as sufficient introduction to Hobbes' work, encouraging readers to proceed further with Hobbes' other writings and Hobbes scholarship. For those who wish to proceed further with Hobbes' original work from this edition's edited content of *Leviathan*, Edwin Curley's edition,[8] including all of Parts III and IV, is an excellent choice.

Introductory Background

Thomas Hobbes was born in Malmesbury, England, in April of 1588. He died in December of 1679, reaching the ripe old age (and an exceptionally old age for his era) of ninety-one. He was acquainted with or established friendships with philosophers and scientists in England and on the Continent, including John Locke, René Descartes, Marin Mersenne, and others; he was employed by British royalty and tutored their children. He was educated at Oxford University, where, after publication of his *Leviathan*, many people detested his work because they thought it atheistic, and some took the opportunity to burn the books he authored. For all this, however, there was no erasing or silencing Hobbes, either in his own time or throughout history to the present. Hobbes' *Leviathan* is an enduring classic and one of the most beautifully crafted works in the history of philosophy.

Hobbes was reviled by some in his own time, and in our own time it is often people who have only nodding acquaintance with his work who claim that it contains a pessimistic account of human nature and a detestable justification for

---

8. Thomas Hobbes, *Leviathan: With Selected Variants from the Latin Edition of 1668*, ed. Edwin Curley (Indianapolis, IN: Hackett, 1994).

absolute government. It is true that there are ways in which to justify the claim that his account of human nature is something less than laudatory—and it is no less true that he did argue for absolute government largely on the basis of his convictions regarding human nature and the ability of rhetorical devices to lead people to act against peace and security. On the basis of this, it is often the case that readers will dismiss his work. Some of our contemporaries and some of his own accuse Hobbes of atheism, dismissing his work out of hand because of that. A contemporary of Hobbes, Bishop Bramhall, with whom Hobbes debated on several issues, claimed that Hobbes' "principles are pernicious both to piety and policy, and destructive to all relations of mankind, between prince and subject, father and child, master and servant, husband and wife; and . . . they who maintain them obstinately, are fitter to live in hollow trees among wild beasts than in any Christian political society."[9] However, Hobbes' work had and continues to have significant influence in philosophy and political science, and his words are often to this day heard in commentaries in the news media when reporters or political pundits use the phrase—made famous by Hobbes in *Leviathan*—regarding the life of man being "solitary, poor, nasty, brutish, and short."

For all the bad press Hobbes has received, his work endures—and for good reason. It is the first systematic statement of modern social contract theory, and in this it contains justification for the contention that government exists legitimately only by the consent of the governed. Hobbes' work has served as a point from which many Western political philosophers built their own political and moral systems by which we continue to order our social and political lives.

Parts of the Work

Hobbes' *Leviathan* is separated into four separate sections, all of which together are a cohesive unit. They move at first from the nature of man (a characterization of humanity, especially the individual human being) in Part I to the nature of commonwealth (society and government, the ultimate cooperative enterprise between and among individual human beings) in Part II. If one is looking simply for something of Hobbes' theory of knowledge, a little of his metaphysics, and the relationship of these areas of inquiry to a conception of human nature leading to Hobbesian social and political theory, it is possible to stop at the end of Part II. That, however, might be to cheat the reader out of one of the most ingenious arguments for the relationship of religious doctrine to political organization ever contrived, which appears in Parts III and IV.

There is some controversy among Hobbes' scholars regarding the status of Parts III and IV of *Leviathan* with respect to whether they are necessary at all since it seems clear from Hobbes himself when he asserts at the beginning of Part III

---

9. Thomas Hobbes, "Questions Concerning Liberty, Necessity, and Chance," in *The English Works of Thomas Hobbes, Vol. V*, ed. William Molesworth (London: John Bohn, 1841), 1–27, 25.

that he has "derived the rights of sovereign power and the duty of subjects up to this time from the principles of nature only such as experience has found true or consent . . . has made so—that is to say from the nature of men known to us by experience and from definitions . . . universally agreed on." In other words, Hobbes has, without consideration of things like ecclesiastical authority or a doctrine of the immortality of the soul, without concern with or necessary dependence on Christianity or any other religion, provided an argument for government power and the organization of political states that is designed by Hobbes to be put into practice by sovereigns (rulers) of states. Doing this is no mean achievement since it serves as a foundational document for the rejection of the traditional divine right of kings and the affirmation of the doctrine that government exists by the consent of the governed.[10]

---

10. The belief that government exists by the consent of the governed was not unique to Hobbes, and in fact it was, according to Johann Sommerville, commonplace during the English Civil War, the time in which Hobbes was writing *Leviathan*. See Johann P. Sommerville, *Thomas Hobbes: Political Ideas in Historical Context* (New York: St. Martin's Press, 1992), 51.

LEVIATHAN

Hobbes' Letter of Dedication

TO MY MOST HONORED FRIEND, MR. FRANCIS GODOLPHIN[1] OF GODOLPHIN

HONORED SIR,

Your most worthy brother, Mr. Sidney Godolphin, was pleased when he lived to think my studies something and otherwise to oblige me . . . with real testimonies of his good opinion, which are great in themselves and greater for his worthiness. There is not any virtue that disposes a man either to the service of God or to the service of his country, to civil society, or to private friendship that did not manifestly appear in his conversation but shone from his generous nature. Therefore, in honor and gratitude to him and with devotion to you, I humbly dedicate to you my discourse of commonwealth. I do not know how the world will receive it nor how it may reflect on those who seem to favor it. For in a way beset with those who contend on one side for too great liberty and on the other side for too much authority, it is hard to pass between the points of both unwounded. But yet I think the endeavor to advance civil power should not be condemned by the civil power nor by private men who, reprehending it, declare that they think that power is too great. Besides, I do not speak of men but of the seat of power and offend none, I think, but those outside or those within who favor them. That which perhaps will most offend are certain texts of Holy Scripture, alleged by me to other purposes than ordinarily used by others.[2] But I have done it with due submission and also necessarily, for they are the outworks of the enemy from whence they impugn the civil power. If, notwithstanding this, you find my labor generally decried, you might excuse yourself and say that I am merely a man who loves my own opinions and think that all I say is true, that I honored both you and your brother and have presumed on that to assume the title of being, as I am,

Sir,

Your most humble, and most obedient servant, Thomas Hobbes
Paris, April 15/25, 1651

---

1. Sidney Godolphin, killed during the English Civil War, was a personal friend of Thomas Hobbes.
2. Hobbes' concern in including in *Leviathan* a significant portion (Parts III and IV) centered on religious doctrine was to show how religious doctrine could be used as a means to justify his moral and political ideas as well as to show, from his point of view, the dangerous consequences of religious doctrine held and defended contrary to the maintenance of peace and security in political society.

Introduction

Nature (the art by which God has made and governs the world) is imitated by the art of man in that it can make an artificial animal. Seeing life is just motion of limbs with the beginning in some principal part inside, why may we not say that all automata (engines that move themselves by springs and wheels like a watch) have an artificial life? For what is the heart but a spring, and the nerves but so many strings, and the joints but so many wheels that give motion to the whole body as intended by the artificer?[3] Art goes further in imitating that rational and most excellent work of nature, man. For it is by art that the great Leviathan, called a commonwealth or state (in Latin, *Civitas*) is created as an artificial man. The artificial man is greater in stature and strength than the natural for whose protection and defense it was intended, and in which sovereignty is an artificial soul giving life and motion to the whole body. The magistrates and other officers of judicature and execution are artificial joints. Reward and punishment are the nerves that do the same in the natural body. The wealth and riches of all individual members are the strength. *Salus Populi* (the people's safety) is its business. Counselors, by whom all things it needs to know are suggested to it, are the memory. Equity and laws are an artificial reason and will. Concord is health. Sedition is sickness. And civil war is death. Lastly, the pacts and covenants by which the parts of this body politic were first made, set together and united, resemble that fiat or the "Let us Make Man," pronounced by God in the Creation.

To describe the nature of this artificial man, I will consider, (1) the matter of it and the artificer, both of which is man, (2) how and by what covenants is it made and what are the rights and just power or authority of a sovereign, and what it is

---

3. This is the first statement in *Leviathan* of Thomas Hobbes' position on the nature of reality (a metaphysical position): that reality is all and only material substance. Materialism is contrasted with metaphysical dualism (the position that reality is composed of matter and spiritual substance) and immaterialism (also called idealism, which is the position that matter does not exist and the whole of reality is composed of "mind," "soul," or "spiritual" substance). For classic statements of dualism and immaterialism, consult René Descartes, *Meditations on First Philosophy*, ed. Donald A. Cress, 3rd ed. (Indianapolis, IN: Hackett, 1993); John Locke, *Essay Concerning Human Understanding*, ed. Kenneth P. Winkler (Indianapolis, IN: Hackett, 1996); George Berkeley, *A Treatise Concerning the Principles of Human Knowledge*, ed. Kenneth Winkler (Indianapolis, IN: Hackett, 1982). The Continental Rationalist Baruch Spinoza argued for monism (the position that all is one and, essentially, that everything is God) in his *Ethics*, ed. Seymour Feldman, trans. Samuel Shirley (Indianapolis, IN: Hackett, 1992). Further, G. W. F. Leibniz argued for a position quite different from any of the others' in holding that the universe is composed of an infinite number of substances called "monads." See Leibniz, "Monadology," in *Discourse on Metaphysics and Other Essays*, trans. Daniel Garber and Roger Ariew, 9th ed. (Indianapolis, IN: Hackett, 1991).

that preserves and dissolves it, (3) what is a Christian commonwealth, and (4) what is the kingdom of darkness.

Concerning the first, there is a saying that wisdom is acquired by reading men, not by reading books. Consequently, persons who for the most part can give no other proof of being wise take great delight in showing what they think they have read in men by uncharitable censures of one another behind their backs. But there is another saying that is today not understood by which they might learn truly to read each other if they would take the pains to do so, and that is . . . to Read Thyself. By this it was not meant—as it is now used—to countenance either the barbarous state of men in power toward their inferiors or to encourage men of low degree to a saucy behavior toward their betters. Instead it is to teach us the similarity of thoughts and passions of one man to the thoughts and passions of another. Anyone who looks into himself and considers what he does when he thinks, opines, reasons, hopes, fears, etc., and upon what grounds he does so, shall thereby read and know the thoughts and passions of all other men on similar occasions.[4] I say the similarity of passions, which are the same in all men such as desire, fear, hope, etc., not the similarity of the objects of the passions,[5] which are things desired, feared, hoped, etc. The objects of the passions depend on the individual and vary by education, and they are easily kept from our knowledge because the character of a man's heart is blotted and confounded with dissembling, lying, counterfeiting, and erroneous doctrines, and are legible only to him who searches hearts. Though by men's actions we sometimes discover their design, to do it without comparing them with our own and distinguishing all circumstances by which the case may be altered is to decipher without a key and be for the most part deceived by too much trust or by too much diffidence[6] as he that reads is himself a good or evil man.

Even if one man reads another person perfectly by his actions, it serves him only with his acquaintances, who are few. He who is to govern a whole nation must read in himself not this or that particular man, but mankind. This is hard to do and harder to learn than any language or science. But when I set down my reading in an orderly fashion, the pains left another will be only to consider if he also finds the same in himself. For this kind of doctrine admits of no other demonstration.

---

4. Hobbes' comment regarding the individual's ability to read his own thoughts and passions—and in doing so read the thoughts and passions of all others in similar circumstances—is a hint at Hobbes' conception of human nature that is more fully developed in Chapters XI–XIV.
5. The distinction between the passions we have and the objects toward which our passions are directed is important in understanding Hobbes' discussion of the causes of quarrel—that is, the causes of war—introduced in Chapter XIII.
6. The term "diffidence" as used by Thomas Hobbes in _Leviathan_ is roughly equivalent to what we might now describe as a defensive stance or a readiness to engage in battle with others arising from uncertainty regarding their intentions. Hobbes lists diffidence as one of the causes of quarrel between individuals (which results in all-out war) in Chapter XIII. There are some limited instances in _Leviathan_ in which the term is used differently to indicate doubt about one's own abilities.

PART I: OF MAN

Chapter I. Of Sense

In this chapter, Hobbes expresses the "empiricist thesis" that all ideas arise from—and only from—experience. Ideas are caused by real things outside ourselves and the qualities of real things (which for Hobbes are completely and only material things) cause ideas in us by the operation of these qualities on our senses. The distinction between appearance and reality makes a difference to Hobbes' political doctrine and it becomes prominent beginning in Chapter V (on reason and science) and in the distinction Hobbes employs throughout the work between "science" and observation.

Hobbes argues that it is important for us not to be misled into believing the doctrines of the "Schools" (that is, the Scholastic philosophers who were influenced by the works of Aristotle) that things like a "visible being seen" are the cause of the ideas received through visual sensation. For Hobbes, the simple fact is that what we perceive (the "fancy" or idea in the mind) is one thing, and the thing itself, which is the cause of sensation, is another. We can be confident that matter exists (even though we have, really, no idea of it at all).

I will consider the thoughts of man first singly and afterward in train or dependence upon one another. Singly, they are each a representation or appearance of some quality or accident of a body outside us which is commonly called an object. The object works on the eyes, ears, and other parts of a man's body. By diversity of working, the object produces diversity of appearances.

The origin of all thoughts is sense (for there is no conception in a man's mind that has not at first, either totally or in part, been begotten upon the organs of sense). The rest are derived from the original. To know the natural cause of sense is not relevant to the business now in hand, and I have elsewhere written of the same.[1] ... Nevertheless, to fill each part of my present method I will briefly deliver the same here.

---

1. For an introductory look at Thomas Hobbes' metaphysics and epistemology, see Yves Charles Zarka, "First Philosophy and the Foundation of Knowledge" in *The Cambridge Companion to Thomas Hobbes*, ed. Tom Sorell (New York: Cambridge University Press, 1996), 62–85. In addition, short sections of Hobbes' metaphysical (and some epistemological) works are included in *Metaphysical Writings: Thomas Hobbes*, ed. Mary Whiton Calkins (La Salle, IL: Open Court, 1905) with excerpts from Hobbes' *Elements of Philosophy* and *Human Nature*.

The cause of sensation is the external body or object which presses the organ corresponding to each sense either immediately, as in taste and touch, or mediately, as in seeing, hearing, and smelling. This pressure by the mediation of nerves, other strings and membranes of the body continues inward to the brain and heart, causing resistance or counterpressure or endeavor of the heart to deliver itself. This endeavor, because it is outward, seems to be some external matter. This seeming (or fancy) is called sense and consists as to the eye in light or color, to the ear in sound, to the nostril in an odor, to the tongue and palate in savor, and to the rest of the body in heat, cold, hardness, softness, and other such qualities discerned by feeling. All these qualities are called sensible and are [not]² in the object that causes them, but are so many motions of matter which press diversely on our organs. In us, they are nothing but diverse motions (since motion produces nothing but motion). Their appearance to us is fancy and the same waking as dreaming. And as pressing, rubbing, or striking the eye makes us fancy a light and pressing the ear produces a din, so the bodies we see or hear produce the same by their strong but unobserved action. If the colors and sounds were in bodies or objects that cause them, they could not be separated from them as by glasses and in echoes by reflection we see they are. Where we know the thing we see is in one place, the appearance is in another. Though at some distance the real object seems invested with the fancy it causes in us, it is still the case that the object is one thing and the image or fancy is

----

2. The word "not" does not appear in the Molesworth and Penguin editions of *Leviathan*, nor in the Clarendon Edition (ed. Noel Malcolm). Nor does it appear in Flathman and Johnston or Oakeshott. It is clear, however, that Hobbes intended to assert that the so-called secondary qualities of objects are not "in" the object itself but are instead dependent upon the perceiver of the object. It is perhaps the case that Hobbes is referring in this line of the work to so-called primary qualities of objects, but in the same paragraph he asserts, "If the colors and sounds were in bodies or objects that cause them, they could not be separated from them as by glasses and in echoes by reflection we see they are." The distinction between primary and secondary qualities does not appreciably affect Hobbes' moral or political doctrines in any case, but the distinction itself is important in the debate in early modern philosophy concerning appearance and reality. Generally speaking, primary qualities of material objects are identified as those that are "really" in the object. They are qualities that remain even when all the apparent qualities of an object have changed. Among the primary qualities are figure, motion, rest, and extension. Secondary qualities are described as perceiver-dependent qualities that are not part of the object itself but are caused in the perceiver by the effect of the motion of primary qualities on perceivers. Among the secondary qualities are colors, tastes, sounds, smells, and tactile sensations. It is also important to note that Hobbes does not use the distinction between primary and secondary qualities in the way in which John Locke used it in the *Essay Concerning Human Understanding*. For Hobbes, as Tom Sorell and Cees Leijenhorst note, both the primary and secondary qualities are perceiver dependent, so it is not the case that the primary qualities are in some way known as a representation in our minds of the way things are. Instead, we know the existence of the external world through causation of ideas in our minds rather than through representation, or a "picture" sort of understanding of the connection between matter and our thoughts. So, for Hobbes, all of our ideas are subjective.

another. So sensation in all cases is nothing but original fancy, caused by the pressure (i.e., by the motion) of external things upon our eyes, ears, and other organs.

But the schools of philosophy through all the universities of Christendom that are grounded in some texts of Aristotle teach a different doctrine. They say that the cause of vision is the thing seen sending forth a visible species, apparition, or aspect, or a "being seen." Receiving this into the eye is seeing. For the cause of hearing, the thing heard sends forth an audible species and "audible being heard," which entering the ear makes hearing. For the cause of understanding, they say the thing understood sends forth "intelligible species," that is, an intelligible being seen, which, coming into the understanding makes us understand. I do not say this to disapprove of the universities. I say it because I am hereafter going to speak of their place in a commonwealth and I must let you see on all occasions what things would be amended in them—among which the frequency of insignificant speech is one.

Chapter II. Of Imagination

Hobbes is concerned in Chapter II with ideas derived from sense experience but that go beyond mere experience to the combinations of ideas in many and varied ways in dreams as well as in waking moments. What may begin to confuse us is the simple fact that there are people who believe that there is some difficulty in distinguishing dreams from waking moments and people who make use of fear and superstition to disguise themselves and their ideas, leading people to believe claims that are not derivable from the ideas they receive from experience. Making clear the difference between what is remembered and imagined and what actually occurred or might be a probable occurrence is essential to ensuring civil peace.

No one doubts that when a thing is lying still it will lie still forever unless something else moves it. It is not as easily assented that when a thing is in motion it will be eternally in motion unless something else stops it even though the reason is the same—that is, nothing changes itself. For men measure not only other men, but all other things by themselves. Because they find themselves subject after motion to pain and lassitude, they think everything else grows weary of motion and seeks repose of its own accord and they little consider whether their desire for rest consists in some other motion. From hence it is, the Schools[3] absurdly say, heavy bodies fall downward out of an appetite to rest and to conserve their nature in a place most proper for them, and ascribe appetite and knowledge of what is good for their conservation to inanimate things (which is more than man has).

When a body is once in motion it moves eternally unless something else hinders it, and whatever hinders it cannot instantly—but instead over time and by degrees—extinguish it. As we see in the water, even when the wind has ceased the waves continue for a long time after. It also happens in that motion which is made in the internal parts of a man when he sees, dreams, etc. For after the object is removed or the eye shut, we still retain an image of the thing seen though it is more obscure than when we see it. This is what the Latins called imagination, from

---

3. The "Schools" to which Hobbes refers are the universities in Europe that taught Aristotelian doctrines and science. Aristotle's metaphysics, which was appropriated by St. Thomas Aquinas in the Middle Ages, includes the notion that all natural things have a perfection or goal toward which they strive such that, for example, acorns grow into oak trees because it is the natural goal of acorns to strive toward betterment (on the assumption that being an oak tree is better and more perfect than being an acorn). Ideas such as this are closely associated with Aristotle's contention that all natural things have a purpose (Aristotle was a teleologist, an adherent to the notion that there is a purpose or goal "built into" things, so to speak, that makes them what they are and that leads them to seek completion and perfection).

the image made in seeing and applying the same, improperly, to all the other senses. But the Greeks call it fancy, which signifies appearance and is as proper to one sense as to another. Imagination, therefore, is nothing but decaying sense and is found in men and many other living creatures, whether sleeping or waking.

The decay of sense in waking is not the decay of the motion made in sense, but it is obscuring it in the manner in which the Sun obscures the light of the stars. The stars do not exercise less the virtue by which they are visible in the day than in the night. Instead, of the many strokes our eyes, ears, and other organs receive from external bodies, only the predominant is sensible. Therefore, the light of the Sun being predominant, we are not affected with the action of the stars. When any object is removed from our eyes the impression it made in us remains, but other objects more present work on us and imagination of the past is obscured and made weak as the voice of a man in the noise of the day. It follows that the longer the time after sight or sense of any object, the weaker is the imagination.

Over time, the continual change of man's body destroys the parts which when sensing were moved so that the distance of time and place has one and the same effect in us. For as at a distance of place that at which we look appears dim and without distinction of smaller parts, and as voices grow weak and inarticulate, so also after great distance of time our imagination of the past is weak, and we lose (for example) many particular streets of cities we have seen and many particular circumstances of actions. This decaying sense when we would express the thing itself (I mean fancy itself) we call imagination. But when we would express decay and signify that the sense is fading, old, and past, it is called memory. So imagination and memory are the same thing for which diverse considerations have diverse names.

Much memory, or memory of many things, is called experience. Again, imagination is only of those things which have been previously perceived by sense either all at once or by parts at several times. The former (which is imagining the whole object as it was presented to the sense) is simple imagination as when one imagines a man or horse which he has seen before. The other is compounded, as when from the sight of a man one time and of a horse at another, we conceive in our mind a centaur. So when a man compounds the image of his own person with the image of the actions of another man, as when a man imagines himself a Hercules or an Alexander (which happens often to those who are much taken with reading of Romans) it is a compound imagination and properly only a fiction of the mind. There are other imaginations that arise in men (even when waking) from the great impression made in sense. [Examples of this occur when] gazing at the Sun, the impression leaves an image of the Sun before our eyes a long time after, and from long attention upon geometrical figures, a man in the dark (though awake) shall have the images of lines and angles before his eyes. This kind of fancy has no particular name[4] because it is not commonly a subject of discussion.

The imaginations of people sleeping are dreams. These also (as all other imaginations) have been in the senses either totally or in part. Because in sense the brain

---

4. Hobbes is referring here to the phenomenon of an afterimage.

and nerves, which are the necessary organs of sense, are so benumbed in sleep as not easily to be moved by the action of external objects, there is in sleep no imagination, and therefore no dream but what proceeds from the agitation of inward parts of a man's body. These inward parts keep the same motion for the connection they have with the brain and other organs when they are distempered. In this case, the imaginations formerly made appear as if a man were waking except that the organs of sense are now benumbed so that there is no new object to master and obscure them with a more vigorous impression. So a dream must be more clear, in this silence of sense, than are our waking thoughts. So it comes to pass that it is thought by many impossible to distinguish exactly between sense and dreaming. For my part, I consider that in dreams I do not often nor constantly think of the same persons, places, objects and actions that I do waking, nor remember so long a train of coherent thoughts dreaming as at other times. Because when awake I often observe the absurdity of dreams, but never dream of the absurdities of my waking thoughts, I am well satisfied that being awake I know I do not dream, though when I dream I think myself awake.

Seeing that dreams are caused by the distemper of some of the inward parts of the body, diverse distempers must cause different dreams. So lying cold breeds dreams of fear and raises the thought and image of the fearful object (the motion from the brain to the inner parts, and from the inner parts to the brain being reciprocal). Since anger causes heat in some parts of the body when we are awake, so when we sleep overheating the same parts causes anger and raises up in the brain the imagination of an enemy. In the same way, as natural kindness when we are awake causes desire and desire makes heat in certain other parts of the body, so too much heat in those parts while we sleep raises in the brain imagination of some kindness shown. In sum, our dreams are the reverse of our waking imaginations such that the motion when we are awake begins at one end, and when we dream, at another.

The most difficult discerning of a dream from waking thoughts is when by some accident we do not observe that we have slept. This easily happens to a man full of fearful thoughts and those whose consciences are much troubled, and those who sleep without going to bed or taking off his clothes, such as one who nods off in a chair. If an uncouth and exorbitant fancy comes to one who takes the pains and industriously lays himself to sleep, he cannot easily think it other than a dream. We read of Marcus Brutus (one who had his life given him by Julius Caesar, and although was his favorite, murdered him) how at Phillip, the night before battling with Augustus Caesar, he saw a fearful apparition commonly related by historians as a vision. Considering the circumstances, one may easily judge it to have been only a short dream. Sitting in his tent, pensive and troubled with the horror of his rash act, it was not hard for him while slumbering in the cold to dream of that which most frightened him. This fear by degrees awakened him, so it must make the apparition vanish by degrees. Having no assurance that he had slept he could have no cause to think it a dream or anything but a vision. This is no very rare accident. For even those who are perfectly awake, if they are timorous and superstitious and possessed with fearful tales and alone in the dark, are subject to the like fancies and believe they see spirits and dead men's ghosts walking in churchyards. It is either their fancy only or the knavery[5] of persons who make use of superstitious fear to pass disguised in the night to places they would not be known to go.

From ignorance of how to distinguish dreams and other strong fancies from vision and sense arise the greatest part of the religion of the Gentiles in the past who worshipped satyrs, fawns, nymphs, and the like. And nowadays, it is the opinion that rude people have of fairies, ghosts, goblins, and of the power of witches. As for witches, I do not think their witchcraft is any real power. Even so, they are justly punished for the false belief they have that they can do such mischief joined with their purpose to do it if they can.[6] Their trade is nearer to a new religion than to a craft or science. For fairies and walking ghosts, I think the opinion of them has been purposely either taught or not confuted to keep in credit the use of exorcism, of crosses, of holy water, and other such inventions of ghostly men.[7] Nevertheless, there is no doubt that God can make unnatural apparitions. But that he does it so often as men need to fear such things, more than they fear the stay or change of the course of nature, which he can also stay and change, is no point of Christian faith. But under the pretext that God can do anything, evil men are so bold as to say anything when it serves their turn even if they think it untrue. It is part of a wise man to believe them no further than right reason makes what they say appear credible. If this superstitious fear of spirits were taken away and with it the prognostications from dreams, false prophecies, and many other things dependent thereon by which crafty, ambitious persons abuse simple people, men would be much more fitted than they are for civil obedience.

This ought to be the work of the schools, but rather they nourish such doctrine. For (not knowing what imagination or the senses are) what they receive, they teach. Some say that imaginations rise of themselves and have no cause. Others say that they rise most commonly from the will, that good thoughts are blown (inspired) into a man by God and evil thoughts by the Devil, or that good thoughts are powered (infused) into a man by God and evil ones by the Devil. Some say the senses receive the species of things and deliver them to common sense and common sense delivers them over to the fancy, and the fancy to the memory, and the memory to the judgment, like handing things from one to another with many words, making nothing understood.

---

5. Trickery. Later in *Leviathan*, Hobbes refers to false prophets as those who engage in trickery and, in doing so, often incite others to political rebellion.
6. While Hobbes speaks of the mischief of witches, he does not believe that those who claim to be or are reputed to be witches actually have any such powers that witches would possess. However, witches have a place in Hobbes' view very similar to that of "ghostly men," to whom he has referred in this chapter. On his view, witches and priests ("ghostly men") not only speak nonsense but are also dangerous to the commonwealth.
7. This comment is one among many, most of which appear in Parts III and IV of *Leviathan*, indicating Hobbes' dislike and distrust of Catholicism.

The imagination that is raised in man or in any other creature with the faculty of imagining by words or other voluntary signs is what we generally call understanding and is common to man and beast. A dog by custom will understand the call or the rating of his master and so will many other beasts. Understanding which is specific to man is understanding not only his will but his conceptions and thoughts by the sequel and context of the names of things into affirmations, negations, and other forms of speech. Of this kind of understanding I shall speak hereafter.

Chapter III. Of the Consequence or Train of Imaginations

While Hobbes' comments in the first two chapters of Leviathan *are designed at least in part to warn readers to be careful in drawing conclusions from their experiences, it is no less true that experience itself is of great value. While the train of our imagination is not always predictable, there are causal connections between the ideas, and the person with the most experience is, generally speaking, the most prudent. Further, however, our imagination is limited exclusively to that which is finite, from which it follows that, for Hobbes, we have no conception of God or of the immortality of the soul. Those who put forth the notion that we do have such conceptions are attempting to deceive us.*

By the consequence or train of thoughts I understand the succession of one thought to another. This is called mental discourse. When a man thinks about anything, his next thought after is not altogether so casual as it seems to be. Not every thought to every thought succeeds indifferently. But as we have no imagination that was not formerly in sense in whole or in parts, we have no transition from one imagination to another whereof we never had the like before in our senses. The reason is that all fancies are motions inside us, relics of those made in the sense, and those motions that immediately succeeded one another in the sense continue together after sense. Insomuch as the former comes again to take place and be predominant, the latter follows by coherence of the matter moved in such manner like water on a plain table is drawn which way any one part of it is guided by the finger. Because in sense to one and the same thing perceived, sometimes one thing and sometimes another follows, it comes to pass in time that in imagining anything there is no certainty what we shall imagine next. Only this is certain: it shall be something that succeeded the same before at one time or another.

The train of thoughts (mental discourse) is of two sorts. The first is unguided and without design. It is inconstant such that where there is no passionate thought to govern and direct those that follow to itself as the end and scope of some desire or other passion. In which case the thoughts are said to wander and seem impertinent to one another as in a dream. Such are commonly the thoughts of men who are not only without company but who are also without care of anything, though even then their thoughts are as busy as at other times but it is without harmony. It is like the sound which a lute out of tune would yield to any man, or in tune to one who could not play. Yet in this wild ranging of the mind, a man may often perceive the way of it and the dependence of one thought upon another. For in a discourse of our present civil war,[8] what could seem more impertinent than to ask (as one did) what was the value of a Roman penny? Yet the coherence to me was manifest enough. For the thought of the war introduced the thought of delivering the king to his enemies. The thought of that brought in the thought of delivering up Christ. That again brought in the thought of the thirty pence[9] which was the price of that treason. From this it easily followed that malicious question and all this in a moment of time, for thought is quick.

The second is more constant, being regulated by some desire and design. The impression made by things we desire or fear is strong and permanent or (if it ceases for a time) quick to return. It is so strong sometimes as to hinder and break our sleep. The thought of some means we have seen to produce the like of that at which we aimed arises from desire. From the thought of that, the thought of means to that mean, and so continually until we come to some beginning within our own power. Because the end, by the greatness of the impression comes often to mind, in case our thoughts begin to wander they are quickly again reduced into the way. . . .

The train of regulated thoughts is of two kinds. One, when we seek the causes or means that produce an imagined effect. This is common to man and to beast. The other is when imagining anything, we seek all the possible effects that can be produced by it. That is to say, we imagine what we can do with it when we have it. I have never seen any sign of this except in man, for this is a curiosity hardly incident to the nature of any living creature that has no other but sensual passion, such as hunger, thirst, lust, and anger. . . . Or of the effects of some present or past cause, sometimes a man seeks what he has lost and from that place and time wherein he misses it, his mind runs back from place to place, and from time to time, to find where and when he had it. That is to say, to find some certain and limited time and place in which to begin a method of seeking. Again . . . his thoughts run over the same places and times to find what action or other occasion might make him lose it. This we call remembrance, or calling to mind. . . . Sometimes a man knows a determinate place within the compass whereof he is to seek. And then his thoughts run over all the parts of it in the same manner as one would sweep a room to find a jewel, or as a Spaniel ranges the field till he finds a scent, or as a man should run over the alphabet to start a rhyme.

Sometimes a man desires to know the event of an action, and then he thinks of some similar past action, and the events thereof one after another and supposes that like events will follow like actions. As he who foresees what will become of a criminal re-cons what he has seen follow on a similar crime before. He has this

---

8. The English Civil War (1642–1651) occurred between royalists and parliamentarians. Thousands of people died in the conflict, most of whom were civilians. This war included the beheading of King Charles I, the exile of his son, Charles II (with whom Hobbes had a close tutorial relationship), and the takeover of the British government by Oliver Cromwell.
9. This is a biblical reference to the betrayal of Jesus by his disciple Judas. Judas was willing to deliver Jesus to those conspiring to kill him for the price of thirty pieces of silver. Later, the story recounts that Judas regretted his decision but it was too late; Jesus was condemned. As a result, Judas committed suicide (Matt. 26.14–16; 27.3–5).

order of thoughts: the crime, the officer, the prison, the judge, and the gallows. This kind of thought is called foresight and prudence, or Providence. Sometimes it is called wisdom, though such conjecture through the difficulty of observing all circumstances is very fallacious. But this is certain: by how much one man has more experience of things past than another, by so much . . . he is more prudent and his expectations more seldom fail him.

The present only has a being in nature. Things past have a being in the memory only, but things to come have no being at all. The future is only a fiction of the mind applying the sequels of past actions to present actions that are present, which with most certainty is done by he who has most experience, but not with certainty enough. And though it is called prudence when the event answers our expectation, yet in its own nature it is only presumption. For the foresight of things to come, which is Providence, belongs only to him by whose will they are to come.[10] From him only, and supernaturally, proceeds prophecy. The best prophet naturally is the best guesser. And the best guesser is he who is most versed and studied in the matters at which he guesses, for he has most signs by which to guess.

A sign is the antecedent event of the consequent; and contrarily it is the consequent of the antecedent when like consequences have been observed before. The more often they have been observed, the less uncertain the sign. Therefore he who has most experience in any kind of business has the most signs by which to guess at the future and consequently is the most prudent. And so much more prudent than he who is new in that kind of business as not to be equaled by any advantage of natural and extemporary wit, though perhaps many young men think the contrary. Nevertheless, it is not prudence that distinguishes man from beast. There are beasts that at a year old observe more, and pursue that which is for their good more prudently, than a child can do at ten.

As prudence is a presumption of the future derived from the experience of time past, so there is a presumption of things past taken from other things (not future but) past also. Upon the sight of the ruin of a state, he who has seen by what courses and degrees a flourishing state has come into civil war and then to ruin will guess the like war and the like causes have been there. But his conjecture has the same uncertainty almost with the conjecture of the future, both being grounded only upon experience.[11]

There is no other act of man's mind that I can remember naturally planted in him so as to need no other thing to exercise it but to be born a man and live with the use of his five senses. Those other faculties of which I shall speak and which seem proper to man only are acquired and increased by study and industry, and of most men learned by instruction and discipline and proceed from the invention of words and speech. For besides sense, thoughts, and the train of thoughts the mind of man has no other motion. By the help of speech and method, the same

---

10. That is, from God. Only God has perfect knowledge of all events, whether past, present, or future.

11. In short, while experience is valuable it is not an infallible guide by which to reach conclusions. Ultimately, only reason provides certainty. See Chapter V on ratiocination.

faculties may be improved to such a height as to distinguish men from all other living creatures.

Whatsoever we imagine is finite. Therefore there is no idea or conception of anything we call infinite. No man can have in his mind an image of infinite magnitude nor conceive the ends and bounds of the thing named because we have no conception of the thing but of our own inability. And therefore the name of God is used not to make us conceive him (for he is incomprehensible and his greatness and power are inconceivable) but that we may honor him. Also because whatever (as I said before) we conceive has been perceived first by sense either all at once or by parts, a man can have no thought representing anything that is not subject to sense. No man therefore can conceive anything except as conceived in some place and imbued with some determinate magnitude and which may be divided into parts. Nor can he conceive that anything is all in this place and all in another place at the same time, nor that two or more things can be in one and the same place at once. For none of these things have or can be incident to sense. They are absurd speeches taken upon credit (without any signification at all) from deceived philosophers and deceived or deceiving Schoolmen.

Chapter IV. Of Speech

Speech is, Hobbes contends, the "most profitable invention" for humanity. It allows us to remember, to name things, and to speak to each other. It ultimately makes our arts and sciences possible. But it is also true that speech may be abused in ways such as to deceive and to "grieve each other." One of the ways in which some people may attempt to deceive others is in the belief in "universals," about which Hobbes vehemently protests. Hobbes was, instead, a nominalist in believing that all existent things are individual things.

Deceptive use of words also affects our understanding of truth and falsehood, which are, for Hobbes, all and only properties of speech. In other words, there are no "true" or "false" things but only true or false sentences. It is when we misunderstand the proper uses of language, and when we lack proper method in reasoning, that error and falsehood occur. To combat errors at their source, Hobbes is convinced that careful use of language in the form of definitions is the beginning of reliable inquiry leading to knowledge.

Even though the invention of printing is ingenious, compared with the invention of letters it is no great matter. . . . [Printing is] a profitable invention for continuing the memory of time past and the conjunction of mankind dispersed into so many and distant regions of the Earth, and [it] proceeds from a watchful observation of the diverse motions of the tongue, palate, lips, and other organs of speech whereby to make as many differences of characters to remember them. But the most noble and profitable invention of all others was that of speech, consisting of names or appellations and their connection whereby men register their thoughts, recall them when they are past, and also declare them to each other for mutual utility and conversation. Without [speech there would be] among men neither commonwealth nor society, nor contract nor peace, no more than among lions, bears, and wolves. The first author of speech was God himself, who instructed Adam how to name such creatures as he presented to his sight [but] the Scripture goes no further in this matter. But this was sufficient to direct him to add more names as the experience and use of the creatures should give him occasion, and to join them in such manner by degrees as to make himself understood. So by succession of time, so much language might be gotten for which he found use though not so copious as an orator or philosopher has need of. For I do not find anything in the Scripture out of which, directly or by consequence can be gathered, that Adam was taught the names of all figures, numbers, measures, colors, sounds, fancies, relations, much less the names of words and speech, such as general, special, affirmative, negative, interrogative, optative, infinitive, all of which are useful; and least of all, of entity, intentionality, quiddity, and other insignificant words of the Schools.

All this language gotten and augmented by Adam and his posterity was again lost at the Tower of Babel, when by the hand of God every man was stricken for his rebellion with oblivion of his former language. Being forced to disperse themselves into several parts of the world, it must be that the diversity of tongues that now is proceeded by degrees from then in such manner as need (the mother of all inventions) taught them, and in tract of time grew everywhere more copious.

The general use of speech is to transfer our mental discourse into verbal discourse, or the train of our thoughts into train of words, and that for two commodities. One is registering the consequences of our thoughts which are apt to slip out of memory and put us to a new labor and can instead be recalled by the words by which they were marked. So the first use of names is to serve for marks or notes of remembrance. Another is when many use the same words to signify (by their connection and order) one to another what they conceive or think of each matter and also what they desire, fear, or have any other passion for. For this use they are called signs.[12] Special uses of speech are, first, to register what by cogitation we find to be the cause of anything present or we find what things present or past may produce or effect, which in sum is acquiring arts. The second is to show to others knowledge we have attained, which is to counsel and teach one another. The third is to make known to others our wills and purposes, so that we may have mutual help of one another. The fourth is innocently to please and delight ourselves and others by playing with our words for pleasure or ornament.

To these uses there are also four correspondent abuses. First is when men register their thoughts incorrectly by the inconstancy of the signification of their words by which they register for their conceptions what they never conceived, and so deceive themselves. Second is when they use words metaphorically, that is, in another sense than that for which they are meant and thereby deceive others. Third is when by words they declare that to be their will which is not. Fourth is when they use them to grieve one another. Seeing nature has armed some living creatures with teeth, some with horns, and some with hands to grieve an enemy, it is an abuse of speech to grieve him with the tongue unless it be one whom we are obliged to govern, and then it is not to grieve, but to correct and amend.

The manner in which speech serves to remember the consequence of causes and effects consists in imposing names and the connection of them.

Some names are proper and singular to only one thing as "Peter," "John," "this man," "this tree" and some are common to many things such as "man," "horse," "tree," all of which though just one name are nevertheless the names of diverse particular things in respect of all which together they are called a universal, there being nothing in the world universal but names because the things named are all individual and singular.[13]

---

12. Hobbes distinguishes between marks (which are personal) and signs (which are social) with respect to words and language.

13. Hobbes shows here that he is a nominalist. Nominalism is the rejection of universals. Universals are properties that exist in multiple tokens of the same type, due to the nature of that type. For example, in a right triangle, the sum of the angles is equal to 180 degrees. The

One universal name is imposed on many things for their similarity in some quality or other accident. And whereas a proper name brings to mind one thing only, universals recall any one of those many. Some universal names are more and some are of less extent. The larger include the less large and some again of equal extent include each other reciprocally. For example, the name "body" is of larger signification than the word "man," and contains it. The names "man" and "rational" are of equal extent, containing mutually one another. But here we must take notice that by a name is not always understood only one word as in grammar, but sometimes the circumlocution of many words together. For all these words, he who in his actions observes the laws of his country makes but one name equivalent to this one word, "Just."

By this imposition of names of which some are of larger and some are of stricter signification, we turn reckoning of the consequences of things imagined in the mind into reckoning the consequences of appellations. For example, if a triangle and two right angles (such as the corners of a square figure) are set before the eyes of a man who has no use of speech at all (such as one who is born and remains perfectly deaf and dumb), he may by meditation compare and find that the three angles of that triangle are equal to those two right angles that stand by it. But if another triangle different in shape from the former is shown to him, he cannot know without more labor whether the three angles of that also are equal to the same. But he who has the use of words, when he observes that such equality was consequent, not to the length of the sides nor to any other particular thing in his triangle, but only that the sides were straight and the angles were three, and that was all for which he named it a triangle will boldly conclude universally that such equality of angles is in all triangles whatsoever. He will register his invention in these general terms that "Every triangle has its three angles equal to two right angles." Thus the consequence found in one particular comes to be registered and remembered as a universal rule and discharges our mental reckoning of time and place and delivers us from all labor of the mind, saving the first, and makes that which was found true here and now to be true in all times and places.

But the use of words in registering our thoughts is in nothing so evident as in numbering. A natural fool who could never learn by heart the order of numeral words such as "one," "two," and "three," may observe every stroke of the clock and nod to it, or say "one," "one," "one" but can never know what hour it strikes. . . . So that without words there is no possibility of reckoning numbers, much less magnitudes, swiftness, force, and other things the reckonings whereof are necessary to the being or well-being of mankind.

---

philosopher who holds to universals would say that this is a property of the shape that constitutes a triangle, and it applies to any triangle that exists, that once existed, and could exist. However, the nominalist denies that this necessarily applies to all triangles, right or not. The nominalist believes the geometer has calculated a feature of this particular triangle, but there is no immediate reason to believe that it applies to any other triangles prior to calculating the sum of the angles in them as well.

When two names are joined together into a consequence or affirmation such as "A man is a living creature," or "If he be a man, he is a living creature," if the latter name "living creature" signifies all that the former name "man" signifies, then the affirmation or consequence is true. Otherwise, it is false. For "true" and "false" are attributes of speech, not of things. Where there is no speech, there is neither truth nor falsehood. There may be error, as when we expect that which shall not be, or suspect what has not been, but in neither case can a man be charged with untruth.

Seeing then that truth consists in the right ordering of names in our affirmations, a man who seeks precise truth must remember what every name he uses stands for, and to place it accordingly. Otherwise, he will find himself entangled in words like a bird in lime twigs. The more he struggles, the more belimed. Therefore in geometry (which is the only science that has pleased God so far to bestow on mankind) men begin at settling the significations of their words. Settling significations they call definitions and place them in the beginning of their reckoning.

By this it appears how necessary it is for any man who aspires to true knowledge to examine the definitions of former authors and either to correct them where they are negligently set down, or to make them himself. For the errors of definitions multiply themselves according as the reckoning proceeds, and lead men into absurdities which at last they see but cannot avoid without reckoning anew from the beginning, in which lies the foundation of their errors. From this it happens that they who trust to books do as they who cast up many little sums into a greater without considering whether those little sums were rightly cast up or not. At last finding the error visible, and not mistrusting their first grounds, they do not know which way to clear themselves but spend time in fluttering over their books as birds entering a chimney and finding themselves enclosed in a chamber, flitter at the false light of a glass window because they do not know which way they came in. So that in the right definition of names lies the first use of speech, which is the acquisition of science. And in wrong or no definitions lies the first abuse from which proceeds all false and senseless tenets which make those men who take their instruction from the authority of books and not from their own meditation[14] to be as much below the condition of ignorant men as men endued with true science are above it. For between true science and erroneous doctrines, ignorance is in the middle. Natural sense and imagination are not subject to absurdity. Nature itself cannot err. And as men abound in copiousness of language, so they become more wise or more mad than ordinary. Nor is it possible without letters for any man to become either excellently wise or (unless his memory is hurt by disease or ill constitution of organs) excellently foolish. For words are wise men's counters. They do but reckon by them. But they are the money of fools, who value them by

---

14. It is not that Hobbes believed books to be sources of error in and of themselves, but instead he (as most modern philosophers) was distrustful simply of claims written down and recited where the recitation often makes people accept a claim to be true simply because it is familiar or written down.

the authority of an Aristotle, a Cicero, or a Thomas [Aquinas], or any other Doctor whatsoever, if but a man.[15]

Whatever can enter into or be considered in an account and added to another to make a sum, or subtracted from another and leave a remainder, is subject to names. The Latins called accounts of money *rationes*, and accounting, *ratiocinatio*. And that which we in bills or books of account call "items," they called *nomina*, that is, "names." It seems to proceed that they extended the word "ratio" to the faculty of reckoning in all other things. The Greeks have but one word, "logos," for both speech and reason. Not that they thought there was no speech without reason, but there is no reasoning without speech. They called the act of reasoning "syllogism,"[16] which signifies summing up the consequences of one saying to another. Because the same things may enter into account for diverse accidents, their names are (to show that diversity) diversely wrested and diversified. This diversity of names may be reduced to four general heads.

First, a thing may enter into account for matter or body, as living, sensible, rational, hot, cold, moved, quiet, by which names the word "matter" or "body" is

---

15. It was common for the philosophers Hobbes is criticizing to appeal to what prior philosophers ("authorities") once said instead of working the problems out by observing nature. He specifically mentions three people here: Aristotle, Cicero, and Thomas Aquinas. Aristotle was a philosopher from ancient Greece who became the most popular and powerful scholarly authority. Thomas Aquinas was a medieval philosopher and theologian who borrowed heavily from Aristotle, synthesizing his views with Christian belief, and became an authority just as strong as Aristotle for later medieval philosophers and on into Hobbes' day. Cicero was an eclectic Roman philosopher who drew in part from the philosophical tradition of Stoicism, though taking liberties of his own when writing.

16. Syllogisms are deductive arguments composed of three statements, of which two are premises (reasons offered in support of a claim) and one is a conclusion (the point at issue that is to be justified by premises). Aristotle is recognized as the inventor of this type of deductive reasoning. Deductive arguments are characterized such that if the premises offered in support of a conclusion are true, the conclusion derived from them must be true as well. In other words, in a valid deductive argument (of any kind), it is impossible for the conclusion to be false when the premises of the argument are true. With all this said, it is also the case that modern philosophers tend to be suspicious of "mere" syllogisms because they have been associated with the reasoning of the "Schools" in which new discovery and certainty are not the goal of inquiry, but instead justifying beliefs or claims already accepted. It is therefore clear that when Hobbes and Descartes, for example, go about breaking down the foundations of uncertain arguments and claims to knowledge to replace them with reliable claims and information, they are doing so to combat the weakness of mere deductive reasoning. Syllogistic reasoning is merely deductive, which means that if the premises of the argument in which statements appear are true, the conclusion must also be true. This, however, is not enough for those on a search for absolute certainty, or "science" in Hobbes' way of conceiving it. Instead, it must be the case that the terms used and the statements formulated are themselves beyond doubt so that the arguments in which they appear are no longer simply "mere" deductions but have become demonstrations (such as the reasoning in geometry, which Hobbes has already identified as the only science with which God has so far seen fit to provide to us).

understood. All are names of matter. Second, it may enter into account or be considered for some accident or quality which we conceive to be in it. As for instance,
being moved, being so long, or being hot. Then, through the name of the thing
itself, by a little change or wrestling it, we make a name for that accident which we
then consider. This is the case for "living" put into the account "life," and the same
for "moved" and "motion," "hot" and "heat," "long" and "length," and the like. All
such names are the names of accidents and properties by which one matter and
body is distinguished from another. These are called "abstract names" because they
are severed from the account of matter but not from matter itself. Third, we bring
into account the properties of our own bodies whereby we make such distinction
as when anything is seen by us, we do not reckon the thing itself, but the sight,
the color, the idea of it in the fancy. When anything is heard, we reckon it only by
hearing or sound, which is our fancy or conception of it by the ear. And such are
names of fancies. Fourth, we bring into account, consider, and give names to names
themselves, and to speeches. "General," "universal," "special," and "equivocal" are
names of names. "Affirmation," "interrogation," "commandment," "narration," "syllogism," "sermon," "oration," and many other such are names of speeches. This is all
the variety of positive names which are used to mark something in nature or that
may be imagined by the mind of man as bodies that are or may be conceived to
be or of the properties of bodies that are or may be imagined or words and speech.

There are also other names called "negative" which are notes to signify that a
word is not the name of the thing in question such as the words "nothing," "no
man," "infinite," "indocible," "three want four," and the like. They are nevertheless
of use in reckoning or in correcting reckoning and call to mind our past thoughts
though they are not names of anything because they make us refuse to admit of
names not used rightly.

All other names are insignificant sounds, and those are of two sorts. One, when
they are new and their meaning not explained by definition, whereof there has
been an abundant number coined by Schoolmen and confused philosophers.
Another occurs when men make a name of two names whose significations are
contradictory and inconsistent such as an "incorporeal body" or (which is the same)
an "incorporeal substance,"[17] and a great number more. For whenever any affirmation is false, the two names of which it is composed put together and made one
signify nothing at all. For example, if it is a false affirmation to say "A quadrangle
is round," the word "round quadrangle" signifies nothing but is a mere sound. So
likewise if it is false to say that virtue can be powered or blown up and down the
words "in-powered virtue" and "in-blown virtue" are as absurd and insignificant as

---

17. When Hobbes contends that "incorporeal substance" is a meaningless phrase, he has
posed significant difficulties in his account of God in any normally recognized and orthodox sense of the term. It seems clear, especially in later chapters of *Leviathan*, particularly in
Part III, that Hobbes considers God to be a material thing that must be infinite. Remember,
too, that Hobbes has already noted above that it is impossible for human beings to have any
conception or idea of God because all that which we perceive (which is the only source of
our ideas) is finite.

a "round quadrangle." Therefore you shall hardly meet with a senseless and insignificant word that is not made up of some Latin or Greek names. . . .

When a man hears any speech and has thoughts which the words of that speech and their connection were intended and constituted to signify, then he is said to understand it. Understanding is nothing else but conception caused by speech. Therefore if speech is peculiar to man, then understanding is peculiar to him also. Therefore there can be no understanding of absurd and false affirmations when they are universal, though many think they understand when they repeat the words softly or con them in their mind. What kinds of speeches signify the appetites, aversions, and passions of man's mind and of their use and abuse, I shall speak when I have spoken of the passions.

The names of things that affect us, that is, which please and displease us, are in common discourse of inconstant signification because all men are not affected in the same way with the same thing nor the same man the same way at all times. For seeing all names are imposed to signify our conceptions, and all our affections are but conceptions, when we conceive the same things differently we can hardly avoid naming them differently. For though the nature of what we conceive is the same, the diversity of our reception of it in respect of different constitutions of body and prejudices of opinion gives everything a tincture of our different passions. Therefore in reasoning, a man must take heed of words, which besides the signification we imagine of their nature, disposition, and interest of the speaker, such as are the names of virtues and vices. For one man calls wisdom what another calls fear; and one cruelty what another calls justice; one prodigality what another calls magnanimity; one gravity what another calls stupidity, etc.[18] Therefore such names can never be true grounds of any ratiocination. Neither can metaphors and tropes of speech. But these are less dangerous because they profess their inconstancy, which the others do not.

---

18. Hobbes' position concerning the "inconstancy" of the names of things that please or displease us is very important in at least two main respects. First, such things as our passions cannot be the subject of ratiocination (science) and, second because of the differences in our attitudes toward things (for example, what I like today I may not like tomorrow; and you and I may disagree on whether a particular thing is desirable), human beings find themselves in often intractable disagreements about them, leading to difficulties that Hobbes ultimately makes clear in Chapter XIII with respect to the "state of war" and why a final arbiter of language (the political sovereign) must be put in place to quell such disagreements.

Chapter V. Of Reason and Science

The appropriate subjects of reason and science are clarified in Chapter V. Reason is nothing more than adding and subtracting the consequences of names. Names are the words on which human beings agree to mark and signify their thoughts. The subject matter of science is therefore founded on words.

Hobbes is careful to note that we reach absurd conclusions by having insufficient method or no method at all for guiding our reasoning. He gives examples, such as statements in which we give the names of material bodies to their qualities, or when we use metaphors, as cases in which the words we use mean and signify nothing. But because science is composed of reasoning about words, it does not mean that the subject matter of science is simply a human invention involving completely arbitrary combinations of terms conjured up with meanings of any kind. Instead, for example, Hobbes notes that since there is nothing in the world except material things, when we make some claims about purportedly nonmaterial things, those claims amount to nonsense and are therefore not the subjects of science and reasoning. A statement such as "The soul is immaterial," is for Hobbes completely meaningless. If there is something we mean by "immaterial" substance, the term does not correspond to anything real. In fact, what is called "immaterial" is the negation of what is "material," and since Hobbes holds that the only things that exist are material things (which include soul or spirit), to claim that the soul or spirit is immaterial is to engage in a contradiction. We must therefore exercise great caution in reasoning since it is essential to the employment of careful method to create consequences. This, for Hobbes, is science.

When a man reasons, he does nothing else but conceive a sum total from addition of parcels or a remainder from subtraction of one sum from another. If it is done by words it is conceiving of the consequence of the names of all the parts to the name of the whole or from the names of the whole and one part to the name of another part. In some things (as in numbers) besides adding and subtracting, men name other operations such as multiplying and dividing. Yet they are the same because multiplication is just addition together of things equal; and division is subtracting of one thing, as often as we can. These operations are not applicable only to numbers, but to all manner of things that can be added together and taken out of another. For as arithmeticians teach to add and subtract in numbers, so geometricians teach the same in lines, figures (solid and superficial), angles, proportions, times, degrees of swiftness, force, power, and the like. Logicians teach the same in consequences of words, adding together two names to make an affirmation; and two affirmations to make a syllogism, and many syllogisms to make a demonstration, and from the sum or conclusion of a syllogism they subtract one proposition to find another. Writers of politics add together pactions to find men's duties, and lawyers find laws and facts to find what is right and wrong in the actions of private men. In sum, wherever there is place for addition and subtraction, there also is place for reason. Where these have no place, reason has nothing at all to do there.

Out of all of which we may define (that is, determine) what is meant by this word "reason" when we reckon it among the faculties of the mind. For reason in this sense is nothing but reckoning (that is, adding and subtracting) the consequences of general names agreed upon for marking and signifying our thoughts. I say marking them, when we reckon by ourselves; and signifying, when we demonstrate or approve our reckonings to other men.

As in arithmetic, unpracticed men must err and professors may often err, and [consequently they] cast up false. So also in any other subject of reasoning it is the case that the ablest, most attentive, and most practiced men may deceive themselves and infer false conclusions. Not that reason itself is always right reason, as well as arithmetic is a certain and infallible art.[19] But no one man's reason nor the reason of any number of men makes certainty any more than an account is therefore well cast up because a great many men have unanimously approved it. Therefore, as when there is a controversy in an account, the parties must by their own accord set up for right reason the reason of some arbitrator or judge to whose sentence they will both stand. Otherwise their controversy must either come to blows or be undecided for want of right reason constituted by nature. So it is also in all debates of whatever kind. When men think themselves wiser than all others they clamor and demand right reason for judge. Yet they seek no more but that things should be determined by no other men's reason but their own. This is as intolerable in the society of men as it is in play after trump is turned to use for trump on any occasion that suit whereof they have most in their hand. . . .[20]

---

19. Hobbes' wording here is a bit confusing in both the Molesworth and Penguin editions of *Leviathan*. Hobbes is saying that all reasoning can be erroneous and lead to falsehood. Even in a case when reasoning itself is done properly (that is, the rules of reasoning are followed), false conclusions will result if the content of the statements made in the process of reasoning are themselves false. Finding out, however, whether a statement with which one begins reasoning is true or false is only possible with certainty in cases in which we have ourselves defined the terms (as is the case with geometry). But when it comes to facts in the world that are the subject matter of that about which we are reasoning, it is simple enough that errors can be made when we cannot be certain that the information with which we start is accurate. Hobbes uses the example of a person accounting for expenses in a household and trusting the list of items and expenses as being accurate in trying to "balance the books." If one of the pieces of information is incorrect, the entire process of reasoning, even in a case in which the reasoning itself is done carefully and without error, leads to error in the final conclusion. It is human error, then, that leads to false conclusions, not the science of how to reason itself. When there are issues or topics that cannot be decided by reasoning itself, it is then, as Hobbes notes, that we must defer to the decision of someone to decide the case. Otherwise, the parties to the disagreement in the accuracy of basic claims may "come to blows."

20. In other words, everyone wants reason to favor the position they already take or that which they think is true. This is "intolerable" in society for the same reason that cheating

The use and end of reason is beginning at first definitions and significations of names to proceed from one consequence to another. It is not finding the sum and truth of one or a few consequences that are remote from first definitions and significations of names. There can be no certainty of the last conclusion without certainty of all the affirmations and negations on which it was grounded and inferred. When a master of a family in taking an account casts up the sums of all the bills of expense into one sum and, not regarding how each bill is summed up by those who give them in account, nor what it is he pays for, he advantages himself no more than if he allowed the account in gross, trusting to every one of the accountants' skill and honesty. So also in reckoning all other things when he takes conclusions on the trust of authors and does not get them from the first items in every reckoning (which are the significations of names settled by definitions) he loses his labor and does not know anything. He only believes.

When a man reckons without the use of words, which may be done in particular things (as when upon the sight of any one thing, we conjecture what was likely to have preceded or is likely to follow upon it) if that which he thought likely to follow does not follow or that which he thought likely to have preceded has not preceded it, it is error, to which even the most prudent men are subject. But when we reason in words of general signification and fall upon a general inference which is false, though it is commonly called error, it is actually an absurdity or senseless speech. This is true because error is just deception in presuming that something is past or to come though it is not past or to come. Yet in this there was no impossibility discoverable. But when we make a general assertion, unless it is a true one, the possibility of it is inconceivable. Words whereby we conceive nothing but the sound are called absurd, insignificant, and nonsense. Therefore if a man should talk to me of a round quadrangle, or accidents of bread in cheese, or immaterial substances, or of a free subject, a free-will, or any free but free from being hindered by opposition,[21] I should not say he were in error, but that his words were without meaning—that is to say, they are absurd.

I have said before (in Chapter II) that man exceeds all other animals in this faculty that when he conceives anything, he is apt to inquire the consequences of it and what effects he could do with it. Now I add this other degree of the same excellence that he can by words reduce the consequences he finds to general rules

---

in cards is intolerable in that social practice. If a player identifies as the trump suit in a card game the type of cards he has most in his hand, he is unfairly advantaging himself, which is taking his own reason for right reason. This is an interesting and important claim that is not often noted by commentators on Hobbes in the context in which it appears. Where Hobbes is suggesting that it is unfair of a person to advantage himself over others where there are constitutive rules of a game in place, Hobbes may be making a claim that belies the common interpretation of his moral views as "psychological egoism."

21. Hobbes is here hinting at what he will explain later in *Leviathan* at several points: that there is no such thing as a "free-will." In fact, for Hobbes the term "free-will" is nonsense or absurdity. Instead only the actor is either free or not free. To be free is not to be hindered in doing what one wants to do.

called theorems or aphorisms. That is, he can reason or reckon not only in number, but in all other things, whereof one may be added to or subtracted from another.

But this privilege is allayed by the privilege of absurdity to which no living creature except man is subject. Men who profess philosophy are of all men most subject to it. For it is most true that Cicero said of them somewhere that there can be nothing so absurd but may be found in the books of philosophers.[22] The reason is obvious. For there is not one of them who begins his ratiocination from the definitions or explications of the names they are to use, which is a method that has been only in geometry, whose conclusions have thereby been made indisputable.

The first cause of absurd conclusions I ascribe to lack of method in that they do not begin their ratiocination from definitions, that is, from settled significations of their words.... Whereas all bodies enter into account upon diverse considerations (which I have mentioned in the preceding chapter) these considerations being diversely named, diverse absurdities proceed from the confusion and unfit connection of their names into assertions. Therefore the second cause of absurd assertions I ascribe to giving names of bodies to accidents or of accidents to bodies, as they do who say that faith is infused or inspired when nothing can be powered or breathed into anything but body, and that extension is body, that phantasms are spirits, etc.

The third I ascribe to giving names of accidents to bodies outside us to the accidents of our own bodies, as they do who say "the color is in the body," "the sound is in the air," etc. The fourth, to giving names of bodies to names or speeches—such as saying that there are universal things, that a living creature is a genus, or a general thing, etc. The fifth, to giving names of accidents to names and speeches as saying that the nature of a thing is in its definition, that a man's command is his will, and the like. The sixth, to the use of metaphors, tropes, and other rhetorical figures instead of proper words. Though it is lawful to say (for example) in common speech, "The way goes," or "lead hither," . . . the Proverb says this or that (whereas ways cannot go, nor Proverbs speak), yet in reckoning and seeking truth, such speeches are not to be admitted. The seventh, to names that signify nothing but are taken up and learned by rote from the Schools, such as "hypostatical," "transubstantiate," "consubstantiate," "eternal-now," and the like canting of Schoolmen.

For one who can avoid these things it is not easy to fall into any absurdity unless it is by the length of an account, wherein he may perhaps forget what went before. For all men by nature reason alike and well when they have good principles. For who is so stupid as both to mistake in geometry and also to persist in it when another points out his error to him?

By this it appears that reason is not, as sense and memory, born with us nor is it gotten only by experience as prudence is. Reason is attained by industry, first in apt imposing of names and second by getting a good and orderly method in proceeding from the elements, which are names, to assertions made by connection

---

22. Hobbes offers a testy comment on the works of Aristotle in Chapter XLVI, in which he asserts, "I believe that scarcely anything can be more absurdly said in natural philosophy than that which now is called Aristotle's *Metaphysics*, nor more repugnant to government than much of what he has said in his *Politics*, nor more ignorantly than a great part of his *Ethics*."

of one of them to another, and so to syllogisms, which are the connections of one assertion to another, until we come to knowledge of all the consequences of names applying to the subject at hand. That is what men call science.[23] Whereas sense and memory are just knowledge of fact which is a thing past and irrevocable, science is knowledge of consequences and dependence of one fact upon another by which, out of what we can presently do, we know how to do something else when we will or the like another time. When we see how anything comes about, upon what causes, and by what manner, when like causes come into our power we see how to make it produce like effects.

Children therefore are not endowed with reason at all until they have attained the use of speech. They are called reasonable creatures for the apparent possibility of having the use of reason in the future. And most men, though they have the use of reasoning a little way, as in numbering to some degree, it serves them to little use in common life in which they govern themselves, some better and some worse, according to their differences of experience, quickness of memory, and inclinations to several ends, but especially according to good or evil fortune and the errors of one another. As for science or certain rules of their actions, they are so far from it that they do not know what it is.

Geometry they have thought conjuring. But for other sciences, they who have not been taught the beginnings and progress in them so that they may see how they are acquired and generated are like children who having no thought of generation are made to believe by women that their brothers and sisters are not born but found in the garden. They who have no science are in better and nobler condition with their natural prudence than men who reason improperly or, by trusting others who reason improperly, fall upon false and absurd general rules. For ignorance of causes and of rules does not set men so far astray as relying on false rules and taking for causes of what they aspire to that those are not so, but rather causes of the contrary.

To conclude, the light of human minds is perspicuous words snuffed and purged from ambiguity by exact definitions. Reason is the pace, increase of science is the way, and the benefit of mankind is the end. On the contrary, metaphors and senseless and ambiguous words are like Ignes Fatui;[24] and reasoning upon them is wandering among innumerable absurdities and their end is contention and sedition, or contempt.

As much experience is prudence, so is much science sapience. Even though we usually have the name of wisdom for them both, the Latins always distinguished between *prudentia* and *sapientia*, ascribing the former to experience and the latter to science. To make their difference appear more clearly, let us suppose one man endowed with excellent natural use and dexterity in handling his arms and another to have added to that dexterity an acquired science where he can offend or be offended by his adversary in every possible posture or guard. The ability of the former would be the ability of the latter, as prudence to sapience, both useful but

---

23. Note that science does not mean what we take it to mean today, that is, like the natural sciences, but instead mathematical—or more accurately, geometrical—reasoning.
24. An odd flickering light.

the latter infallible. They who trust only the authority of books follow the blind blindly, and are like the person who trusts to the false rules of the master of fence and ventures presumptuously upon an adversary who either kills or disgraces him.[25]

Some signs of science are certain and infallible while some are uncertain. Signs are certain when he who claims the science of anything can teach it—that is to say, demonstrates the truth perspicuously to another. It is uncertain when only some particular events answer to his claim, and upon many occasions prove so as he says they must. Signs of prudence are all uncertain because to observe by experience and to remember all circumstances that may alter success is impossible. But in any business in which a man does not have infallible science by which to proceed, to forsake his own natural judgment, and to be guided by general sentences read in authors and subject to many exceptions is a sign of folly and generally scorned as pedantry. Even of politics and history, very few do it in their domestic affairs where their particular interest is concerned. They have prudence enough for their private affairs, but in public they study more the reputation of their own wit than the success of another's business.[26]

---

25. It is no accident that Hobbes uses an analogy regarding the potential for death in fencing in which one believes himself well equipped to fight but is actually in possession of bad rules and ends up dead or disgraced. The same serious consequences are found in cases in which people follow the nonsense of Aristotelian metaphysics and ethics in forming political organizations and find themselves in war. See esp. Chapter XIII.

26. Hobbes is again giving a hint of what is to come at the end of Part I and throughout Part II of *Leviathan*. Just as a person may do an acceptable or good job in managing his own individual or family affairs, applying individual prudential knowledge to larger groups is subject to many problems, not the least of which has to do with reputation, in which a person tries to appear to know more than he actually does, blinding himself to other information and knowledge that might be helpful and beneficial.

Chapter VI. Of the Interior Beginnings of Voluntary Motions Commonly Called the Passions and the Speeches by Which They Are Expressed

Human beings are nothing more than bodies in motion. "Animal motion" is voluntary and the beginning of all voluntary motion is in the imagination. We are moved by desire and aversion, corresponding to what we want (that toward which we move) and that which we wish to avoid (that away from which we move). In short, this chapter is about human desires and aversions. Because motion is change, and because our desires and aversions are motions, there is nothing static about that which we love (desire) or that which we hate (aversion). This means, too, that sometimes we call a particular thing or event good and another time we call the same thing evil, depending on whether we desire it or are averse to it at that time. Therefore, there is nothing simply and absolutely good and nothing simply and absolutely bad or evil, and instead the terms "good" and "evil" are used with respect to and relative to a person.

Note that Hobbes' discussion of the terms "religion" and "superstition" in this chapter is closely related to conceptions of good and evil. The things we call "bad" or "good" are determined by us to be such based on the power or quality of a thing corresponding to our aversion or desire. Sometimes, the things we fear are "invisible" powers that are the product of imagination, and Hobbes specifically refers to "fear of invisible power" as "religion" when it is publicly approved. It is superstition otherwise.

We deliberate about things we find desirable or offensive, and the last appetite or aversion is "will." Will is the action resulting from deliberation about things we find desirable or objects of aversion. Regularly obtaining the things we desire is happiness in this life.

There are two sorts of motions unique to animals. One is called vital, begun in generation, and continued without interruption through their whole life such as are the course of the blood, the pulse, breathing, concoctions, nutrition, excretion, etc., to which motions no help of imagination is needed. The other is animal motion, otherwise called voluntary motion, as to go, to speak, to move any of our limbs in a manner as first fancied in our minds.

Motion is the sense in the organs and interior parts of man's body caused by the action of the things we see, hear, etc. Fancy is just the relics of the same motion remaining after sense, which has been already said in Chapters I and II. It is evident that the imagination is the first internal beginning of all voluntary motion because going, speaking, and the like voluntary motions always depend upon a precedent thought of whither, which way, and what. Even though unstudied men do not conceive any motion at all to be there where the thing moved is invisible, or the space in which it is moved is (for the shortness of it) insensible, that does not mean that such motions do not exist. Let a space be ever so little, what is moved over a greater space whereof that little one is part must first be moved over that. Endeavor is the small beginnings of motion within the body of man before they appear in walking, speaking, striking, and other visible actions.

Endeavor is called appetite or desire when it is toward something which causes it. Desire is the general name and appetite often restrained to signify the desire of food, namely hunger and thirst. When the endeavor is away from something, it is generally called aversion. The words "appetite" and "aversion" we have from the Latins and they both signify the motions of approaching and of retiring. So also do the Greek words for the same, which are *orme* and *aphorme*. For nature itself often presses upon men those truths which afterward, when they look for something beyond nature, they stumble at. For the schools find in mere appetite to go, or move, no actual motion at all. But because they must acknowledge some motion, they call it "metaphorical motion," which is absurd speech, for though words may be called metaphorical, bodies and motions cannot.

That which men desire they are also said to love, and hate those things for which they have aversion. So desire and love are the same thing except by desire we always signify the absence of the object and by love, most commonly the presence of the object. So also by aversion we signify the absence and by hate the presence of the object.

Some appetites and aversions are born with men, such as appetite of food, of excretion, and exoneration (which may also and more properly be called aversions, from something they feel in their bodies) and some other appetites, not many. The rest, which are appetites of particular things, proceed from experience and trial of their effects on themselves or other men. Of things we do not know at all or that we believe not to exist we can have no further desire than to taste and try. But we have aversion for things we know have hurt us and also for those we do not know whether they will hurt us or not.

We have contempt for things which we neither desire nor hate. Contempt is nothing but an immobility or contumacy of the heart in resisting the action of certain things, and proceeding from that the heart is already moved otherwise by either more potent objects or from lack of experience of them. Because the constitution of man's body is in continual mutation it is impossible that all the same things should always cause in him the same appetites and aversions. Much less can all men consent in the desire of almost any one and the same object.

Good is whatever is the object of any man's appetite or desire. The object of his hate and aversion is evil. The object of his contempt is vile and inconsiderable. For the words "good," "evil," and "contemptible" are used with relation to the person who uses them. There is nothing simply and absolutely so, nor is there any common rule of good and evil to be taken from the nature of the objects themselves. Instead, good and evil are taken from the person of the man (where there is no commonwealth) or (in a commonwealth) from the person who represents it.[27] Or they can be taken from an arbitrator or judge whom men who disagree shall set up by consent and make his sentence the rule of it.

The Latin tongue has two words whose significations approach those of good and evil, but they are not precisely the same. They are *pulchrum* and *turpe*. The former signifies that which by some apparent signs promise good and the latter that which promises evil. But in our tongue we do not have so general names to express them. Instead, for *pulchrum*, we say in some things "fair," or "beautiful," or "handsome," or "gallant," or "honorable," or "comely," or "amiable." For *turpe*, "foul," "deformed," "ugly," "base," nauseous," and the like as the subject shall require. All these words in their proper places signify nothing else but the manner or countenance that promises good and evil. So there are three kinds of good: good in the promise, that is *pulchrum*; good in effect, as the end desired, which is called *jucundum*, "delightful"; and good as the means, which is called "utile," "profitable." And as many of evil. For evil in promise, they call *turpe*; evil in effect and end is *molestum*, "unpleasant," "troublesome"; and evil in the means, "inutile," "unprofitable," "hurtful."

As in sense, that which is really within us is (as I have said before) only motion caused by the action of external objects. But it is in appearance. To the sight, light and color; to the ear, sound; to the nostril, odor, etc. So when the action of the same object is continued from the eyes, ears, and other organs to the heart, the real effect there is nothing but motion or endeavor, which consists in appetite or aversion to or from the object moving. But the appearance or sense of that motion is what we either call delight or trouble of the mind.

The motion which is called appetite and for the appearance of it "delight" and pleasure seems to be a corroboration of vital motion and a help to it. Therefore such things that cause delight were not improperly called *jucunda* from helping or fortifying; and the contrary, *molesta*, "offensive," from hindering and troubling the vital motion.

Therefore pleasure (or delight) is the appearance or sense of good; and molestation or displeasure is the appearance or sense of evil. Consequently all appetite, desire, and love are accompanied with more or less delight; and all hatred and aversion with more or less displeasure and offense.

Some pleasures or delights arise from the sense of a present object and those may be called pleasures of sense (the word "sensual" as it is used by those only who condemn them have no place until there are laws). Of this kind are all onerations and exonerations of the body, as also all that is pleasant in the sight, hearing, smell, taste, or touch. Others arise from the expectation that proceeds from foresight of the end or consequence of things, whether those things in the sense please or displease. These are pleasure of the mind of him who draws those consequences and are generally called joy. In like manner, some displeasures are in the senses and are called pain. Others, in the expectation of consequences, are called grief.

---

27. The issue of the nature of good and evil appears again in more detail in Chapter XIII, where it is related to the causes of disagreement and quarrel between people when they desire the same thing(s).

These simple passions called "appetite," "desire," "love," "aversion," "hate," "joy," and "grief" have their names for diverse considerations diversified. As first, when one succeeds another, they are diversely called from the opinion men have of the likelihood of attaining what they desire. Second, from the object loved or hated. Third, from the consideration of many of them together. Fourth, from the alteration or succession itself.

For appetite with an opinion of attaining is called hope. The same, without such opinion, despair. Aversion, with opinion of hurt from the object, fear. The same, with hope of avoiding that hurt by resistance, courage.

Sudden courage is anger. Constant hope is confidence of ourselves. Constant despair is diffidence of ourselves. Anger for great hurt done to another, when we conceive the same to be done by injury, is indignation. Desire of good to another is benevolence, good will, or charity. If to a man generally, it is good nature.

Desire of riches, covetousness, is a name used always to signify blame because men contending for riches are displeased with one another's attaining them. Though the desire in itself is to be blamed or allowed according to the means by which those riches are sought. Desire of office, or precedence, is ambition. It is a name used also in the worse sense, for the reason before mentioned.

Desire of things that conduce but a little to our ends and fear of things that are but of little hindrance is pusillanimity. Contempt of little helps and hindrances is magnanimity. Magnanimity in danger of death or wounds is valor or fortitude. Magnanimity in the use of riches is liberality. Pusillanimity, in the same, is wretchedness, miserableness; or parsimony as it is liked or disliked.

Love of persons for society is kindness. Love of persons for pleasing the sense only is natural lust. Love of the same, acquired from rumination, that is imagination of pleasure past, is luxury. Love of one singularly, with desire to be singularly beloved, is the passion of love. The same, with fear that the love is not mutual, is jealousy. Desire, by doing hurt to another, to make him condemn some fact of his own, is revengefulness.

Desire to know why, and how, is curiosity such as is in no living creature but man. So man is distinguished not only by his reason but also by this singular passion from other animals in whom the appetite of food and other pleasures of sense, by predominance, take away the care of knowing causes. Knowing causes is a lust of the mind that, by a perseverance of delight in the continual and indefatigable generation of knowledge, exceeds the short vehemence of any carnal pleasure.

Fear of invisible power, feigned by the mind or imagined from tales publicly allowed, is religion. Not allowed is superstition. When the power imagined is truly such as we imagine, it is true religion. Fear, without the apprehension of why or what, is panic terror. It is called so from the fables that make Pan the author of them. Whereas in truth there is always in him who so fears first some apprehension of the cause, though the rest run away by example, every one supposing his fellow to know why. And therefore this passion happens to none but in a throng, or multitude of people.

Joy, from apprehension of novelty, is admiration. It is proper to man, because it excites the appetite of knowing the cause. Joy, arising from imagination of a man's own power and ability, is that exultation of the mind which is called glorying. If grounded upon the experience of his own former actions is the same with confidence. But if grounded on the flattery of others, or only supposed by himself for delight in the consequences of it, is called vain-glory. This name is properly given because a well-grounded confidence begets attempt, whereas supposing power does not and is therefore rightly called vain. Grief, from opinion of want of power, is called dejection of mind.

The vain-glory which consists in feigning or supposing abilities in ourselves which we know we do not have is most incident to young men and nourished by the histories or fictions of gallant persons and is often corrected by age and employment. Sudden glory is the passion which makes those grimaces called laughter and is caused either by some sudden act of their own that pleases them or by the apprehension of some deformed thing in another, by comparison whereof they suddenly applaud themselves. It is incident most to those who are conscious of the fewest abilities in themselves who are forced to keep themselves in their own favor by observing the imperfections of other men. Therefore much laughter at the defects of others is a sign of pusillanimity. Of great minds, one of the proper works is to help and free others from scorn and compare themselves only with the most able.

On the contrary, sudden dejection is the passion that causes weeping and is caused by accidents such as suddenly having some vehement hope or some prop of their power taken away. Those who rely principally on external helps (such as women and children) are most subject to it. Therefore, some weep for the loss of friends, others for their unkindness, others for the sudden stop made to their thoughts of revenge by reconciliation. But in all cases, both laughter and weeping are sudden motions. Custom takes them both away for no man laughs at old jests or weeps for an old calamity.

Grief for the discovery of some defect of ability is shame or the passion that discovers itself in blushing and consists in the apprehension of something dishonorable. In young men it is a sign of the love of good reputation and commendable. In old men it is a sign of the same, but because it comes too late, it is not commendable. Contempt of good reputation is called impudence.

Grief for the calamity of another is pity and arises from the imagination that the like calamity may befall himself, and therefore is also called compassion and in the phrase of this present time a fellow feeling. Therefore, for calamity arising from great wickedness, those who have least pity are those who are the best men and those who think themselves least susceptible to it. Contempt, or little sense of the calamity of others, is that which men call cruelty, proceeding from security of their own fortune. I do not conceive it possible that any man should take pleasure in other men's great harms without other end of his own.

Grief, for the success of a competitor in wealth, honor, or other good, if it is joined with endeavor to enforce our own abilities to equal or exceed him, is called emulation. But joined with endeavor to supplant or hinder a competitor, it is envy.

When in the mind of man appetites, aversions, hopes, and fears concerning one and the same thing arise alternately, it is deliberation. Diverse good and evil consequences of doing or omitting the thing propounded come successively into our thoughts so that sometimes we have an appetite to it, sometimes an aversion from it.

Sometimes we have hope to be able to do it, sometimes despair or fear to attempt it. The whole sum of desires, aversions, hopes, and fears continued until the thing is either done or thought impossible is deliberation.

Therefore there is no deliberation of things in the past because they are manifestly impossible to change. Nor of things known to be impossible, or thought so because men know or think such deliberation vain. Of things impossible which we think possible we may deliberate, not knowing it is in vain. It is called deliberation because it is putting an end to the liberty we had of doing or omitting according to our own appetite or aversion. This alternate succession of appetites, aversions, hopes, and fears is no less in other living creatures than in man and therefore beasts also deliberate. Every deliberation is then said to end when that about which they deliberate is either done or thought impossible, because until then we retain the liberty of doing or omitting according to our appetite or aversion.

In deliberation, the last appetite or aversion immediately adhering to the action or to the omission thereof is what we call the will.[28] It is the act, not the faculty, of willing. Beasts having deliberation must necessarily also have will. The definition of the will given commonly by the Schools, that it is a rational appetite, is not good. For if it were, then there could be no voluntary act against reason. For a voluntary act is that which proceeds from the will, and no other. But if instead of a rational appetite, we shall say an appetite resulting from a preceding deliberation, then the definition is the same that I have given here. Will, therefore, is the last appetite in deliberating. Though we say in common discourse that a man had a will once to do a thing that nevertheless he forbore to do, that is actually an inclination, which makes no action voluntary, because the action depends not on it but on the last inclination or appetite. For if the intervenient appetites make any action voluntary, then by the same reason all intervenient aversions should make the same action involuntary, and so one and the same action should be both voluntary and involuntary. By this it is clear that not only actions that have their beginning from covetousness, ambition, lust, or other appetites to the thing propounded, but also those that have their beginning from aversion or fear of those consequences that follow the omission are voluntary actions.[29]

The forms of speech by which the passions are expressed are partly the same and partly different from those by which we express our thoughts. First generally,

---

28. Note here that "will" is not a "thing" but is instead the result of a process of deliberation. So what is willed is the act attended with the last point in a process of deliberation. As noted previously, will is neither free nor unfree. The only thing to which the term "free" applies is actions when they are not hindered or, more specifically, a person is free when he is not hindered in doing what he has willed to do. Hobbes agrees with Aristotle (see *Nicomachean Ethics*, trans. Terence Irwin, 2nd ed. [Indianapolis, IN: Hackett, 1999]) where he asserts that "among those things up to us, we deliberate about and [consequently] desire to do. Hence also decision will be deliberative desire to do an action that is up to us; for when we have judged [that it is right] as a result of deliberation, we desire to do it in accord with our wish." (36)

29. The notion that an action proceeding from fear is voluntary is important to Hobbes' argument for the creation of government power in the form of sovereignty, which is the result of the fear of death. See esp. Chapters XIII through XXXI.

all passions may be expressed indicatively as "I love," "I fear," "I joy," "I deliberate," "I will," "I command." But some of them have particular expressions by themselves which nevertheless are not affirmations unless they serve to make other inferences, besides that of the passions from which they proceed. Deliberation is expressed subjunctively, which is a speech proper to signify suppositions with their consequences, such as "If this be done, then this will follow," and does not differ from the language of reasoning except that reasoning is in general words, but deliberation for the most part is of particulars. The language of desire and aversion is imperative, as "Do this; forbear that," which when the party is obliged to do or to forbear is command. Otherwise, it is prayer or counsel. The language of vain-glory, of indignation, pity, and revengefulness is optative. But of the desire to know, there is a peculiar expression called interrogative, as "What is it?", "When shall it?", "How is it done?", and "Why so?" I find no other language of the passions. Cursing, swearing, reviling, and the like do not signify as speech, but as the actions of an accustomed tongue.

These forms of speech . . . are expressions or voluntary signs of our passions, but they are not certain signs because they may be used arbitrarily, whether they who use them have such passions or not. The best signs of passions present are either in the countenance, motions of the body, actions and ends, or aims which we otherwise know the man to have.

Good or evil effect depends on foresight of a long chain of consequences which very few men are able to see to the end, because in deliberation the appetites and aversions are raised by foresight of the good and evil consequences of the action about which we deliberate. But for so far as a man sees, if the good in those consequences is greater than the evil, the whole chain is that which writers call "apparent" or "seeming good." And contrarily, when evil exceeds good, the whole is apparent or seeming evil, so that he who has by experience or reason the greatest and surest prospect of consequences deliberates best and is able, when he will, to give the best counsel to others.

Continual success in obtaining those things which a man desires from time to time—that is to say, continual prospering—is felicity. I mean the felicity of this life. For there is no such thing as perpetual tranquility of mind while we live here because life itself is but motion and can never be without desire,[30] nor without fear, no more than without sense. What kind of felicity God has ordained to them who devoutly honor him a man shall no sooner know than enjoy. . . .

The form of speech by which men signify their opinion of the goodness of anything is praise. That whereby they signify the power and greatness of anything is magnifying. And that whereby they signify the opinion they have of a man's felicity is called *makarismos* by the Greeks, for which we have no name in our tongue. And thus much is sufficient for the present purpose to have been said of the passions.

---

30. In this claim, Hobbes agrees with Aristotle that in this life there is continual motion and that one desire is always replaced by another. Later in *Leviathan* (Chapter XI), Hobbes reiterates this general sentiment in claiming that human life is characterized by a "perpetual and restless desire for power after power that ceases only in death."

Chapter VII. Of the Ends or Resolutions of Discourse

We engage in discourse—the operations of the mind in thinking—in order to reach our ends or goals. One of our goals is to find truth. Just as the last action resulting from deliberation is will, so the last opinion in our search for truth is judgment. In the process of thinking about our goals and how to reach them, we often find ourselves in doubt. Doubt, for Hobbes, is nothing more than recognition of a chain of different opinions. When it comes to facts—that is, to occurrences in the world of material things—there is no absolute knowledge. This does not mean that because there is no absolute knowledge of facts it is not knowledge at all. It is simply that it is not characterized by certainty. Recall that if we seek certainty, we utilize science. The catch, however, is that knowledge of consequences from science (in Hobbes' meaning of the term) is conditional and about names, not about "things" or natural objects. Any other information we possess (if it is neither knowledge of fact nor knowledge from science) is nothing more than opinion.

At the end of Chapter VII Hobbes speaks of faith, properly understood, as being in the one who speaks and as different from belief. Belief can be in both the person who speaks and in the truth of the statements made. So when, for example, we believe only on the authority of authors and on what they write, it is faith in a human being, not faith in the thing about which the human being speaks.

Of all discourse governed by the desire of knowledge there is at last an end, either by attaining or by giving over. In the chain of discourse, wherever it is interrupted, there is an end for that time. If the discourse is merely mental, it consists of thoughts that the thing will be, and will not be, or that it has been and has not been, alternately. So that wherever you break off the chain of a man's discourse, you leave him in a presumption of "It will be," or "It will not be" or "It has been," or "It has not been." All of this is opinion. That which is alternate appetite in deliberating concerning good and evil, the same is alternate opinion in the enquiry of the truth of past and future. As the last appetite in deliberation is called the will, so the last opinion in search of the truth of past and future is called the judgment or resolute and final sentence of he who discourses. As the whole chain of appetites alternate in the question of good and bad is called deliberation, so the whole chain of opinions alternate in the question of true or false is called doubt.

No discourse can end in absolute knowledge of fact from the past or into the future because knowledge of fact is originally in sense and later in memory. For the knowledge of consequence, which I have said before is called science, it is not absolute but conditional. No man can know by discourse that this or that is, has been, or will be, which is to know absolutely. He knows only that "If this be, that is," "If this has been, that has been," "If this shall be, that shall be," which is to know conditionally, and that is not the consequence of one thing to another, but it is of one name of a thing to another name of the same thing.

Therefore, when discourse is put into speech and begins with the definitions of words and proceeds by connection of the same into general affirmations, and of these into syllogisms, the end or last sum is called the conclusion. The thought of the mind signified by it is conditional knowledge, or knowledge of the consequence of words, which is commonly called "science." But if the first ground of such discourse is not definitions, or if the definitions are not rightly joined together into syllogisms, then the end or conclusion is again opinion of the truth of something said, though sometimes in absurd and senseless words without possibility of being understood. When two or more men know of one and the same fact, they are said to be conscious of it to one another which is as much as to know it together. Because such are fittest witnesses of the facts of one another or of a third, it was and always will be considered a very evil act for any man to speak against his conscience or to corrupt or force another to do so. The plea of conscience has always been harkened unto very diligently. Afterward, men made use of the same word metaphorically for the knowledge of their own secret facts and secret thoughts, and therefore it is rhetorically said that the conscience is a thousand witnesses. Last of all, men who are vehemently in love with their own new opinions—regardless of how absurd—and obstinately bent to maintain them gave their opinions to those who reverenced the name of conscience as if they would have it seem unlawful to change or to speak against them, and so pretend to know they are true when they know at most that they think so.

When a man's discourse does not begin at definitions and instead begins at some other contemplation of his own, it is still called opinion. If it begins at some saying of another person whose ability to know the truth and whose honesty is not doubted, the discourse is not so much concerning the thing as the person. The resolution is called belief and faith. Faith is in the man. Belief is both of the man and of the truth of what he says. So then in belief there are two opinions. One is the saying of the man. The other is of his virtue. To have faith in or to trust, or to believe a man, signifies the same thing—an opinion of the veracity of the man. But to believe what is said signifies only an opinion of the truth of the saying. But we are to observe that this phrase, "I believe in," is never used except in the writings of divines. In other writings are put "I believe him," "I have faith in him," "I rely on him," and this singularity of the ecclesiastical use of the word has raised many disputes about the right object of the Christian faith.

But by believing in, as it is in the creed, is not meant trust in the person but confession and acknowledgment of the doctrine. For not only Christians but all manner of men believe in God as to hold all for truth they hear him say whether they understand it or not. This is all the faith and trust that can possibly be had in any person. But they do not all believe the doctrine of the creed.

From this we infer that when we believe a saying to be true from arguments— and not from the thing itself or from the principles of natural reason—and from the authority and good opinion we have of the person who said it, then we believe in or trust in the speaker and that person's words are the object of our faith. The honor done in believing is done to him only. Consequently when we believe that the Scriptures are the Word of God, having no immediate revelation from God himself, our belief, faith and trust is in the Church whose word we take and in which we acquiesce. They who believe that which a prophet relates to them in the name of God takes the word of the prophet and honors him and trusts him, and believes, touching the truth of what he relates whether he is a true or a false prophet.[31] So it is with all other history. For if I should not believe all that is written by historians of the glorious acts of Alexander or Caesar, I do not think the ghost of Alexander or of Caesar had any just cause to be offended, or anybody else but the historian. If Livy said the gods once made a cow speak, and we do not believe it, we do not therein distrust God, but Livy. So it is evident that whatever we believe upon no other reason than what is drawn only from authority of men and their writings, whether they are sent from God or not, is faith in men only.

---

31. Since in this chapter Hobbes is writing about truth, falsehood, belief, and faith, it is easy to understand why he will turn to a discussion of faith in persons and belief in doctrines and how these are related to each other. There is more to it, however, in that it has implications later for the nature of prophecy and for the faith one is to put in prophets. Ultimately, Hobbes argues that the ultimate prophet of God is the political sovereign, a position that surely was not considered orthodox in Hobbes' time and is not in modern democratic societies or with respect to the supposed independence of religious doctrine from that of the state.

Chapter VIII. Of the Virtues Commonly Called Intellectual and Their Contrary Defects

The topic of intellectual virtues and defects follows naturally from the previous chapters. If it is true, as Hobbes indicates, that objects of love are associated with movements toward the things we find desirable, and objects of hate are those away from which we move because we find them to be objects of aversion, it must also be the case that those things we desire, which we call good, are matters of our own individual judgment. Here in Chapter VIII Hobbes contends that desire for power causes difference of wit, and among the sources of one's reputation (which is a social phenomenon) are a person's intelligence, wit, prudence, and wisdom. Hobbes is giving us a preview of his arguments about the causes of quarrel between individuals that lead, ultimately, to the need for the establishment of an absolute sovereign power to manage or overrule disagreements. Hobbes is careful to add, in addition, that a form of "madness" is also characteristic of people who hold beliefs in religious concepts such as transubstantiation and who, we might reasonably assume, become just as much enraged when beliefs they hold with vehement passion are challenged.

In all sorts of subjects virtue generally is valued for eminence and consists in comparison. For if all things were equally in all men, nothing would be prized. Intellectual virtues are always understood as abilities of the mind men praise, value, and desire should be in themselves, and are commonly called "good wit," though the same word, "wit," is also used to distinguish one certain ability from the rest.

These virtues are of two sorts—natural and acquired. By "natural" I do not mean that which a man has from his birth. It is not considered among the virtues because it is only sense in which men differ little from each other and from brute beasts. I mean wit which is gotten by use only, and experience, without method, culture, or instruction. Natural wit consists principally in two things: celerity of imagining (that is, swift succession of one thought to another) and steady direction to some approved end. On the contrary, a slow imagination makes defect or fault of the mind commonly called dullness, stupidity, and sometimes by other names that signify slowness of motion or difficulty to be moved.

Difference of quickness is caused by difference of men's passions. Some love and dislike one thing, and some another. Therefore some men's thoughts run one way, some another, and are held to and observe differently the things that pass through their imagination. Whereas in succession of men's thoughts there is nothing to observe in the things they think on, but either in what they are like one another, or in what they are unlike, or for what they serve or how they serve a purpose. Those who observe their similarities when they are rarely observed by others are said to have a good wit, which in this case is meant a good fancy. But they who observe their differences and dissimilarities (which is called distinguishing and discerning and judging between things) when discerning is not easy are said to have good judgment. Particularly in matters of conversation and business, where times, places, and persons are to be discerned, this virtue is discretion. The former, fancy, is not commended as a virtue without the help of judgment, but the latter which is judgment and discretion is commended for itself, without the help of fancy. Besides the discretion of times, places, and persons necessary to a good fancy, regular application of his thoughts to their end is also required, that is to say, to some use to be made of them. . . .

Both judgment and fancy are required in a good poem (whether it is epic or dramatic) and in sonnets, epigrams, and other pieces. Fancy must be more eminent because they please for the extravagancy, but ought not to displease by indiscretion. In a good history, judgment must be eminent because goodness consists in the method, in the truth, and in the choice of the actions that are most profitable to be known. Fancy has no place except in adorning style.

In orations of praise and in invectives, fancy is predominant because the intent is not truth, but to honor or to dishonor, which is done by noble or vile comparisons. Judgment suggests what circumstances make an action laudable or culpable. In hortatives and pleadings, as truth or disguise serves best to the design in hand, so is the judgment or the fancy most required.

In demonstration, in counsel, and all rigorous search for truth, judgment does all—except sometimes the understanding has need to be opened by some apt similarity, and then there is so much use of fancy. But for metaphors, they are in this case utterly excluded. For seeing they openly profess deceit, to admit them into counsel or reasoning is obvious folly.

In any discourse, if the defect of discretion is apparent, no matter how extravagant the fancy, the whole discourse will be taken for a sign of lack of wit. It will never be taken for lack of wit when discretion is manifest, though the fancy be never so ordinary.

The secret thoughts of a man run over all things holy, profane, clean, obscene, grave, and light without shame or blame, which verbal discourse cannot do farther than the judgment shall approve of the time, place, and persons [to whom a thing is said]. An anatomist or a physician may speak or write his judgment of unclean things because it is not to please but to profit. But for another man to write his extravagant and pleasant fancies of the same, is as if a man from being tumbled into the dirt should come and present himself before good company. It is lack of discretion that makes the difference. Again, in reminiscence of mind and familiar company a man may play with the sounds and equivocal significations of words, and many times with encounters of extraordinary fancy. But in a sermon or in public, or before persons unknown or whom we ought to revere, there is no gingling[32] of words that

---

32. This term is probably the same as "jingling," and with respect to words in this context, it means that words are made to be striking, to be loud, or to draw attention.

will not be accounted folly and the difference is only in lack of discretion. So that where wit is wanting, it is not fancy that is wanting, but discretion. Therefore, judgment without fancy is wit, but fancy without judgment is not.

When the thoughts of a man who has a design in hand that runs over a multitude of things observes how they do or may conduce to a design, if his observations are not easy or usual, his wit is called prudence and depends on much experience and memory of similar things and their consequences. In this there is not so much difference of men as there is in their fancies and judgments because the experience of men equal in age is not much unequal in quantity but lies in different occasions, everyone having his private designs. To govern well a family and a kingdom are not different degrees of prudence but different sorts of business, no more than to draw a picture in little or as great, or greater, than the life are different degrees of art. A plain husbandman is more prudent in affairs of his own house than a privy counselor in the affairs of another man.

If you add the use of unjust or dishonest means to prudence like those usually prompted in men by fear or want, you have crooked wisdom, which is called craft and is a sign of pusillanimity. For magnanimity is contempt of unjust or dishonest helps. What the Latins call *versutia* (translated into English, shifting) is putting off a present danger or incommodity by engaging a greater, such as when a man robs one to pay another, and it is but a shorter sighted craft called *versutia* from *versura*, which signifies taking money at usury for the present payment of interest.

As for acquired wit (I mean acquired by method and instruction) there is none but reason which is grounded on the right use of speech and produces the sciences. But of reason and science, I have already spoken in Chapters V and VI. The causes of difference of wits are in the passions, and the difference of passions proceeds partly from the different constitution of the body and partly from different education. For if the difference proceeded from the temper of the brain and the organs of sense, either exterior or interior, there would be no less difference of men in their sight, hearing, or other senses than in their fancies and discretions. It proceeds therefore from the passions, which are different not only from the difference of men's complexions, but also from their difference of customs and education.

The passions that most of all cause differences of wit are principally the more or less desire of power, of riches, of knowledge, and of honor. All of which may be reduced to the first, that is desire of power. For riches, knowledge and honor are just several sorts of power.

And therefore a man who has no great passion for any of these things but is indifferent, though he may be so far a good man as to be free from giving offense, he cannot possibly have either a great fancy or much judgment. For the thoughts are to the desires as scouts and spies to range abroad and find the way to the things desired. All steadiness and quickness of the mind's motion proceeds from this. To have no desire is to be dead, to have weak passions is dullness, and to have passions indifferently for everything is giddiness and distraction. To have stronger and more vehement passions for anything than is ordinarily seen in others is that which men call madness, whereof there are almost as many kinds as of the passions themselves.

Sometimes the extraordinary and extravagant passion proceeds from the evil constitution of the organs of the body or harm done to them, and sometimes the hurt and indisposition of the organs is caused by the vehemence or long continuance of the passion. But in both cases the madness is of one and the same nature. The passion whose violence or continuance makes madness is either vain-glory, which is commonly called pride and self-conceit, or great dejection of mind.

Pride subjects a man to anger, the excess of which is the madness called "rage" and "fury." Thus it comes to pass that excessive desire of revenge, when it becomes habitual, hurts the organs and becomes rage. Excessive love with jealousy also becomes rage. Excessive opinion of a man's own self, for divine inspiration, for wisdom, learning, form, and the like becomes distraction and giddiness. The same, joined with envy, is rage. Vehement opinion of the truth of anything that is contradicted by others is rage.

Dejection subjects a man to causeless fears which is a madness commonly called melancholy, apparent also in diverse manners as in haunting of solitudes and graves, in superstitious behavior, and in fearing someone or some particular thing. In sum, all passions that produce strange and unusual behavior are called by the general name of madness. But of the several kinds of madness, he who would take the pains might enroll a legion. If the excess is madness, there is no doubt but the passions themselves, when they tend to evil, are degrees of the same.

For example, the effect of folly in those who possess an opinion of being inspired is not visible always in one man by any very extravagant action that proceeds from such passion. Yet when many of them conspire together, the rage of the whole multitude is visible enough. For what argument of madness can there be greater than to clamor, strike, and throw stones at our best friends? Yet this is somewhat less than such a multitude will do. They will clamor, fight against, and destroy those by whom all their lifetime before they have been protected and secured from injury.[33] If this is madness in the multitude, it is the same in every particular man. For as in the midst of the sea, though a man perceives no sound of that part of the water next to him, yet he is well assured that part contributes as much to the roaring of the sea as any other part of the same quantity. So also, though we perceive no great unquietness in one or two men, yet we may be well assured that their singular passions are parts of the seditious roaring of a troubled nation. If there was nothing else that betrayed their madness, arrogating such inspiration to themselves is argument enough. If some man in Bedlam should entertain you with sober discourse and you desire to know who he is so that you might at some other time requite his civility and he tells you he is God the Father, I think you need not expect

---

33. Hobbes is describing the behavior of mobs and rioters. We tend in our time to think it peculiar that rioters, for example, will burn down and loot businesses in their own neighborhoods. It is beyond the scope of this work to comment on such issues beyond saying that Hobbes was an astute observer of human behavior, which seems over the past three and a half centuries not to have changed much.

extravagant action for argument of his madness. Opinion of inspiration, commonly called "private spirit," begins very often from luck in finding an error generally held by others and not knowing or remembering by what conduct of reason they came to so singular a truth (as they think it, though it may be an untruth), they presently admire themselves as being in the special grace of God Almighty, who has revealed the same to them supernaturally, by his spirit.

Again, madness being nothing but too much appearing passion may be gathered out of the effects of wine, which are the same with those of the evil disposition of the organs. For the variety of behavior in men who have drunk too much is the same with that of madmen. Some of them rage, others love, others laugh, all extravagantly, but according to their several domineering passions. The effect of the wine removes dissimulation and takes from them the sight of the deformity of their passions. For (I believe) the most sober men, when they walk alone without care and employment of the mind, would be unwilling that the vanity and extravagance of their thoughts at that time should be publicly seen. This is a confession that passions unguided are for the most part mere madness.

The opinions of the world in ancient times and later ages concerning the causes of madness have been two. Some, deriving them from the passions, some from either good or bad demons or spirits which they thought might enter into a man, possess him, and move his organs in such strange and uncouth manner as madmen use to do. The former sort therefore called such men madmen but the latter sometimes called them "demoniacs" (that is, possessed with spirits), sometimes *energumeni* (that is, agitated or moved with spirits), and now in Italy they are called not only "pazzi," madmen, but also *spiritati*, men possessed. . . .

There is another fault in the discourses of some men which may also be counted among the sorts of madness, namely, the abuse of words as absurdity that I have spoken of before in the Chapter V. That is when men speak such words put together having no signification but are fallen upon by some misunderstanding of the words and repeated by rote. By others, from intention to deceive by obscurity. This is incident to none but those who converse in questions of incomprehensible matters such as the Schoolmen or in questions of abstruse philosophy. The common sort of men seldom speaks insignificantly and are therefore by those other egregious persons counted idiots. But to be assured their words are without anything correspondent to them in the mind there would need some examples which, if any man requires, let him take a Schoolman into his hands and see if he can translate any one chapter concerning any difficult topic such as the Trinity, the Deity, the nature of Christ, transubstantiation, free-will, etc., into any of the modern languages so as to make it intelligible, or into Latin. . . . What is the meaning of these words? "The first cause does not necessarily inflow anything into the second by force of the essential subordination of the second causes by which it may help it to work?" They are the translation of the title of the sixth chapter of Suarez's first Book, of the *Concourse, Motion, and Help of God.*[34] When men write whole volumes of such stuff,

---

34. Francisco Suarez was a Spanish Scholastic priest whose works in the sixteenth and early seventeenth centuries were considered nearly as important as those of St. Thomas Aquinas.

are they not mad or intend to make others so? And particularly in the question of transubstantiation, where after certain words are spoken that they say the whiteness, roundness, magnitude, quality, corruptibility, all of which are incorporeal, etc., go out of the wafer into the body of our Blessed Savior, do they not make those "nesses," "tudes," and "ties" to be so many spirits possessing his body? For by spirits they always mean things, being incorporeal, are nevertheless movable from one place to another. So that this kind of absurdity may rightly be numbered among the many sorts of madness. . . . And thus much of the intellectual virtues and defects.

Chapter IX. Of the Several Subjects of Knowledge

It is in Chapter IX that it is possible from previous discussions of science, method, and the nature of causation to clarify the division of the sciences in table form. As you can see, there are two types of knowledge. One is of "fact" and the other is conditional. Hobbes has already explained at several points that knowledge of fact is at best only probable when reasoning into the future (and "absolute" when a matter of memory of that which in fact has occurred), while knowledge of conditionals yields certainty. In short, subject matter that is of our own creation (what we create through definitions and the proper application of sound method) yields certainty. This chapter is intended to clarify the division of the sciences and ultimately to make it obvious why the science of politics, the crowning achievement of Leviathan, *is among the most pure and reliable of all.*

There are two kinds of knowledge. One is of fact and the other is knowledge of the consequence of one affirmation to another. The former is nothing else but sense and memory and is absolute knowledge such as when we see a fact occurring or remember it done. This is the knowledge required in a witness. The latter is called science and is conditional as when we know that if the figure shown is a circle, then any straight line through the center shall divide it into two equal parts. This is the knowledge required in a philosopher who pretends to reason.

The register of knowledge of fact is called history. Of this there are two sorts. One is natural history, which is the history of such facts or effects of nature that have no dependence on man's will. Such are the histories of metals, plants, animals, regions, and the like. The other is civil history, which is the history of the voluntary actions of men in commonwealths.

The registers of science are such books that contain the demonstrations of consequences of one affirmation to another and are commonly called books of philosophy, whereof the sorts are many according to the diversity of the matter and may be divided in such manner as I have divided them in the following table.

Science: Knowledge of Consequences, called Philosophy

I. Consequences from accidents of political bodies, called politics and civil philosophy

Consequences from institution of commonwealths to the rights and duties of the body politic, or sovereign	Consequences from the same to the duty and right of the subjects

II. Consequences from the accidents of natural bodies, called natural philosophy

A. Consequences from the accidents common to all natural bodies, which are quality and motion

Consequences from quality and motion indeterminate, which being principles or first foundation of philosophy, called philosophia prima	Consequences from motion and quantity determined	
PHILOSOPHIA PRIMA	Consequences from quantity and motion determined	Consequences from motion and quantity of bodies in special
	By figure or By number, in Mathematics for the sciences of GEOMETRY AND ARITHMETIC	Consequences from motion and quantity of the great parts of the world, as the Earth and stars, in ASTRONOMY, GEOGRAPHY Consequences from the motion of special kinds and figures of body, in mechanics and the doctrine of weight for the sciences of ENGINEERS, ARCHITECTURE, AND NAVIGATION

B. Physics, or consequences from qualities

Consequences from the qualities of bodies permanent.

Consequences from qualities of bodies transient, such as sometimes appear, sometimes vanish, for the science of METEOROLOGY	Consequences of the qualities from liquid bodies that fill the space between the stars, such as are the air or ethereal substance	Consequences from the qualities of the stars		Consequences from the qualities of terrestrial bodies	
		Consequences from the light of the stars. Out of this, and the motion of the Sun, is made the science of SCIOGRAPHY	Consequences from the influence of the stars, ASTROLOGY	Consequences from the qualities of minerals, as stones, metals, etc. Consequences of the qualities of vegetables	Consequences from the qualities of animals in general, include: consequences from vision, for OPTICS, consequences from sounds, for MUSIC, consequences from the rest of the senses Consequences from the qualities of men in special include: consequences of the passions of men, for ETHICS, consequences of speech: in magnifying, vilifying, etc., for POETRY, in persuading, for RHETORIC, in reasoning, for LOGIC, in contracting, for the science of JUST AND UNJUST

Chapter X. Of Power, Worth, Dignity, Honor, and Worthiness

Chapter X is very important as an introduction to Hobbes' conception of human behavior. Beginning with Chapter X and continuing through Chapter XIII, Hobbes presents his position on human personality and some of the elements of the clashes between human beings when their preferences, their honor, and their very survival are threatened. It is in this chapter that Hobbes' position is alive with implications regarding human dignity and value, both of which are intimately connected to survival or, more specifically for Hobbes, they are intimately connected to avoiding the summum malum,[35] death.

The power of a man (to take it universally) is his present means to obtain some future apparent good. It is either original or instrumental. Natural power is eminence of the faculties of body or mind such as extraordinary strength, form, prudence, art, eloquence, liberality, or nobility. Instrumental powers are those acquired by these means or by fortune and are means and instruments to acquire more, such as riches, reputation, friends, and the secret working of God, which men call good luck. For the nature of power is in this point like fame, increasing as it proceeds—or like the motion of heavy bodies, the further they go, the more haste they make.

The greatest of human powers is compounded of the powers of most men united by consent in one person, natural or civil, who has the use of all their powers depending on his will such as is the power of a commonwealth. Or depending on the wills of each particular, such as is the power of a faction or of diverse factions leagued. Therefore to have servants is power, to have friends is power, for they are strengths united.

Also riches joined with liberality is power because it procures friends and servants. Without liberality, it is not so because in this case they do not defend but expose men to envy, as a prey. Reputation of power is power because it draws with it the adherence of those who need protection. So reputation of love of a man's country is called popularity, for the same reason. Also, whatever quality makes a man beloved or feared by many or the reputation of such quality is power, because it is a means to have the assistance and service of many.

Good success is power because it makes reputation of wisdom or of good fortune, which makes men either fear him or rely on him. Affability of men already in power is increase of power because it gains love. Reputation of prudence in the conduct of peace or war is power because to prudent men we commit the

---

35. Ultimately bad occurrence, thing, or state of affairs; the ultimate evil.

government of ourselves more willingly than to others. Nobility is power, but not in all places and only in those commonwealths where it has privileges, for in such privileges consists their power. Eloquence is power because it is seeming prudence. Form is power because being a promise of good it recommends men to the favor of women and strangers.

The sciences are small power because they are not eminent and therefore they are not acknowledged in any man, nor are they at all but in a few—and in them, but of a few things. For science is such that one can understand it to be but those as in a good measure have attained it.

Arts of public use such as fortification, making engines, and other instruments of war, because they confer to defense and victory, are power. Though the true mother of them is science, namely mathematics, because they are brought into the light by the hand of the artificer, they are esteemed (the midwife passing with the vulgar for the mother) as his issue.

The value or worth of a man is as of all other things his price, that is to say, so much as would be given for the use of his power and it is therefore not absolute, but dependent upon the need and judgment of another. An able conductor of soldiers is of great price in time of present or imminent war, but not in peace. A learned and corrupt judge is much worth in time of peace, but not so much in war. As in other things, so in men, not the seller but the buyer determines the price. For let a man (as most men do) rate themselves at the highest value they can, their true value is no more than it is esteemed by others.

The manifestations of the value we set on one another are that which is commonly called honoring and dishonoring. To value a man at a high rate is to honor him; at a low rate, is to dishonor him. But high and low in this case is to be understood by comparison to the rate that each man sets on himself.

The public worth of a man, which is the value set on him by the common-wealth, is that which men commonly call dignity. The value of him by the commonwealth is understood by offices of command, judicature, public employment, or by names and titles introduced for distinction of such value.

To pray to another for aid of any kind is to honor, because it is a sign we have an opinion he has power to help, and the more difficult the aid, the more is the honor. To obey is to honor, because no man obeys those whom they think have no power to help or hurt them. And consequently, to disobey is to dishonor.

To give great gifts to a man is to honor him, because it is buying protection and acknowledging power. To give little gifts is to dishonor because it is but alms and signifies an opinion of the need of small helps. To be sedulous in promoting another's good, also to flatter, is to honor as a sign we seek his protection or aid. To neglect is to dishonor.

To give way or place to another in any commodity is to honor, being a confession of greater power. To arrogate is to dishonor. To show any sign of love or fear of another is to honor, for both to love and to fear is to value. To contemn, or less to love or fear than he expects is to dishonor, for it is undervaluing.

To praise, magnify, or call happy is to honor because nothing but goodness, power, and felicity is valued. To revile, mock, or pity is to dishonor. To speak to another with consideration, to appear before him with decency and humility, is to honor him as signs of fear to offend. To speak to him rashly, to do anything before him obscenely, slovenly, impudently, is to dishonor.

To believe, to trust, to rely on another is to honor him, a sign of opinion of his virtue and power. To distrust or not to believe is to dishonor. To hearken to a man's counsel or discourse of whatever kind is to honor as a sign we think him wise, eloquent, or witty. To sleep or go forth, or talk the while, is to dishonor.

To do those things to another which he takes for signs of honor or which the law or custom makes so is to honor because in approving the honor done by others, he acknowledges the power which others acknowledge. To refuse to do them is to dishonor. To agree with him in opinion is to honor, as being a sign of approving his judgment and wisdom. To dissent is dishonor and an upbraiding of error; and (if the dissent is in many things) of folly.

To imitate is to honor, for it is vehemently to approve. To imitate one's enemy is to dishonor. To honor those another honors is to honor him as a sign of approbation of his judgment. To honor his enemies is to dishonor him.

To employ in counsel or in actions of difficulty is to honor as signs of opinion of his wisdom or other power. To deny employment in the same cases to those who seek it is to dishonor.

All these ways of honoring are natural, both within as without commonwealths. But in commonwealths, where he or they who have the supreme authority can make whatsoever they please to stand for signs of honor, there are other honors.

A sovereign honors a subject with a title or office, or employment or action that he himself will have taken for a sign of his will to honor him. The king of Persia honored Mordecai when he appointed he should be conducted through the streets in the king's garment, upon one of the king's horses, with a crown on his head and a prince before him, proclaiming, "Thus shall it be done to him that the king will honor." And yet either another king of Persia or the same another time gave permission to one who demanded some great service to wear one of the king's robes, but with his addition: that he should wear it as the king's fool, and then it was dishonor. So that of civil honor such as are magistracy, offices, titles, and in some places coats and painted scutcheons, and men honor those who have them as having so many signs of favor in the commonwealth, which favor is power.

Honorable is whatsoever possession, action, or quality is an argument and sign of power. Therefore to be honored, loved, or feared of many is honorable as arguments of power. To be honored by few or none is dishonorable.

Good fortune (if lasting) is honorable as a sign of the favor of God. Ill fortune and losses are dishonorable. Riches are honorable because they are power. Poverty is dishonorable. Magnanimity, liberality, hope, courage, confidence are honorable for they proceed from the conscience of power. Pusillanimity, parsimony, fear, and diffidence are dishonorable.

Timely resolution or determination of what a man is to do is honorable as being the contempt of small difficulties and dangers. Irresolution is dishonorable as a sign of too much valuing of little impediments and little advantages. For when a man has weighed things as long as the time permits and does not resolve, the difference of weight is little and therefore if he does not resolve, he overvalues little things, which is pusillanimity.

All actions and speeches that proceed or seem to proceed from much experience, science, discretion, or wit are honorable, for all these are powers, actions, or words that proceed from error, ignorance, or folly, and are dishonorable. Gravity, as far as it seems to proceed from a mind employed on something else, is honorable because employment is a sign of power. But if it seems to proceed from a purpose to appear grave, it is dishonorable. For the gravity of the former is like the steadiness of a ship laden with merchandise, but for the latter, like the steadiness of a ship ballasted with sand and other trash.

To be conspicuous, that is to say, to be known for wealth, office, great actions, or any eminent good is honorable as a sign of the power for which he is conspicuous. On the contrary, obscurity is dishonorable. To be descended from conspicuous parents is honorable because they more easily attain the aid and friends of their ancestors. On the contrary, to be descended from obscure parentage is dishonorable.

Actions proceeding from equity, joined with loss, are honorable as signs of magnanimity. For magnanimity is a sign of power. On the contrary, craft, shifting, neglect of equity is dishonorable. Nor does it alter the case of honor, whether an action that is great and difficult and consequently a sign of much power is just or unjust. For honor consists only in the opinion of power. Therefore the ancient heathen did not think they dishonored but instead greatly honored the gods when they introduced them in their poems, committing rapes, thefts, and other great but unjust or unclean acts. . . .

Until great commonwealths were constituted, it was thought no dishonor to be a pirate or a highway thief but rather a lawful trade. This was the case among the Greeks and all other nations as is clear by ancient histories. At this day, in this part of the world private duels are and always will be honorable, though unlawful, until such time as there shall be honor ordained for them who refuse and ignominy for those who make the challenge. For duels also are many times effects of courage, and the ground of courage is always strength or skill which are power, though for the most part they are effects of rash speaking and the fear of dishonor in one or both the combatants, who, engaged by rashness, are driven into the lists to avoid disgrace.

Where they have any eminent privileges, scutcheons, and coats of hereditary arms are honorable. Otherwise they are not. Their power consists either in such privileges or in riches or some such thing as is equally honored in other men. This kind of honor, commonly called gentry, has been derived from the ancient Germans. For there never was any such thing known where the German customs were unknown. Nor is it now anywhere in use where the Germans have not inhabited. When they went to war, the ancient Greek commanders had their shields painted with such devices as they pleased. An unpainted buckler was a sign of poverty and of a common soldier, but they did not transmit the inheritance of them. The Romans transmitted the marks of their families, but they were images, not the devices of their ancestors. Among the people of Asia, Africa, and America, there is not nor was there ever any such thing. The Germans only had that custom from whom it has been derived into England, France, Spain, and Italy when in great numbers they either aided the Romans or made their own conquests in these Western parts of the world. . . .

Titles of honor such as duke, count, marquis, and baron are honorable as signifying the value set on them by the sovereign power of the commonwealth. These titles were in old times titles of office and command, some derived from the Romans, some from the Germans and French. Dukes, in Latin *duces*, were generals in war. Counts . . . bear the general company out of friendship and were left to govern and defend places conquered and pacified. Marquises . . . were counts who governed the marches or bounds of the empire. Titles of duke, count, and marquis came into the empire about the time of Constantine the Great from the customs of the German militia. But baron seems to have been a title of French and signifies a great man such as were the king's or princes' men whom they employed in war about their persons. The term seems to be derived from *vir*, to *ber* and *bar*, that signified the same in the language of the French that *vir* does in Latin, and thence to *bero* and *baro*, so that such men were called *berones*, and after *barones*, and (in Spanish) *varones*. . . . Over time these offices of honor, by occasion of trouble and for reasons of good and peaceable government, were turned into mere titles serving for the most part to distinguish the precedence, place, and order of subjects in the commonwealth and men were made dukes, counts, marquises, and barons of places wherein they had neither possession nor command, and other titles also were devised to the same end.

Worthiness is a thing different from the worth or value of a man, and also from his merit or desert, and consists in a particular power or ability for which he is said to be worthy. This particular ability is usually named fitness or aptitude. He is worthiest to be a commander, to be a judge, or to have any other charge who is best fitted with the qualities required to discharge it well and worthiest of riches who has the qualities most requisite for using them well. If any of the qualities are absent, one may nevertheless be a worthy man and valuable for something else. Again, a man may be worthy of riches, office, and employment that nevertheless can plead no right to have it before another and therefore cannot be said to merit or deserve it. For merit presupposes a right, and that the thing deserved is due by promise. Of this I shall say more hereafter when I shall speak of contracts.

Chapter XI. Of the Difference of Manners

By manners, Hobbes refers to "qualities" of mankind concerning our ability to live in peace and unity. We are honor seekers because honor indicates power, and we are, Hobbes notes, in a "perpetual and restless desire for power after power that ceases only in death." It is not enough simply to acquire what one needs to survive at any given time because our desires recur as well as change over time. Hobbesian people are not satisfied with just good enough—they want to be assured of continual success in obtaining what they need to live and to live well. One of the ways to ensure such success is to receive benefits from and to provide benefits to others.

Benefits received from and provided to others are not simple matters, however, since there is room for comparisons of value between the giver and the receiver as well as cases in which what is received from another person is hurtful in some way rather than beneficial. It is in such cases that questions of revenge and forgiveness become important and lead to contention. Further, power is associated with fear, and every person constantly searching for power may be associated with lies, ignorance, and deceit as well as fear of "invisible" things and powers, which are the "seed of religion." Hobbes is setting the stage for the development of his political conclusions that are closely related to the ways in which human beings deal with fear, desire, power, and differences in conceptions of things they fear or desire.

By manners I do not mean decency of behavior as how one man should salute another or how a man should wash his mouth or pick his teeth before company and such other points of small morals, but those qualities of mankind that concern living together in peace and unity. To which end we are to consider that the felicity of this life does not consist in the repose of a satisfied mind. For there is no such *finis ultimus* (utmost aim) nor *summum bonum* (greatest good) as is spoken of in the books of the old moral philosophers.[36] Nor can a man any more live whose desires

---

36. These terms refer to concepts deriving from the ancient philosophers, especially from Aristotle, with respect to the notion that there is some ultimate aim or ultimate good toward which things tend. So, for example, the final aim of an acorn is an oak tree (because it is the "perfection" of an acorn to become an oak tree). The final aim (goal) of human beings is also the ultimate good (*summum bonum*), which for Aristotle is happiness. It is both interesting and important to note that while Hobbes denies that there is an ultimate good or an ultimate aim, he still holds the position that there is an ultimate fear (death) and that safety is one of the most important goals of human life. He contends, "But by *safety* must be understood, not the sole preservation of life in what condition soever, but in order to its happiness. For to this end did men freely assemble themselves, and *institute* a government, that they might, as much

are at an end than he whose senses and imaginations are at a stand. Felicity is a continual progress of the desire from one object to another. Attaining the former is still the way to the latter. The cause of this is that the object of man's desire is not to enjoy once only and for one instant of time, but to assure forever the way of his future desire. Therefore the voluntary actions and inclinations of all men tend not only to procuring but also to assuring a contented life and differ only in the way which arises partly from the diversity of passions in diverse men and partly from the difference of the knowledge or opinion each one has of the causes which produce the desired effect.

So that in the first place, I put for a general inclination of all mankind a perpetual and restless desire of power after power that ceases only in death. The cause of this is not always that a man hopes for a more intensive delight than he has already attained or that he cannot be content with moderate power, but because he cannot assure the power and means to live well which he has present without the acquisition of more. Thus kings, whose power is greatest, turn their endeavors to assuring it at home by laws or abroad by wars, and when that is done, there succeeds a new desire—in some of fame from new conquest, in others of ease and sensual pleasure, in others of admiration, or being flattered for excellence in some art or other ability of the mind.

Competition of riches, honor, command, or other power inclines to contention, enmity, and war because the way of one competitor to attain his desire is to kill, subdue, supplant, or repel the other. Particularly, competition of praise inclines to a reverence of antiquity. For men contend with the living, not with the dead, to these ascribing more than due that they may obscure the glory of the other.

Desire for ease and sensual delight disposes men to obey a common power because by such desires a man abandons the protection for which he might hope from his own industry and labor. Fear of death and wounds disposes to the same and for the same reason. On the contrary, needy men and hardy men who are not content with their present condition—as well as men who are ambitious for military command—are inclined to continue the causes of war and to stir up trouble and sedition because there is no military honor except by war. Desire of knowledge and arts of peace inclines men to obey a common power. For such desire contains a desire of leisure and consequently protection from some other power than their own.

Desire of praise disposes to laudable actions such as please the people whose judgment they value. We contemn the praises of men whom we contemn. Desire of fame after death does the same. And though after death there is no sense of the praise given us on Earth, as being joys that are either swallowed up in the unspeakable joys of Heaven or extinguished in the extreme torments of Hell. Such fame is not vain because men have a present delight in it from the foresight of it and from the benefit that may go thereby to their posterity. They do not now see the benefit,

---

as their human condition would afford, live delightfully" (*Man and Citizen [De Homine and De Cive]*, ed. Bernard Gert [Indianapolis, IN: Hackett, 1991], 259).

but they imagine it, and anything that is pleasure in the sense is also pleasure in the imagination.

To have received greater benefits than there is hope to requite from one to whom we think ourselves equal disposes to counterfeit love, but really to secret hatred and puts a man into the estate of a desperate debtor that in declining the sight of his creditor, tacitly wishes him where he might never see him again. For benefits oblige and obligation is thraldom, which is hateful to one's equal. But to have received benefits from one whom we acknowledge our superior inclines to love because the obligation is no new depression and cheerful acceptation (which men call gratitude) is such an honor done to the obliger as is taken generally for retribution. To receive benefits from an equal or inferior as long as there is hope of requital disposes to love. For in the intention of the receiver, the obligation is of aid and mutual service, and from this proceeds an emulation of who shall exceed in benefiting, which is the most noble and profitable contention possible, where the victor is pleased with his victory and the other is revenged by confessing it.

To have done more hurt to a man than he can or is willing to expiate inclines the doer to hate the sufferer. For he must expect revenge or forgiveness, both of which are hateful.[37]

Fear of oppression disposes a man to anticipate or to seek aid by society. There is no other way by which a man can secure his life and liberty.

Men who distrust their own subtlety are in tumult and sedition, better disposed for victory than they who suppose themselves wise or crafty. For they love to consult the other (fearing to be circumvented) to strike first. And in sedition, since men are always in the precincts of battle, to hold together and use all advantages of force is a better strategy than any proceeding from subtlety of wit.

Vainglorious men such as those who are not conscious of their own great sufficiency delight in supposing themselves gallant men and are inclined only to ostentation, but not to attempt. Because when danger of difficulty appears, they look for nothing but to have their insufficiency discovered. Vainglorious men are those who estimate their sufficiency by the flattery of other men or the fortune of some preceding action and who do not have assured ground of hope for true knowledge of themselves. They are inclined to engage in rash action and to retire if they can because when they do not see the way of safety they would rather hazard their honor, which may be salved with an excuse, rather than to hazard their lives for which no salve is sufficient.

Men who have a strong opinion of their own wisdom in matters of government are disposed to ambition. Without public employment in counsel or magistracy, the

---

37. Revenge and forgiveness are both hateful because they are harmful to the person who has done wrong. Revenge is some physical, monetary, or reputational slight against a person, which does damage to him since it is a diminution of power. Forgiveness is hateful because the forgiver has shown that the harm done to him is slight and that he is superior to the person who has harmed him.

honor of their wisdom is lost. Therefore eloquent speakers are inclined to ambition, for eloquence seems to be wisdom, both to themselves and to others.

Pusillanimity disposes men to irresolution and consequently to lose the occasions and fittest opportunities of action. For after men have been in deliberation until the time of action approaches, if it is not then manifest what is best to be done, it is a sign that difference of motives one way and the other are not great. Therefore, not to resolve them is to lose the occasion by weighing trifles, which is pusillanimity.

Frugality (though in poor men a virtue) makes a man unapt to achieve such actions as require the strength of many men at once. It weakens their endeavor which is to be nourished and kept in vigor by reward.

Eloquence with flattery disposes men to confide in them who have them, because the former is seeming wisdom. The latter is seeming kindness. Add to them military reputation, and it disposes men to adhere and subject themselves to those men who have them. The two former give them caution against danger from him, the latter gives them caution against danger from others.

Want of science (ignorance of causes) disposes—or rather constrains—a man to rely on the advice and authority of others. For all men whom the truth concerns, if they do not rely on their own they must rely on the opinion of some other whom they think wiser than themselves and do not see why he should deceive them.

Ignorance of the signification of words, which is lack of understanding, disposes men to take on trust not only the truth that they do not know, but also the errors and—which is more—the nonsense of those they trust. For neither error nor nonsense can be detected without perfect understanding of words. It follows that men give different names to one and the same thing from the difference of their own passions, as they who approve a private opinion call it opinion, but they who dislike it call it heresy. . . .

It also follows that men cannot distinguish without study and great understanding between one action of many men and many actions of one multitude, as, for example, between the one action of all the senators of Rome in killing Catiline and the many actions of a number of senators in killing Caesar. Therefore they are disposed to take for the action of the people that which is a multitude of actions done by a multitude of men, led perhaps by the persuasion of one.

Ignorance of the causes and original constitution of right, equity, law, and justice disposes a man to make custom and example the rule of his actions so that he thinks that to be unjust what has been customarily punished—and they think to be just the impunity and approbation of which they can produce an example . . . or a precedent, like little children who have no other rule of good and evil manners but the correction they receive from their parents and masters. But children are constant to their rule whereas men are not. Because grown strong and stubborn, they appeal from custom to reason, and from reason to custom as it serves their purpose, receding from custom when their interest requires it and setting themselves against reason as often as reason is against them. This is the reason that the doctrine of right and wrong is perpetually disputed both by the pen and the sword. The doctrine of lines and figures is not disputed this way because men do not care in that subject what is truth because it is a thing that crosses no man's ambition, profit, or lust. I do not doubt if the three angles of a triangle being equal to two angles of a square was contrary to any man's right of dominion or interest, the doctrine would have been disputed or all the books of geometry would have been burned as far as the concerned person was able.

Ignorance of remote causes disposes men to attribute all events to immediate and instrumental causes. These are all the causes they perceive. Therefore it comes to pass that in all places, men who are grieved with payments to the public discharge their anger on the publicans, i.e., farmers, collectors, and other officers of the public revenue and adhere to those who find fault with the public government. When they have engaged themselves beyond hope of justification, they fall upon the supreme authority for fear of punishment or shame of receiving pardon.

Ignorance of natural causes disposes a man to credulity so as to believe many impossibilities. Such people know nothing to the contrary but that they may be true since they are unable to detect the impossibility. Because men love to be heard in company, credulity disposes them to lying so that ignorance itself without malice is able to make a man both to believe lies and to tell them, and sometimes also to invent them. Anxiety for the future disposes men to inquire into causes of things because knowledge of them makes men better able to order the present to their best advantage.

Curiosity, or love of the knowledge of causes, draws a man from consideration of the effect to seek the cause, and again, the cause of that cause, until of necessity he must come finally to the thought that there is some cause for which there is no former cause, but is eternal, which men call God.[38] So it is impossible to make any profound inquiry into natural causes without being inclined to believe there is one eternal God, though they cannot have any idea of him in their mind answerable to his nature. As a man who is born blind who hears men talk of warming themselves by the fire, and warming himself by it, he may easily conceive and assure himself that there is something there and it is the cause of the heat he feels. But he cannot

---

38. The reasoning in which Hobbes engages here concerning God is probably the closest he comes to a "proof" or argument for the existence of God. He has already made it clear that it is impossible for us to have an idea of God, and in addition Hobbes had disdain rather than respect for the philosophers who offered such proofs (e.g., Aristotle, St. Thomas Aquinas, and others). However, Hobbes' statement that human beings seek causes and the causes of causes until they come finally to a cause that has no cause and is eternal is at least a nod to the Cosmological Argument for God's existence, which is found in Aristotle's *Metaphysics* XII (see *Metaphysics* in *Introduction to Aristotle*, ed. Richard McKeon [New York: Modern Library, 1947]) and in St. Thomas Aquinas' *Summa Theologica* I.Q.2.A.3 (*The Summa Theologiae of Saint Thomas Aquinas: Latin-English Edition. Volume I: Prima Pars, Q. 1–64* [Scotts Valley, CA: CreateSpace, 2008]). The general format of the argument is that everything in sense experience has a cause, and nothing may come from nothing. An infinite series of causes is impossible, so there must be some first cause. We identify or call the first cause "God." It follows according to those who adopt this argument, then, that God exists. Hobbes, on the other hand, holds that the word "God" does not imply anything about existence that we may observe or experience but is instead a term of honor for that which is the first, eternal cause of all that is.

imagine what it is like nor have an idea of it in his mind such as they have who see it. So also by the visible things of this world and their admirable order a man may conceive there is a cause of them which men call God and yet not have an idea or image of him in his mind.

Those who do not inquire or inquire little into natural causes and who have fear deriving from ignorance of what has the power to do them good or harm are inclined to suppose and imagine several kinds of invisible powers. They invoke when in distress as well as in time of expected good success to give them thanks, making the creatures they imagine into gods. . . . From the innumerable variety of fancy, men have created in the world innumerable sorts of gods. This fear of invisible things is the natural seed of that which everyone calls religion. Those who worship or fear that power differently call it superstition.

In this seed of religion . . . some who have observed it have been inclined to nourish, dress, and form it into laws and to add through their own invention any opinion of the causes of future events by which they thought they should best be able to govern others and make for themselves the greatest use of their powers.

Chapter XII. Of Religion

In Chapter XII, Hobbes combines the importance of knowledge (which is power) with religion. He continues here to pave the way for Part II of Levia-than, "Of Commonwealth," and its relationship to Part III, "Of a Christian Commonwealth," with respect to the most powerful creation of human beings, the political state. So he begins Chapter XII by reminding us that we all seek knowledge of causes because we wish to be able to control the sequence of causes and effects. We naturally reason that whatever has a beginning must have a cause for its existence. Sometimes, however, we are not able to determine the causes of the things we experience and instead imagine what they are, or we trust those we think friendly to us or more wise and adopt their views. Whatever the case may be, our acceptance of the identified "cause" leads to anxiety about a future time.

Religion comes about, then, either from the invention of human beings or from God's commands and direction. When religion is created by human beings, religion is necessarily related to politics and the duty of subjects to a king. In the second case, the seed of religion is divine politics and concerns the duty of subjects to the Kingdom of God.

Being that there are no signs and no fruit of religion except in man, there is no reason to doubt that the seeds of religion are also only in man and consist in some peculiar quality—or at least some eminent degree thereof—not found in other living creatures. First, it is specific to the nature of man to be inquisitive about the causes of the events they see, some more and some less. All men are curious in the search of the causes of their own good and evil fortune. Second, upon the sight of anything that has a beginning, it is part of the nature of man to think it also had a cause that determined it to begin when it did, rather than sooner or later. Third, beasts have no felicity other than enjoying their daily food, ease, and lusts because they have little or no foresight of the future because of their lack of observation and memory of the order, consequence, and dependence of the things they see. Man observes how one event has been produced by another and remembers them in antecedence and consequence. When he cannot assure himself of the true causes of things (for the causes of good and evil fortune are for the most part are invisible) he supposes causes of them either as his own fancy suggests or trusts to the authority of other men he thinks to be his friends and wiser than himself.

The first two cause anxiety because, being assured that there are causes of all things that have occurred or shall occur later, it is impossible for a man who continually endeavors to secure himself against the evil he fears and procure the good he desires not to be in a perpetual anxiety of the time to come. So that every man—especially those who are over provident—is in an estate like that of Prometheus. For as Prometheus (which interpreted is The Prudent Man) was bound to the hill Caucasus ... where an Eagle, feeding on his liver, devoured as much in the day as was repaired in the night. So that man who looks too far before him in the care of future time has his heart all day long gnawed on by fear of death, poverty, or other calamity and has no repose nor pause of his anxiety but in sleep.

This perpetual fear that always accompanies mankind in the ignorance of causes must have something for its object. Therefore when there is nothing to be seen, there is nothing but some power or invisible agent to accuse of their good or evil fortune. In this sense perhaps it was that some of the old poets said that the gods were at first created by human fear (or at least this is true of the many gods of the Gentiles). But acknowledging one eternal God, infinite and omnipotent, may be more easily derived from the desire men have to know the causes of natural bodies and their virtues and operations than from the fear of what was to befall them in the future. For he who reasons from any effect he sees to the next and immediate cause, and from that to the cause of the cause, and plunges himself profoundly in the pursuit of causes shall at last come to the conclusion that there must be (as even the heathen philosophers confessed) one First Mover and that is a First and an eternal cause of all things, which is what men mean by the name of God. And all this without thought of their fortune, the solicitude of which both inclines to fear and hinders them from the search of the causes of other things and gives occasion to invent as many gods as there are men who invent them. . . . Therefore men who by their own meditation arrive at the acknowledgment of one infinite, omnipotent, and eternal God choose to confess he is incomprehensible and above their understanding rather than to define his nature by incorporeal spirit and then confess their definition to be unintelligible. Or, if they give him such a title, it is not dogmatically with the intention to make the divine nature understood, but piously, to honor him with attributes and of significations as remote as they can be from the grossness of visible bodies.

Then, for the way by which they think these invisible agents caused their effects ... men who do not know what it is that we call "causing" (that is, almost all men) have no other rule by which to guess but to observe and remember what they have seen preceding the like effect at some other time or times before without seeing between the antecedent and consequent event any dependence or connection at all. Therefore from similar things past, they expect similar things to come and hope for good or evil luck, superstitiously, from things that have no part at all in causing it. . . . In like manner, they attribute their fortune to a bystander, to a lucky or unlucky place, to words spoken, especially if the name of God is among them, as charming and conjuring (the liturgy of witches) insomuch as to believe they have power to turn a stone into bread, bread into man, and anything into anything.

Third, for the worship which men naturally exhibit to invisible powers, it is by expressions of their reverence as they would use toward men, such as gifts, petitions, thanks, submission of body, considerate addresses, sober behavior, premeditated words, swearing (i.e., assuring one another of their promises) by invoking them.

Beyond that, reason suggests nothing but leaves them either to rest there for further ceremonies or to rely on those they believe to be wiser than themselves.

Last, concerning how these invisible powers declare to men things which shall happen in the future, especially concerning their good or evil fortune in general or in particular, men are naturally at a stand. Except that using to conjecture of the time to come by the time past they are very apt not only to take causal things after one or two encounters for prognostications of the like encounter ever after, but also to believe the like prognostications from other men from whom they have once heard a good opinion.

And in these four things—opinion of ghosts, ignorance of second causes, devotion toward what men fear, and taking casual things for prognostications—consists the natural seed of religion. By reason of the different fancies, judgments, and passions of many men has grown up into ceremonies so different that those used by one man are for the most part ridiculous to another.

These seeds have received culture from two sorts of men. One sort have been those who have nourished and ordered them according to their own invention. The other have done it by God's commandment and direction. Both sorts have done it with a purpose to make those men who relied on them more apt to obedience, laws, peace, charity, and civil society. So the religion of the former sort is a part of human politics and teaches part of the duty which earthly kings require of their subjects. The religion of the latter sort is divine politics and contains precepts to those who have yielded themselves subjects in the Kingdom of God. Of the former sort were all the founders of commonwealths and the lawgivers of the Gentiles. Of the latter sort were Abraham, Moses, and our Blessed Savior, who have derived and given to us the laws of the Kingdom of God.

And for that part of religion that consists of opinions concerning the nature of invisible powers, there is almost nothing that has a name that has not been esteemed among the Gentiles in one place or another, a God, a Devil, or feigned by their poets to be inanimate, inhabited, or possessed by some spirit or other. . . .[39]

Therefore the first founders and legislators of commonwealths among the Gentiles, whose ends were only to keep the people in obedience and peace, have in all places taken care first, to imprint in their minds a belief that those precepts which they gave concerning religion were not thought to proceed from their own device but from the dictates of some God or spirit or that they of higher nature than mere mortals so that laws are more easily received. So Numa Pompilius pretended to

---

39. What follows is a lengthy section that was omitted because Hobbes discusses similar issues elsewhere in later chapters in Part III. Something in this section worth mentioning from the omitted text is that Hobbes begins framing his criticism of private inspiration. Those who claim to hear prophetic messages directly from God and do not agree with the doctrine set forth by the sovereign "sometimes in the insignificant speeches of madmen, supposed to be possessed with a divine spirit, which possession they called enthusiasm; and these kinds of foretelling events were accounted theomancy, or prophecy" Hobbes calls madmen. He dismisses their messages as the talk of an insane person, a rhetorical theme that he will continue in following chapters.

receive the ceremonies he instituted among the Romans from the Nymph Egeria and the first king and founder of the kingdom of Peru pretended himself and his wife to be the children of the Sun. To set up his new religion, Muhammad pretended to have conferences with the Holy Ghost in the form of a dove. Second, they have taken care to make it believed that the same things were displeasing to the gods which were forbidden by the laws. Third, to prescribe ceremonies, supplications, sacrifices, and festivals by which they were to believe the anger of the gods might be appeased, and that ill success in war, great contagions of sickness, earthquakes, and each man's private misery came from the anger of the gods and their anger from neglect of their worship or forgetting or mistaking some point of the ceremonies required. Though among the ancient Romans men were not forbidden to deny what is written by the poets of the pains and pleasures after this life, yet that belief was always more cherished than the contrary.

By these and other such institutions they obtained in order to their end—which was the peace of the commonwealth—that common people were less apt to mutiny against their government when the fault lies on neglect or error in their ceremonies or disobedience to the laws. Being entertained with the pomp and pastime of festivals and public games made in honor of the gods, they needed nothing else but bread to keep them from discontent, murmuring, and commotion against the state. Therefore the Romans who had conquered the greatest part of the then known world made no scruple of tolerating any religion whatsoever in the city of Rome itself unless it had something in it inconsistent with their civil government. Nor do we read that there was any religion forbidden there but that of the Jews, who (being the peculiar Kingdom of God) thought it unlawful to acknowledge subjection to any mortal king or state whatsoever. Thus you see how the religion of the Gentiles was part of their policy.

Where God planted religion by supernatural revelation, he also created a specific kingdom and gave laws of behavior toward himself and also toward one another. Thereby in the Kingdom of God, the policy and civil laws are part of religion and thus the distinction of temporal and spiritual domination has no place. It is true that God is king of all the Earth, yet he may be king of a peculiar and chosen nation. For there is no more incongruity therein than that he who has the general command of the whole army should have a particular regiment or company of his own. God is the king of all the Earth by his power, but of his chosen people he is king by covenant. But to speak more largely of the Kingdom of God, both by nature and by covenant, I have in the following discourse assigned another place.[40]

From the propagation of religion, it is not hard to understand the causes of the resolution of it into its first seeds or principles. These are only an opinion of a deity that has invisible and supernatural powers that can never be abolished out of human nature but that new religions may again be made to spring out of them by the culture of men. . . .

All formed religion is founded at first upon the faith which a multitude has in some one person whom they believe to be a wise man and to labor to procure their

---

40. See Chapter XXXV.

happiness, and also to be a holy man to whom God himself vouchsafes to declare his will supernaturally. It follows necessarily when they who have government of religion come to have either the wisdom, sincerity, or love suspected, or that they shall be unable to show any probable token of divine revelation, that the religion which they desire to uphold must be suspected likewise and (without the fear of the civil sword) contradicted and rejected.

That which takes away the reputation of wisdom in a person who formed a religion or added to it after being formed is enjoining belief in contradictories.[41] Both parts of a contradiction cannot possibly be true and therefore to enjoin the belief in them is an argument of ignorance which is evident in the author in that and discredits him in all other things he claims to come from supernatural revelation. A man may indeed have revelation of many things above, but of nothing against natural reason.

Reputation of sincerity is taken away when a person does or says things that are signs that he really does not believe what he requires other men to believe. All such doings or sayings are therefore called scandalous because they are stumbling blocks that make men fall in the way of religion as injustice, cruelty, profaneness, avarice, and luxury. Who can believe that he who ordinarily does such actions that proceed from any of these roots believes there is any such invisible power to be feared and frightens other men for lesser faults?

Being detected of private ends takes away the reputation of love; the same for when the belief they require of others conduces, or seems to conduce, to acquiring dominion, riches, dignity, or securing pleasure only to themselves, or to themselves specially. For that by which men reap benefit to themselves they are thought to do for their own sakes and not for love of others.

Last, the testimony that men can render of divine calling can be no other than the operation of miracles or true prophecy (which is also a miracle) or extraordinary felicity. Therefore, to points of religion received from those who did miracles, those added by miracles that do not approve their calling by some miracle receive no greater belief than what customs and laws of places where they are educated have created in them. As in natural things, men of judgment require natural signs and arguments; and in supernatural things they require supernatural signs (miracles) before they consent inwardly and from their hearts.

---

41. Contradictory statements cannot both be true, nor can they both be false at the same time. That is, if a statement such as "All dogs are mammals" is true, it is impossible for "Some dogs are not mammals" to be true and in fact the latter must be false. And if a statement such as "No horse is a dog" is true, it must be the case (that is, it is necessarily true) that "Some horses are dogs" is false. These pairs of statements differ both in the number of things (everything and nothing) to which they refer and in the way in which they refer to them (one is an affirmation and the other is a negation). In Aristotle's traditional square of opposition, the relationships between statements that differ in both quantity and quality are contradictories. A person who contradicts herself is uttering a falsehood. In some cases, such falsehood indicates not simply a lack of wisdom but also a lie.

All causes of weakening men's faith appear in the following examples. First, we have the example of the children of Israel. When Moses who had approved his calling to them by miracles and the happy conduct of them out of Egypt and was absent for forty days, they revolted from the worship of the true God recommended to them by him. And setting up (Exod. 32.1, 2) a golden calf for their God, relapsed into the idolatry of the Egyptians from whom they had been delivered. After Moses, Aaron, Joshua, and that generation which had seen the great works of God in Israel (Judg. 2.11) were dead, another generation arose and served Baal. So that when miracles failed, faith also failed. When the sons of Samuel (1 Sam. 8.3) . . . received bribes and judged unjustly, the people of Israel refused to have God to be their king in other manner than he was king of other people and therefore cried out to Samuel to choose them a king after the manner of the nations.[42] So that when justice failed, faith also failed insomuch as they deposed their God from reigning over them.

Whereas in planting Christianity oracles ceased in all parts of the Roman Empire and the number of Christians increased wonderfully every day and everywhere by preaching of apostles and evangelists. A great part of the success may reasonably be attributed to the contempt into which the priests of the Gentiles of that time had brought themselves by their uncleanness, avarice, and juggling between princes. Also the religion of the Church of Rome was abolished in part for the same reason in England and many other parts of Christendom insomuch as the failing of virtue in the pastors makes faith fail in the people; and partly from bringing philosophy and doctrines of Aristotle into religion by the Schoolmen.[43] From them arose so many contradictions and absurdities it brought the clergy into a reputation both of ignorance and of fraudulent intention and inclined people to revolt from them either against the will of their own princes, as in France and Holland, or with their will as in England.

Last, among the points by the Church of Rome declared necessary for salvation there are some obviously of advantage to the pope and of his spiritual subjects residing in the territories of other Christian princes. If it were not for the mutual emulation of those princes, they might without war or trouble exclude all foreign authority as easily as it has been excluded in England. Who is there who does not see to whose benefit it is to believe that a king does not have his authority from

---

42. It may seem strange to a contemporary reader that Hobbes cites biblical texts to support his argument since he appeals so insistently to rejecting authority and instead using reason. While there is some controversy over the sincerity of Hobbes' religious claims, at the very least, much of the audience he would want to persuade would care a great deal about what scripture had to say. If Hobbes did not use it to support his argument, his critics would use it to attack his argument—and they did.

43. Hobbes is discussing the Protestant Reformation, which is the creation of Protestantism in breaking away from Catholicism and most of Catholic doctrine. Descartes (who was a contemporary of Hobbes) seems to have been sincere in his own religious convictions (and a Catholic), but even he was intent on using reason rather than tradition and authority to engage in argumentation concerning proof for the existence of God and the immortality of the soul.

Christ unless a bishop crowns him? That a king, if he is a priest, cannot marry? That whether a prince is born in lawful marriage or not must be judged by authority from Rome? That subjects may be freed from their allegiance if by the court of Rome the king is judged a heretic? That a king (as Chilperique of France) may be deposed by a pope (as Pope Zachary) for no cause and his kingdom given to one of his subjects? That the clergy and regulars in any country shall be exempt from the jurisdiction of their king in criminal cases? Or who does not see to whose profit the fees of private masses and the vales of Purgatory go, with other signs of private interest enough to mortify the most lively faith if (as I said) the civil magistrate and custom did not more sustain it than any opinion they have of the sanctity, wisdom, or probity of their teachers? So I may attribute all the changes of religion in the world to one and the same cause: unpleasing priests and those not only among Catholics but even in the Church that has presumed most of Reformation.[44]

---

44. Hobbes' concern, as the reader will see clearly in Part III, is that if ecclesiastical power supersedes that of civil or political authority, there is danger to the stability of the political commonwealth, resulting in civil unrest and, ultimately, civil war.

Chapter XIII. Of the Natural Condition of Mankind as Concerning Their Felicity and Misery

Chapter XIII is the point at which Hobbes begins the central task of arguing that agreement between and among people is necessary in order to establish government. It is in this chapter that the scope of Hobbes' science of politics becomes very clear. The goal of science is to control conclusions by creating conditions leading to them. We want to create peace, for which the establishment of government is necessary. It is only with the existence of strong political organization that peace is possible and, as you will see, strong political organization is founded on the laws of nature.

Hobbes describes a condition called the "state of nature" in which there is no government, no organized society, no religious institutions, and no established law. From this condition, the progression of the argument hinges on the assertion that all human beings are naturally equal. While Hobbes already noted that people desire different things, there are enough who desire the same things or the same sorts of things—especially things necessary to maintain their lives—to cause immediate trouble while trying to amass whatever objects and powers they think are necessary for survival. This, it is clear, leads to conflict, competition, and disagreements—and ultimately to war. The most famous and well-known phrase from Hobbes regarding human existence in the state of nature is that the life of man is "solitary, poor, nasty, brutish, and short." There must therefore be something that Hobbesian natural persons can do to alleviate the unbearable conditions in which they find themselves. Hobbes suggests that there are "convenient articles of peace" that rational people will recognize and that, if utilized, will lead them out of the state of nature and the state of war. Those "convenient articles" are the laws of nature.

Nature has made men so equal in the faculty of body and mind that even though there is one man sometimes manifestly stronger in body or of quicker mind than another, when all is reckoned together the difference between people is not so considerable as that one man can claim to himself any benefit that another may also claim. As to the strength of the body, the weakest has strength enough to kill the strongest, either by secret machination or by confederacy with others who are in the same danger as himself.

As to faculties of the mind: if the arts grounded on words and especially skill from general and infallible rules—that is, science—are set aside, very few have it since it is not a native faculty with which we are born nor is it attained while we do something else. Even those who have this art typically have it only in a few things.

This aside, concerning the faculties of the mind, I find a greater equality among men than strength. Prudence is experience which equal time bestows on all men in that which they equally apply themselves. What perhaps makes such equality incredible is vain conceit of one's own wisdom, which almost all men think they have in a greater degree than the vulgar—that is, than all men except themselves and a few others who, by fame or agreeing with themselves, they approve. Such is the nature of men that no matter that they acknowledge many others to be more witty, eloquent, or learned, they do not believe there are many who are so wise as themselves. For they see their own wit at hand and other men's at a distance. But this proves rather that men are equal in that point rather than unequal. For there is not ordinarily a greater sign of the equal distribution of anything than that every man is contented with his share.

From equality of ability arises equality of hope in attaining our ends. Therefore if any two men desire the same thing that they cannot both enjoy, they become enemies, and in the way to their end (which is principally their own conservation and sometimes only their delectation) endeavor to destroy or subdue one another. From this it comes to pass that where an invader has no more to fear than another man's single power, if one plants, sows, builds, or possesses a convenient seat, others may probably be expected to come prepared with forces united to dispossess and deprive him of the fruit of his labor and also his life or liberty. The invader again is in the like danger of another.

From diffidence of one another there is no way for any man to secure himself so reasonably as anticipation—that is, by force or wiles—to master all the men he can until he sees no other power great enough to endanger him. This is no more than his own conservation requires and is generally allowed. Also, because there are some who take pleasure in contemplating their own power in acts of conquest, they pursue farther than their security requires.[45] If others who would otherwise be glad to be at ease within modest bounds did not increase their power by invasion they would not be able for long to subsist only by defending themselves. Consequently, augmentation of dominion over men, being necessary to a man's conservation, ought to be allowed to him.

Again, men have no pleasure—but on the contrary a great deal of grief—in keeping company where there is no power able to overawe them all. For every man looks that his companion should value him at the same rate he sets upon himself. Upon all signs of contempt or undervaluing, naturally endeavors as far as he dares (which among them who have no common power to keep them quiet is enough to make them destroy each other) to extort a greater value from those who have contempt for him by damage and from others by example.

So that in the nature of man we find three principal causes of quarrel. First, competition; second, diffidence; third, glory. The first makes men invade for gain, the second for safety, and the third for reputation. The first uses violence to make

---

45. Even in conditions in which one might not reasonably expect that others are likely to invade for gain, there are people who will invade another's person and property simply for the glory or excitement of it.

themselves the masters of other men's persons, wives, children, and cattle; the second to defend them; the third for trifles such as a word, a smile, a different opinion, and any other sign of undervalue, either direct in their persons or by reflection in their relatives, their friends, their nation, their profession, or their name.

Hereby it is manifest that during the time men live without a common power to keep them all in awe, they are in the condition of war. Such a war is of every man against every man. For war consists not in battle only, or in the act of fighting, but in a tract of time wherein the will to contend by battle is sufficiently known, and therefore the notion of time is to be considered in the nature of war as it is in the nature of weather. As the nature of foul weather does not lie in a shower or two of rain, but in an inclination to it of many days together, so the nature of war does not consist in actual fighting but in the known disposition toward it during all the time there is no assurance to the contrary.[46] All other time is peace.

Whatever therefore is consequent to a time of war where every man is enemy to every man, the same is consequent to the time wherein men live without security other than that which their own strength and invention shall furnish them. In such condition there is no place for industry because the fruit of it is uncertain, and consequently there is no culture of the Earth; no navigation nor use of the commodities that may be imported by sea; no commodious building; no instruments of moving or removing things that require much force; no knowledge of the face of the Earth; no account of time; no arts; no letters; no society; and which is worst of all, continual fear and danger of violent death; and the life of man, solitary, poor, nasty, brutish, and short.[47]

It may seem strange to some who have not well weighed these things that nature should thus dissociate and render men apt to invade and destroy one another, and he may therefore desire to have the same confirmed by experience because he does not trust to this inference made from passions. Let him therefore consider that when taking a journey he arms himself and seeks to go well accompanied. When going to sleep he locks his doors. When even in his house he locks his chests, and this when he knows there are laws and armed public officers to revenge all injuries done to him. What opinion he has of his fellow subjects when he rides armed; of his fellow citizens when he locks his doors; and of his children and servants when

---

46. To contemporary readers, Hobbes is describing a condition similar to that after World War II in which the Soviet Union and its Eastern Bloc satellites were in a condition of Cold War with the United States and its Western allies. This is a condition in which two or more sides to disagreement or contention are always prepared and preparing for actual war.

47. This is probably the most famous of all quotations from the works of Thomas Hobbes. In the condition of war, the life of man is "solitary, poor, nasty, brutish, and short." This does not, however, mean that the only consideration to take into account is the maintenance of life itself. There are some commentators who have argued that Hobbes was concerned only with mere survival and that he was a psychological egoist. Others have argued that Hobbes' position is not as severe as it may at first seem to be. One hint from one of Hobbes' other works, *De Cive*, that he did not argue for mere survival in any sort of miserable condition is when he asserts that the goal in instituting government is not simply to live in any condition whatsoever but so that people may "live delightfully."

he locks his chests. Does he not there as much accuse mankind by his actions as I do by my words? But neither of us accuses man's nature in it. The desires and other passions of man are in themselves no sin. No more are the actions that proceed from those passions until they know a law that forbids them, which until laws are made they cannot know, nor can any law be made until they have agreed upon the person who shall make it.[48]

It may be thought there was never such a time nor condition of war as this, and I believe it was never generally so all over the world. But there are many places where they live so now. For the savage people in many places of America, except the government of small families[49] that depend on natural lust for concord, have no government at all and live this day in that brutish manner. . . . Howsoever, it may be perceived what manner of life there would be where there was no common power to fear; by the manner of life which men who have formerly lived under a peaceful government use to degenerate into a civil war.

But though there had never been any time in which particular men were in a condition of war against another, yet in all times kings and persons of sovereign authority, because of their independency, are in continual jealousies and in the state and posture of gladiators, having their weapons pointing and their eyes fixed on one another—that is, their forts, garrisons, and guns upon the frontiers of their kingdoms and continual spies upon their neighbors, which is a posture of war.[50] But because they uphold thereby the industry of their subjects, there

---

48. Hobbes' claim that the desires and passions leading people to behave as they would in a condition of war are not sinful is often overlooked in a cursory reading of Hobbes' work. Those who persist in claiming that Hobbes has described human beings in the natural condition in the state of war as immoral or amoral beasts have clearly got it wrong. In that condition, there is no common power to enforce rules of any kind. There can be no breach of law, and so no sin, until there is a power sufficient in force to guarantee compliance or punishment for transgressions.

49. The claim that the government of small families can exist in a natural condition (regardless of whether Hobbes has his facts straight concerning "the savage people in many places of America") is clear indication that Hobbes did not believe, as some commentators and cursory readers of his works have contended, that in a state of nature everyone is isolated from everyone else and there is no social existence at all. The existence of families is admitted and emphasized by Hobbes in explaining the need for strong central government, which "little monarchies" (families) are unable to provide for themselves due to their severely limited size and strength.

50. This is Hobbes' affirmation of the notion that war is more than actual fighting. It is an important point in clarifying why Hobbes thought that people would continue to be acquisitive and constantly on guard. It describes conditions between states in his time as well as in ours, in which nations are sufficiently prepared either in fact or in principle to take up arms against each other. Again, Hobbes is describing a condition that we in the twenty-first century recognize from the conditions of the Cold War in the twentieth century after World War II.

does not follow from it that misery which accompanies the liberty of particular men.[51]

To this war of every man against every man this also is consequent—that nothing can be unjust. The notions of right and wrong, justice and injustice have there no place. Where there is no common power, there is no law; where no law, no injustice. Force and fraud are in war the two cardinal virtues. Justice and injustice are none of the faculties neither of the body nor mind. If they were, they might be in a man who was alone in the world as well as his senses and passions. They are qualities that relate to men in society, not in solitude. It is consequent also to the same condition that there be no propriety, no dominion, no mine and thine distinct, but only that to be every man's that he can get, and for so long as he can keep it. And thus much for the ill condition which man by mere nature is actually placed, though with a possibility to come out of it consisting partly in the passions, partly in his reason.

The passions that incline men to peace are fear of death, desire of things necessary to commodious living, and a hope by their industry to obtain them. Reason suggests convenient articles of peace upon which men may be drawn to agreement. These articles are called the laws of nature, whereof I shall speak more particularly in the two following chapters.

---

51. Hobbes is highlighting what he takes to be the fact that individual people, their families, and their friends are more secure under a strong central government than they are in trying to secure themselves alone or in small groups.

Chapter XIV. Of the First and Second Natural Laws, and of Contracts

Hobbes distinguishes between rights and laws as freedoms and obligations, respectively. A person is free when she or he lacks external impediments to action. For Hobbes, every person is naturally free to defend his own life. Further, however, every person is obligated to preserve his life, from which it follows that it is necessary for every person to agree with every other person to give up the "right to all things" and "be contented with so much liberty against other men as he would allow other men against himself." In other words, continuing to behave as though one possesses a right to everything is bound to result in clashes with others, who also believe they have a right to all things. Agreement (contract) is necessary in order to begin the process of establishing peace among people who are natural competitors with each other and seek possession of scarce resources needed for survival.

The right of nature, which writers commonly call *Jus Naturale*, is the liberty each man has to use his own power as he sees fit for the preservation of his own nature—that is to say, of his own life—and consequently of doing anything which in his own judgment and reason he conceives are the best means to do so.

By liberty is understood—according to the proper signification of the word—the absence of external impediments, which impediments may often take away part of a man's power to do what he would, but cannot hinder him from using the power left to him according as his judgment and reason shall dictate to him.[52]

A law of nature (*Lex Naturalis*) is a precept or general rule found out by reason by which a man is forbidden to do that which is destructive to his life or takes away the means of preserving it, and to omit that by which he thinks it may be best preserved. . . . *Jus* and *lex* (right and law) ought to be distinguished because right consists in the liberty to do or to forbear, whereas law determines and binds to one of them. So that law and right differ as much as obligation and liberty, which in one and the same matter are inconsistent.

Because the natural condition of man (as has been declared in the preceding chapter) is a condition of war of every one against everyone, in which case

---

52. Hobbes was a compatibilist with respect to the question of "freedom" of the will. That is, Hobbes believed that necessitation or "determinism" is consistent with "freedom." For the most part, Hobbes' discussions of "freedom" or "liberty" in *Leviathan* are centered on absence of constraints in a political condition, but the meaning is essentially the same for his metaphysical view of the issue. It is sufficient at this point to note that Hobbes was convinced that people are free when they are not hindered in doing what they want to do. There is no such thing, for Hobbes, as "free-will," and in fact he considers the phrase to be absurd.

everyone is governed by his own reason, there is nothing he can make use of that may not be a help to him in preserving his life against his enemies. It follows that in such a condition, every man has a right to everything, even to another's body. Therefore as long as this natural right of every man to everything endures, there can be no security to any man (no matter how strong or wise he is) of living out the time which nature ordinarily allows men to live.

Consequently, it is a precept or general rule of reason, "that every man ought to endeavor peace as far as he has hope of obtaining it, and when he cannot obtain it, that he may seek and use all helps and advantages of war." The first branch of this rule contains the first, the fundamental law of nature, which is "to seek peace and follow it." The second, the sum of the right of nature, is "by all means we can, to defend ourselves."

From this fundamental law of nature by which men are commanded to endeavor peace is derived this second law: "that a man be willing, when others are too, as far as for peace and defense of himself he shall think it necessary, to lay down his right to all things and be contented with so much liberty against other men as he would allow other men against himself." As long as every man holds this right of doing anything he likes, so long are men in the condition of war. But if other men will not lay down their right as well as he, then there is no reason for anyone to divest himself of his because that would be to expose himself to prey (which no man is bound to) rather than to dispose himself to peace. This is that law of the Gospel, "Whatsoever you require that others should do to you, do you to them." And that law of all men, *Quod tibi feiri non vis, alteri ne feceris.*[53]

To lay down a man's right to anything is to forfeit the liberty of hindering another person to use his right to the same thing. For he who renounces or passes away his right does not give to any other man a right which he did not have before because there is nothing to which every man did not have a right by nature. Instead, he only stands out of another's way so he may enjoy his original right without hindrance. . . . So the effect which comes to one man by another man's defect of right is so much diminution of impediments to the use of his own original right.

Right is laid aside either by simply renouncing it or by transferring it to another. Simple renunciation is done when he does not care to whom the benefit goes. By transferring, he intends the benefit to some certain person or persons. When a man has in either manner abandoned or granted away his right, then he is said to be obliged or bound not to hinder those to whom such a right is granted or abandoned, and the benefit of it. He ought, and it is his duty, not to make void that voluntary act of his own and that such hindrance is injustice and injury, as being *sine jure,*[54] the right being before renounced or transferred. So that injury or injustice in the controversies of the world is something like what scholars in their disputations called absurdity. For as it is there called an absurdity to contradict what one maintained in the beginning, so in the world it is called injustice and injury voluntarily

---

53. "Do not do unto others what you would not want done to yourself" or "What you do not want done to yourself, do not do to another."
54. "Without right."

to undo that which from the beginning he had voluntarily done. The way by which a man either simply renounces or transfers his right is a declaration or signification by some voluntary and sufficient sign or signs that he does so renounce or transfer, or has so renounced or transferred the same to he who accepts it. These signs are either words only, or actions only, or (as it happens most often) both words and actions. And the same are the bonds by which men are bound and obliged. They are bonds that do not have their strength from their own nature (for nothing is more easily broken than a man's word) but from fear of some evil consequence upon the rupture.

Whenever a man transfers or renounces his right, it is either in consideration of some right reciprocally transferred to himself or for some other good for which he hopes by doing so. This is the case because it is a voluntary act, and of the voluntary actions of every man, the object is some good to himself. Therefore there are some rights which no man can be understood by any words or other signs to have abandoned or transferred. A man cannot lay down the right of resisting those who assault him by force to take away his life, because he cannot be understood to aim thereby at any good to himself. The same may be said of wounds and chains and imprisonment, both because there is no benefit consequent to such patience as there is to the patience of suffering another to be wounded or imprisoned. Also because a man cannot tell when he sees men proceed against him by violence whether they intend his death or not. And last, the motive, an end for which renouncing and transferring a right is introduced is nothing else but the security of a man's person in his life and in the means of preserving his life as not to be weary of it. Therefore, if a man by words or other signs seems to despoil himself of the end for which those signs were intended, he is not to be understood as if he meant it or that it was his will, but that he was ignorant of how such words and actions were to be interpreted.

The mutual transfer of a right is that which men call contract. There is a difference between transferring right to a thing and transferring or delivering the thing itself. For the thing may be delivered together with the translation of the right, as in buying and selling with ready money or exchange of goods or lands, and it may be delivered sometime after.

One of the contractors may deliver the thing contracted for on his part and leave the other to perform his part at some determinate time after and in the meantime be trusted. And then the contract on his part is called pact or covenant. Or both parts may contract now and perform hereafter, in which case he who is to perform in time to come, being trusted, his performance is keeping of promise or faith and failing performance (if it is voluntary) is violation of faith.

When transferring of right is not mutual but one of the parties transfers in hope thereby to gain friendship or service from another or from his friends or in hope to gain the reputation of charity or magnanimity, to deliver his mind from the pain of compassion, or in hope of reward in Heaven, it is not contract but gift, free-gift, or grace. These words signify one and the same thing.

Signs of contract are either express or by inference. Express are words spoken with understanding of what they signify. Such words are either of present or past, indicated by "I give," "I grant," "I have given," "I have granted," "I will that this be yours," or of the future as "I will give," "I will grant," where words of the future are promise.

Signs by inference are sometimes the consequence of words and sometimes the consequence of silence. Sometimes they are the consequence of forbearing an action. Generally, a sign by inference of any contract is whatever sufficiently argues the will of the contractor.

Words alone, if they are of a time to come and contain a bare promise, are an insufficient sign of a free-gift and therefore they are not obligatory. For if they are of the time to come (such as "Tomorrow I will give") they are a sign that I have not yet given and consequently that my right is not transferred but remains until I transfer it by some other act. But if the words are of the present time, or past, as "I have given, or do give to be delivered tomorrow," then my right tomorrow is given away today, and that by the virtue of the words even though there was no other argument of my will. There is a great difference in the signification of these words . . . "I will that this be yours tomorrow," and "I will give it to you tomorrow." For the word "I will," in the former manner of speech signifies an act of the present will. But in the latter, it signifies a promise of an act of the will to come and therefore the former words, because they are of the present, transfer a future right. The latter that are of the future transfer nothing.[55] But if there are other signs of the will to transfer a right besides words, then though the gift is free, the right may yet be understood to pass by words of the future such as if a man promises a prize to he who comes first in a race, the gift is free and though the words are of the future, the right passes. Because if he would not have his words understood this way, he should not have said them.

In contracts, the right passes not only where the words are of the present or past, but also where they are of the future because all contract is mutual transfer or change of right. Therefore, he who promises only because he has already received the benefit for which he promised is to be understood as if he intended the right should pass. For unless he was content to have his words so understood, the other would not have performed his part first. And for that cause in buying, selling, and other acts of contract, a promise is equivalent to a covenant and therefore it is obligatory.

He who performs first in the case of contract is said to merit that which he is to receive by the performance of the other, and he has it as his due. Also, when a prize is offered to many which is to be given only to he who wins, or money is thrown among many to be enjoyed by those who catch it to win or to catch is to merit and to have it as due even though this is free-gift. The right is transferred in propounding the prize and in throwing down the money, though it is not determined in advance who wins and instead it is determined by the event of the contention. There is between these two sorts of merit the difference that in contract, I merit

---

55. The reason that promises referring to the future transfer nothing is that, as Hobbes indicated earlier in Part I, statements about the future can have no meaning because the future itself has no existence.

by virtue of my own power and the contractor's need. But in the case of free-gift, I am enabled to merit only by the benignity of the giver. In contract, I merit at the contractor's hand that he should depart with his right. In this case of gift, I do not merit that the giver should part with his right, but that when he has parted with it, it should be mine rather than another person's. . . . Only this I say, when a gift is given indefinitely, as a prize to be contended for, he who wins merits and may claim the prize as due.

In the condition of mere nature, which is a condition of war of every man against every man, if a covenant is made in which neither of the parties performs immediately but trust one another, it is void. But if there is a common power set over them both, with right and force sufficient to compel performance it is not void. For he who performs first has no assurance the other will perform after because the bonds of words are too weak to bridle men's ambition, avarice, anger, and other passions without the fear of some coercive power which, in the condition of mere nature where all men are equal and judges of the justness of their own fears, cannot possibly be supposed. Therefore he who performs first betrays himself to his enemy, contrary to the right (he can never abandon) of defending his life and means of living. But in a civil estate where there is a power set up to constrain those who would otherwise violate their faith, that fear is no longer reasonable because the first to perform according to the covenant is obliged to do so.

The cause of fear which makes such a covenant invalid must always be something arising after the covenant, such as some new fact or other sign of the will not to perform, or else it cannot make the covenant void. For that which could not hinder a man from promising should not be admitted as a hindrance to performing.

He who transfers any right transfers the means of enjoying it as far as lies in his power. He who sells land is understood to transfer the herbage and whatever grows upon it. Nor can he who sells a mill turn away the stream that drives it. They who give to a man the right of government in sovereignty are understood to give to him the right of levying money to maintain soldiers and of appointing magistrates for the administration of justice.

To make covenant with brute beasts is impossible because they do not understand our speech and cannot accept any transfer of right. Nor can they transfer any right to another. Without mutual acceptation, there is no covenant.

It is impossible to make a covenant with God except by mediation of those to whom God speaks either by supernatural revelation or by lieutenants who govern under him and in his name. Otherwise we do not know whether our covenants are accepted.[56] Therefore, vowing anything contrary to any law of nature is to vow in vain because it is unjust to pay such a vow. And if it is a thing commanded by the law of nature, it is not the vow but the law that binds them.

The matter or subject of a covenant is always something that falls under deliberation (for to covenant is an act of the will, that is, an act and the last act of

---

56. As the reader will see in Part III, Hobbes' point here is that only the sovereign is able to covenant with God on behalf of the people over whom he (or she) rules. This point is essential to Hobbes' religious justification for the existence and power of the civil sovereign.

deliberation) and is therefore always understood to be something to come, and which it is judged possible for he who covenants to perform. Therefore, to promise what is known to be impossible is not a covenant. If it proves impossible afterward, which was before thought possible, the covenant is valid and binds (though not to the thing itself) yet to the value. Or if that is also impossible, it binds to the honest endeavor of performing as much as is possible, for no more no man can be obliged.[57]

Men are freed from their covenants in two ways—by performing or by being forgiven. Performance is the natural end of obligation and forgiveness the restitution of liberty, as being a retransferring of that right in which the obligation consisted.

Covenants entered into by fear in the condition of mere nature are obligatory. For example, if I covenant to pay a ransom or service for my life to an enemy I am bound by it. For it is a contract in which one receives the benefit of life and the other is to receive money or service for it. Consequently where no other law (as in the condition of mere nature) forbids the performance, the covenant is valid. Therefore if prisoners of war are trusted with the payment of their ransom they are obliged to pay it. If a weaker prince makes a disadvantageous peace with a stronger out of fear, he is bound to keep it unless (as has been said before) there arises some new and just cause to fear to renew the war. Even in commonwealths, if I am forced to redeem myself from a thief by promising him money, I am bound to pay it until the civil law discharges me. For whatever I may lawfully do without obligation, the same I may lawfully covenant to do through fear and what I lawfully covenant, I cannot lawfully break.[58]

A former covenant makes void a later. For a man who has passed away his right to one man today does not have it to pass tomorrow to another, and therefore the later promise passes no right, but is null.

A covenant not to defend myself from force by force is always void. For (as I have showed before) no man can transfer or lay down his right to save himself from death, wounds, and imprisonment (avoiding these is the only end in laying down any right) and therefore the promise of not resisting force in no covenant transfers

---

57. Say, for example, that you promise in a written contract with a bank or loan company to pay for the car for which the company has advanced funds for you to buy. If a condition arises in which you are no longer able to make payments, the fact is that upon the execution of the contract, both you and the bank believed that you would make and be able to make the payments required, so even if something happens after the agreement has been made and you are for whatever reason not able to repay the loan, you are required instead to do your best to live up to the contract.

58. Hobbes' position regarding covenants made through fear may seem problematic on the whole, but for the argument Hobbes is advancing, it would be impossible to institute a political sovereign if agreements made in fear were *not* valid. Hobbes notes that it is from fear of each other that we make an agreement to form government and institute a sovereign power, and regardless of the source or reason for enacting the agreement, it is justified just so long as it was freely entered into. On the whole, however, Hobbes' conception of the notion of freely made agreements remains problematic.

any right, nor is it obliging. For though a man may covenant thus, "Unless I do so or so, kill me," he cannot covenant thus, "Unless I do so or so, I will not resist you when you come to kill me." For man by nature chooses the lesser evil, which is danger of death in resisting rather than the greater, which is certain and present death in not resisting. And this is granted to be true by all men in that they lead criminals to execution and prison with armed men, notwithstanding that such criminals have consented to the law by which they are condemned.[59]

A covenant to accuse oneself without assurance of pardon is, likewise, invalid. For in the condition of nature where every man is judge, there is no place for accusation, and in the civil state the accusation is followed with punishment which, being force, a man is not obliged not to resist.[60] The same is true also of the accusation of those whose condemnation a man falls into misery, as of a father, wife, or benefactor. For the testimony of such an accuser, if it is not willingly given, is presumed to be corrupted by nature and therefore not to be received. Where a man's testimony is not to be credited, he is not bound to give it. Also, accusations upon torture are not to be reputed as testimonies, for torture is to be used but as a means of conjecture and light in the further examination and search of truth.[61] What is in that case confessed tends to the ease of he who is tortured and not to informing the torturers, and therefore ought not to have the credit of sufficient testimony. Whether he delivers himself by true or false accusation, he does it by the right of preserving his own life.

The force of words being (as I have formerly noted) too weak to hold men to the performance of their covenants, there are in man's nature but two imaginable helps to strengthen it. Those are either a fear or the consequence of breaking their word or a glory or pride in appearing not to need to break it. This latter is a generosity too rarely found to be presumed on, especially in the pursuers of wealth, command, or sensual pleasure, which are the greatest part of mankind. The passion to be reckoned upon is fear, of which there are two very general objects. One is the power of invisible spirits, the other the power of those men they shall therein offend. Of these two, even though the former is the greater power, the fear of the latter is commonly the greater fear.[62] The fear of the former is in every man his own religion which has place in the nature of man before civil society. The latter

---

59. In other words, while it is to be expected that prisoners sentenced to death will try to break free and avoid death to preserve their lives, they have submitted to the laws that were applied leading to the sentence.

60. The meaning of the claim that a person is not required to accuse himself without promise of pardon is amply expressed much later in the U.S. Constitution's provision in the Fifth Amendment that no person may be required to be a witness against himself in any criminal proceeding and may, instead, remain silent.

61. Hobbes does not claim that torture is never to be used but, instead, that information gained from it is unreliable.

62. As Hobbes makes clear through Part III of *Leviathan* on the power of the political sovereign as supreme prophet of God, the combination of great power in the commonwealth and great fear of God make the political sovereign's power irresistible in principle even if not in fact.

does not have such a place, at least not place enough to keep men to their promises. Because in the condition of mere nature, the inequality of power is not discerned but by the event of battle. So that before creation of civil society, or in the interruption of it by war, there is nothing that can strengthen a covenant of peace agreed on against the temptations of avarice, ambition, lust, or other strong desire but the fear of that invisible power which everyone worships as God; and fear as a revenger of their perfidy. All therefore that can be done between two men not subject to civil power is to put one another to swear by the God he fears. Swearing such an oath is a form of speech, added to a promise, by which he who promises signifies that unless he performs, he renounces the mercy of his God or calls to him for vengeance on himself. Such was the heathen form, "Let Jupiter kill me else as I kill his beast." So is our form, "I shall do thus and thus, so help me God." And this, with the rites and ceremonies which everyone uses in his own religion that the fear of breaking faith might be the greater.

By this it appears that an oath taken according to any other form or rite than his who swears is in vain, and is not an oath. There is no swearing by anything which the swearer does not think God. For though men have sometimes sworn by their kings for fear or flattery, they would not have it thereby understood that they attributed to them divine honor. Swearing unnecessarily by God is profaning his name, and swearing by other things as men do in common discourse is not swearing, but an impious custom gotten by too much vehemence of talking.

It also appears that the oath adds nothing to the obligation because a covenant, if lawful, binds in the sight of God without the oath as much as with it. If unlawful, it does not bind at all though it is confirmed with an oath.

Chapter XV. Of Other Laws of Nature

In this chapter, Hobbes begins the process of deriving other laws of nature. All of them are the result of reason and derive in part from the right of nature that each person has to defend her or his own life. They are rules of reason, and in fact Hobbes contends that what is more is that the laws of nature are the origin of the only true moral philosophy (more specifically, they are part of a science of politics) that has ever existed.

From the law of nature requiring us to transfer right to another that, being retained, hinder the peace, there follows a third law of nature: That men perform the covenants that they made, without which covenants are in vain and but empty words, and the right of all men to all things remaining, we are still in the condition of war.

The fountain and origin of justice is in this law. For where no covenant has preceded, there has been no transfer of right and every man has right to everything. Consequently, no action can be unjust. But when a covenant is made, to break it is unjust. The definition of injustice is no other than not performing covenant. Whatsoever is not unjust, is just.

Even though the origin of justice is making covenants, where there is fear of nonperformance on either part (as has been said in the former chapter), covenants of mutual trust are invalid. Yet, there can actually be no injustice until the cause of fear is removed. This cannot be done while men are in the natural condition of war. Therefore before the names of just and unjust can have place, there must be some coercive power to compel men equally to the performance of their covenants by the fear of some punishment greater than the benefit they expect by breach of covenant. Power to make good the propriety acquired by mutual contract as compensation for the universal right abandoned does not exist before the creation of commonwealth. This is also to be gathered out of the ordinary definition of justice in the Schools. For they say that "Justice is the constant will of giving to every man his own." . . . Therefore where there is no coercive power erected, that is, where there is no commonwealth, there is no propriety since all men have a right to all things. Therefore where there is no commonwealth, there is nothing unjust. So that the nature of justice consists in keeping valid covenants, but the validity of covenants begins with the constitution of a civil power sufficient to compel men to keep them. And then it is also that propriety begins.

The fool has said in his heart there is no such thing as justice, and sometimes also with his tongue, seriously alleging that since every man's conservation and contentment is committed to his own care, there could be no reason why every man might not do what he thought conduced to it. Therefore also to make or not make, to keep or not keep covenants was not against reason when it conduced to one's benefit. He does not therein deny that there are covenants and they are sometimes broken, sometimes kept, and that breach of them may be called injustice and the observance of them justice. He questions whether injustice, taking away the fear of God (for the same fool has said in his heart there is no God) may not sometimes stand with that reason which dictates to every man his own good. Particularly then, when it conduces to such a benefit, as shall put a man in a condition to neglect not only the dispraise and revilings, but also the power of other men. The Kingdom of God is gotten by violence, but what if it could be gotten by unjust violence?[63] Were it against reason to get it that way, when it is impossible to receive hurt by it? And if it is not against reason, it is not against justice, or else justice is not to be approved for good. From such reasoning as this, successful wickedness has obtained the name of virtue and some who in all other things have disallowed the violation of faith have allowed it when it is for getting a kingdom. . . . A man will be very prone to infer that when the heir apparent of a kingdom shall kill him who is in possession, even though it is his father, you may call it injustice or by what other name you will, yet it can never be against reason seeing that all the voluntary actions of men tend to the benefit of themselves.[64] Those actions are most reasonable that conduce most to their ends. This specious reasoning is nevertheless false because the question is not of mutual promises where there is no security of performance on either side, as when there is no civil power erected over the parties promising for such promises are not covenants. But either where one of the parties has performed already or where there is a power to make him perform, there is the question whether it is against reason, that is, against the benefit of the other to perform or not. And I say it is not against reason. For the manifestation of it we are to consider, first, that when a man does a thing which tends to his own destruction, howsoever some accident which he could not expect may turn to his benefit. Yet such events do not make it reasonably or wisely done. Second, that in a condition of war wherein every man is an enemy to every man because there is no common power to keep them all in awe, there no man can hope by his own strength or wit to defend himself from destruction without the help of confederates, where everyone expects the same defense by the confederation that anyone else does. Therefore he who declares he thinks it reasonable to deceive those who help him can in reason expect no other means of safety than what can be had from his own single power. He therefore who breaks his covenant, and consequently declares that he thinks he may do so with reason, cannot be received into any society that unite themselves for peace and defense except by the error of those who receive him. Nor when he is received may he be retained in it without seeing the danger of their error, which errors a man cannot reasonably reckon upon as the means of his security. Therefore if he is left or cast out of society, he perishes; and if he lives in society, it is by the errors of

---

63. Hobbes is referencing Matt. 11.12.
64. Here, again, when Hobbes insists that all voluntary actions performed are done with a view to one's own benefit, it does not imply that one's voluntary actions may not be performed also for the benefit of others.

other men which he could not foresee nor reckon upon, and consequently against the reason of his preservation. So, all men who do not contribute to his destruction forbear him only out of ignorance of what is good for themselves.

There is only one way imaginable to gain secure and perpetual felicity of Heaven, and that is not breaking, but keeping, covenant. As for the instance of attaining sovereignty by rebellion, it is obvious that though the event follows, it could not have been reasonably expected. Instead the contrary is reasonably expected and because by gaining it in this way, others are taught to gain the same in a similar way and the attempt is against reason. Justice, therefore—that is to say, keeping of covenant— is a rule of reason by which we are forbidden to do anything destructive to our life, and consequently a law of nature.

There are some who proceed further and will not admit the law of nature to be rules conducing to the preservation of man's life on Earth, but to attaining eternal felicity after death to which breach of covenant may be conducive and consequently be just and reasonable. Such are they who think it a work of merit to kill or depose or rebel against the sovereign power constituted over them by their own consent. But because there is no natural knowledge of man's estate after death much less of the reward that is then to be given to breach of faith, but only a belief grounded upon other men's saying, that they know it supernaturally, or that they know those who knew them who knew others who knew it supernaturally. Breach of faith cannot be called a precept of reason or nature.

Others who allow for a law of nature, the keeping of faith, nevertheless make exception of certain persons such as heretics and those who do not perform their covenants to others. And this is also against reason. For if any fault of a man is sufficient to discharge our covenant, the same ought reasonably to have been sufficient to have hindered making it.

When the names of just and unjust are attributed to men they signify one thing, and when they are attributed to actions, another. When they are attributed to men they signify conformity or inconformity of manners to reason. But when they are attributed to actions, they signify the conformity or inconformity to reason—not of manners or manner of life but—of particular actions. A just man therefore is he who takes all the care he can that his actions may be all just. And an unjust man is he who neglects it. Such men are more often in our language styled by the names of righteous and unrighteous than just and unjust, though the meaning is the same. Therefore a righteous man does not lose that title by one or a few unjust actions that proceed from sudden passion or mistake of things or persons. Nor does an unrighteous man lose his character for such actions as he does or forbears to do for fear because his will is not framed by the justice but by the apparent benefit of what he is to do. That which gives to human actions the relish of justice is a certain nobleness or gallantness of courage (rarely found) by which a man scorns to be beholding for the contentment of his life to fraud or breach of promise.[65] Justice of

---

65. Another way to put the case is that actions that are truly just are the actions of a person who is noble and courageous enough not to be satisfied with his safety and happiness being gained by fraud and lies. It is also important to see that the distinction here is one with a very

manners is that which is meant where justice is called a virtue and injustice a vice. But the justice of actions denominates men not just but guiltless, and injustice of the same (which is also called injury) gives them the name of guilty.

Again, the injustice of manners is the disposition or aptitude to do injury and is injustice before it proceeds to act and without supposing any individual person injured. But the injustice of an action (that is to say, injury) supposes an individual person injured—namely he to whom the covenant was made. Therefore, many times the injury is received by one man when the damage redounds to another. As, for example, when the master commands his servant to give money to a stranger, if it is not done, the injury is done to the master whom he had before covenanted to obey, but the damage redounds to the stranger to whom he had no obligation and therefore he could not injure him. So also in commonwealths, private men remit to one another their debts, but by robbers or other violences they are damaged because detaining debt is an injury to themselves. But robbery and violence are injuries to the person of the commonwealth.

Whatever is done to a man consistent with his own will and signified to the doer is not injury to him. For if he who does it has not passed away his original right to do what he pleases by some antecedent covenant, there is no breach of covenant, and therefore no injury done to him. And if he has, then his will to have it done being signified is a release of that covenant and so again there is no injury done to him.

Justice of actions is divided by writers into commutative and distributive. The former consists in arithmetical proportion, the latter in geometrical proportion. Commutative justice is placed in the equality of value of things contracted for. Distributive is in the distribution of equal benefit to men of equal merit. As if it were injustice to sell dearer than we buy, or to give more to a man than he merits. The value of all things contracted for is measured by the appetite of the contractors, and therefore the just value is that which they are contented to give. Merit (besides that which is by covenant where the performance on one part merits the performance of the other and falls under commutative justice, not distributive) is not due by justice, but is rewarded of grace only. Therefore this distinction in the sense wherein it used to be expounded is not right.

To speak properly, commutative justice is the justice of a contractor—that is, performance of covenant in buying and selling, hiring and letting to hire, lending and borrowing, exchanging, bartering, and other acts of contract. Distributive justice is the justice of an arbitrator—that is to say, the act of defining what is just. Wherein (being trusted by them who make him arbitrator) if he performs his trust, he is said to distribute to every man his own, and his is indeed just distribution and may be called (though improperly) distributive justice, but more properly equity, which is also a law of nature, as shall be shown in due place.

As justice depends on antecedent covenant, so gratitude depends on antecedent grace—that is to say, antecedent free-gift, and is the fourth law of nature which may

---

significant difference. In the natural condition, the two cardinal virtues are force and fraud. After the institution of the sovereign, this is no longer the case.

be conceived in this form. "That a man who receives benefit from another of mere grace endeavors that he who gives it has no reasonable cause to repent him of his good will." For no man gives except with the intention of good to himself because gift is voluntary, and of all voluntary acts the object is to every man his own good, of which if men see they shall be frustrated, there will be no beginning of benevolence or trust, nor consequently of mutual help, nor of reconciliation of one man to another, and therefore they are to remain still in the condition of war, which is contrary to the first and fundamental law of nature which commands men to seek peace. The breach of this law is called ingratitude and has the same relation to grace that injustice has to obligation by covenant.

A fifth law of nature is complaisance—that is to say, "That every man strives to accommodate himself to the rest." For the understanding of this we may consider that there is in men's aptness to society diversity of nature arising from their diversity of affections not unlike what we see in stones brought together for building an edifice. As from the asperity and irregularity of figure in a stone takes more room from others than it itself fills, and for its hardness cannot be easily made plain and thereby hinders the building, it is cast away as unprofitable and troublesome by the builders. So also a man who by asperity of nature strives to retain those things which to himself are superfluous and to others necessary, and for the stubbornness of his passions cannot be corrected is to be left or cast out of society as cumbersome to it. Every man not only by right, but also by necessity of nature, is supposed to endeavor all he can to obtain that which is necessary for his conservation. He who shall oppose himself against it for things superfluous is guilty of the war that thereupon is to follow, and therefore he does what is contrary to the fundamental law of nature which commands to seek peace. The observance of this law may be called sociable. . . . The contrary are stubborn, insociable, froward, intractable.

A sixth law of nature is this: "That upon caution of the future time, a man ought to pardon the past offenses of those who repent and desire it." For pardon is nothing but granting peace, which though granted to them who persevere in their hostility is not peace but fear. Yet not granted to them who give caution of the future time is a sign of aversion to peace and therefore contrary to the law of nature.

A seventh is, "That in revenges (that is, retribution of evil for evil) men look not at the greatness of the past evil, but the greatness of the good to follow." Whereby we are forbidden to inflict punishment with any other design than for correction of the offender or direction of others. For this law is consequent to the one before it that commands pardon upon security of a future time. Besides, revenge without respect to the example and profit to come is a triumph or glorying in the hurt of another, tending to no end (for the end is always something to come) and glorying to no end is vain-glory and contrary to reason. And to hurt without reason tends to the introduction of war which is against the law of nature and is commonly styled by the name of cruelty.

Because all signs of hatred or contempt provoke to fight since most men choose rather to hazard their life than not to be revenged, we may set down in the eighth place for a law of nature this precept, "That no man by deed, word, countenance, or gesture, declare hatred or contempt of another." The breach of which law is commonly called contumely.

The question who is the better man has no place in the condition of mere nature where (as has been shown before) all men are equal. The inequality that now is has been introduced by the civil laws. I know that for a foundation of his doctrine, in the first book of his *Politics* Aristotle makes some men by nature more worthy to command, meaning the wiser sort (such as he thought himself to be for his philosophy), others to serve (meaning those who had strong bodies, but were not philosophers as he) as if master and servant were not introduced by consent of men but by difference of wit, which is not only against reason but also against experience. For there are very few so foolish who would not rather govern themselves than be governed by others. Nor when the wise in their own conceit contend by force with them who distrust their own wisdom always, or often, or almost at any time, get the victory. If nature therefore has made men equal, that equality is to be acknowledged, or if nature has made men unequal, because men think themselves equal, they will not enter into conditions of peace but upon equal terms, such equality must be admitted. Therefore for the ninth law of nature I put this, "That every man acknowledge another for his equal by nature." The breach of this precept is pride.

On this law depends another, "That at the entrance into conditions of peace, no man require to reserve to himself any right which he is not content should be reserved to every one of the rest." As it is necessary for all men who seek peace to lay down certain rights of nature, that is to say, not to have liberty to do all they wish, so it is necessary for man's life to retain some such as a right to govern their own bodies, to enjoy air, water, motion, and ways to go from place to place, and all things else without which a man cannot live or not live well. If in this case at the making of peace men require for themselves that which they would not have granted to others, they do contrary to the preceding law that commands the acknowledgment of natural equality and therefore also against the law of nature. The observers of this law are those we call modest, and the breakers arrogant men. The Greeks call the violation of this law pleonexia, that is, a desire of more than their share.

Also, "If a man be trusted to judge between man and man," it is a precept of the law of nature "that he deal equally between them." For without that, the controversies of men cannot be determined except by war. He therefore who is partial in judgment does what he is able to deter men from the use of judges and arbitrators and consequently (against the fundamental law of nature) is the cause of war. The observance of this law from the equal distribution to each man of which in reason belongs to him, is equity and (as I have said before) distributive justice. The violation is acceptance of persons, prosopolepsia.

From this follows another law, "That such things that cannot be divided, be enjoyed in common if it can be, and if the quantity of the thing permits, without stint. Otherwise, proportionately to the number of them who have right." For otherwise the distribution is unequal and contrary to equity.

But there are some things that can neither be divided nor enjoyed in common. Then, the law of nature, which prescribes equity, requires "That the entire right, or else (making the use of alternate) the first possession be determined by lot." For equal distribution is of the law of nature and other means of equal distribution cannot be imagined.

Of lots there are two sorts, arbitrary and natural. Arbitrary is that which is agreed on by the competitors. Natural is either primogeniture (which the Greek calls *kleronomia*, which signifies "given by lot") or first seizure. Therefore, those things which cannot be enjoyed in common nor divided ought to be adjudged to the first possessor and is in some cases to the first born as acquired by lot.

It is also a law of nature "That all men who mediate peace be allowed safe conduct." For the law that commands peace as the end commands intercession as the means, and to intercession the means is safe conduct.

And because, though men are never so willing to observe these laws, there may nevertheless arise questions concerning a man's action. First, whether it was done or not done. Second (if done), whether against the law or not against the law, the former is called a question of fact and the latter a question of right. Therefore, unless the parties to the question covenant mutually to stand to the sentence of another, they are as far from peace as ever. This other, to whose sentence they submit, is called an arbitrator. Therefore it is of the law of nature, "That they who are at controversy submit their right to the judgment of an arbitrator."

Seeing every man is presumed to do all things in order to his own benefit, no man is a fit arbitrator in his own cause, and if he were never so fit, yet equity allowing to each party equal benefit, if one is admitted to be judge, the other is to be admitted, and so the controversy, that is, the cause of war, remains and is against the law of nature.

For the same reason no man in any cause ought to be received for arbitrator to whom greater profit, honor, or pleasure apparently arising out of the victory of one party than the other. For he has taken (though an unavoidable bribe) yet a bribe. And no man can be obliged to trust him. And thus also the controversy and the condition of war remains, contrary to the law of nature.

In a controversy of fact, the judge is to give no more credit to one than to the other and if there be no other arguments must give credit to a third or to a third and fourth, and more. For otherwise the question is undecided and left to force, contrary to the law of nature.

These are the laws of nature, dictating peace, for a means of the conservation of men in multitudes, and which only concern the doctrine of civil society. There are other things tending to the destruction of particular men such as drunkenness and all other parts of intemperance, which may therefore also be reckoned among those things which the law of nature has forbidden, but are not necessary to be mentioned nor are they pertinent enough to this place.

Though this may seem too subtle a deduction of the laws of nature to be taken notice of by all men, the most part are too busy in getting food and the rest too negligent to understand, yet to leave all men inexcusable, they have been contracted into one easy sum, intelligible even to the meanest capacity. And that is, "Do not do to another which you would not have done to yourself," which shows him that he has no more to do in learning the laws of nature but, when weighing the actions of other men with his own they seem too heavy to put them into the other part of the balance, and his own into their place, that his own passions and self-love may add nothing to the weight, and then there are none of these laws of nature that will not appear to him very reasonable.

But in effect then only when there is security the laws of nature oblige *in foro interno*, that is to say, they bind to a desire they should take place. But not always *in foro externo*, that is, to putting them in act. For he who should be modest and tractable and perform all he promises in such time and place where no other man should do, should make himself a prey to others, and procure his own certain ruin, which is contrary to the ground of all laws of nature which tend to nature's preservation. And again, he who shall observe the same laws toward him but does not observe them himself does not seek peace, but war, and consequently the destruction of his nature by violence.

Whatever laws bind *in foro interno* may be broken not only by a fact contrary to the law but also by a fact according to it in a case a man thinks it contrary. For though his action in this case is according the law, which where the obligation is *in foro interno* is a breach.

The laws of nature are immutable and eternal, for injustice, ingratitude, arrogance, pride, iniquity, acception of persons, and the rest, can never be made lawful. For it can never be that war shall preserve life, and peace destroy it.

The same laws, because they oblige only to a desire and endeavor, I mean an unfeigned and constant endeavor, are easy to be observed. For in that they require nothing but endeavor, he who endeavors their performance fulfills them, and he who fulfills the law is just.

The science of them is the true and only moral philosophy.[66] For moral philosophy is nothing else but the science of what is good and evil in the conversation and society of mankind. Good and evil are names that signify our appetites and aversions, which in different tempers, customs and doctrines of men are different. And diverse men differ not only in their judgment on the sense of what is pleasant and unpleasant to the taste, smell, hearing, touch, and sight, but also of what is conformable or disagreeable to reason in the actions of common life. The same man in diverse times differs from himself and one time praises—that is, calls good—what in other times he dispraises and calls evil. From this arise disputes, controversies, and at last, war. Therefore so long as man is in the condition of mere nature (which is a condition of war), as private appetite is the measure of good and evil, and consequently all men agree on this that peace is good and therefore also the way

---

66. Note that in Chapter IX in the table of the sciences, Hobbes has placed ethics squarely in the category of natural philosophy while politics is civil philosophy. So ethics can precede government through the laws of nature that make political society (through civil philosophy) possible. However, it is civil philosophy that enforces what is good or right. Prior to the institution of the sovereign, every person is governed morally by his own preferences and desires and his own estimation of the distinction between what is good and what is not.

or means of peace which (as I have shown before) are justice, gratitude, modesty, equity, mercy, and the rest of the laws of nature are good, that is to say, moral virtues, and their contrary vices are evil. Now, the science of virtue and vice is moral philosophy and therefore the true doctrine of the laws of nature is the true moral philosophy. But the writers of moral philosophy, even though they acknowledge the same virtues and vices, not seeing wherein consisted their goodness, nor that they come to be praised as the means of peaceable, sociable, and comfortable living, place them in a mediocrity of passions as if not the cause, but the degree of daring made fortitude or not the cause but the quantity of a gift made liberality.

These dictates of reason men used to call by the name of laws, but improperly. For they are but conclusions or theorems concerning what conduces to the conservation and defense of themselves, whereas law, properly is the word of him who by right has command over others. But yet if we consider the same theorems as delivered in the Word of God who by right commands all things, then they are properly called laws.[67]

---

67. Hobbes is not wavering on the contention that the laws of nature are laws. It is simply the fact that the laws of nature ought to be followed because they are beneficial to peace and continued survival, but it is also possible for people to violate them for whatever reason. Since "law" comes properly only from a command, the only way in which to understand the laws of nature in the natural condition of mankind is to understand them as coming to us as commands of God. Interestingly, however, Hobbes' explanation of the laws of nature as conclusions or theorems about what is conducive to preservation and self-defense allows his moral and political doctrines to apply even to those who do not believe in the existence of God.

Chapter XVI. Of Persons, Authors, and Things Personated

In this chapter, Hobbes introduces the concept of representation. A representative "personates" another in acting or representing herself or himself or another person. In the latter case, the artificial person in representing another, acts in the "name" of the other. Hobbes gives examples of those who may personate another, including a representative, an attorney, or an actor. When one person authorizes another to act or to speak for him, the actor (the person authorized) may make an agreement that binds the author as if the author made the agreement himself. So, for example, when a political sovereign enters into a contract with another political state, it is "as if" the people who gave authority to the actor made the agreement themselves. So the authors "own" the actions and words of the actor.

The distinction between author and actor is important because a commonwealth is formed through the institution of the sovereign by the multitude of people being represented by one person or assembly by their consent. For Hobbes, it is essential to note that it is not the unity of those who are represented but instead the unity of the representative that makes the person one. It is a simple distinction: if the multitude of people were themselves "one," there could by definition be no disagreements between people, in which case there would be no need for the creation of sovereign power at all.

This chapter is central to Hobbes' political thought because it sets up the conditions and particular aspects of commonwealth presented in Part II of Leviathan, *and it is the first fully formulated, modern statement of the notion that government exists by the consent of the governed.*

A person is he "whose words or actions are considered either as his own or as representing the words or actions of another man, or of any other thing to whom they are attributed, whether truly or by fiction." When they are considered as his own, then he is called a natural person. And when they are considered as representing the words and actions of another, then he is a feigned or artificial person.

The word "person" is Latin. The Greeks have *prosopon* which signifies the face in the way that *persona* in Latin signifies the disguise or outward appearance of a man, counterfeited on stage. And sometimes more particularly that part of it which disguises the face as a mask or a visard, and from the stage has been translated to any representer of speech and action in tribunals as well as in theaters. So that a person is the same as an actor both on the stage and in common conversation, and to personate is to act or to represent himself or another, and he who acts another is said to bear his person or act in his name (in which sense Cicero uses it where he says "... I bear three persons; my own, my adversary's, and the judges'") and is called on diverse occasions a representer, a representative, a lieutenant, a vicar, an attorney, a deputy, a procurator, an actor, and the like.

Some artificial persons have their words and actions owned by those whom they represent. Then the person is the actor, and he who owns his words and actions is the author, in which case the actor acts by authority. For that which in speaking of goods and possessions is called an owner and in Latin *Dominus*, in Greek *Kurios*. Speaking of actions is called author. As the right of possession is called dominion, so the right of doing any action is called authority. So that by authority is always understood a right of doing any act. An act done by authority is done by commission or license from him whose right it is.

It follows that when the actor makes a covenant by authority, he binds thereby the author no less than if he had made it himself and no less subjects him to all the consequences of the same. Therefore all that has been said formerly (Chapter XIV) of the nature of covenants between man and man in their natural capacity is true also when they are made by their actors, representers, or procurators that have authority from them, so far forth as is in their commission but no farther.

Therefore he who makes a covenant with the actor or representer, not knowing the authority he has, does it at his own peril. This is true because no man is obliged by covenant of which he is not author, nor consequently by a covenant made against or beside the authority he gave. When the actor does anything against the law of nature by command of the author, if he is obliged by former covenant to obey him, not he but the author breaks the law of nature. For though the action is against the law of nature, yet it is not his but contrarily to refuse to do it is against the law of nature that forbids breach of covenant.

He who makes a covenant with the author by mediation of the actor, not knowing what authority he has but only takes his word, in case such authority is not made manifest to him upon demand is no longer obliged. For the covenant made with the author is not valid without his counter-assurance. But if he who so covenants knew beforehand he was to expect no other assurance than the actor's word, then the covenant is valid because the actor in this case makes himself the author. Therefore, when the authority is evident the covenant obliges the author, not the actor. So when the authority is pretended it obliges the actor only, there being no author but himself.

There are few things that are not capable of being represented by fiction. Inanimate things, as a church, a hospital, or a bridge, may be personated by a rector, master, or overseer. But inanimate things cannot be authors nor therefore give authority to their actors. Yet the actors may have authority to procure their maintenance, given them by those who are owners or governors of those things. And therefore, such things cannot be personated before there is some state of civil government.

Likewise, children, fools, and madmen who have no use of reason may be personated by guardians or curators, but cannot be authors during that time of any action done by them longer than when they shall recover the use of reason they shall judge the same reasonable. Yet during the folly, he who has right of governing them may give authority to the guardian. But this again has no place but in a civil state because before such state, there is no dominion of persons.

An idol or mere figment of the brain may be personated as were the gods of the heathen, which by such officers as the state appointed were personated and held possessions and other goods and rights which men from time to time dedicated and consecrated unto them. But idols cannot be authors, for an idol is nothing. The authority proceeded from the state, and therefore before introduction of civil government, the gods of the heathen could not be personated.

The true God may be personated as he was, first, by Moses who governed the Israelites (who were not his, but God's people) not in his own name ... but in God's name. Second, by the son of man, his own Son, our Blessed Savior Jesus Christ, who came to reduce the Jews and induce all nations into the kingdom of his Father, not as himself, but as sent from his Father. And third, by the Holy Ghost, or Comforter, speaking and working in the apostles, which Holy Ghost was a Comforter who came not of himself, and proceeded from them both.

A multitude of men are made one person when they are represented by one man or one person so that it is done with the consent of every one of that multitude. For it is the unity of the representer, not the unity of the represented, that makes the person one. And it is the representer that bears the person and but one person. Unity cannot otherwise be understood in multitude.

Because the multitude naturally is not one, but many, they cannot be understood for one but instead for many authors of everything their representative says or does in their name. Every man giving their common representer authority from himself in particular, and owning all the actions the representer does, they give him authority without stint. Otherwise, when they limit him in what and how far he shall represent them, none of them owns more than they gave him commission to act.

If the representative consists of many men the voice of the greater number must be considered as the voice of them all. For if the lesser number pronounce (for example) in the affirmative and the greater in the negative, there will be more than enough negatives to destroy the affirmatives, and thereby the excess of negatives, standing uncontradicted, are the only voice the representative has.

A representative of even number—especially when the number is not great—whereby the contradictory voices are often equal, is therefore often mute and incapable of action. Yet in some cases contradictory voices that are equal in number may determine a question such as in condemning or absolving. . . . For when a cause is heard, not to condemn is to absolve; but on the contrary to say that not absolving is condemning is not true. It is like this in a deliberation of executing presently or deferring until another time. For when the voices are equal, not decreeing execution is a decree of dilation. If the number is odd, as three or more (men or assemblies) whereof everyone has by a negative voice authority to take away the effect of the affirmative voices of the rest, this number is not representative because by the diversity of opinions and interests of men it becomes often and in cases of the greatest consequence a mute person and unapt as for many things, so for the government of a multitude, especially in a time of war.

There are two sorts of authors. The first simply so called, which I have before defined to be him who owns the actions of another simply.[68] The second is he who owns an action or covenant of another conditionally—that is to say, he undertakes to do it if the other does not do it at or before a certain time. And these conditional authors are generally called sureties and sponsors and particularly for debt and for appearance before a judge or magistrate.

---

68. The political sovereign is authorized simply by the authors (individual people who are part of the multitude), and the authors "own" all the actions of the sovereign who is the actor (representative) of them.

PART II. OF COMMONWEALTH

Chapter XVII. Of the Causes, Generation, and Definition of a Commonwealth

    Chapter XVII begins Part II of Leviathan *on commonwealth, which is the political structure created as a result of sovereign authorization. Hobbes defines commonwealth as "One person of whose acts a great multitude, by covenants with another, have made themselves every one the author to the end he may use the strength and means of them all as he shall think expedient for their peace and common defense." Because following the laws of nature is contrary to our natural passions, it is necessary for those who love "liberty and dominion over others" to restrain themselves. They achieve restraint through fear of punishment for not observing the laws of nature. In short, as Hobbes puts it, covenants "without the sword" are insufficient to secure anyone.*

    The only way to create a common power is for individuals to transfer power and strength to one man or assembly. For Hobbes, this is to reduce their wills into one will. That common power will bear their person and submit all their wills to his will. Here, Hobbes contends that this is more than simple consent and that it is real unity. People give up their right to govern themselves to this power, and their unity in one person (the sovereign) constitutes the commonwealth. The culmination of the transfer of right, consent into unity, and creation of commonwealth creates a condition in which the wills of all people turn toward internal peace and defense from external threats.

    The essence of commonwealth is in the artificial person (the sovereign) which is "One person of whose acts a great multitude, by covenants with another, have made themselves every one the author to the end he may use the strength and means of them all as he shall think expedient for their peace and common defense." Anyone who is part of the multitude that authorized the sovereign is a subject. But not all commonwealths are formed by simple agreement. Some are instead formed by force. This distinction is political commonwealth (by institution) and commonwealth by acquisition, respectively.

The final cause, end, or design of men (who naturally love liberty and dominion over others) in the introduction of that restraint upon themselves (in which we see them live in commonwealths) is the foresight of their own preservation and of a more contented life thereby. That is to say, of getting themselves out from the miserable condition of war which is necessarily consequent (as has been shown) to the natural passions of men where there is no visible power to keep them all in awe and tie them by fear of punishment to the performance of their covenants and observance of these laws of nature set down in Chapters XIV and XV.

For the laws of nature (as justice, equity, modesty, mercy and in sum doing to others as we would be done to) if they are without the terror of some power to cause them to be observed, are contrary to our natural passions that carry us to partiality, pride, revenge, and the like. Covenants without the sword are but words and of no strength to secure a man at all. Therefore notwithstanding the laws of nature (which everyone has then kept, when he has the will to keep them when he can do it safely) if there be no power erected or not great enough for our security, every man will and may lawfully rely on his own strength and art for caution against all other men. In all places where men have lived by small families to rob and spoil one another there has been trade, and so far from being reputed against the law of nature that the greater spoils they gained the greater was their honor, and men observed no others laws therein but the laws of honor—that is, to abstain from cruelty, leaving to men their lives and instruments of husbandry. As small families did then so now do cities and kingdoms which are but greater families (for their own security) enlarge their dominions upon all pretenses of danger and fear of invasion or assistance that may be given to invaders—endeavor as much as they can to subdue or weaken their neighbors by open force and secret arts, for want of other caution, justly. They are remembered for it in later ages with honor.

Nor is it the joining together of a small number of men that gives them this security because in small numbers, small additions on one side or the other makes the advantage of strength so great as is sufficient to carry the victory and therefore gives encouragement to an invasion. The multitude sufficient to confide in our security is not determined by any certain number but by comparison with the enemy we fear. It is then sufficient when the odds of the enemy are not of so visible and conspicuous moment to determine the event of war as to move him to attempt.

Be there never so great a multitude, if their actions are directed according to their particular judgments and appetites, they can thereby expect no defense or protection against a common enemy or against the injuries of one another. For being distracted in opinions concerning the best use and application of their strength, they do not help but hinder one another and reduce their strength by mutual opposition to nothing, whereby they are easily not only subdued by a very few who agree together but also when there is no common enemy, they make war upon each other for their particular interests. For if we could suppose a great multitude of men to consent in the observation of justice and other laws of nature without a common power to keep them all in awe, we might as well suppose all mankind to do the same, and then there neither would be, nor would there need to be, any civil government or commonwealth at all, because there would be peace without subjection.[1]

It is not enough for the security which men desire that it should last all the time of their life that they be governed and directed by one judgment for a limited time as in one battle or one war. Even though they obtain a victory by their unanimous endeavor against a foreign enemy, afterward when they have no common enemy or when there is someone considered an enemy by one ground and a friend to another, they must by the difference of their interests dissolve and again fall into war among themselves.

It is true that certain living creatures, such as bees and ants, live sociably with one another (which are therefore numbered by Aristotle among the political creatures) and yet have no other direction than their particular judgments and appetites. Nor do they have speech whereby one of them can signify to another what he thinks expedient for the common benefit. Therefore some man may perhaps desire to know why mankind cannot do the same, to which I answer, first, that men are continually in competition for honor and dignity while these creatures are not. Consequently among men there arises on that ground envy and hatred and finally war, but among these, it is not the case. Second, among these creatures the common good does not differ from the private, and being by nature inclined to their private interest, they thereby obtain the common benefit. But man, whose joy consists in comparing himself with other men, can relish nothing but what is eminent. Third, these creatures, unlike man in not having the use of reason, do not see nor think they see any fault in the administration of their common business. Whereas among men, there are very many who think themselves wiser and more able to govern the public better than the rest and they strive to reform and innovate one this way, another that way, and thereby bring it into distraction and civil war. Fourth, these creatures—though they have some use of voice in making known to one another their desires and other affections—do not have the art of words by which some men can represent to others that which is good in the likeness of evil, and evil in the likeness of good, and augment or diminish the apparent greatness of good and evil, discontenting men and troubling their peace at their pleasure. Fifth, irrational creatures cannot distinguish between injury and damage and therefore as long as they are at ease they are not offended with their fellows, whereas man is most troublesome when he is most at ease, for it is then that he loves to show his wisdom and control the actions of those who govern the commonwealth. Last, the agreement of these creatures is natural while that of men is by covenant only, which is artificial. Therefore it is no wonder there is something else required (besides covenant)

---

1. Hobbes intends this comment as an argument against those who think, like Aristotle in his *Politics*, for example, that human beings are naturally social or political animals. If we could cooperate with each other naturally, all the time, there would be no need for agreement to enter into political organization. This comment also serves as a reminder (as noted in the division of the sciences in Chapter IX) that the science of politics is man-made.

to make their agreement constant and lasting, which is a common power to keep them all in awe and to direct their actions to the common benefit.

The only way to erect such a common power that may be able to defend them from the invasion of foreigners and the injuries of one another, and thereby to secure them so that as by their own industry and by the fruits of the Earth they may nourish themselves and live contentedly, is to confer all their power and strength upon one man or upon one assembly of men that may reduce all their wills by plurality of voices into one will. This is as much as to say to appoint one man or assembly of men to bear their person, and every one to own and acknowledge himself to be author of whatsoever he who bears their person shall act or cause to be acted in those things which concern the common peace and safety, and therein to submit all their wills to his will and their judgments to his judgment. This is more than consent or concord—it is a real unity of them all, in one and the same person,[2] made by covenant of every man with every man in such manner as if every man should say to every man, "I authorize and give up my right of governing myself to this man or to this assembly of men on this condition, that you give up your right to him and authorize all his actions in like manner." This done, the multitude so united in one person is called a commonwealth, in Latin, *civitas*. This is the generation of that great Leviathan, or rather (to speak more reverently) of that mortal God to which we owe under the immortal God our peace and defense. For by this authority, given him by every particular man in the commonwealth, he has the use of so much power and strength conferred on him that by terror thereof, he is enabled to form the wills of them all to peace at home and mutual aid against their enemies abroad.

In him consists the essence of the commonwealth, which (to define it) is "One person of whose acts a great multitude, by covenants with another, have made themselves every one the author to the end he may use the strength and means of them all as he shall think expedient for their peace and common defense."[3] He who carries this person is called sovereign, and said to have sovereign power and everyone else is his subject.

---

2. The creation of the sovereign in this manner is the act of authorization that Hobbes described in Chapter XVI. Note that in Chapter XVI, Hobbes emphasizes that it is the "unity of the representer, not the unity of the represented, that makes the person one." The "person" who is authorized is an artificial person such as Hobbes described in the introduction to *Leviathan*, comparing it with the workings of a natural man. The authorization of sovereign power in this way highlights the fact that Hobbes considers politics, or civil philosophy, to be among the sciences and, in fact, superior to all other sciences in that we have created it ourselves and so can determine the consequences of it in geometrical (that is, scientific) fashion.

3. The apparently problematic nature of the agreement to institute a sovereign revolves around Hobbes' position that agreements in the state of nature are "but words." If that is the case, one may justifiably wonder how the agreement to institute a sovereign will be upheld. Hobbes also does not explain in detail the process by which a sovereign by institution would be chosen except that it would be by majority vote.

Sovereign power is attained by two ways. One is by natural force, as when a man makes his children submit themselves and their children to his government, being able to destroy them if they refuse, or by war subdue his enemies to his will, giving them their lives on that condition. The other is when men agree among themselves to submit to some man or assembly of men voluntarily, on confidence to be protected by him against all others. This latter may be called a political commonwealth, or commonwealth by institution; and the former a commonwealth by acquisition. First I shall speak of commonwealth by institution.

Chapter XVIII. Of the Rights of Sovereigns by Institution

Even though the title of Chapter XVIII is "Of the Rights of Sovereigns by Institution," all the rights of sovereigns are exactly the same regardless of the method or means of its creation. With respect to commonwealth by institution, there may be a vote of some sort by the people in the natural condition to determine who will be sovereign, and for Hobbes, those who voted against the sovereign who is ultimately chosen are obligated in the same way and to the same extent as those who voted in favor. To deny this is to put oneself into a state of war with others. Once the sovereign exists, the form of government cannot be changed. The rights of all individuals are transferred to the sovereign as a matter of agreement, and since the sovereign is not part of the agreement, it is impossible for the sovereign to violate it. There are many rights of the sovereign, including the right to be judge of the expression and dissemination of opinions and doctrines and who may be a public spokesperson or censor. The reason for this is that securing peace includes "well-governing of opinions" because opinions lead to actions.[4] Recognizing that there are different commonwealths in the world but that each one is to be governed by the same principles Hobbes presents in Leviathan, *he notes carefully that the sovereign also prescribes rules, but that "these rules of propriety and of good and evil, lawful and unlawful actions of subjects are the civil laws. They are the laws of each commonwealth in particular." This is important in that particular, specific laws concerning property might vary between commonwealths, but for all that it does not mean that the sovereign in each individual commonwealth is for that reason not absolute in the prescription of rules. They are absolute within their own spheres of influence inside their own commonwealths.*

A commonwealth is said to be instituted when a multitude of men agree and covenant with each other that whatsoever a man or assembly of men shall be given by the major part, the right to present the person of them all (that is to say, to be their representative) every one, those who voted for it as well as those who voted against it, shall authorize all the actions and judgments of that man or assembly of men in the same manner as if they were his own, to the end to live peaceably among themselves and be protected against other men.

---

4. Remember from Part I, "Of Man," that Hobbes plainly indicated that actions proceed from "imagination" and the contents of imagination include the ideas people have received from "books."

The consequences of such institution are, first, that the subjects cannot change the form of government.[5] From this institution of a commonwealth by consent of the assembled people are derived all the rights and faculty of him or they on whom sovereign power is conferred. First is because the covenant to institute commonwealth is to be understood that the people are no longer obliged by former covenant to anything that would be repugnant to the current covenant. Consequently they who have already instituted a commonwealth are bound to own the actions, and judgments of one cannot lawfully make a new covenant among themselves to be obedient to any other in anything without his permission. Therefore, they who are subjects to a monarch cannot without his permission cast off monarchy and return to the confusion of a disunited multitude nor transfer their person from him to another man or another assembly. This is because they are bound, every man to every man, to own and be reputed author of all that he who is already his sovereign shall do and judge fit to be done. So if any one man dissents and all the rest break their covenant made to him, it is injustice. Every man has also given the sovereignty to him who bears their person and therefore if they depose him they take from him what is his own, and this is again injustice. Besides, if a person who attempts to depose his sovereign is killed or punished by him for the attempt, he is the author of his own punishment, being by the institution author of all his sovereign does. Because it is injustice for a man to do anything for which he may be punished by his own authority, he is unjust. Whereas some men have pretended for their disobedience to their sovereign a new covenant—made not with men, but with God—this is also unjust because there is no covenant with God except by mediation of some body that represents God's person and no one does this other than God's lieutenant (Jesus) who has sovereignty under God. This pretense of covenant with God is so evidently a lie even in the pretender's conscience that it is not only an act of an unjust man, but also of a vile and unmanly disposition.

Sovereign power cannot be forfeited, second, because the right of bearing the person of them all is given to the person they make sovereign by covenant only of one to another and not of sovereign to any of them, there can be no breach of covenant on the part of the sovereign. Consequently, none of his subjects by any pretense of forfeiture can be freed from his subjection. It is obvious that the sovereign can make no covenant with his subjects beforehand because he must make it either with the whole multitude as one party to the covenant or he must make several covenants with every man.[6] It is impossible that it should be with the whole

---

5. Since the subjects cannot change the form of government, there is no legal (or even moral) justification for revolution. Hobbes recognized that revolutions happen, and in discussing the rights and duties of sovereigns, he is careful to warn sovereigns who read *Leviathan* that while the sovereign power is absolute, there is care to be taken in managing a commonwealth and making laws to ensure in a reasonable way that subjects will not revolt. He makes it clear, for example, in Chapter XIX that no king can be rich whose subjects are poor, nor strong when the subjects are weak.

6. Not all those who adhere to a social contract theory of government deny that the people have a covenant or agreement *with* the sovereign. See, for example, John Locke's *Second*

as one party because as yet they are not one person. If he makes so many covenants as there are men, those covenants after he has sovereignty are void. This is the case because whatever act can be pretended by one of them for breach is the act both of himself and all the rest because done in the person and by right of every one of them in particular. Besides, if any one or more of them pretends a breach of covenant made by the sovereign at his institution, and one or more subjects or himself alone pretend there was no such breach, there is in this case no judge to decide the controversy. It returns therefore to the sword again and every man recovers the right to protect himself by his own strength, which is contrary to the design they had in instituting the sovereign. It is therefore in vain to grant sovereignty by way of precedent covenant. The opinion that any monarch receives his power by covenant—that is to say on condition—proceeds from lack of understanding the easy truth that covenants, being only words and breath, have no force to oblige, contain, constrain, or protect any man but what it has from the public sword. That is, from the united hands of that man or assembly of men having the sovereignty and whose actions are avouched by them all and performed by the strength of them all in him united. When an assembly of men is made sovereign, then no man imagines such covenant to have passed in the institution. No man is so dull as to say, for example, the people of Rome made a covenant with the Romans to hold sovereignty on such and such conditions, which if not performed, the Romans might lawfully depose the Roman people. Men not seeing the reason to be the same in monarchy and in a popular government proceeds from the ambition of some who prefer government of an assembly in which they hope to participate than of monarchy which they despair to enjoy.

Third, no man can without injustice protest against the institution of the sovereign declared by the major part. The major part has by consenting voices declared a sovereign. The person dissenting must now consent with the rest, that is, be contented to avow all the actions he shall do or justly be destroyed by the rest. If he voluntarily entered into the congregation of those assembled, he sufficiently declared his will by doing it (therefore tacitly covenanting) to stand with what the major part ordains. Therefore if he refuses to stand or protests against any of their decrees, he does contrary to his covenant. This is unjust. Whether he is of the congregation or not, and whether his consent is asked or not, he must either submit to their decrees or be left in the condition of war in which he was before in which he might without injustice be destroyed by anyone.

Fourth, the sovereign's actions cannot be justly accused by the subject. Because every subject is by institution author of all the actions and judgments of the sovereign, it follows that whatever he does cannot be injury to any of his subjects nor ought he to be by any of them accused of injustice. He who does anything by authority from another does no injury to him by whose authority he acted. By the

---

Treatise of Government, ed. C. B. Macpherson (Indianapolis, IN: Hackett, 1980) and Thomas Paine, "The Rights of Man," in *Common Sense and Other Political Writings*, ed. Nelson F. Adkins (Indianapolis, IN: Bobbs-Merrill, 1953). Those who hold that the contract institutes the sovereign and creates government do not, like Hobbes, forbid revolution.

institution of a commonwealth, every particular man is author of all the sovereign does and consequently he who complains of injury from his sovereign complains of that of which he is himself author and therefore ought not to accuse any man but himself nor do injury to himself because to do injury to oneself is impossible. It is true that they who have sovereign power may commit iniquity, but they cannot commit injustice or injury in the proper signification.[7]

Fifth, and consequently, whatever the sovereign does is unpunishable by the subject. No man who has sovereign power can justly be put to death or otherwise in any manner be punished by his subjects. Seeing every subject is author of the actions of the sovereign, he punishes another for the actions committed by himself.

Because the end of this institution is peace and defense of them all, and whoever has a right to the end has right to the means, it belongs rightly to whatever man or assembly that has sovereignty to be judge of both the means of peace and defense and of the hindrances and disturbances of them. This includes doing whatever is necessary to be done beforehand for preserving peace and security, by preventing discord at home and hostility from abroad, and when peace and security are lost, for recovery of the same. . . .

Sixth, it is annexed to the sovereignty to be judge of what opinions and doctrines are averse and what conducing to peace and consequently on what occasions, how far, and what men are to be trusted in speaking to multitudes, and who shall examine the doctrines of all books before they are published. The actions of men proceed from their opinions, and well-governing of opinions consists of well-governing of men's actions in order to their peace and concord. Though in matter of doctrine nothing ought to be regarded but the truth, it is not repugnant to regulate the same by peace because doctrine that is repugnant to peace can no more be true than peace and concord can be against the law of nature. It is true that due to negligence and unskillfulness of governors and teachers in a commonwealth that false doctrines are generally received and contrary truths may be generally offensive. But the most sudden and rough bustling in of a new truth never breaks the peace but only sometimes awakes the war. For men who are so remissly governed that they dare to take up arms to defend or introduce an opinion are still in war and their condition is not peace but only cessation of arms for fear of one another and they live in the precincts of battle continually. It belongs therefore to him who has sovereign power to be judge and to constitute all judges of opinions and doctrines as necessary to peace to prevent discord and civil war.[8]

---

7. Since there is no agreement or covenant with the sovereign, and injustice has already been defined (Chapter XIV) as not performing covenants, there is by definition no way in which the sovereign can be accused of injustice. Further, however, when Hobbes claims that the sovereign may commit iniquity, which is unfair action or action against duty, it indicates that the sovereign, while not held to account for law, is held to account for morality.

8. Hobbes is arguing for a very strong conception of censorship. At the same time, however, that he asserts that a person's actions are governed by his opinions, Hobbes does in fact indicate that freedom of thought is impossible to control and that with which the

Seventh, the whole power of prescribing the rules is annexed to sovereignty. By these rules every man may know what goods he may enjoy and what actions he may do without being molested by any of his fellow subjects. Men call this propriety. Before constitution of sovereign power (as has already been shown) all men had a right to all things. This necessarily causes war, and therefore his propriety being necessary to peace and depending on sovereign power is the act of the power to ensure the public peace. These rules of propriety and of good and evil, lawful and unlawful actions of subjects are the civil laws. They are the laws of each commonwealth in particular. . . .⁹

Eighth, the right of judicature—of hearing and deciding all controversies which may arise concerning either civil or natural law or concerning fact—is annexed to the sovereignty. Without decision of controversies, there is no protection of one subject against the injuries of another, the laws of *meum* and *tuum* (mine and yours) are in vain, and to every man remains, from the natural and necessary desire of his own conservation, the right of protecting himself by private strength. This is the condition of war and contrary to the end for which every commonwealth is instituted.

Ninth, the right of making war and peace with other nations—that is, of judging when it is for the public good and how great forces are to be assembled, armed, and paid, and to levy money upon the subjects to defray the costs—is annexed to the sovereignty. For the power by which people are to be defended consists in their armies and the strength of an army in the union of their strength under one command. The sovereign has this strength because the command of the militia without other institution makes him who has it sovereign. Therefore no matter who is made general of an army, he who has the sovereign power is always generalissimo.¹⁰

Tenth, it is annexed to sovereignty both in peace and war to choose all counselors, ministers, magistrates and officers. Seeing the sovereign is charged with the end—common peace and defense—he is understood to have power to use such means as he shall think most fit for the purpose.

Eleventh, the power of rewarding with riches and honor and of punishing with corporal or pecuniary punishment, or with ignominy, every subject according to the law he has formerly made. If there is no law made, according as he shall judge most conducive to encouraging men to serve the commonwealth or deterring them from doing disservice to it.

---

commonwealth is to be concerned is the actions of people with respect to whether they act in accordance with the laws of nature and civil laws created by the sovereign.

9. The fact that Hobbes states here that different commonwealths may have different laws does not make him a moral relativist. Moral laws, which are the laws of nature, are found out solely by reason (in which case they should, in principle, be the same for all human beings no matter where they are or under what form of government they live). A sovereign, however, is the interpreter of the natural laws and has sole responsibility for instituting civil laws.

10. "Generalissimo" is a term for the supreme commander of an army or armed forces generally. Citizens of the United States would recognize this as roughly equivalent to "commander in chief."

Last, considering what values men are naturally apt to set upon themselves, what respect they look to from others, and how little they value other men, from which continually arise among them emulation, quarrels, factions, and at last war to destroy one another, and the diminution of their strength against a common enemy. It is necessary that there be laws of honor and a public rate of their worth of men[11] who deserve or are able to deserve well of the commonwealth and that there be force in the hands of some to put those laws in execution. It has already been shown that not only the whole militia or forces of the commonwealth and also the judicature of all controversies is annexed to the sovereignty. It therefore belongs also to the sovereign to give titles of honor and to appoint what order of place and dignity each man shall hold and what signs of respect in public or private meetings they shall give to one another.

These are the rights which make the essence of sovereignty and are the marks by which a man may discern in what man or assembly the sovereign power is placed and resides. These are incommunicable and inseparable. The power to coin money, to dispose of the estate and persons of infant heirs, to have preemption in markets and all other statute prerogatives may be transferred by the sovereign. And yet the power to protect his subject is retained. If he transfers the militia, he retains judicature for want of execution of the laws. Or if he grants away the power of raising money the militia is in vain, or if he gives away the government of doctrines men will be frightened into rebellion with the fear of spirits.[12] So if we consider any one of the said rights we will presently see that holding all the rest will produce no effect in the conservation of peace and justice, which is the end for which all commonwealths are instituted. Of this division it is said "A kingdom divided in itself cannot stand." . . . If there had not first been an opinion received of the greatest part of England that these powers were divided between the king and the lords and the House of Commons, the people had never been divided and fallen into civil war, first between those who disagreed in politics and after between the dissenters about the liberty of religion which have so instructed men in this point of sovereign right that there are few now in England who do not see these rights are inseparable. . . .

Because they are essential and inseparable rights, it follows necessarily that in whatever words any of them seem to be granted away, if the sovereign power itself is not in direct terms renounced and the name of sovereign no more given by the grantees to him who grants them, the grant is void. When he has granted all he can, if we grant back sovereignty, all is restored as inseparably annexed to sovereignty.

Because this great authority is indivisible and inseparably annexed to the sovereignty, there is little ground for the opinion of those who say of sovereign kings

---

11. Hobbes has already indicated in Chapter X that any inequality that exists between subjects of a commonwealth has come from the civil laws. By nature, all human beings are equal in principle.

12. "Fear of spirits" must refer primarily if not solely to religious doctrines, and the comment here regarding the government of doctrines clearly applies to Hobbes' position regarding the subordinate position of religion in the political state in Part III and regarding the danger of religious doctrines that are not accepted by the state or sovereign as "superstition."

who are of greater power than every one of their subjects that they are of less power than them all together. If by all together they mean not the collective body as one person, then all together and every one signify the same, the speech is absurd. But if by all together they understand them as one person (which person the sovereign bears) then the power of all together is the same with the sovereign's power and so again the speech is absurd. They see the absurdity well enough when the sovereignty is in an assembly of the people. But in a monarch they do not see it and yet the power of sovereignty is the same in whomever it is placed.[13]

The honor—just as the power—of the sovereign ought to be greater than that of any or all of the subjects. For the sovereign is the fountain of honor. Dignities of lord, earl, duke, and prince are his creatures. As in the presence of the master the servants are equal and without any honor at all, so are the subjects in the presence of the sovereign. And though they shine some more, some less, when they are out of his sight, in his presence they shine no more than the stars in the presence of the Sun.

Sovereign power is not as hurtful as the want of it. The hurt proceeds for the greatest part from not submitting readily to less. But a man may object that the condition of subjects is very miserable, being obnoxious to the lusts and other irregular passions of him or them who have so unlimited power in their hands. Commonly they who live under a monarch think it the fault of monarchy, and they who live under government of democracy or other sovereign assembly attribute all the inconveniences to that form of commonwealth. It is actually the case that the power in all forms—if they are perfect enough to protect them—is the same not considering the estate of man can never be without some incommodity or other and that the greatest in any form of government can possibly happen to the people in general is hardly sensible in respect of the horrible calamities accompanying a civil war or the dissolute condition of masterless men.[14] In those cases, men are without subjection to laws and a coercive power to tie their hands from rapine and revenge. The greatest pressure of sovereign governors proceeds not from delight or profit they can expect in damaging or weakening their subjects in whose vigor their own selves consist, that unwillingly contributing to their own defense make it necessary for their governors to draw from them what they can in time of peace so they may have means in any emergency or sudden need to resist or take advantage of their enemies. For all men are by nature provided of notable multiplying glasses (that is, their passions and self-love) through which every little payment appears a great grievance, but are destitute of those prospective glasses (namely, moral and civil science) to see far off the miseries that hang over them and that cannot be avoided without such payments.

---

13. Contrary to what many readers and commentators may think, for Hobbes it makes no difference whether a government is in democratic form, aristocratic form, or a monarchy—the rights of sovereignty are all the same and absolute. Bernard Gert has clarified this position in his *Hobbes: Prince of Peace* (Malden, MA: Polity Press, 2010), 127.

14. In other words, any government is better than no government at all.

Chapter XIX. Of the Several Kinds of Commonwealth by Institution, and of Succession to the Sovereign Power

With respect to the specific type of commonwealth instituted, Hobbes had a decided preference for monarchy, but he argues in Chapter XIX that the power of the sovereign is the same whether it is an individual, a small group, or many in a democracy. He discusses problems of various forms of sovereignty, making clear distinctions between types of government and why they are all characterized by absolute power.

The difference between commonwealths consists in the difference in the sovereign or the person representative of all and every one of the multitude. Because the sovereignty is either in one man or assembly of more than one, and into that assembly either every man has the right to enter or not everyone but certain men distinguished from the rest, it is clear that there can be only three kinds of commonwealth. The representative must be one man or more. If more than one, then it is the assembly of all or of a part. When the representative is one man, the commonwealth is a monarchy. When an assembly of all who come together, it is a democracy or popular commonwealth. When an assembly of only a part, it is an aristocracy. Other kinds of commonwealth are not possible, for either one or more or all must have sovereign power (which I have shown to be indivisible) entire.

There are other names of government in the histories and books of policy such as tyranny and oligarchy. But they are not the names of other forms of government, but of the same forms disliked. For they who are discontented under monarchy call it tyranny. They who are displeased with aristocracy call it oligarchy. They who find themselves grieved under democracy call it anarchy (which signifies lack of government) and yet I think no man believes the lack of government is any new kind of government. By the same reason they ought not to believe that the government is of one kind when they like and another when they dislike it or are oppressed by the governors.[15]

It is clear that men who are in absolute liberty may, if they please, give authority to one man to represent all of them as well as to give such authority to any assembly of men. Consequently they may subject themselves to a monarch as absolutely as to any other representative if they think it good. Therefore, where there is already a

---

15. Aristotle makes this sort of distinction in *Nicomachean Ethics*, VIII.10. Hobbes, however, held that this distinction is unjustified since the form of government does not change based on whether citizens like or dislike it.

sovereign power, there can be no other representative of the same people but only to certain particular ends limited by the sovereign. For that would be to erect two sovereigns and every man would have his person represented by two actors that, by opposing each other, must divide that power which (if men will live in peace) is indivisible and thereby reduce the multitude into the condition of war, which is contrary to the end for which all sovereignty is instituted. Therefore it is absurd to think that a sovereign assembly that invites the people of their dominion to send their deputies with power to make known their advice or desires should therefore hold such deputies rather than themselves for the absolute representative of the people. So it is absurd to think the same in a monarchy. I do not know how such an obvious truth should be lately so little observed that in monarchy he who has sovereignty from a descent of 600 years was alone called sovereign and had the title of Majesty from every one of his subjects and was unquestionably taken by them for their king was not ever considered as their representative. The name without contradiction passing for the title of those men who at his command were sent up by the people to carry their petition and give him (if he permitted it) their advice. This may serve as a warning for those who are the true and absolute representative of a people to instruct men in the nature of that office and to take heed how they admit of any other general representation upon any occasion if they mean to discharge the truth committed to them.

The difference between these three kinds of commonwealth consists in the difference of convenience or aptitude to produce the peace and security of the people, for which end they were instituted. To compare monarchy with the other two we may observe, first, that whoever bears the person of the people or is one of the assembly bearing it also bears his own natural person. Though he is careful in his political person to procure the common interest, he is more, or at least no less, careful to procure the private good to himself, his family, kindred, and friends. For the most part if public interest chances to cross the private, he prefers the private. For the passions of men are commonly more potent than their reason. From this it follows that where the public and private interests are most closely united, the public is most advanced. In monarchy, the private interest is the same as the public. The riches, power, and honor of a monarch arise only from the riches, strength, and reputation of his subjects. For no king can be rich, glorious, or secure whose subjects are either poor or contemptible or too weak through want or dissention to maintain a war against their enemies. In a democracy or aristocracy, public prosperity confers not so much to the private fortune of who is corrupt or ambitious as does many times a perfidious advice, a treacherous action or a civil war.

Second, a monarch receives counsel of whom, when, and where he pleases. Consequently he may hear the opinion of men of any rank and quality who are versed in the matter about which he deliberates as long before the time of action and with as much secrecy as he will. But when a sovereign assembly has need of counsel, none are admitted but those who have a right from the beginning, who for the most part are those who have been versed more in the acquisition of wealth than of knowledge and are to give their advice in long discourses which may and do commonly excite men to action, but not govern them in it. For the understanding is by the flame of the passions never enlightened, but dazzled. Nor is there any place or time wherein an assembly can receive counsel with secrecy because of their own multitude.

Third, the resolutions of a monarch are subject to no other inconstancy than that of human nature. But in assemblies, besides that of nature, there arises inconstancy from the number. For the absence of a few who would have the resolution once taken continue firm (which may happen by security, negligence, or private impediments) or the diligent appearance of a few of the contrary opinion undoes today all that was concluded yesterday.

Fourth, a monarch cannot disagree with himself out of envy or interest, but an assembly may and to such a height as may produce a civil war.

Fifth, in monarchy there is this inconvenience that any subject, by the power of one man for enriching a favorite or flatterer, may be deprived of all he possesses, which I confess is a great and inevitable inconvenience. But the same may as well happen where the sovereign power is in an assembly for their power is the same and they are as subject to evil counsel and to be seduced by orators as a monarch by flatterers. Becoming one another's flatterers, they serve one another's covetousness and ambition. Whereas the favorites of an assembly are many and the kindred much more numerous than of any monarch. Besides, there is no favorite of a monarch which cannot as well succor his friends as hurt his enemies. But orators, that is to say, favorites of sovereign assemblies, have great power to hurt but have little to save. For to accuse requires less eloquence (such is man's nature) than to excuse; and condemnation resembles justice more than absolution.

Sixth, it is an inconvenience in monarchy that sovereignty may descend upon an infant or one who cannot discern between good and evil. The use of his power must be in the hands of another man or of some assembly of men who are to govern by his right and in his name, such as curators and protectors of his person and authority. But to say there is inconvenience in putting the use of the sovereign power into the hands of a man or an assembly of men is to say that all government is more inconvenient than confusion and civil war. Therefore all the danger that can be pretended must arise from the contention of those who become competitors for an office of so great honor and profit. To make it appear that this inconvenience does not proceed from monarchy, we are to consider that the precedent monarch has appointed who shall have the tuition of his infant successor either expressly by testament or tacitly, by not controlling the custom in that case received. Then such inconvenience (if it happens) is not to be attributed to monarchy but to the ambition and injustice of the subjects, which is in all kinds of government where the people are not well instructed in their duty and the rights of sovereignty. Otherwise, the preceding monarch has not provided for such tuition, and then the law of nature has provided this sufficient rule that the tuition shall be to him who has by nature most interest in preserving the authority of the infant and to whom least benefit can accrue by his death or diminution. For seeing every man by nature seeks his own benefit and promotion, to put an infant into the power of those who can promote themselves by his destruction or damage is not tuition, but treachery. So if sufficient provision has been taken against all quarrel about the government under a child, if any contention arises that disturbs the public peace, it is not attributed to the form of monarchy but to the ambition of the subjects and ignorance of their duty. On the other side, there is no great commonwealth where the sovereignty is in a great assembly which is not in the same condition as if the government was in a child with respect to consultation of peace and war and making laws. As a child lacks the judgment to dissent from the counsel given him and is thereby necessitated to take the advice of them or him to whom he is committed, so an assembly lacks the liberty to dissent from the counsel of the major part, be it good or bad. And as a child has need of a tutor or protector to preserve his person and authority, so also (in great commonwealths) the sovereign assembly in all great dangers and troubles has need of dictators or protectors of their authority. They are as much as temporary monarchs to whom for a time they may commit the entire exercise of their power and have (at the end of that time) been more often deprived thereof than infant kings by their protectors, regents, or any other tutors.

Though the kinds of sovereignty are, as I have shown, three—that is to say, monarchy where one man has it, democracy where the general assembly of subjects has it, or aristocracy where it is in an assembly of certain persons nominated or otherwise distinguished from the rest—he who shall consider particular commonwealths that have been and are in the world will not perhaps easily reduce them to three. He may thereby be inclined to think there are other forms arising from these mingled together. As, for example, elective kingdoms where kings have the sovereign power put into their hands for a time, of kingdoms wherein the king has a limited power, which governments are nevertheless by most writers called monarchy. Likewise if a popular or aristocratical commonwealth subdues an enemy's country and governs the same by president, procurator, or other magistrate, this may seem perhaps at first sight to be a democratic or aristocratic government. But it is not so. Elective kings are not sovereigns but ministers of the sovereign, nor are limited kings sovereigns. They are ministers of them who have the sovereign power. Nor are those provinces which are in subjection to a democracy or aristocracy of another commonwealth democratically or aristocratically governed, but monarchically.

. . . If an elective king with power limited to his life has right to appoint his successor, he is not elective but hereditary. If he has no power to elect his successor, then there is some other man or assembly known which after his death may elect anew or the commonwealth dies and dissolves with him and returns to the condition of war. If it is known who has the power to give the sovereignty after his death, it is known also that the sovereignty was in them before. For none have the right to give that which they have not right to possess, and keep to themselves if they think it good. But if there are none who can give the sovereignty after the death of he who was first elected, then the sovereign has power and is obliged by the law of nature to provide by establishing his successor to keep those who had trusted him with the government from relapsing into the miserable condition of civil war. Consequently he was, when elected, an absolute sovereign.

Second, the king whose power is limited is not superior to him or them who have the power to limit it, and he who is not superior is not supreme—that is to say, not sovereign. The sovereignty therefore was always in that assembly which had the right to limit him and by consequence the government is not monarchy but either democracy or aristocracy. . . .

Third, . . . where the people are governed by an assembly chosen by themselves out of their own number, the government is called a democracy or aristocracy. When they are governed by an assembly not of their own choosing, it is a monarchy of one people over another people, not of one man over another man.

Of all these forms of government, the sovereign is mortal. It is necessary for the conservation of the peace of men that as there was order taken for an artificial man so there be order also taken for an artificial eternity of life without which men who are governed by an assembly should return to the condition of war in every age, and they who are governed by one man as soon as their governor dies. This artificial eternity is that which men call the right of succession.

There is no perfect form of government where disposing of the succession is not in the present sovereign. For if it is in any other particular man or private assembly, it is in a person and may be assumed by the sovereign at his pleasure. Consequently the right is in himself. If it is in no particular man but left to a new choice, then the commonwealth is dissolved and the right is in him who can get it, contrary to the intention of those who instituted the commonwealth for their perpetual, not temporary, security.

In a democracy, the whole assembly cannot fail unless the multitude that are to be governed fail. Therefore, questions of the right of succession have in that form of government no place at all. In an aristocracy, when any of the assembly dies, the election of another into his room belongs to the assembly as the sovereign to whom belongs the choosing of all counselors and officers. For that which the representative does as actor, every one of the subjects does as author. Though the sovereign assembly may give power to others to elect new men for supply of their court, yet it is still by their authority that the election is made and by the same it may (when the public shall require it) be recalled.

The greatest difficulty about the right of succession is in monarchy. The difficulty arises from this—that at first sight it is not manifest who is to appoint the successor, nor many times who it is whom he has appointed. For in both of these cases, there is required a more exact ratiocination than every man is accustomed to use. As to the question who shall appoint the successor of a monarch who has the sovereign authority, that is to say (for elective kings and princes do not have sovereign power in propriety but in use only) we are to consider that either he who is in possession has the right to dispose of the succession or else that right is again in the dissolved multitude. For the death of he who has sovereign power in propriety leaves the multitude without any sovereign at all, that is, without any representative in whom they should be united and be capable of doing any one action at all. Therefore they are incapable of electing any new monarch, every man having equal right to submit himself to such as he thinks best able to protect him or if he can, protect himself by his own sword, which is a return to confusion and to the condition of war of every man against every man, contrary to the end for which monarchy had its first institution. Therefore it is manifest that by the institution of monarchy, disposing of the successor is always left to the judgment and will of the present possessor. Who the monarch in possession has designed to succession and inheritance of his power is determined by the monarch's express words and testament or by other tacit sufficient signs.

Succession passes by express words or testament when it is declared by him in his lifetime verbally or by writing. . . . For the word "heir" does not of itself imply the children or nearest kindred of a man, but whomever he shall in any way declare who would succeed him in his estate. If, therefore, a monarch declares expressly by word or writing that such a man shall be his heir, then that man is invested in the right of being monarch immediately after the death of his predecessor.

Where testament and express words are lacking, other natural signs of the will are to be followed, one of which is custom. Therefore where the custom is that the next of kin succeeds absolutely, there the next of kin has right to the successor. If the will of him who was in possession had been otherwise, he might easily have declared it in his lifetime. Likewise, where the custom is that the next of male kindred succeeds, there the right of succession is in the next of the male kindred for the same reason. So it is if the custom were to advance the female. For whatever custom a man may control by a word and does not, it is a natural sign he would have the custom stand.

Where neither custom nor testament has preceded, there it is understood first that a monarch's will is that the government remain monarchical because he has approved that government in himself. Second, that a child of his own, male or female, is preferred before any other because men are presumed to be more inclined by nature to advance their own children than the children of other men and of their own, a male rather than a female because men are naturally fitter than women for actions of labor and danger.[16] Third, where his own issue fails, a brother rather than a stranger, and so still the nearer in blood rather than the more remote because it is always presumed that the nearer of kin is the nearer in affection. It is evident that a man always receives, by reflection, the most honor from the greatness of his nearest kindred.

If it is unlawful for a monarch to dispose of the succession by words of contract or testament, men may perhaps object as a great inconvenience that he may sell or give his right to govern to a stranger which, because strangers (that is, men not used to living under the same government or not speaking the same language)

---

16. It is interesting—as well as a bit troubling—that Hobbes has gone to great lengths in Part I, Chapter XIII to make it clear that all human beings are naturally equal and he then asserts in this chapter that male monarchs are preferable to female monarchs due to women being less fit for "actions of labor and danger." But perhaps this is where the difference resides. In the natural condition there is equality; but after the institution of commonwealth, any inequalities are the result of civil law. On the other hand, how could it be that "civil law" could produce in women less ability to engage in "actions of labor and danger"? An act of law does not create such abilities or lack of abilities. It is therefore probably the case that the reason Hobbes prefers males to females as monarchs is due to social custom or to inherent misogyny. It does not seem reasonable to believe that his conclusion is due to misogyny, however, since if it is, it would have been more consistent for him to claim female inequality in the state of nature.

commonly undervalue one another and may turn to the oppression of his subjects, which is indeed a great inconvenience. But it does not proceed necessarily from the subjection to a stranger's government but from the unskillfulness of governors who are ignorant of the true rules of politics. Therefore when the Romans had subdued many nations to make their government digestible they were likely to take away that grievance as much as they thought necessary by sometimes giving to whole nations and sometimes to principal men of every nation they conquered the name of Romans, not just the privileges of Romans, and took many of them into the senate and offices of charge even in Rome itself. This was what our most wise king, James, aimed at in endeavoring the union of his two realms of England and Scotland. If he could have obtained it, it would have in all likelihood prevented the civil wars which make both of those kingdoms miserable at this time. It is not therefore any injury for the monarch to dispose of the succession by will, though it has sometimes been found inconvenient by the fault of many princes. It is also an argument of the lawfulness of it that whatever inconvenience can arrive by giving a kingdom to a stranger may also arrive by marrying with strangers as the right of succession may descend upon them. Yet this by all men is accounted lawful.

Chapter XX. Of Paternal and Despotical Dominion

Chapter XX is interesting in its discussion of the distinction between despotical and paternal power. Hobbes had indicated earlier that the manner in which sovereignty is instituted has no effect on the rights and powers of sovereigns, but what he did not explain before—or at least not as completely—are some of the finer distinctions between the ways in which dominion of one person over another or over many others is acquired. Among such distinctions are those of the position of mothers and fathers in families and the obligations of children to their parents.

A commonwealth by acquisition is that in which the sovereign power is acquired by force. It is acquired by force when for fear of death or bonds, men singly or many together by the plurality of voices authorize all the actions of that man or assembly that has their lives and liberties in his power.

This kind of dominion or sovereignty differs from sovereignty by institution only in that men who choose their sovereign do it for fear of one another and not of him whom they institute. In this case, they subject themselves to the person they are afraid of. In both cases they do it for fear. It is to be noted by those who hold all such covenants that proceed from fear of death or violence to be void that if it were true, no man in any kind of commonwealth could be obliged to obedience. It is true that in a commonwealth once instituted or acquired that promises proceeding from fear of death or violence are neither covenants nor obliging when the thing promised is contrary to the laws. But the reason is because he who promises has no right in the thing promised, not because it was made upon fear. In addition, when he may lawfully perform and does not it is the sentence of the sovereign that absolves him, not the invalidity of the covenant. Otherwise, whenever a man lawfully promises, he unlawfully breaks. But when the sovereign, who is the actor, acquits him then he is acquitted by he who extorted the promise as by the author of such absolution.

The rights and consequences of sovereignty are the same in both. His power cannot be transferred to another without his consent. He cannot forfeit it and he cannot be accused by any of his subjects of injury. He cannot be punished by them. He is the judge of what is necessary for peace and he is the judge of doctrines. He is the sole legislator and supreme judge of controversies and of the times and occasions of war and peace. To him belongs the choice of magistrates, counselors, commanders, and all other offices and ministers, and to determine rewards and punishments, honor, and order. The reasons for this are the same which are alleged in the preceding chapter for the same rights and consequences of sovereignty by institution.

Dominion is acquired in two ways—by generation and by conquest. The right of dominion by generation is that which the parent has over his children. It is called paternal. It is not derived from the generation as the parent has dominion over his child because he begat him, but from the child's consent. The child's consent is either express or by other sufficient declared arguments.[17] As to generation, God has ordained to man a helper and there are always two who are equally parents. But that the dominion therefore over the child should belong equally to both and he is equally subject to both is impossible, for no man can obey two masters. Whereas some have attributed dominion only to the man as being the more excellent sex, they misreckon in it. This is the case because there is not always difference of strength or prudence between the man and the woman as that the right can be determined without war. In commonwealths, the controversy is decided by the civil law and for the most part (but not always) the sentence is in favor of the father because for the most part commonwealths have been erected by fathers and not by mothers of families. But the question now lies in the state of mere nature where there are supposed no laws of matrimony and no laws for the education of children but the law of nature and the natural inclination of the sexes to one another and to their children. In the condition of mere nature, either the parents dispose of the dominion over the child between themselves by contract or they do not dispose of it at all. If they dispose the dominion the right passes according to the contract. We find in history that the Amazons contracted with the men of neighboring countries to whom they had recourse for issue that the male child should be sent back but the female remain with themselves so that the dominion of the females was in the mother.

If there is no contract, the dominion is in the mother. For in the condition of mere nature where there are no matrimonial laws it cannot be known who is the father unless it is declared by the mother. Therefore, the right of dominion over the child depends on her will and is consequently hers. Again, seeing the infant is first in the power of the mother so that she may either nourish it or expose it, if she nourishes it, it owes its life to the mother and is therefore obliged to obey her rather than any other. By consequence, dominion over it is hers. But if she exposes it and another person finds and nourishes it, the dominion is in him who nourishes it. It ought to obey him by whom it is preserved because preservation of life is the end for which one man becomes subject to another and every man is supposed to promise obedience to him in whose power it is to save or destroy him.[18]

---

17. While it is clear that infants and children cannot actually give "consent" to their parent(s), since every person naturally desires her or his own preservation, if the parent provides protection and preserves the lives of children, then children are bound to their parents in the same way that a political subject is bound to the political sovereign by tacit consent.
18. The dominion of a mother over her children is the same in this case as the dominion of a sovereign over subjects. The sovereign's power lasts so long as the sovereign is able to sufficiently protect the subject from early, violent death. The same is true of a mother. If she "exposes" it (the child)—that is, if she fails to care properly for her child—anyone else who does do so has dominion over the child and the child thereby promises obedience to that person.

If the mother is the father's subject, the child is in the father's power. If the father is the mother's subject (as when a sovereign queen marries one of her subjects) the child is subject to the mother because the father is also her subject. If a man and a woman who are monarchs of two different kingdoms have a child and they contract concerning who shall have dominion of the child, the right of dominion passes by the contract. If they do not contract, dominion follows the dominion of the place of his residence. For the sovereign of each country has dominion over all who reside there. He who has dominion over the child has dominion also over their children's children. For he who has dominion over the person of a man has dominion over all that is his, without which dominion would be only a title without effect. The right of succession to paternal dominion proceeds in the same manner as the right of succession to monarchy, of which I have already spoken in the preceding chapter.

Dominion acquired by conquest or victory in war is what some writers call despotical . . . which signifies a lord or master and is the dominion of a master over his servant. This dominion is then acquired to the victor when the vanquished covenants either in express words or sufficient signs of the will to avoid the present stroke of death and where the victor shall have the use of his life and liberty of his body at his pleasure so long as life and liberty of his body are allowed him. After such covenant is made, and not before, the vanquished is a servant. For by the word "servant" (whether derived from *servire*, to serve or from *servare*, to save, which I leave to grammarians to dispute) is not meant a captive who is kept in prison or bonds until the owner of him who took him or bought him of one who did shall consider what to do with him. For such men (commonly called slaves) have no obligation at all but may break their bonds or the prison and kill or carry away their master as captive and do so justly.[19] But one who is taken and has corporal liberty allowed him and promises not to run away or do violence to his master is trusted by him.

It is his own covenant and not the victory, therefore, that gives the right of dominion over the vanquished. Nor is he obliged because he is conquered—that is to say, beaten and taken or put to flight—but because he comes in and submits to the victor. Nor is the victor obliged by an enemy rendering himself (without promise of life) to spare him for yielding to discretion which does not oblige the victor longer than in his own discretion he thinks fit.

That men do when they demand (as it is now called) quarter . . . is to evade the present fury of the victor by submission and to offer the victor ransom or service for the preservation of their life. Therefore, he who has quarter does not have his life given but deferred until further deliberation. It is not yielding on condition of life but to discretion. Then only is his life secure and his service due when the victor has trusted him with corporal liberty. For slaves who work in prisons or fetters do not do it out of duty but to avoid the cruelty of their task masters.

---

19. Because the master over a slave has absolute power of life and death over another person, the slave is not bound in any way and is justified in escaping or in killing him.

The master of the servant is master also of all he has and may exact the use of it—that is to say of his goods, his labor, his servants and his children—as often as he thinks fit. For he holds his life of his master by the covenant of obedience. That is, he owns and authorizes whatever the master shall do. In case the master kills him if he refuses or casts him into bonds or otherwise punishes him for his disobedience, he is himself the author of the same and cannot accuse him of injury.

In sum, the rights and consequences of both paternal and despotical dominion are the very same as those of a sovereign by institution for the same reasons. The reasons are set down in the preceding chapter. So a man who is monarch of diverse nations in which one sovereignty is by institution and another is by conquest (that is, by the submission of each particular to avoid death or bonds) to demand more of the conquered nation than the other is an act of ignorance of the rights of sovereignty. For the sovereign is absolute over both alike or there is no sovereignty at all. So every man may lawfully protect himself with his own sword if he can, which is the condition of war.

By this it appears that if a great family is not part of some commonwealth, it is as to the rights of sovereignty a little monarchy whether the family consists of a man and his children or a man and his servants or of a man and his children and servants together in which the father or master is the sovereign. But a family is not properly a commonwealth unless it is of power by its own number or by other opportunities not to be subdued without the hazard of war. Where a number of men are too weak to defend themselves united, every one may use his own reason in time of danger to save his own life either by flight or submission to the enemy as he thinks best. In the same manner as a very small company of soldiers who are surprised by an army may cast down their arms and demand quarter or run away rather than be put to the sword. Thus much shall suffice concerning what I find by speculation and deduction of sovereign rights from the nature, need, and designs of men in erecting commonwealths and putting themselves under monarchs or assemblies entrusted with power enough for their protection.

Let us now consider what Scripture teaches on the same point. To Moses, the children of Israel say "Speak thou to us and we will hear you, but let not God speak to us lest we die."[20] This is absolute obedience to Moses. God himself by the mouth of Samuel said concerning the right of kings, "This shall be the right of the king you will have to reign over you. He shall take your sons. . . . He shall take your daughters to make perfumes, to be his cooks and bakers. He shall take your fields, your vineyards and olive-yards and give them to his servants. . . . He shall take your man-servants and your maid-servants and the choice of your youth. . . . and you shall be his servants."[21] This is absolute power and summed up in the last words, "you shall be his servants." . . . When the people heard what power their king was to have, they consented and said thus, "We will be as all other nations and our King shall judge our causes and go before us to conduct our wars." This confirms the rights that sovereigns have both to the militia and to judicature which contains

---

20. Exod. 20.19.
21. 1 Sam. 8.11–17.

absolute power that one man can transfer to another. . . . The prayer of King Solomon to God was this: "Give to your servant understanding to judge your people and to discern between good and evil."[22] It therefore belongs to the sovereign to be judge and to prescribe the rules of discerning good and evil, which rules are laws, and therefore in him is the legislative power . . . and his commands are not to be disputed.

It appears plainly to my understanding both from reason and from Scripture that the sovereign power, whether in one man in a monarchy or in one assembly as in popular and aristocratic commonwealths, is as great as men can possibly imagine to make it. Though of so unlimited power men may fancy many evil consequences, the consequences of the want of it which is perpetual war of every man against his neighbor are much worse. The condition of man in this life shall never be without inconveniences but there happens in no commonwealth any great inconvenience except what proceeds from the subject's disobedience and breach of covenants from which the commonwealth had its being. Whoever thinks sovereign power too great will seek to make it less and must subject himself to the power that can limit it—that is to say, to a greater power.[23]

The greatest objection is that of the practice of men asking where and when such power has been acknowledged by the subjects. But one may ask them again when or where there has been a kingdom long free from sedition and civil war. In those nations whose commonwealths have been long-lived and not destroyed but by foreign war, the subjects never did dispute of the sovereign power. Regardless, an argument for the practice of men who have not sifted to the bottom and weighed the causes and nature of commonwealth with exact reason and suffer daily those miseries that proceed from the ignorance thereof is invalid. For though in all places of the world men should lay the foundation of their houses on sand, it could not from this be inferred that it ought to be that way. The skill of making and maintaining commonwealths consists in certain rules (as do arithmetic and geometry and not, as tennis, on practice only) which rules neither poor men who do not have the leisure nor those who have the leisure have so far had the curiosity or method to find out.

---

22. 1 Kings 3.9.

23. Just as Hobbes has previously noted that there is no justification for revolution, he now provides a specifically logical reason: a person who seeks to limit or replace sovereign power in order not to be subjected to that power must, ironically, submit himself to an even greater power to do so. It is therefore logically absurd and self-defeating to attempt to limit the power of the sovereign or to depose him (or her).

Chapter XXI. Of the Liberty of Subjects

Liberty, for Hobbes, is nothing more than being free from external impediments to one's actions. Power is part of the constitution of a human being, making it possible to act as one wishes to act. As Hobbes had previously explained, "free-will" simply means the liberty a person has to do what he has a will, desire, or inclination to do. There is nothing inside a human being called "the will" that is part of human anatomy. It is, instead, the last act in deliberation. So when an impediment to motion is in the constitution of a thing or being, the thing or being lacks power, not freedom. Hobbes' concern in Chapter XXI is with individuals or the political state creating (or removing) hindrances to motion in doing what one wishes to do.

For Hobbes, liberty and necessity are consistent since every act of will and every desire and inclination proceeds from a cause that is part of a chain of causes leading back to the first cause (God), and all of this must proceed from necessity. What a person does, therefore, is part of the will of God or of doing God's will. But when liberty has to do with personal life organization, Hobbes leaves it open to the individual that she or he has the liberty to do whatever is thought most profitable or beneficial to themselves—except in cases in which the law has forbidden it.

Hobbes notes that the commonwealth has all the same liberties that every person would have if there were no civil wars and no commonwealth, in that the commonwealth through the sovereign has the liberty to do anything it sees as most productive of its benefit. In this, commonwealths, like individuals in the state of nature, are in a condition of perpetual war. And since the commonwealth is in perpetual war, a monarch who is vanquished and subjects himself to the victor now creates a condition in which the subjects are obliged to the new sovereign.

Liberty, or freedom, signifies (properly) the absence of opposition (by opposition I mean external impediments of motion) and may be applied no less to irrational and inanimate creatures than to rational. For whatever is tied or environed such that it cannot move but within a certain space (where space is determined by the opposition of some external body) we say it does not have liberty to go further. So of all living creatures while they are imprisoned or restrained with walls or chains, and of water while kept in by banks or vessels that otherwise would spread itself into a larger space, we used to say that they are not at liberty to move in such manner as they would without those external impediments. When the impediment of motion is in the constitution of the thing itself, we do not say that it lacks the liberty but the power to move such as when a stone lies still or a man is fastened to his bed by sickness.[24]

---

24. Hobbes' conception of the nature of "liberty" has been discussed in previous chapters, but here he adds a clarifying point: if some particular characteristic of a person that is internal

According to this proper and generally received meaning of the word, a free-man is "he, who in those things which by his strength and wit he is able to do, is not hindered to do what he has a will to." But when the words "free" and "liberty" are applied to anything but bodies they are abused. For that which is not subject to motion is not subject to impediment. Therefore, when it is said (for example) the way is free, no liberty of the way is signified but of those who walk in it without stopping. When we say a gift is free, we do not mean the gift itself has any liberty; what is meant is that the giver has liberty and was not bound by any law or covenant to give it. So when we speak freely, it is not liberty of his voice or pronunciation, but it is the liberty of the man whom no law has obliged to speak otherwise than he did.[25] Last, from the use of the word "free-will," no liberty can be inferred to the will, desire, or inclination, but the liberty of the man, which consists in that he finds no stop in doing what he has the will, desire, or inclination to do.

Fear and liberty are consistent. For example, when a man throws his goods into the sea for fear the ship would sink, he does it nevertheless very willingly and may refuse to do it if he will. It is therefore the action of one who was free so a man sometimes pays his debt only for fear of imprisonment, which because nobody hindered him from detaining was the action of a man at liberty.[26] Generally all actions which men do in commonwealths, for fear of the law, or actions, which the doers had liberty to omit, are free.

---

to himself keeps him from doing what he wishes to do, it is not that he lacks liberty. Instead, it is that he lacks power to do as he wishes to do. So the person who is too ill to get out of bed is not "restrained" but instead lacks power in himself to be able to rise. In the case of submission to sovereign power, which is by definition the greatest of all human powers, the analogy works well except with respect to the analog's reference to "sickness." A person who submits to sovereign power has now put himself into a position in which he lacks the power to do anything at all he wishes to do and has constrained himself to a greater power. Since he voluntarily submitted himself to sovereign power, the actions he is bound to perform by sovereign decree are his own (through authorization), in which case he lacks power to do as he might wish to do at that time, but the actions he performs because he is bound to them by his voluntary submission are by his own design. That is, the actions of the sovereign, which includes the creation of laws that limit individuals' actions, are authorized by the subjects. So the subject is free in acting according to the laws and rules of the sovereign.

25. The distinction here is between positive and negative freedom. Positive liberty is the liberty to perform some action. Negative liberty is freedom from the constraint or interference of others.

26. This is another instance in which Hobbes is in agreement with Aristotle regarding actions done freely. An almost identical example is given in *Nicomachean Ethics*, III.1, where Aristotle notes that a ship's captain who decides during a storm to throw cargo overboard in the attempt to secure safety has done it voluntarily. Aristotle, however, adds that this is really a "mixed" action—that is, it is both free as well as necessitated. Aristotle adds that the ship's captain is responsible for the action because he performed it voluntarily even while under duress.

Liberty and necessity are consistent[27] as in water that has not only liberty to descend, but necessity of descending by the channel. So likewise in the actions which men voluntarily do which (because they proceed from their will) proceed from liberty. Yet because every act of man's will and every desire and inclination proceeds from some cause, which causes in a continual chain (whose first link is the hand of God the first of all causes) proceed from necessity. To he who could see the connection of those causes, the necessity of all men's voluntary actions would appear manifest. Therefore God, who sees and disposes all things, sees also that the liberty of man in doing what he will is accompanied with the necessity of doing that which God wills and no more nor less. For though men may do many things which God does not command and is therefore not author of them, yet they can have no passion or appetite of anything of which appetite God's will is not the cause. If his will did not assure the necessity of man's will and consequently of all that on man's will depends, the liberty of men would be a contradiction and impediment to the omnipotence and liberty of God.[28] This shall suffice (as to the matter in hand) of that natural liberty which only is properly called liberty.

Men have made an artificial man called a commonwealth for attaining peace and self-preservation. They have also made artificial chains by mutual covenants called civil laws which they have fastened at one end to the lips of that man or assembly to whom they gave sovereign power and at the other end to their own ears. These bonds in their own nature are weak but may nevertheless be made to hold by the danger of breaking them, though not by the difficulty.

It is the liberty of subjects in relation to these bonds only. For being that there is no commonwealth in the world for regulating all the actions and words of men (being a thing impossible) it follows necessarily that in all kinds of actions [about which no law has been recognized or about which law is silent],[29] men have the liberty of doing what their own reason shall suggest for the most profit to themselves. If we take liberty in the proper sense for corporal liberty—that is to say, freedom from chains and prison—it would be very absurd for men to clamor as they do for the liberty they so obviously enjoy. Again, if we take liberty for an exemption to

---

27. This is an explicit statement of Hobbes' compatibilism—that is, that liberty and necessity are compatible with each other, and that one is responsible for his own actions that are done without hindrance.

28. Another way to put the case is that if human beings had free-will in the radical sense of a will determined by nothing at all, it would amount to a logical contradiction in that God's liberty and power would be denied. A popular example to explain such logical absurdities with respect to God's power is the "rock problem" in which the question is posed whether it is possible for God to create a rock so heavy that he cannot lift it. If the answer is that God can create such a rock, there is something God cannot do: lift it. And if God can lift it, then it is impossible (that is, there is something God cannot do) for God to create it. In essence, absolute human free-will leads to logical absurdity and, as such, it cannot be the case that human beings have free-will while God is infinite and therefore absolutely powerful and knowing. A similar claim is made by Aquinas in *Summa Theologica* 1.25.iii–xi.

29. Hobbes uses the term "praetermitted."

the laws it is no less absurd for men to demand as they do that liberty by which all other men may be masters of their lives.[30]

Yet as absurd as it is, this is what they demand when they do not know that the laws are of no power to protect them without a sword in the hands of a man or men to cause the laws to be executed. The liberty of a subject therefore lies only in those things which, in regulating their action, the sovereign has not prohibited by law. Such is the liberty to buy and sell and otherwise contract with one another to choose their own abode, diet, trade of life, and rear their children as they think fit, and the like.

Nevertheless, we are not to understand that by such liberty the sovereign power of life and death is either abolished or limited. For it has already been shown that nothing the sovereign representative can do to a subject for whatever reason can properly be called injustice or injury. Because every subject is author of every act the sovereign does, he never wants right to anything other than as he is subject to God and thereby bound to observe the laws of nature. Therefore it may and does often happen in commonwealths that a subject may be put to death by command of the sovereign power and yet not do the other wrong. . . .[31]

The liberty of which there is so frequent and honorable mention in histories and philosophy of the ancient Greeks and Romans, and in the writings and discourse of those who have received all their learning in politics from them, is the liberty of the commonwealth. It is not the liberty of particular men. The liberty of the commonwealth is the same as that which every man should have if there were no civil wars and no commonwealth at all. The effects of it are also the same. For as among masterless men there is perpetual war of every man against his neighbor, no inheritance to transmit to the son or to expect from the father, no propriety of goods or lands, and no security but a full and absolute liberty in every particular man. So in states and commonwealths that are not dependent on one another, every commonwealth (not every man) has absolute liberty to do what it shall judge (that is, what the man or assembly that represents it shall judge) most conducive to their benefit. But they live in the condition of perpetual war and upon the confines of battle with their frontiers armed and cannons planted against their neighbors. The Athenians and Romans were free—that is, [they had a] free commonwealth—not that any particular man had the liberty to resist their own representative but that their representative had the liberty to resist or to invade other people. On the turrets of the city of Luca there is written in great characters the word *libertas*, yet no man can from this infer that a particular man has more liberty or immunity from

---

30. Again, liberty is corporal liberty to do as one pleases. Hobbes emphasizes that if by "liberty" anyone means that he wishes to be free of the law, it is as absurd (because it is identical to) as saying that they wish others to be masters over them. The laws created and enforced by the sovereign, in other words, keep human beings free from the arbitrary, unpredictable, and dangerous conditions of the state of nature.

31. It is possible for the sovereign to do harm to a subject, but not to do injury to a subject. This is the case because "injury" is specific to "injustice," and it is impossible for a sovereign to commit any injustice since the sovereign is, like God, above the laws as creator of them.

the service of the commonwealth. . . . Whether a commonwealth is monarchical or popular, the freedom is still the same.

It is easy for men to be deceived by the specious name of liberty and for lack of judgment to distinguish and mistake that for their private inheritance and birthright what is the right only of the public. When the same error is confirmed by the authority of men in reputation for their writings on this subject, it is no wonder if it produces sedition and change of government. In these western parts of the world we are made to receive our opinions concerning the institution and rights of commonwealths from Aristotle, Cicero, and other men—Greeks and Romans—living under popular states. Those holding these opinions derived those rights not from the principles of nature but transcribed them into their books out of the practice of their own commonwealths which were popular. . . . Because the Athenians were taught (to keep them from desire to change their government) that they were free-men and all who lived under monarchy were slaves, Aristotle puts it down in his *Politics* (VI.2), "In democracy liberty is to be supposed: for it is commonly held that no man is free in any other government." And as Aristotle, so Cicero and other writers have grounded their civil doctrine on the opinions of the Romans who were taught to hate monarchy. . . . By reading of these Greek and Latin authors, from childhood men have gotten a habit (under a false show of liberty) of favoring tumults and licentious controlling actions of their sovereigns, and again of controlling those controllers with the effusion of so much blood as I think may truly say there was never anything so dearly bought as these Western parts have bought the learning of Greek and Latin tongues.

To come now to the particulars of the true liberty of a subject—that is to say, what are the things which though commanded by the sovereign he may nevertheless without injustice refuse to do—we are to consider what rights we pass away when we make a commonwealth or . . . what liberty we deny ourselves by owning all the actions (without exception) of the man or assembly we make our sovereign. In the act of submission consists both our obligation and our liberty which must therefore be inferred by arguments, there being no obligation on any man which does not arise from some act of his own. For all men are by nature equally free. Because such arguments must either be drawn from the express words, "I authorize all his actions," or from the intention of he who submits himself to his power (which intention is to be understood by the end for which he submitted) the obligation and the liberty of the subject is derived either from those words (or their equivalent) or from the end of the institution of sovereignty, namely, the peace of the subjects within themselves and their defense against a common enemy.

First, seeing sovereignty by institution is by covenant of every one to everyone and sovereignty by acquisition is by covenants of the vanquished to the victor[32] or

---

32. Even though Hobbes insists throughout *Leviathan* that there is no contract or covenant between a subject and a sovereign, this is (as previously noted) the single apparent exception to that rule. It is an exception, however, that does no damage to Hobbes' argument since the agreement between the victor and the vanquished is simply the promise of the vanquished to submit to the victor and the promise of the victor is not to kill the vanquished in return for

child to the parent, it is clear that every subject has liberty in all those things of which right cannot be transferred by covenant. I have shown before in Chapter XIV that covenants not to defend a man's own body are void. Therefore, if the sovereign commands a man (though justly condemned) to kill, wound, or maim himself or not to resist those who assault him or to abstain from the use of food, air, medicine, or any other thing without which he cannot live, he has the liberty to disobey. If a man is interrogated by the sovereign or his authority concerning a crime done by himself he is not bound (without assurance of pardon) to confess it because no man (as I have shown in the same chapter) can be obliged by covenant to accuse himself.

Again, the consent of a subject to sovereign power is contained in the words, "I authorize and take upon me all his actions," in which there is no restriction at all of his own former natural liberty. For by allowing him to kill me, I am not bound to kill myself when he commands me. It is one thing to say "Kill me, or my fellow, if you please," and another thing to say, "I will kill myself or my fellow." It follows therefore that no man is bound by the words themselves either to kill himself or any other man. Consequently, the obligation a man may sometimes have upon command of the sovereign to execute dangerous or dishonorable office does not depend on the words of our submission but on the intention, which is to be understood by the end. When therefore our refusal to obey frustrates the end for which sovereignty was ordained, then there is no liberty to refuse,[33] otherwise, there is.

Upon this ground, a man who is commanded as a soldier to fight against the enemy, though his sovereign has right enough to punish his refusal with death, may nevertheless in many cases refuse without injustice, as when he substitutes a sufficient soldier in his place. For in this case he deserts not the service of the commonwealth. And there is allowance to be made for natural timorousness, not only to women (of whom no such dangerous duty is expected) but also to men of feminine courage. When armies fight, there is on one side or both a running away, yet when they do it not out of treachery but fear, they are not esteemed to do it unjustly but dishonorably. For the same reason, to avoid battle is not injustice but cowardice. But he who volunteers to be a soldier or takes imprest money takes away the excuse of a timorous nature and is obliged both to go to battle and also not to run from it

---

doing so. It is therefore the case that this type of agreement between subject and sovereign is not truly an agreement between *them* as sovereign and subject at all. The reason is that the vanquished person does not become a subject until he has agreed to submit to the sovereign, so the victor is not, at the time of agreement, making an agreement with his subject.

33. Hobbes' position regarding a sovereign order for one person to kill another is complicated, but not insurmountable. Because the law of nature obliges a person prior to the institution of sovereignty not to do anything destructive to his life, the sovereign can in fact order a subject to kill himself or someone else, but the subject is not bound to do so by the moral law contained in the laws of nature and the subject is free to do anything that self-preservation requires. On the other hand, since the subject has freely entered into authorization of the sovereign and creation of the commonwealth, and the purpose in doing so is creation of peace and order, if the order to kill oneself or another is disobeyed and disobeying is contrary to the reason for which sovereignty was instituted, the subject does not have liberty to refuse.

without his captain's permission. When the defense of the commonwealth requires at once the help of all who are able to bear arms, everyone is obliged. Otherwise, the institution of commonwealth which they do not have the purpose or courage to preserve was in vain.

No man has liberty to resist the sword of the commonwealth in defense of another man, whether guilty or innocent, because such liberty takes away from the sovereign the means of protecting us and is therefore destructive of the very essence of government. But in case a great many men together have already resisted sovereign power unjustly or committed some capital crime for which every one of them expects death, do they have the liberty then to join together and assist and defend each other? Certainly they have. For they but defend their lives, which the guilty man may as well do as the innocent. There was indeed injustice in the first breach of their duty. Bearing arms subsequently to it—though it is to maintain what they have done—is no new unjust act. If it is only to defend their persons it is not unjust at all. But the offer of pardon takes from them to whom it is offered the plea of self-defense and makes their perseverance in assisting or defending the rest unlawful.

Other liberties depend on the silence of the law. In cases where the sovereign has prescribed no rule, there the subject has the liberty to do or forbear according to his own discretion.[34] Therefore such liberty is in some places more and in some less and in some times more and other times less according as they who have sovereignty think most convenient. For example, there was a time in England when a man might enter in to his own land (and dispossess anyone who wrongfully possessed it) by force. But in after times, that liberty of forcible entry was taken away by a statute made in Parliament. In some places of the world men have liberty of many wives and in other places such liberty is not allowed.

If a subject has a controversy with his sovereign of debt or right possession of lands or goods or concerning any service required at his hands or concerning any corporal or pecuniary penalty grounded on precedent law, he has the same liberty to sue for his right as if it were against a subject and before such judges as are appointed by the sovereign. For seeing the sovereign demands by force a former law and not by virtue of his power, he declares thereby that he requires no more than shall appear to be due by that law. The suit therefore is not contrary to the will of the sovereign and consequently the subject has the liberty to demand the hearing of his cause and sentence according to that law. But if he demands or takes anything by pretense of his power there lies in that case no action of law. For all that is done by him in virtue of his power is done by the authority of every subject and consequently he who brings an action against the sovereign brings it against himself.

---

34. This will help shape Hobbes' account of religion. He allows for freedom of religion so long as it does not break any laws that the sovereign has established. How much diversity is allowed in worship depends on what the sovereign has decreed. Anything not explicitly commanded or forbidden is permissible, so long as it does not subvert or threaten the sovereign's authority. To preserve the covenant or social contract is always the law. With respect to that about which the laws are silent or what the law has omitted, Hobbes uses the term "praetermitted."

If a monarch or sovereign assembly grants a liberty to all or any subjects rendering him unable to provide for their safety, the grant is void unless he directly renounces or transfers the sovereignty to another. In that he might openly (if it had been his will) and in plain terms have renounced or transferred it and did not, it is to be understood it was not his will but that the grant proceeded from ignorance or the repugnancy between such a liberty and the sovereign power. Therefore if the sovereignty is still retained the powers which are necessary to exercising it are retained such as are the power of war and peace, of judicature, appointing officers and counselors, or levying money and the rest named in the Chapter XVIII.

The obligation of subjects to the sovereign is understood to last as long and no longer than the power lasts by which he is able to protect them. For the right they have by nature to protect themselves when no one else can protect them can be relinquished by no covenant. The sovereignty is the soul of the commonwealth. Once it is departed from the body the members no longer receive their motion from it. The end of obedience is protection which nature applies his obedience to it and his endeavor to maintain it no matter whether protection is in his own or in another's sword. Though immortal sovereignty is intended by those who make it, it is in its own nature not only subject to violent death by foreign war but also through ignorance and passions of men it has many seeds of natural mortality by internal discord from its very institution.

If a subject is taken prisoner in war or his person or means of life are within the guards of his enemy and has his life and corporal liberty given to him on condition that he will be subject to the victor, he has liberty to accept the condition. Having accepted it, he is the subject of he who took him because he had no other way to preserve himself. The case is the same if he is detained on the same terms in a foreign country. But if a man is held in prison or bonds or is not trusted with the liberty of his body, he cannot be understood to be bound by covenant and therefore if he can, he may make his escape by any means.

If a monarch relinquishes the sovereignty both for himself and his heirs, his subjects return to the absolute liberty of nature because it depends on his will (as has been said in the preceding chapter) who shall be his heir. This is true even though nature may declare who are his sons and who are the nearest of his kin. If therefore he will have no heir there is no sovereignty nor subjection. The case is the same if he dies without known kindred and without declaration of his heir. Then there can be no heir known and consequently no subjection is due.

If the sovereign banishes a subject, during the banishment he is not subject. But he who is sent on a message or has leave to travel is still subject. It is by contract between sovereigns that this is the case, not by virtue of the covenant of subjection. For whoever enters into another's dominion is subject to all the laws of it unless he has a privilege of the amity of the sovereigns or by special license.[35]

---

35. An example of having the amity of sovereigns or special license is manifested in diplomats with diplomatic immunity.

If a monarch subdued by war renders himself subject to the victor, his subjects are delivered from their former obligation and become obliged to the victor. But if he is held prisoner or does not have the liberty of his own body he is not understood to have given away the right of sovereignty and therefore his subjects are obliged to yield obedience to magistrates formerly placed who govern in his place but not their own. For his right remains and the question is only of the administration—that is to say, of the magistrates and officers he is supposed to approve that he had formerly appointed if he does not have the means to name them.

Chapter XXII. Of Subject, Political, and Private Systems

Chapter XXII concerns subsidiary "bodies politic," such as conquered foreign lands, corporations set up for profit, and natural family relationships. Hobbes refers in this chapter to things that may lead to the dissolution or weakening of a commonwealth as well as some that are part of its functioning well. Sometimes, factions arise in a commonwealth that are formed for mutual defense. Hobbes' position regarding them is that they are unlawful and dangerous to civil peace.

After speaking of the generation, form, and power of a commonwealth, I am in order to speak of its parts. First of systems, which resemble the similar parts or muscles of a natural body, I understand any number of men joined in one interest or one business of which some are regular and some irregular. Regular are those where one man or assembly of men is constituted representative of the whole number. All others are irregular.

Of regular, some are absolute and independent and subject to none but their own representative. These are commonwealths only of which I have spoken already in the last five preceding chapters. Others are dependent, that is, subordinate to some sovereign power to which everyone including their representative is subject.

Some subordinate systems are political and some are private. Political (otherwise called political bodies and persons in law) are those which are made by authority of the sovereign of the commonwealth. Private are those which are constituted by subjects among themselves or by authority from a stranger. For no authority derived from foreign power within the dominion of another is public.

Some private systems are lawful and some are unlawful. Lawful are those which are allowed by the commonwealth. All others are unlawful. Irregular systems are those which have no representative and consist only in concourse of the people which, if not forbidden by the commonwealth nor made on evil design (e.g., conflux of people to markets or shows or any other harmless end) are lawful. But when the intention is evil or (if the number is considerable) unknown, then they are unlawful.

In all political bodies the power of the representative is always limited and that which prescribes its limits is the sovereign power. For unlimited power is absolute sovereignty. The sovereign in every commonwealth is the absolute representative of all the subjects and therefore no other can be representative of any part of them but so far forth as the sovereign shall give leave. To give leave to a political body of subjects to have an absolute representative for all intents and purposes would be to abandon the government of so much of the commonwealth and to divide the dominion contrary to their peace and defense. This the sovereign cannot be understood to do by any grant that does not plainly and directly discharge them of their subjection. For consequences of words are not signs of his will when other consequences are signs of the contrary and rather are signs of error and misreckoning to which all mankind is too prone.

The bounds of the power which is given to the representative of a political body are to be taken notice of from two things. One is their writ or letters from the sovereign. The other is the law of the commonwealth.

For though in the institution or acquisition of a commonwealth that is independent, there needs no writing because the power of the representative has no other bounds but what are set out by the unwritten law of nature. In subordinate bodies, there are such diversities of limitation necessary concerning their businesses, times, and places as can neither be remembered without letters nor taken notice of unless such letters be patent that they may be read to them and sealed or testified with the seals or other permanent signs of the sovereign authority.

Because such limitation is not always easy or perhaps possible to be described in writing, the ordinary laws that are common to all the subjects must determine what the representative may lawfully do in all cases where the letters themselves are silent. Therefore in a political body, if the representative is one man, whatever he does in the person of the body which is not the act of the body nor of any other member of it besides himself is his action only. Because further than his letters or the laws limit, he represents no man's person but his own. But what he does according to these is the act of every one. For every one is the author of the act of the sovereign because he is their unlimited representative. And the act of he who does not recede from the letters of the sovereign is the act of the sovereign and therefore every member of the body is author of it.

But if the representative is an assembly, whatever that assembly decrees that is not warranted by their letters or the laws is the act of the assembly or political body. It is the act of every one by whose vote the decree was made, but it is not the act of any man who was present and voted to the contrary nor of any man who was absent unless he voted for it by procuration. It is the act of the assembly because it was voted by the major part and if it is a crime the assembly may be punished as far forth as it is capable by dissolution or forfeiture of their letters (which is capital to such artificial and fictitious bodies) or by pecuniary mulct in the case that the assembly has a common stock in which none of the innocent members have propriety. For nature has exempted all political bodies from corporal penalties. But they who did not give their vote are therefore innocent because the assembly cannot represent any man in things unwarranted by their letters and consequently are not involved in their votes. . . .[36]

Regular private and lawful bodies are those constituted without letters or other written authority, saving the laws common to all other subjects. Because they are united in one representative person, they are held considered regular, such as are

---

36. At this point, Hobbes gives some lengthy examples of debt and lending to illustrate these points.

families in which the father or master orders the whole family. For he obliges his children and servants as far as the law permits, though not further, because none of them are bound to obedience in those actions which the law has forbidden to be done. In all other actions during the time they are under domestic government, they are subject to their fathers and masters as to their immediate sovereigns. For the father and master is before the institution of commonwealth absolute sovereign in their own families, they lose afterward no more of their authority than the law of the commonwealth takes from them.

Unlawful private regular bodies . . . are those that unite themselves into one representative person without any public authority at all, such as are corporations of beggars, thieves, and gypsies, the better to order their trade of begging and stealing, and the corporations of men that by authority from any foreign person unite themselves in another's dominion for easier propagation of doctrines and for making party against the power of the commonwealth.[37]

Irregular systems in their nature are but leagues or sometimes mere concourse of people having no union to any particular design and no obligation to one another. They proceed only from similarity of wills and inclinations and become lawful or unlawful according to the lawfulness or unlawfulness of every particular man's design therein. His design is to be understood by the occasion.

The leagues of subjects (because leagues are commonly made for mutual defense) in a commonwealth (which is no more than a league of all the subjects together) are for the most part unnecessary and savor of unlawful design and are for that reason unlawful and go commonly by the name of factions or conspiracies. Because a league is a connection of men by covenants, if there is no power given to any one man or assembly (as in mere nature) to compel them to performance it is only valid as long as there arise no just cause of distrust. Therefore, leagues between commonwealths over whom there is no human power established to keep them all in awe are not only lawful but profitable for the time they last. But the leagues of the subjects of one and the same commonwealth, where every one may obtain his right by means of the sovereign power are unnecessary to maintaining peace and justice and (in case the design of them is evil, or unknown to the commonwealth) unlawful. For all uniting of strength by private men is, if for evil intent, unjust, and if for unknown intent, dangerous to the public and unjustly concealed.[38]

If the sovereign power is in a great assembly and a number of men who are part of the assembly and without authority consult a part to contrive the guidance of

---

37. An example of a corporation of men that would unite by authority of a foreign person against the power of the commonwealth is a spy ring that attempts to undermine the government under which they are living.

38. Hobbes, as is evident, would have been no supporter of the U.S. constitutional right of assembly in the First Amendment to the Constitution. Interestingly, for a philosopher whose concern seems to have been (according to some of his apologists, such as Bernard Gert) to offer a political theory in *Leviathan* intended to convince people of the need to understand properly and to reason clearly, especially about matters of truth, the lack of right of assembly and freedom of inquiry seems antithetical to the purpose.

the rest, this is a faction or unlawful conspiracy. It is unlawful because it is a fraudulent seducing of the assembly for their particular interest. But if he whose private interest is to be debated and judged in the assembly make as many friends as he can, in him it is no injustice because in this case he is no part of the assembly. And though he hires such friends with money (unless there is an express law against it) yet it is not injustice. For sometimes (as men's manners are) justice cannot be had without money and every man may think his own cause just until it is heard and judged.

In all commonwealths, if a private man entertains more servants than the government of his estate and lawful employment he has for them requires, it is faction and unlawful. For having the protection of the commonwealth, he does not need the defense of a private force. And whereas in nations not thoroughly civilized, several numerous families have lived in continual hostility and invaded one another with private force, it is evident enough that they have done unjustly, or else that they had no commonwealth.

And as factions for kindred, so also factions for government of religion, as of Papists, Protestants, etc., or of the state as patricians and plebeians of old time . . . are unjust as being contrary to the peace and safety of the people and taking of the sword out of the hand of the sovereign.

Concourse of people is an irregular system, the lawfulness or unlawfulness whereof depends on the occasion and on the number of them who are assembled. If the occasion is lawful and manifest, the concourse is lawful as the usual meeting of men at church or at a public show in usual numbers. If the numbers are extraordinarily great, the occasion is not evident and consequently he who cannot render a particular and good account of his being among them is to be judged conscious of an unlawful and tumultuous design.[39] It may be lawful for a thousand men to join in a petition to be delivered to a judge or magistrate, yet if a thousand men come to present it, it is a tumultuous assembly because there needs but one or two for that purpose. But in such cases as these, it is not a set number that makes the assembly unlawful, but a number as the present officers are not able to suppress and bring them to justice.

When an unusual number of men assemble against a man whom they accuse, the assembly is an unlawful tumult because they may deliver their accusation to the magistrate by a few or by one man. Such was the case of St. Paul at Ephesus, where Demetrius and a great number of other men brought two of Paul's companions before the magistrate, saying with one voice, "Great is Diana of the Ephesians," which was their way of demanding justice against them for teaching the people such doctrine as was against their religion and trade. The occasion here, considering

---

39. The extent to which Hobbes justifies the power of the sovereign to regulate even the public meeting of people for worship in a church or amusement at a show is striking. He requires that a person who attends such a large gathering must have a good reason to be in attendance. While it does not appear that Hobbes would find signing a petition problematic, he would certainly not allow public demonstrations, sit-ins, or public protest.

the laws of that people, was just. Yet their assembly was judged unlawful and the magistrate reprehended them for it. . . . Where he calls an assembly, whereof men can give no just account, a sedition and such as they could not answer for. And this is all I shall say concerning systems and assemblies of people which may be compared (as I said) to the similar parts of man's body, such as are lawful to the muscles, such as are unlawful to wens, biles, and apostemes, engendered by the unnatural conflux of evil humors.

Chapter XXIII. Of the Public Ministers of Sovereign Power

Public ministers are an important part of the Hobbesian commonwealth in that they do the business of the sovereign in the sovereign's name. Among public ministers are governors, tax collectors, and teachers. They are needed for the proper administration of the commonwealth for the simple reason that no sovereign as a human being is capable of performing every function necessary for the proper ordering of society.

In this chapter I shall speak of the organic parts of the commonwealth which are public ministers. A public minister is he who is employed by the sovereign in any affairs with authority to represent in that employment the person of the commonwealth. Whereas every man or assembly that has sovereignty represents two persons or (as the more common phrase is) has two capacities, one natural and another political (as a monarch has the person not only of the commonwealth but also of a man, and a sovereign assembly has the person not only of the commonwealth but also of the assembly). They who are servants to them in their natural capacity are not public ministers, but only those who serve them in the administration of the public business. Therefore neither ushers, nor sergeants, nor other officers who wait on the assembly, for no other purpose but the commodity of the men assembled in an aristocracy, or democracy; nor stewards, chamberlains, cofferers, or any other officers of the household of a monarch are public ministers in a monarchy.

Some public ministers have a charge committed to them of a general administration either of the whole dominion or a part of it. The whole administration of his kingdom may be committed by the predecessor of an infant king during his minority to a protector or regent. In this case every subject is obliged to obedience to his ordinances and commands given in the king's name and that are not inconsistent with his sovereign power. It is administration of part of a province when either a monarch or sovereign assembly gives general charge of it to a governor, lieutenant, or viceroy. In this case every one of the province is obliged to all he shall do in the name of the sovereign that is not incompatible with the sovereign's right. Protectors, viceroys, and governors have no other right except what depends on sovereign will and no commission can be given them that can be interpreted as a will to transfer sovereignty without express and perspicuous words to that purpose. This kind of public minister resembles the nerves and tendons that move the limbs of the natural body.

Others have special administration—that is to say, charges of some special business at home or abroad. First, those who have authority at home concerning the treasure as tributes, impositions, rents, fines, or whatever public revenue to collect, receive, issue, or take the accounts are public ministers for the economy of a commonwealth. They are ministers because they serve the representative person and can do nothing against his command nor without his authority. They are public because they serve him in his political capacity.

Second, they who have authority concerning the militia to have custody of arms, forts, ports, to levy, pay, conduct soldiers, or to provide for anything necessary for the use of war by land or sea are public ministers. But a soldier without command does not represent the person of the commonwealth because there is none to represent it to even though he fights for the commonwealth. For everyone who has command represents it only to them whom he commands.

They who have authority to teach or enable others to teach the people their duty to the sovereign power is a public minister who instructs them in the knowledge of what is just and unjust, thereby rendering them more apt to live in godliness and in peace among themselves and resist the public enemy. They are ministers in that they do not do it by their own authority but by another's. They are public because they do it (or should do it) by no authority but that of the sovereign. The monarch or the sovereign assembly only has immediate authority from God to teach and instruct the people and no man but the sovereign receives his power . . . from the favor of anyone but God.[40] All others receive theirs from the favor and Providence of God and their sovereign. . . .

Those to whom jurisdiction is given are public ministers because in their seats of justice they represent the person of the sovereign and their sentence is his sentence. For (as has been declared before) all judicature is essentially annexed to the sovereignty and therefore all judges are but ministers of him or them who have the sovereign power. As controversies are of two sorts, namely of fact and of law, so are some judgments of fact and some of law. Consequently in the same controversy there may be two judges—one of fact and another of law.

In both these controversies there may arise controversy between the party judged and the judge. Because they are both subjects to the sovereign they ought in equity to be judged by men agreed on by consent of both since no man can be judge in his own cause. But the sovereign is already agreed on for judge by them both and is therefore either to hear the cause and determine it himself or appoint a judge on which they shall both agree. This agreement is then understood to be made between them in different ways. First, if the defendant is allowed to take exception against judges whose interest makes him suspect them (as to the complaint he has already chosen his own judge) those which he does not except against are judges on which he himself agrees. Second, if he appeals to any other judge he

---

40. At this point, Hobbes is referring to authority coming from God for matters involving civil government, but Hobbes will later use the same concept to argue for the political sovereign's ecclesiastical authority.

can appeal no further because his appeal is his choice. Third, if he appeals to the sovereign himself and he by himself or by delegates on which the parties agree give sentence, that sentence is final for the defendant is judged by his own judges—that is to say, by himself.

Having considered the properties of just and rational judicature, I cannot help but to observe the excellent constitution of courts of justice established both for common and for public pleas in England. Common pleas are those where both the complainant and defendant are subjects. By public (which are also called pleas of the crown) those where the complainant is the sovereign. For whereas there were two orders of men in which one was lords and the other commons, the lords had the privilege to have judges in all capital crimes be none but lords and of them, as many as would be present and acknowledged as a privilege of favor, their judges were those they had themselves desired. In all controversies, every subject (also in civil controversies the lords) had judges who were men of the country where the matter in controversy lay, against which he might make his exceptions until twelve men without exception were agreed on, they were judged by those twelve. Because he has his own judges, nothing could be alleged by the party why the sentence should not be final. These public persons with authority from the sovereign either to instruct or to judge the people are such members of the commonwealth as may fitly be compared to the organs of voice in a natural body.

Public ministers are also those who have authority from the sovereign to pursue execution of judgments given to publish sovereign commands, to suppress tumults, to apprehend and imprison malefactors, and other acts tending to the conservation of the peace. Every act they do by such authority is the act of the commonwealth and their service is like the hands in a natural body.

Those who represent the person of their own sovereign to foreign states are public ministers abroad. They are ambassadors, messengers, agents, and heralds sent by public authority and on public business. But those who are sent by authority only of some private party of a troubled state are neither public nor private ministers of the commonwealth because none of their actions have the commonwealth for author.

Similarly, an ambassador sent from a prince to congratulate, condole or to assist in a solemn occasion does so through public authority but the business is private and belongs to him in his natural capacity as a private person. Also, if a man is sent secretly into another country to explore their counsels and strength, he is a private minister because there is no one to take notice of any person in him but his own even though both the authority and the business are public. This person may be compared to an eye in the natural body. Those who are appointed to receive the petitions or other information of the people, like public ears, are public ministers and represent their sovereign.

A counselor or a council of state with no authority of judicature of command who only gives advice to the sovereign when required or offers it when it is not required is not a public person. This is because the advice is addressed to the sovereign only and his person cannot in his own presence be represented to him by another. But a body of counselors has some other authority either of judicature or immediate administration. In a monarchy, they represent the monarch in delivering his commands to public ministers. In a democracy, the council or senate propounds the result of their deliberations to the people as a council. But when they appoint judges or hear causes or give audience to ambassadors, it is in the quality of a minister of the people. In an aristocracy the counsel of the state is the sovereign assembly itself and gives counsel only to themselves.

Chapter XXIV. Of the Nutrition and Procreation of a Commonwealth

Some of the functions of the commonwealth are provided by its people and not by public ministers. Nature itself provides every commonwealth with some abundant resources, or at least most commonwealths can produce something more than they require. Any excess is available for trade. While the subjects provide the labor and own what they produce by virtue of the existence of the sovereign, by definition all "real" property and products are ultimately the property of the sovereign. Further, business decisions such as providing laws of employment, commerce, and exchange of money are to be determined by the sovereign for the safety of the commonwealth.

The nourishment of a commonwealth consists in the commodities of sea and land. The nutrition of a commonwealth consists in the plenty and distribution of materials conducing to life. In concoction or preparation, and (when concocted) in the conveyance of it by convenient conduits to the public use.

The plenty of materials is limited by nature to those commodities which from (the two breasts of our common mother) land and sea, God usually either freely gives or for labor sells to mankind. The matter of this nutriment consists in animals, vegetables, and minerals. God has freely laid them before us in or near to the face of the Earth so that nothing more is needed but the labor and industry of receiving them. Plenty depends (next to God's favor) merely on the labor and industry of men.

This matter, commonly called commodities, is partly native and partly foreign. Native is that which is to be had within the territory of the commonwealth. Foreign is that which is imported from outside. Because there is no territory under the dominion of one commonwealth (except when it is of very vast extent) that produces all things needed for the maintenance and motion of the whole body and few who do not produce something more than necessary. The superfluous commodities to be had within become superfluous no more and instead supply wants at home by importation of that which may be had abroad either by exchange or by just war or by labor, for a man's labor is also a commodity exchangeable for benefit as well as anything else. There have been commonwealths having no more territory that served them for habitation but they have not only maintained but also increased their power partly by the labor of trading from one place to another and partly by selling the manufactured things made from materials brought in from other places.

Distribution of materials of nourishment is the constitution of mine and thine and his—that is to say, in one word, propriety. Propriety belongs in all kinds of commonwealth to the sovereign power for where there is no commonwealth, there is (as has already been shown) a perpetual war of every man against his neighbor. Therefore everything is his who gets it and keeps it by force and this is neither propriety nor community, but is uncertainty. This is so evident that even Cicero (a passionate defender of liberty) in a public pleading attributes all propriety to the civil law. "Let the civil law," said he, "be once abandoned or but negligently guarded (not to say oppressed) and there is nothing that any man can be sure to receive from his ancestor or leave to his children." And again, "Take away the civil law and no man knows what is his own and what another man's."[41] Therefore, seeing the introduction of propriety is an effect of commonwealth . . . it is the act only of the sovereign and consists in the laws that no one can make who does not have sovereign power. . . .

In this distribution the first law is for division of the land itself in which the sovereign assigns to every man a portion according as he and not according as any subject or any number of subjects judge agreeable to equity and the common good. . . . Though people coming into possession of land by war do not always exterminate the ancient inhabitants . . . but leave to many or most all of them their estates, it is clear they hold them afterward as of the victor's distribution as the people of England held all theirs of William the Conqueror.

From this we may see that the propriety a subject has in his lands consists in a right to exclude all other subjects from the use of them but not to exclude their sovereign. . . . Seeing the sovereign, i.e., the commonwealth (whose person he represents) is understood to do everything in order to the common peace and security, this distribution of lands is to be understood as done for the same reason. Consequently, whatever distribution he shall make in prejudice of it is contrary to the will of every subject who committed his peace and safety to his discretion and conscience and therefore by the will of every one of them it is reputed void. It is true that a sovereign monarch or the majority of a sovereign assembly may ordain doing many things in pursuit of their passions and contrary to their own consciences. This is a breach of trust and the law of nature. But this is not enough to authorize any subject to make war upon or even to accuse of injustice or any way to speak evil of their sovereign because they have authorized all his actions and made them their own in bestowing sovereign power. In what cases the commands of the sovereign are contrary to equity and the law of nature is to be considered in another place.

In the distribution of land, the commonwealth may be conceived to have a portion and possess and improve it by their representative and that the portion may be made sufficient to sustain the whole expense to the common peace and is necessary for defense. This would be very true if there could be any representative conceived to be free from human passions and infirmities. But the nature of men being as it is, setting forth of public land or any certain revenue for the commonwealth is in

---

41. Hobbes is citing Cicero's *Pro Caecina* XXV, ed. and trans. H. Grose Hodge (Cambridge, MA: Harvard University Press, 1927), 167–69.

vain and tends to dissolution of government and the condition of mere nature and war as soon as sovereign power falls into the hands of a monarch or assembly that are either too negligent with money or too hazardous in engaging the public stock into a long or costly war. Commonwealths can endure no diet. Seeing expense is not limited by their own appetite but by external accidents and appetites of their neighbors, public riches cannot be limited by other limits than those which emergent occasions require. Whereas in England there were by the Conqueror [William] diverse lands reserved to his own use (besides forests and chases for his recreation or for preservation of woods) and diverse services reserved on the land he gave to his subjects, it seems they were not reserved for his maintenance in his public capacity, but in his natural capacity. He and his successors laid arbitrary taxes on subject's land when they judged it necessary. Or if public lands and services were ordained as sufficient maintenance of the commonwealth, it was contrary to the scope of the institution being (as it appeared by those ensuing taxes) insufficient and (as it appears by the late revenue of the crown) subject to alienation and diminution. It is therefore vain to assign a portion to the commonwealth which may sell or give it away and does not do so when it is done by their representative.

It belongs also to the sovereign to assign the distribution of lands at home in what places and for what commodities the subject shall traffic abroad. For if it did belong to private persons to use their own discretion in it, some of them would be drawn for gain to furnish the enemy with means to hurt the commonwealth and hurt it themselves by importing things pleasing to men's appetites that are nevertheless noxious or at least unprofitable to them. Therefore it belongs to the commonwealth (that is, to the sovereign only) to approve or disapprove both the places and matter of foreign traffic.

It is necessary that men distribute what they can spare and transfer their propriety mutually to one another by exchange and mutual contract. This is true because it is not enough to sustain a commonwealth for every man to have a propriety in a portion of land or in a few commodities or a natural property in some useful art. There is no art in the world that is not necessary either for the being or well-being of almost every particular man. Therefore, it belongs to the commonwealth (that is, the sovereign) to appoint in what manner all kinds of contract between subjects (buying, selling, exchanging, borrowing, lending, letting, and hiring) are to be made and by what words and signs they will be understood as valid. This much (considering the model of the whole work) is sufficient for the matter and distribution of nourishment to the members of the commonwealth.

I understand by concoction reducing all commodities that are not presently consumed and instead reserved for nourishment in the future to something of equal value and portably so not to hinder the emotion of men from place to place. This way, a man may have in any place such nourishments as the place affords. This is nothing else but gold and silver and money. For gold and silver are (as it happens) highly valued in almost all countries of the world, it is a commodious measure for the value of all other things between nations. And money (of any matter coined by the sovereign of a commonwealth) is sufficient measure of the value of all other things between the subjects of the commonwealth. By means of these measures all movable and immovable commodities are made to accompany a man to all places inside and outside his place of residence and the same passes from man to man within the commonwealth . . . , nourishing (as it passes) every part of it. This concoction is the sanguinification of the commonwealth. For natural blood is in a similar way made of the fruits of the Earth and circulating, nourishes every member of the body of man.

Because silver and gold have their value from matter itself, they have, first, this privilege that their value cannot be altered by the power of one or a few commonwealths since they are a common measure of the commodities of all places. But base money may easily be enhanced or abased. Second, they have the privilege to make commonwealths move and stretch out their arms when needed into foreign countries and supply whole armies and private subjects with provision. Coin which is not considerable for that matter but for the stamp of the place being unable to endure change of air has its effect at home only where it is also subject to the change of laws and thereby to have value diminished to the prejudice many times of those who have it.

The conduits and ways by which money is conveyed to the public use are of two sorts. One is conveying it to the public coffers. The other is issuing the same out again for public payments. Of the first sort are collectors, receivers, and treasurers. Of the second sort are the treasurers again and the officers appointed for payment of several public or private ministers. In this also the artificial man maintains his resemblance with the natural whose veins receive blood from many parts of the body and carry it to the heart where it is made vital and the heart sends it out again by the arteries to enliven and enable motion for all members.

The procreation or children of a commonwealth are all plantations or colonies which are numbers of men sent out from commonwealth under a conductor or governor to inhabit a foreign country that is either void of inhabitants or voided by war. When a colony is settled, they are a commonwealth of themselves when discharged of their subjection to the sovereign who sent them . . . in which case the commonwealth from which they went was called their metropolis or mother and requires no more of them than fathers require (honor and friendship) of children they emancipate and make free from their domestic government. Or they remain united to their metropolis . . . and then they are not commonwealths but are provinces and parts of the commonwealth that sent them. So the right of colonies (saving honor and league with their metropolis) depends wholly on their license or letters by which the sovereign authorized them to plant.

Chapter XXV. Of Counsel

Since the sovereign as a natural person is a human being and is not omni-scient, it is necessary to make use of counselors to give advice to the sovereign for their own benefit as well as for the benefit of the person to whom they give advice. There is a difference in the implications of the results of counsel for a sovereign and for an individual citizen since a sovereign by definition can do no injustice even in a case in which a sovereign acts on the basis of the bad advice of counsel. The case is not the same for individual citizens, however, because they are responsible to the sovereign. But whether sovereign or individual citizen, anyone who seeks the counsel of another must take care to ensure that the interests of the counselor align with the interests of the person counseled.

How fallacious it is to judge the nature of things by ordinary and inconstant use of words appearing in nothing more than the confusion of counsels and commands arising from the imperative manner of speaking. . . . For the words "Do this" are the words of him who commands and also of him who gives counsel and of him who exhorts. Yet there are but few who do not see that these are very different things or that cannot distinguish between them when they perceive who it is who speaks and to whom the speech is directed and on what occasion. Finding those phrases in men's writings and not being able or willing to enter into consideration of the circumstances, they sometimes mistake precepts of counselors for the precepts of those who command, and sometimes the contrary, according as it best agrees with the conclusion they would infer or the actions they approve. To avoid these mistakes and render to those terms of commanding, counseling and exhorting their proper and distinct significations, I define them as follows.

Command is where a man says "Do this" or "Do not do this" without expecting other reason than the will of him who says it. From this it obviously follows that he who commands intends his own benefit because the reason of his command is his own will and the proper object of every man's will is some good to himself.

Counsel is where a man says "Do" or "Do not do this" and deduces his own reasons from the benefit that comes to him from it and to whom he said it. From this it is evident that he who gives counsel pretends only (whatsoever he intends) the good of him to whom he gives it.

Therefore one great difference between counsel and command is directed to a man's own benefit and counsel to the benefit of another man. From this arises another difference. A man may be obliged to do what he is commanded—as when he has covenanted to obey. But he cannot be obliged to do as he is counseled because the hurt of not following it is his own. Or if he should covenant to follow it then he has turned the counsel into the nature of a command. A third difference between them is that no man can pretend a right to be of another man's counsel because he is not to pretend benefit to himself by it but to demand right to counsel another and argues a will to know his designs or to gain some other good to himself which (as I said before) is the proper object of every man's will.

It is also incident to the nature of counsel that whatever it is, he who asks for it cannot in equity accuse or punish it. For to ask counsel of another is to permit him to give counsel as he shall think best. Consequently, he who gives counsel to his sovereign (whether monarch or assembly) when he asks it cannot in equity be punished for it no matter whether it is conformable to the opinion of the most or not, so it is to the proposition in debate. This is true because if the sense of the assembly can be noticed before the debate ends they should neither ask nor take any further counsel. The sense of the assembly is the resolution of the debate and the end of all deliberation. Generally he who demands counsel is author of it and therefore cannot punish it and what the sovereign cannot do, no other man can. But if one subject gives counsel to another to do anything contrary to the laws, whether the counsel proceeds from evil intention or only from ignorance, it is punishable by the commonwealth because ignorance of the law is no good excuse where every man is bound to take notice of the laws to which he is subject.

Exhortation and dehortation is counsel combined with signs in him who gives counsel of vehement desire to have it followed. Or to say it more briefly, it is counsel vehemently pressed. For he who exhorts does not deduce the consequences of what he advises to be done and tie himself to the rigor of true reasoning, but encourages the person he counsels to action as he who dehorts deters him from it. Therefore they have in their speeches regard to the common passions and opinions of men in deducing their reasons and make use of similitudes, metaphors, examples, and other tools of oratory to persuade their hearers of the utility, honor, or justice of following their advice.

From this it may be inferred, first, that exhortation and dehortation is directed to the good of him who gives counsel and not of him who asks it, which is contrary to the duty of a counselor who (by the definition of counsel) ought not to regard his own benefits but the benefits of the person he advises. That he directs his counsel to his own benefit is clear enough by the long and vehement urging or the artificial giving of it which is not required of him and consequently proceeding from his own occasions is directed principally to his own benefit and accidentally to the good of the person who is counseled—or not at all.

Second, the use of exhortation and dehortation lies only where a man is to speak to a multitude. This is true because when speech is addressed to one that one may interrupt and examine his reasons more rigorously than can be done in multitude because they are too many to enter into dispute and dialogue with him who speaks indifferently to them all at once. Third, they who exhort and dehort are corrupt counselors and bribed by their own interest when they are required to give counsel. For though the counsel they give is good, he who gives it is no more a good counselor than he who gives a just sentence for a reward is a just judge. But where a man may lawfully command, such as a father in his family or a leader in an army, his exhortations and dehortations are not only lawful but also necessary and laudable. Then they are not counsels but commands which, when they are for execution of sour labor, sometimes necessity and humanity always requires to be sweetened in the delivery by encouragement and in tune and phrase of counsel rather than the harsher language of command.

Examples of the difference between command and counsel may be taken from the forms of speech expressed in Holy Scripture. "Have no other Gods but me; Make to thy self no graven image. Take not God's name in vain. Sanctify the Sabbath. Honor thy parents. Kill not. Steal not," etc., are commands because we are to obey them from the will of God our king whom we are obliged to obey. But these words, "Sell all you have, give it to the poor, and follow me" are counsel because the reason we are to do so is drawn from our own benefit, which is that we shall have "Treasure in Heaven." . . .

The differences between apt and inept counselors may be derived from the difference between counsel and command in that benefit or hurt that may arise to the person to be counseled by necessary or probable consequences of actions propounded. Experience is memory of consequences of like actions formerly observed and counsel is the speech by which that experience is made known to another, so the virtues and defects of counsel are the same with the virtues and intellectual defects. To the person of a commonwealth, his counselors serve him in place of memory and mental discourse. But there is one dissimilitude of great importance joined with this resemblance of a commonwealth to a natural man. It is that a natural man receives experience from the natural objects of sense that work upon him without passion or interest of their own. But they who give counsel to the representative person of a commonwealth may and often have their particular ends and passions that render their counsels always suspected and many times unfaithful. Therefore we may set down for the first condition of a good counselor that his ends and interest are not inconsistent with the ends and interest of him he counsels.

Second, because when an action comes into deliberation, the office of a counselor is to make manifest the consequences of it in a manner such that he who is counseled may be truly and evidently informed, so the counselor ought to propound his advice in a form of speech to make the truth most evidently appear. That is to say, with as firm ratiocination as significant and proper language and as briefly as the evidence will permit. Therefore rash and unevident inferences (which are obtained only from examples or the authority of books and are not arguments of what is good and evil but witnesses of fact or opinion) obscure, confused and ambiguous expressions, and metaphorical speeches that tend to stir up passion . . . are repugnant to the office of a counselor.

Third, because the ability of counseling proceeds from experience and long study. And no man is presumed to have experience in all those things that are necessary to the administration of a great commonwealth, so no man is presumed to be a good counselor except in such business in which he has been much versed in and also much meditated on and considered. Seeing the business of a commonwealth is to preserve the people at home and defend them against foreign invasion, we find it requires great knowledge of the disposition of mankind of the rights of government and the nature of equity, law, justice, and honor that are not to be attained without study. It also requires knowledge of the strength, commodities, and places both of their own country and their neighbors as also of the inclinations and designs of all nations that may any way annoy them. This is not attained without much experience. Of things which not only the whole sum but every one of the particulars requires the age and observation of a man in years and of more than ordinary study. The wit required for counsel, as I have said before in Chapter VIII, is judgment. The differences of men in that point come from different education of some to one kind of study or business and of others to another. For doing anything there are infallible rules (as in engines and edifices and the rules of geometry), all the experience of the world cannot equal his counsel who has learned or found out the rule. When there is no such rule, he who has most experience in that particular kind of business has the best judgment and is the best counselor.

Fourth, to be able to give counsel to a commonwealth in a business that has reference to another commonwealth it is necessary to be acquainted with the intelligences and letters that come from there and all the records of treaties and other state transactions between them. None can do this but the person the representative thinks fit. By this we may see that they who are not called to counsel can have no good counsel in such cases to obtrude.

Fifth, if the number of counselors is equal, a man is better counseled by hearing them apart than in an assembly. This is true for many reasons. First, in hearing them separately, you have the advice of every man. But in an assembly many of them deliver their advice with I or No or with their hands or feet. They are not moved by their own sense but by the eloquence of another or for fear of displeasing some who have spoken or fear of the whole assembly by contradiction, or for fear of appearing duller than those who have applauded the contrary opinion. Second, in an assembly of many, there are some whose interests are contrary to that of the public and their interests make these passionate, and passion makes them eloquent, and eloquence draws others to the same advice. For the passions of men which are separately moderate like the heat of one brand are like many brands that inflame one another . . . in an assembly, setting the commonwealth on fire under pretense of counseling it. Third, in hearing every man separately, one may examine (when there is need) the truth or probability of his reasons and of the grounds of the advice he gives by frequent interruptions and objections. This cannot be done in an assembly where in every difficult question a man is rather astonished and dazzled with the variety of discourse upon it rather than informed of the course he ought to take. Besides, there cannot be an assembly of many called together for advice where there are not some who have the ambition to be thought eloquent and learned in politics and do not give their advice with care of the business at hand but instead of the applause of their motley orations . . . which is an impertinence that at least takes away time for serious consultation. In the secret way of counseling separately this is easily avoided. Fourth, in deliberations that ought to be kept secret (of which there are many occasions in public business) the counsels of many and especially in assemblies are dangerous. Therefore great assemblies are necessitated to commit such affairs to lesser numbers and of such persons who are most versed and in whose fidelity they have most confidence.

To conclude, who is there who approves taking counsel from a great assembly of counselors when he wishes for or would accept their plans when there is a question of marrying his children, disposing of his lands, governing his household, or managing his private estate, especially if there is among them someone who does not wish his prosperity? A man who does this business with help of many and prudent counselors, with every one consulting separately in his proper element, does it best. . . . He does next best who uses only his own judgment. . . . But he who is carried up and down to his business in a framed counsel that cannot move except by the plurality of consenting opinions does it worst of all . . . and most of all when there is one or more among them who desire to have him lose. Though it is true that many eyes see more than one, it is not to be understood of many counselors but then only when the final resolution is in one man. Otherwise, because many eyes see the same thing in different lines and are apt to look asquint toward their private benefit, they who desire not to miss their mark, even when they look about with two eyes, never aim but with one. Therefore no great popular commonwealth was ever kept up by a foreign enemy that united them or by the reputation of an eminent man among them or by the secret counsel of a few, or by the mutual fear of equal factions, and not by the open consultations of the assembly. There is no human wisdom that can uphold little commonwealths, whether popular or monarchical, longer than the jealousy lasts of their potent neighbors.

Chapter XXVI. Of Civil Laws

The laws promulgated by the sovereign are not counsels or advice to the people because laws are commands. But commands, like counsel, often require interpretation; thus, care must be taken in the interpretation of laws so that they are clear in themselves and clear in their origin. There are, for example, people who might take what they think are God's commandments as law. It must be made clear that the one and only source of law is the sovereign and the only legitimate laws are those declared by the sovereign to be laws of the commonwealth.

I understand by civil laws the laws that men are bound to observe because they are members of a commonwealth, not of this or that commonwealth in particular. For the knowledge of particular laws belongs to those who profess the study of the laws of their countries, but knowledge of civil law in general to any man. . . . My design is not to show what is law here and there, but what is law as Plato, Aristotle, Cicero, and others have done without taking upon them the profession of the study of the law.

First it is manifest that law in general is not counsel but command. Nor is it a command of any man to any man, but only of him whose command is addressed to one formerly obliged to obey him. The civil law adds only the name of the person commanding which is *persona civitas*, the person of the commonwealth. So I define civil law in this manner. "Civil law is to every subject those rules which the commonwealth has commanded him by word, writing, or other sufficient sign of the will to make use of for the distinction of right and wrong." . . .

In this definition there is nothing that is not at first sight evident because every man sees that some laws are addressed to all the subjects in general, some to particular provinces, some to particular vocations, and some to particular men and are therefore laws to all of those to whom the command is directed and to no one else. Laws are the rules of just and unjust and nothing is reputed unjust that is not contrary to some law. Likewise, none can make laws but the commonwealth because our subjection is to the commonwealth only and commands are to be signified by sufficient signs because a man does not know otherwise how to obey them. Therefore whatever can be deduced from this definition by necessary consequence ought to be acknowledged for truth. Now I deduce from it what follows.

The legislator in all commonwealths is only the sovereign whether he is one man (as in a monarchy) or one assembly of men (as in democracy or aristocracy). The legislator is he who makes the law and the commonwealth only prescribes and commands the observation of those rules we call law. Therefore the commonwealth is the legislator, but the commonwealth is no person nor does it have the capacity to do anything but by the representative (that is, the sovereign) and therefore the sovereign is the sole legislator. For the same reason no one can abrogate a law made except the sovereign because a law is not abrogated except by another law that forbids it to be put in execution.

The sovereign of a commonwealth, whether an assembly or one man, is not subject to the civil laws. For having power to make and repeal laws, he may when he pleases free himself from that subjection by repealing the laws that trouble him and making new, and consequently he was free before. For he is free who can be free when he will. Nor is it possible for any person to be bound to himself because he who can bind can release and therefore he who is bound to himself only is not bound.[42]

When long use obtains the authority of law, it is not the length of time that makes the authority but the will of the sovereign signified by his silence (for silence is sometimes an argument of consent) and if it is no longer law, then the sovereign shall be silent. Therefore if the sovereign has a question of right not grounded on his present will but upon formerly made laws, the length of time shall bring no prejudice to his right but the question shall be judged by equity because many unjust actions and unjust sentences go uncontrolled longer than any man can remember. Our lawyers account no customs law except those that are reasonable and that evil customs are to be abolished. But the judgment of what is reasonable and of what is to be abolished belongs to him who makes the law, which is the sovereign assembly or monarch.

The law of nature and the civil law contain each other and are of equal extent because the laws of nature . . . depend on the condition of mere nature (as I have said before in the end of Chapter XV) and are not properly laws but qualities that dispose men to peace and obedience.[43] When a commonwealth is once settled, then they are actually laws and not before because then they are the commands of the commonwealth and therefore they are also civil laws. For it is the sovereign power that obliges men to obey them. This is true because in the differences of private men to declare what is equity, what is justice, what is moral virtue, and to make them binding there is need of ordinances of the sovereign power and punishments to be ordained for those who break them, which ordinances are therefore part of the civil law. The law of nature therefore is part of the civil law in all

---

42. The notion that the person who has the power to make (and repeal) laws is not subject to them is very important both for the civil sovereign as sovereign and for the sovereignty of God. If God, for example, was subject to his own laws, God would be limited; but since he who makes laws can just as well repeal them, it is the person who has sovereignty who is ultimately free and therefore, in other words, unlimited in power.

43. Hobbes' claim that the laws of nature are not "properly laws" is important since the laws of nature are the foundation of the science of morals (that is, the laws of nature are the subject matter of ethics) and ethics is a branch of natural science (observational, regarding human behavior). The state, however, is the subject matter of civil philosophy and, being the result of human invention, has the capacity to take moral requirements and transform them into laws. That is, laws are enforceable with the power of the sovereign.

commonwealths of the world. It is also true reciprocally that the civil law is part of the dictates of nature. For justice, i.e., performance of covenant and giving to every man his own, is a dictate of the law of nature. But every subject in a commonwealth has covenanted to obey the civil law (either with one another as when they assemble to make a common representative or with the representative itself when, subdued by the sword, they promise obedience that they may receive life). Therefore obedience to the civil law is also part of the law of nature. Civil and natural laws are not different kinds but different parts of the law of which one part written is called civil and the other, unwritten, natural. But the right of nature, i.e., the natural liberty of man, may be abridged and restrained by the civil law. The end of making laws is no other but such restraint without which there cannot possibly be any peace. Law was brought into the world for nothing else but to limit natural liberty of particular men[44] in such manner as they might not hurt but assist one another and join together against a common enemy.

If the sovereign of one commonwealth subdues a people who have lived under other written laws and afterward governs them by the same laws by which they were governed before, those laws are the civil laws of the victor and not of the vanquished commonwealth. For the legislator is not he by whose authority the laws were first made but by whose authority they continue to be laws. Therefore where there are diverse provinces within the dominion of a commonwealth and in those provinces diversity of laws which are commonly called the customs of each province, we are to understand that those customs have their force and are now laws by the constitution of their present sovereign and not by virtue of the prescription of time. But if an unwritten law in all the provinces of a dominion are generally observed and no iniquity appears in the use of them that law can be no other but a law of nature that equally obliges all mankind.

Seeing then that all laws, written and unwritten, have their authority and force from the will of the commonwealth . . . a man may wonder the source of such opinions as found in the books of lawyers of eminence in several commonwealths directly or by making the legislative power depend on private men or subordinate judges. For example, as "That the common law has no controller but the Parliament," which is true only where a Parliament has sovereign power and cannot be assembled or dissolved except by their own discretion. If there is a right in any other to dissolve them there is also right to control them and consequently to control their controllings. And if there is no such right, then the controller of laws is not *parlamentum*, but *Rex in Parlamento*. Where a Parliament is sovereign if it should assemble never so many or so wise men from the countries subject to them for whatever cause, there is no man who will believe that such an assembly has acquired to themselves a legislative power. Also, the two arms of a commonwealth

---

44. In limiting the natural liberty of particular men, Hobbes is referring to the law of nature requiring that every person give up his right to all things. The right of nature is for each person to have the liberty to do whatever he deems appropriate for the maintenance of life. So civil law limits the right of nature—not absolutely, as has been shown by Hobbes previously, but in those things that tend toward civil unrest and that are therefore dangerous to peace.

are force and justice. The first is in the king. The other is deposited in the hands of Parliament. As if a commonwealth could consist where the force was in any hand which justice did not have the authority to command and govern.

Our lawyers agree that law can never be against reason and that which is according to the intention of the legislator, not the letter (that is, every construction of it) is the law. And it is true, but the doubt is of whose reason shall be received for law. It is not meant of any private reason because then there would be as much contradiction in the laws as there is in the schools nor yet . . . an artificial perfection of reason obtained by long study, observation and experience. . . .[45] For it is possible that long study may increase and confirm erroneous sentences. Where men build on false grounds the more they build the greater the ruin, and of those who study and observe with equal time and diligence the reasons and resolutions must remain discordant. Therefore it is the reason of this our artificial man the commonwealth and his command that makes law, not the wisdom of subordinate judges. The commonwealth being in their representative only one person, there cannot easily arise any contradiction in the laws and when there is, the same reason is able by interpretation or alteration to take it away. In all the courts of justice, the sovereign (who is the person of the commonwealth) is he who judges. The subordinate judge ought to have regard to the reason which moved the sovereign to make such law that his sentence may be according thereunto, which then is his sovereign's sentence. Otherwise it is his own and an unjust one.

From this, we understand that the command of the commonwealth is law only to those who have means to take notice of it since law is a command and a command consists in declaration or manifestation by voice, writing or some other sufficient argument of the will of he who commands. There is no law over natural fools, children or madmen any more than over brute beasts, nor are they capable of the title of just or unjust because they never had power to make any covenant or to understand the consequences of it. Consequently they never took upon themselves to authorize the actions of any sovereign as those do who make a commonwealth. Those from whom nature or accident has taken away notice of all laws in general and every man from whom any accident not proceeding from his own fault has taken away the means to take notice of any particular law is excused if he does not observe it. To speak properly, that law is no law to him. It is therefore necessary to consider in this place what arguments and signs are sufficient for knowledge of the law—that is to say, what is the will of the sovereign in monarchies as well as in other forms of government.

First, if it is a law that obliges all subjects without exception and it is not written or otherwise published in such places they may take notice, it is a law of nature. Whatever men are to take knowledge of for law from his own reason and not upon other men's words must be agreeable to the reason of all men, and that can be no law but the law of nature. The laws of nature therefore do not need to be published or proclaimed since they are contained in this one sentence and approved by all

---

45. Hobbes is paraphrasing Edward Coke, an English author and politician Hobbes criticized.

the world, "Do not do that to another what you think unreasonable to be done by another to yourself."

Second, if it is a law that obliges only some conditions of men or one particular man and is not published by word, then it is also a law of nature and known by the same arguments and signs that distinguish those in such a condition from other subjects. For whatever law is not written or in some way published by he who makes it a law, it can be known in no way but by the reason of the person who is to obey it. It is therefore not only a civil law but natural. For example, if the sovereign employs a public minister without written instructions what to do, he is obliged to take for instructions the dictates of reason. And if he makes a judge, the judge is to take notice that this sentence ought to be according to the reason of his sovereign to which he is bound by the law of nature as understood to be equity. Or if an ambassador, he is (in all things not contained in his written instructions) to take for instruction that which reason dictates to be most conducive to his sovereign's interest. And so of all other public and private ministers of the sovereignty. All the instructions of natural reason may be comprehended under the name of fidelity which is a branch of natural justice.

With the exception of the law of nature, it belongs to the essence of all other laws to be made known to every man who shall be obliged to obey. They are to be made known either by word or writing or other acts known to proceed from sovereign authority. For the will of another cannot be understood except by his own word or act or by conjecture taken from his scope and purpose, which in the person of the commonwealth is supposed always consonant to equity and reason. In ancient time before letters were in common use, the laws were often put into verse so that the rude people might more easily retain them in memory by taking pleasure in singing or reciting them. For the same reason Solomon advises a man to bind the Ten Commandments upon his ten fingers. . . .[46]

Nor is it enough for the laws to be written and published. There must also be clear signs that it proceeds from the will of the sovereign. For private men may publish for laws what they please with or without legislative authority when they have or think they have force enough to secure their unjust designs and convey them safely to ambitious ends. There is therefore requisite sufficient signs of the author and authority, not only a declaration of the law. The author or legislator is supposed in every commonwealth to be evident because he is sovereign. Being constituted by the consent of everyone he is supposed by everyone to be sufficiently known. Though the ignorance and security of men is for the most part as that when the memory of the first constitution of their commonwealth is worn out, they do not consider by whose power they were defended against their enemies and to have their industry protected and to be righted when injury is done to them. Because no man who considers can make question of it, no excuse can be derived from the ignorance of where sovereignty is placed. It is a dictate of natural reason and consequently an evident law of nature that no man ought to weaken the power of the

---

46. This is a reference to Prov. 7.1–3.

protection whereof he has himself demanded or wittingly received against others.[47] Therefore no man except by his own fault (regardless of what evil men suggest) can have any doubt of who is sovereign. The difficulty consists in the evidence of authority derived from him, the removal of it depending on knowledge of public registers, public counsels, public ministers, and public seals by which all laws are sufficiently verified. Laws are verified, I say, not authorized. For verification is but the testimony and record, not the authority of the law which consists in the command only of the sovereign.

If therefore a man has a question of injury depending on the law of nature—that is to say, on common equity—the sentence of the judge who has authority by commission to recognize such causes is a sufficient verification of the law of nature in that individual case. For though the advice of one who professes the study of the law is useful for avoiding contention, it is only advice. It is the judge who must tell men what is law upon hearing the controversy.

When the question is of injury or crime upon a written law, every man by recourse to the registers by himself or by others may (if he will) be sufficiently informed before he does such injury or commits the crime whether it is an injury or not. He ought to do so for when a man doubts whether the act he goes about is just or unjust and may inform himself (if he will) that the doing is unlawful. Similarly, he who thinks himself injured might complain before he consults with the law. In this case he does so unjustly and betrays a disposition rather to vex other men than to demand his own right.[48]

If the question is of obedience to a public officer, to have seen his commission with the public seal and heard it read or to have had the means to be informed of it . . . is a sufficient verification of his authority. For every man is obliged to do his best to inform himself of all written laws that may concern his own future actions.

When the legislator is known and the laws are sufficiently published either by writing or by the light of nature, there is needed another material circumstance to make them obligatory. For it is not the letter but the intent or meaning—that is to say, the authentic interpretation of the law (which is the sense of the legislator) in which the law consists. Therefore the interpretation of all laws depends on sovereign authority and the interpreters are none but those which the sovereign (to whom only the subject owes obedience) shall appoint. For otherwise by the craft of an interpreter the law may be made to bear a sense contrary to that of the sovereign by which means the interpreter becomes the legislator.

All written and unwritten laws need interpretation. The unwritten law of nature is easy to interpret without partiality and passion and leaves violators without excuse. But considering there are very few—perhaps none—who in some cases are not blinded by self-love or some other passion makes the law of nature of all laws the most obscure and has consequently the greatest need of able interpreters. If the written laws are short they are easily misinterpreted from diverse significations

---

47. This is an additional law of nature to be added to those appearing in Chapters XIII and XIV. In his various works on social and political topics, there are about twenty laws of nature.
48. We might recognize this comment as applying to frivolous lawsuits.

of a word or two. If they are long, they are more obscure by the diverse significations of many words insomuch as no written law that is delivered in a few or many words can be well understood without a perfect understanding of the final causes for which the law was made. Knowledge of final causes is in the legislator. To him therefore there cannot be any knot in the law that is insoluble either by finding out the ends by which to undo it or by making what ends he will (as Alexander did with his sword in the Gordian knot) by the legislative power which no other interpreter can do.

Interpretation of the laws of nature in a commonwealth do not depend on the books of moral philosophy. The authority of writers does not make their opinions law no matter whether they are true without the authority of the commonwealth.[49] That which I have written in this treatise concerning the moral virtues and of their necessity for procuring and maintaining peace, though it is evident truth, is not therefore presently law, but because it is in all commonwealths in the world it is part of the civil law. Though it is naturally reasonable, it is by the sovereign power that it is law. Otherwise, it is a great error to call the laws of nature unwritten law of which we see so many volumes published and so many contradictions between and within themselves.

The interpretation of the law of nature is the sentence of the judge constituted by the sovereign authority to hear and determine such controversies as depend thereon, and consists in the application of the law to the present case. In the act of judicature, the judge does no more than consider whether the demand of the party is consonant to natural reason and equity. The sentence he gives is therefore of the law of nature and is authentic because he gives it by authority of the sovereign, not because it is private sentence, whereby it becomes the sovereign's sentence which is law for that time to the pleading parties.

Because there is no judge subordinate nor sovereign who may err in a judgment of equity, if there is another case later that he finds more consonant to equity to give a contrary sentence, he is obliged to do it. No man's error becomes his own law nor obliges him to persist in it. Neither (for the same reason) does it become a law to other judges though sworn to follow it. If he knows and allows it, a wrong sentence given by authority of the sovereign in laws that are mutable is constitution of a new law in cases in which every little circumstance is the same. Yet in immutable laws, such as are the laws of nature, they are not laws to the same or other judges in like cases ever after. Princes succeed one another and one judge passes, and another comes. Even Heaven and Earth shall pass, but not one title of the law of nature shall pass for it is the eternal law of God. Therefore all the sentences of preceding judges

---

49. Again, Hobbes will have nothing to do with the claim that there are justifiable means by which anyone may claim to be an interpreter of laws except the sovereign. This is also another indication of not trusting the "authority of books" or famous authors. Just as the individual human being has the capacity and perhaps the obligation to determine for himself what is true or false, so also the sovereign person, as the sole legislator, has the right, the capacity, and the obligation to determine and interpret the natural law. For anyone else to do so is to leave open the possibility of civil war.

that have ever been cannot all together make a law contrary to natural equity. Nor can any examples of a former judge warrant an unreasonable sentence or discharge the present judge of the trouble of studying what is equity (in the case he is to judge) from the principles of his own natural reason. For example, it is against the law of nature to punish the innocent and he is innocent who acquits himself judicially and is acknowledged innocent by the judge. Consider the case now when a man is accused of a capital crime. Seeing the powers of malice of some enemy and the frequent corruption and partiality of judges he runs away for fear of the event and afterward is taken, brought to a legal trial, and makes it sufficiently appear that he was not guilty of the crime. Being acquitted of it, he is nevertheless condemned to lose his goods and this is a clear condemnation of the innocent. I say therefore that there is no place in the world where this can be an interpretation of a law of nature or made a law by the sentences of preceding judges who had done the same. For he who judged it first judged unjustly and no injustice can be a pattern of judgment to succeeding judges. A written law may forbid innocent men to flee and they may be punished for fleeing. But that fleeing for fear of injury should be taken for presumption of guilt after a man is already absolved of the crime judicially is contrary to the nature of a presumption which has no place after judgment is given. Yet this is set down by a great lawyer for the common law of England. "If a man," said he, "who is innocent is accused of a felony, . . . he shall notwithstanding his innocence forfeit all his goods, chattels, debts, and duties. For as to the forfeiture of them, the law will admit no proof against the presumption in law grounded upon his flight." Here you see an innocent man, judicially acquitted, notwithstanding his innocence (when no written law forbade him to fly) after his acquittal, upon presumption in law condemned to lose all the goods he has. If the law ground upon his flight a presumption of fact (which was capital) the sentence ought to have been capital. If the presumption was not of the fact for that, then ought he to lose his goods? This therefore is no law of England nor is the condemnation grounded upon a presumption of law. It is grounded upon the presumption of judges. It is also against law to say that no proof shall be admitted against a presumption of law. For all judges, sovereign and subordinate, refuse to do justice if they refuse to hear proof. Though the sentence is just, the judges who condemn without hearing the proofs offered are unjust judges and their presumption is prejudice which no man ought to bring with him to the seat of justice no matter what preceding judgments or examples he pretends to follow. There are other things of this nature in which men's judgments have been perverted by trusting to precedents. But this is enough to show that though the sentence of the judge is a law to the pleading party, yet it is not law to any judge who shall succeed him in that office.

In like manner he is not the interpreter of laws who writes commentary on them when the question is the meaning of written laws. For commentaries are commonly more subject to cavil than the text. Therefore there need other commentaries—and so there will be no end of such interpretation. Therefore, unless there is an interpreter authorized by the sovereign from which the subordinate judges are not to recede, the interpreter can be no other than ordinary judges in the same manner as they are in cases of unwritten law. Their sentences are to be taken by them who plead for laws in that particular case but not to bind other judges in like cases to give like judgments. For a judge may err in the interpretation even of written laws, but no error of a subordinate judge can change the law which is the general sentence of the sovereign.

Men used to distinguish between the sentence and the letter of the law in written laws. When by the letter it is meant whatever can be gathered from bare words, it is well distinguished. For the significations of almost all words are either in themselves or in the metaphorical use of them ambiguous and may be drawn in argument to make many senses. But there is only one sense of the law. If by the letter is meant the literal sense, then the letter and the sentence or intention of the law is all one. For the literal sense is that which the legislator is always supposed to be equity. It is a great contumely for a judge to think otherwise of the sovereign. He ought therefore—if the word of the law does not fully authorize a reasonable sentence—to supply it with the law of nature. Or if the case is difficult, to respite judgment until he has received more ample authority. For example, a written law ordains that he who is thrust out of his house by force shall be restored by force. It happens that a man by negligence leaves his house empty and returning is kept out by force in which case there is no special law ordained. It is evident that this case is contained in the same law, otherwise there is no remedy for him at all, which is supposed to be against the intention of the legislator. Again, the word of the law commands to judge according to evidence. A man is falsely accused of a fact which the judge saw himself done by another and not by he who is accused. In this case neither shall the letter of the law be followed to the condemnation of the innocent nor shall the judge give sentence against the evidence of the witness because the letter of the law is to the contrary. But procure of the sovereign that another be made judge and himself witness. The incommodity that follows the bare words of a written law may lead him to the intention of the law whereby to interpret the same the better, though no incommodity can warrant a sentence against the law. For every judge of right and wrong is not judge of what is commodious or incommodious to the commonwealth.

The abilities required in a good interpreter of the law—that is to say, in a good judge—are not the same with those of an advocate, namely the study of the laws. As a judge ought to take notice of the fact from none but witnesses, so also he ought to take notice of the law from nothing but statutes and constitutions of the sovereign. These may be alleged in the pleading. They may also be declared to him by some who have authority from the sovereign to declare them. . . . For it shall be given him what he shall say concerning the fact by witnesses and what he shall say in point of law from those who shall in their pleadings show it and by authority interpret it upon the place. The lords of Parliament in England were judges and most difficult causes have been heard and determined by them. Yet few of them were much versed in the study of the laws and fewer had made a profession of them, and though they consulted with lawyers who were appointed to be present for the purpose, yet they alone had authority to give sentence. In like manner in the ordinary trials of right, twelve men of the common people are judges and give sentence not only of the fact but of the right and pronounce simply for the complainant or for the defendant. That is to say, they are judges not only of the fact but of the right and in question of crime they determine not only whether it was done or not done, but also whether it is murder, homicide, felony, assault, and the like, which are determinations of law. But because they are not supposed to know the law themselves, there is one who has authority to inform them of it in the particular case in which they are to be judge. But if they do not judge according to what he tells them, they are not subject thereby to any penalty unless it is made to appear they did it against their consciences or had been corrupted by reward. The things that make a good judge or good interpreter of the laws are, first, a right understanding of that principal law of nature called equity. It does not depend on the readings of other men's writings but, on the goodness of a man's own natural reason and meditation, it is presumed to be most in those who have the most leisure and most inclination to meditate thereon. Second, contempt of unnecessary riches and preferment. Third, to be able in judgment to divest himself of all fear, anger, hatred, love, and compassion. Fourth, and last, patience to hear, diligent attention in hearing, and memory to retain, digest, and apply what he has heard.

The difference and division of laws has been made in different ways according to the different methods of those men who have written of them. For it is a thing depending on the scope of the writer and is subservient to every man's proper method and not dependent upon nature. . . .

Laws are also divided into natural and positive. Natural are those which have been laws from all eternity and are called not only natural but also moral laws and consist in the moral virtues such as justice, equity, and all the habits of the mind that conduce to peace and charity, of which I have already spoken in Chapters XIV and XV.

Positive laws are those which have not been laws for eternity but have been made by the will of those who have had sovereign power over others and are either written or made known to men by some other argument of the will of their legislator. Again, some positive laws are human and some are divine and of human positive laws some are distributive and some are penal. Distributive laws are those that determine the rights of subjects, declaring to every man what it is by which he acquires and holds a propriety in lands or goods and a right or liberty of action. These speak to all the subjects. Penal laws are those that declare what penalty shall be inflicted on those who violate the law and speak to the ministers and officers ordained for execution. For though everyone ought to be informed of the punishments ordained beforehand for their transgression, the command is not addressed to the delinquent (who cannot be supposed will faithfully punish himself) but to public ministers appointed to see the penalty executed. These penal laws are for the most part written together with the distributive laws and are sometimes called judgments. For all laws are general judgments or sentences of the legislator and also every particular judgment is law to him whose case is judged.

Divine positive laws (or natural laws, being eternal and universal, are all divine) are those which are commandments of God (not from all eternity or universally addressed to all men but only to certain people or to certain persons) are declared to be so by those God has authorized to declare them. How can the authority of a man to declare what are the positive laws of God be known? God may command a man by supernatural means to deliver laws to other men. But because it is of the essence of law that he who is obliged be assured of the authority of him who declares it—which we cannot naturally take notice to be from God—how can a man without supernatural revelation be assured of the revelation received by the declarer? How can he be bound to obey them? It is evidently impossible for a man to be assured of the revelation of another without a revelation particularly to himself. For though a man may be induced to believe such revelation from the miracles they see him do or from seeing the extraordinary sanctity of his life or from seeing the extraordinary wisdom or felicity of his actions—all of which are marks of God's extraordinary favor—yet they are not assured evidence of special revelation. Miracles are marvelous works, but that which is marvelous to one may not be so to another. Sanctity may be faked and the visible felicities of this world are most often the work of God by natural and ordinary causes. Therefore no man can infallibly know by natural reason that another has had a supernatural revelation of God's will, but only a belief. Everyone (as the signs thereof shall appear greater or lesser) a firmer or weaker belief.

How he can be bound to obey them in the second case is not so hard. For if the declared law is not against the law of nature (which is undoubtedly God's law) and he undertakes to obey it, he is bound by his own act. He is bound to obey it but not bound to believe it, for men's beliefs and interior thoughts are not subject to the commands, but only to the ordinary or extraordinary operation of God. Faith of supernatural law is not fulfilling but only assenting to the same and not a duty that we exhibit to God. It is a gift which God freely gives to whom he pleases as also unbelief is not a breach of any of his laws but a rejection of all of them except natural laws. But this that I say will be made even clearer by the examples and testimonies concerning this point in Holy Scripture. The covenant God made with Abraham (in a supernatural manner) was thus (Gen. 17.10) "This is the covenant which you shall observe between me and yourself and your seed after you." Abraham's seed did not have this revelation nor yet did they exist, but they are a party to the covenant and bound to obey what Abraham should declare to them for God's law which they could not be but in virtue of the obedience they owed to their parents, who (if they are subject to no other earthly power, as here in the case of Abraham) have sovereign power over their children and servants. Again, where God said to Abraham, "In you all Nations of the Earth are blessed: for I know you will command your children and your house after you to keep the way of the Lord and to observe righteousness and judgment," it is manifest the obedience of his family, who had no revelation, depends on their former obligation to obey their sovereign. At Mount Sinai Moses only went up to God. The people were forbidden to approach on pain of death, yet they were bound to obey all that Moses declared to them for God's law. Upon what ground, but on this submission of their own, "Speak to us, and we will hear you; but let not God speak to us, lest we die?" By which two places it sufficiently appears that in a commonwealth a subject who has no certain and assured revelation particularly to himself concerning the will of God is to obey for such is the command of the commonwealth. For if men were at liberty to take for God's commandments their own dreams and fancies, or the dreams and fancies of private men, scarce two men would agree upon what is God's commandment. And yet in respect of them, every man would despise the commandments of the commonwealth. I conclude, therefore, that in all things not contrary to the moral law (that is to say, to the law of nature) all subjects are bound to obey that for divine law which is declared to be so by the laws of the commonwealth. Which also is evident to any man's reason, for whatsoever is not against the law of nature may be made law in the name of them who have the sovereign power. And there is no reason men should be less obliged by it when it is propounded in the name of God. Besides, there is no place in the world where men are permitted to pretend other commandments of God than are declared for such by the commonwealth. Christian states punish those who revolt from Christian religion, and all other states, those that set up any religion forbidden by them. For in whatsoever is not regulated by the commonwealth, it is equity (which is the law of nature and therefore an eternal law of God) that every man equally enjoy his liberty.

There is also another distinction of laws into fundamental and not fundamental. But I could never see in any author what a fundamental law signifies. Nevertheless, one may very reasonably distinguish laws in that manner.

A fundamental law in every commonwealth is that, when taken away, the commonwealth fails and is utterly dissolved, as a building whose foundation is destroyed. Therefore a fundamental law is that by which subjects are bound to uphold whatsoever power is given to the sovereign, whether a monarch or a sovereign assembly, without which the commonwealth cannot stand, such as is the power of war and peace, of judicature, of election of officers, and of doing whatever he shall think necessary for the public good. A law is not a fundamental law when its abrogation does not draw with it the commonwealth's dissolution, such as laws concerning controversies between subjects. . . .

I find the words *Lex Civilis* and *Jus Civile* (law and civil right) promiscuously used for the same thing even in the most learned authors. This nevertheless ought not to be so. For right is liberty, namely that liberty which the civil laws leave us. But civil law is an obligation and takes from us the liberty which the law of nature gave us. Nature gave a right to every man to secure himself by his own strength and to invade a suspected neighbor by way of prevention. But the civil law takes away that liberty in all cases where the protection of the law may be safely assured. So *Lex* and *Jus* are as different as obligation and liberty.

Likewise, laws and charters are taken promiscuously for the same thing. But charters are donations of the sovereign and not laws and are instead exemptions from law. The phrase of a law is "I command, and enjoin." The phrase of a charter is "I have given, I have granted." But what is given or granted to a man is not forced upon by him by a law. A law may be made to bind all the subjects of a commonwealth. A liberty or charter is only to one man or some single part of the people. For to say all the people of a commonwealth have liberty in any case whatsoever is to say that in such case there has been no law made or if it has been made, it is now abrogated.

Chapter XXVII. Of Crimes, Excuses, and Extenuations

Hobbes is careful to provide an explanation of times and cases in which people may be excused for breaking laws. Sometimes, there are extenuating circumstances that mitigate responsibility for a crime; sometimes, a person may be excused for breaking a law. And sometimes, there are no excuses. Hobbes explains the difference between such cases, noting the relevance of understanding, reasoning, passions, the wide publication and distribution of information on laws, and the capacity of the subjects to understand them. Chapter XXVII's most striking feature is that Hobbes will not allow that what a person intends, or about which he thinks, may be considered a crime. Another way to put the case is that no one can be accused and punished by the state for his thoughts or intentions or even for his beliefs (or lack of them), but only for his actions.

A sin is both a transgression of a law and any contempt of the legislator. Such contempt is a breach of all his laws at once and therefore may consist not only in the commission of a fact or in speaking words forbidden by law or in the omission of what the law commands, but also in the intention or purpose to transgress. This is true because to break the law is some degree of contempt of him to whom it belongs to see it executed. To be delighted in the imagination only of being possessed of another man's goods, servants, or wife without any intention to take them by force or fraud is not a breach of the law that says, "Thou shalt not covet." Nor is the pleasure a man has in imagining or dreaming of the death of him from whose life he expects nothing but damage and displeasure a sin. But resolving to put some act in execution that tends thereto is a sin. To be pleased in the fiction of what would please a man if it were real is a passion so connected to the nature both of a man and every other living creature as to make it a sin would be to make it a sin to be a man. The consideration of this has made me think them too severe toward themselves and others who maintain that the first motions of the mind (though checked with the fear of God) are sins.[50] But I confess it is safer to err on that hand than on the other.

A crime is a sin consisting in committing (by deed or word) of what the law forbids or the omission of what it has commanded. So every crime is a sin but not every sin is a crime. To intend to steal or kill is a sin even if it never appears in word

---

50. This is contrary to many Christian theologians, who taught it is possible to sin, even through an act not committed outwardly. See Matt. 5.28 and Augustine's *Civitate Dei* [*City of God*], XIX.13 (*City of God*, trans. Henry Bettenson [New York: Penguin Classics, 2003]).

or fact. . . . But . . . crime signifies the sin of which one man may accuse another. There is no place for human accusation for intentions, which never appear by any outward act. . . .

From the relation of sin to law and of crime to civil law, it may be inferred, first, that where law ceases, sin ceases. But because the law of nature is eternal, violations of covenants, ingratitude, arrogance and all facts contrary to any moral virtue can never cease to be sin. Second, that when civil law ceases, crimes cease because when there is no other law remaining but that of nature, there is no place for accusation with every man being his own judge and accused only by his own conscience and cleared by the uprightness of his own intention. Therefore, when his intention is right, his fact is no sin. If otherwise, his fact is a sin but not a crime. Third, when the sovereign power ceases, crime also ceases because where there is no such power, there is no protection from the law and therefore everyone may protect himself by his own power. Everyone may protect himself by his own power because no man in the institution of sovereign power can be supposed to give away the right of preserving his own body, for the safety whereof all sovereignty was ordained. But this is to be understood only of those who have not themselves contributed to taking away the power that protected them because that is a crime from the beginning.

A defect of the understanding or some error in reasoning, or some sudden force of the passions is the source of every crime. Defect in understanding is ignorance. Defect in reasoning is erroneous opinion. Again, ignorance is of three sorts—of the law, of the sovereign, and of the penalty. Ignorance of the law of nature excuses no man because every man who has attained the use of reason is supposed to know he ought not to do to another that which he would not have done to himself. Therefore, if he does anything contrary to that law it is a crime no matter into what place he comes. If a man comes here from the Indies and persuades men here to receive a new religion or teach them anything tending to disobedience of the laws of this country—no matter how well persuaded of the truth of what he teaches—commits a crime and may be justly punished for it not only because his doctrine is false but also because he does what he would not approve in another, namely, that coming from here he should try to alter the religion there.[51] But ignorance of the civil law shall excuse a man in a strange country until it is declared to him—because until then no civil law is binding.[52]

---

51. Missionaries, or anyone who attempts to change laws or the established religion—Hobbes has already contended that "religious" beliefs not accepted by the sovereign are actually only superstitions—are therefore, for Hobbes, dangerous to the commonwealth and have committed a crime.

52. It might be the case, for example, that there is a civil law in a country requiring payment of tax on a particular service rendered by another person. If the laws in a stranger's country do not include this and if the country in which that stranger is now visiting or residing does include it but the law is not made clear (for example, the law is buried in a dense book of laws and not widely published), the person is excused. Hobbes has been careful regarding his explanation of laws, saying that ignorance of law is not an excuse except in cases in which ignorance of law is not the fault of the person who violates it. See below in this chapter, for example, Hobbes' explanation of laws that are not widely or clearly published.

In a similar way, if the civil law of a man's own country is not sufficiently declared so that he may know it if he wishes to know it, nor the action against the law of nature, ignorance is a good excuse. In other cases, ignorance of the civil law does not excuse. Ignorance of sovereign power in the place of a man's ordinary residence does not excuse him because he ought to take notice of the power by which he has been protected there. Ignorance of the penalty where the law is declared excuses no one. For in breaking the law, the law was only vain words to him without a fear of penalty to follow, he undergoes the penalty even though he does not know what it is. This is true since whoever voluntarily does any action accepts all known consequences of it and punishment is a known consequence of the violation of laws in every commonwealth. He is subject to punishment already determined by the law. If this is not the case, then he is subject to arbitrary punishment. For this reason, when he does injury without other limitation than his own will, he should suffer punishment without other limitation than that of the person's will whose law is thereby violated.

When a penalty is either annexed to the crime in the law or has been usually inflicted in similar cases, the delinquent is excused from greater penalty. If the punishment foreknown is not great enough to deter men from the action, it is an invitation to it. When men compare the benefit of their injustice with the harm of their punishment, they choose by necessity of nature what appears best for themselves, and therefore when they are punished more than the law had formerly determined or more than others were punished for the same crime, the law tempted and deceived them.

No law made after a fact is done can make it a crime because if it is against the law of nature, the law existed before the fact and a positive law cannot be taken notice of before it is made. And therefore it cannot be obligatory. But when the law forbidding a fact is made before the fact is done, he who does it is liable to the penalty ordained after in a case in which no lesser penalty was made known before either by writing or by example for the reason already alleged.

From defect in reasoning (i.e., from error), men are prone to violate the laws in three ways. First, by presumption from false principles such as when men have observed how in all places and ages unjust actions have been authorized by the force and victories of those who committed them. Potent men break through the laws of their country like cobwebs and the weaker sort, like those who have failed in their enterprises, have been considered the only criminals and have thereupon taken for principles and grounds of their reasoning "that justice is but a vain word. That whatever a man can get by his own industry and hazard is his own: that the practice of all nations cannot be unjust; that examples of former times are good arguments for doing the same again," and many more of that time. If these are granted, no act in itself can be a crime but must be made so (not by the law but) by the success of those who commit it. And the same fact is virtuous or vicious as fortune pleases. . . . Second, teachers who either misinterpret the law of nature and make it repugnant to the civil law or who teach doctrines of their own or traditions of former times as laws are inconsistent with the duty of a subject.

Third, by erroneous inferences from true principles (which happens commonly to men who are hasty and precipitate in concluding and resolving what to do such as those who have both great opinion of their own understanding and believe things of this nature do not require time and study but only common experience and a good natural wit). Of this no man thinks himself unprovided, whereas knowledge of right and wrong which is no less difficult no man will pretend to without great and long study. Of those defects in reasoning, there is none that can excuse (though some of them may extenuate) a crime in any man who pretends to the administration of his own private business and much less in them who undertake a public charge because they pretend to the reason upon the want of which they would ground their excuse.

Of the passions that most frequently are causes of crime one is vain-glory—or foolish overrating of their own worth—as if difference of worth was an effect of their wit or riches or blood or some other natural quality that does not depend on the will of those who have sovereign authority. From this proceeds a presumption that the punishments ordained by the laws and extended generally to all subjects ought not to be inflicted on them with the same rigor they are inflicted on poor, obscure, and simple men comprehended under the name of the vulgar.

Therefore it commonly happens that those who value themselves by the greatness of their wealth adventure on crimes upon the hope of escaping punishment by corrupting public justice or obtaining pardon by money or other rewards. Those who have many potent relatives and popular men who have gained reputation among the multitude take courage to violate the laws from hope of oppressing the power to whom it belongs to put them in execution. Those who have a great and false opinion of their own wisdom take upon them to reprehend the actions and call in question the authority of those who govern and unsettle the laws with their public discourse saying that nothing shall be a crime but what their own designs require should be so. It happens also to the same men to be prone to all such crimes that consists in craft and in deceiving their neighbors because they think their designs are too subtle to be perceived. I say these actions are effects of false presumption of their own wisdom. For of them who are first movers in the disturbance of commonwealth (which can never happen without a civil war) very few are left alive long enough to see their new designs established so that the benefit of their crimes redounds to posterity and such as would least have wished it. This argues that they are not as wise as they thought they were. Those who deceive upon hope of not being observed commonly deceive themselves (the darkness in which they believe they lie hidden is nothing but their own blindness) and are no wiser than children who think all is hidden by hiding their own eyes. And generally, all vain-glorious men (unless they are completely timorous) are subject to anger as being more prone than others to interpret for contempt the ordinary liberty of conversation. And there are few crimes that may not be produced by anger.

What crimes the passions of hate, lust, ambition, and covetousness are apt to produce is obvious to every man's experience and understanding as there needs nothing to be said of them except that they are infirmities so annexed to the nature of both man and all other living creatures as that their effects cannot be hindered except by ordinary use of reason or a constant severity in punishing them. For in those things men hate, they find continual and unavoidable molestation whereby either a man's patience must be everlasting or he must be eased by removing the power of that which molests him. The former is difficult and the latter is many times impossible without some violation of the law. Ambition and covetousness are passions that are perpetually incumbent and pressing while reason is not perpetually present to resist them. Therefore whenever the hope of impunity appears, their effects proceed. For lust, what it wants in lasting it has in vehemence which suffices to weigh down the apprehension of all easy or uncertain punishments.

Of all the passions, the one which inclines men least to break the laws is fear. In fact (except for some generous natures) it is the only thing (when there is appearance of profit or pleasure by breaking the laws) that makes men keep them. And yet in many cases a crime may be committed through fear. For not every fear justifies the actions it produces but the fear only of corporeal hurt which we call bodily fear and from which a man cannot see how to be delivered except by the action. A man is assaulted and fears present death from which he does not see how to escape except by wounding the person who assaulted him. If he wounds him to death this is not a crime because no man is supposed at the making of commonwealth to have abandoned the defense of his life or limbs where the law cannot arrive in time to assist him. But to kill a man because from his actions or threats I may argue he will kill me when he can (seeing I have time and means to demand protection from the sovereign power) is a crime. Again, a man receives words of disgrace or some little injuries (for which they who made the laws assigned no punishment and did not think it worthy of a man who has the use of reason to take notice of) and is afraid that unless he revenges it he will fall into contempt and consequently be obnoxious to the like injuries from others. To avoid this, he breaks the law and protects himself for the future by the terror of his private revenge. This is a crime. For the hurt is not corporeal but fantastical and (though in this corner of the world made sensible by a custom not many years since begun among young and vain men) so light as a gallant man and one assured of his own courage cannot take notice of. Also, a man may stand in fear of spirits either through his own superstition or through too much credit given to other men who tell him of strange dreams and visions and thereby he is made to believe they will hurt him for doing or omitting different things which nevertheless to do or to omit is contrary to the laws. That which is so done or omitted is not to be excused by this fear but is a crime. For (as I have shown before in the Chapter II) dreams are naturally the fancies remaining in sleep after the impressions our senses had formerly received in waking. When men are for whatever reason not sure they have slept they seem to be real visions. Therefore he who presumes to break the law upon his own or another's dream, pretended vision, or the fancy of the power of invisible spirits . . . breaks the law of nature which is a certain offense. It follows the imagery of his own or another private man's brain. He can never know whether it signifies anything or nothing or whether he who tells his dream says truly or lies. If every private man should have leave to do (as they must by the law of nature if anyone has it) there could be no law made to hold and so all commonwealths would be dissolved.

From these different sources of crimes it appears already that all crimes are not (as the stoics of old time maintained) of the same type. There is place not only for excuse by which that which seemed a crime is proved not to be one at all but also for extenuation by which the crime that seemed great is made less. For though all crimes equally deserve the name of injustice as all deviation from a straight line is equally crookedness, which the stoics rightly observed. Yet it does not follow that all crimes are equally unjust any more than that all crooked lines are equally crooked, which the stoics did not observe and held it as great a crime to kill a hen against the law as to kill one's father.

That which totally excuses a fact and takes away from it the nature of a crime is none but that which at the same time takes away the obligation of the law. If he who committed a fact against the law is obliged to the law, there can be no other than a crime.

The want of means to know the law totally excuses. For the law of which a man has no means to inform himself is not obligatory. But lack of diligence to inquire shall not be considered a want of means nor shall any man who pretends to reason enough for the government of his own affairs be supposed to want the means to know the laws of nature because they are known by the reason to which he pretends. Only children and madmen are excused from offenses against the natural law.

Where a man is captive or in the power of the enemy (and he is then in the power of the enemy when his person or his means of living is so) if it is not his own fault, the obligation of the law ceases because he must obey the enemy or die. And consequently such obedience is not a crime for no man is obliged (when the protection of the law fails) not to protect himself by the best means he can.

If by the terror of present death a man is compelled to do a fact against the law, he is totally excused because no law can oblige a man to abandon his own preservation. And supposing such a law was obligatory, a man would reason thus: "If I do not do it, I die now. If I do it, I die afterward. Therefore, by doing it there is time of life gained." Nature therefore compels him to the fact.

When a man is destitute of food or other things necessary for his life and cannot preserve himself any other way but by some fact against the law, as if in great famine he takes the food by force or stealth that he cannot obtain for money or charity or in defense of his life he snatches away another man's sword, he is totally excused for the reason previously alleged.

Again, facts done against the law by authority of another are by that authority excused against the author because no man ought to accuse his own fact in another that is but his instrument. But it is not excused against a third person thereby injured because in the violation of the law both the author and the actor are criminals. From this it follows that when that man or assembly that has sovereign power commands a man to do what is contrary to a former law, doing it is totally excused. For he ought not to condemn it himself because he is the author and what cannot justly be condemned by the sovereign cannot be justly punished by any other. Besides, when the sovereign commands anything to be done against his own former law, the command as to that particular fact is an abrogation of the law.

If the man or assembly having sovereign power disclaims any right essential to sovereignty and there accrues from this to the subject any liberty inconsistent with sovereign power—that is to say with the very being of a commonwealth if the subject refuses to obey the command in anything contrary to the liberty granted—this is a sin and contrary to the duty of the subject. For he ought to take notice of what is inconsistent with the sovereignty because it was erected by his own consent and for his own defense and that such liberty that is inconsistent with it was granted through ignorance of the evil consequence of it. But if he not only disobeys but also resists a public minister in the execution of it then it is a crime because he might have been righted (without any breach of the peace) upon complaint.

The degrees of crime are taken on diverse scales and measured first by the malignity of the source or cause, second by the contagion of the example, third by the mischief of the effect, and fourth by the concurrence of times, places, and persons.

If the same fact done against the law proceeds from presumption of strength, riches, or friends to resist those who are to execute the law, it is a greater crime than if it proceeds from hope of not being discovered or of escape by flight. For presumption of impunity by force is a root from which springs at all time and upon all temptations a contempt of all laws. Whereas in the latter case the apprehension of danger that makes a man fly renders him more obedient for the future. A crime which we know to be so is greater than the same crime proceeding from a false persuasion that it is lawful. For he who commits it against his own conscience presumes on his force or other power which encourages him to commit the same again. But he who does it by error after the error is shown to him is conformable to the law.

He whose error proceeds from the authority of a teacher or a publicly authorized interpreter of the law is not so faulty as he whose error proceeds from a peremptory pursuit of his own principles and reasoning. For what is taught by one who teaches by public authority is taught by the commonwealth and has a resemblance of law until the same authority controls it. All crimes that do not contain denial of sovereign power and that are not against evident law are excused totally, while he who grounds his actions on his private judgment ought according to the rectitude or error thereof to stand or fall.[53]

---

53. With liberty and reason come responsibility. It is consistent with Hobbes' contention—and that of other modernists—that government exists by the consent of the governed and that the subjects are responsible for what the sovereign does. The same goes for reasoning where reason is sovereign. Hobbes explains that if a person commissioned by the commonwealth to teach subjects teaches them something unlawful, the subjects are not as culpable (i.e., blameworthy or guilty) because what they have been taught is a matter of power and rule of the commonwealth. On the other hand, if a person makes a judgment and acts on it on his own, he is more culpable because he has only his own reason for a guide. While this may seem at first glance to be an argument for not trusting one's own reason, it clearly is not. Individual reason is one of the hallmarks of modernity. Just as we take responsibility for the creation of the commonwealth, so also we take responsibility for any and all actions we undertake as a result of our own reasoning.

If the same fact has been constantly punished in other men it is a greater crime than if there have been many preceding examples of impunity. For those examples are so many hopes of impunity given by the sovereign himself. Because he who furnishes a man with such hope and presumption of mercy that encourages him to offend has his part in the offense and cannot reasonably charge the offender with the whole.

A crime arising from sudden passion is not so great as when the same arises from long meditation. For in the former case there is a place for extenuation in the common infirmity of human nature. But he who does it with premeditation has used circumspection and cast his eye on the law, on the punishment, and on the consequence of it to human society, all of which in committing the crime he has contemned and postponed to his own appetite. But there is no suddenness of passion sufficient for a total excuse. For all the time between first knowing the law and the commission of the fact shall be taken for a time of deliberation because he ought by meditation of the law to rectify the irregularity of his passions.

Where the law is publicly and with assiduity before all the people read and interpreted, a fact done against it is a greater crime than where men are left without such instruction to inquire of it with difficulty, uncertainty, and interruption of their callings and be informed by private men. For in this case, part of the fault is discharged upon common infirmity but in the former there is apparent negligence which is not without some contempt of the sovereign power. Tacit approbation of the sovereign extenuates those facts which the law expressly condemns but the lawmaker by other manifest signs of his will tacitly approves. They are less crimes than the same facts condemned by both the law and lawmaker. For seeing the will of the lawmaker is a law there appears in this case two contradictory laws which would totally excuse if men were bound to take notice of the sovereign's approbation by other arguments than are expressed by his command. But because there are punishments that are consequent not only to transgression of his law but also to observing it, he is in part a cause of the transgression and therefore cannot reasonably impute the whole crime to the delinquent. For example, the law condemns duels and the punishment is made capital. On the contrary part, he who refuses a duel is subject to contempt and scorn without remedy and sometimes is thought by the sovereign himself to be unworthy to have any charge or preferment in war. If based on this he accepts a duel he ought not in reason to be rigorously punished because all men lawfully endeavor to obtain the good opinion of them who have sovereign power. Part of the fault may be discharged on the punisher. I say this not as wishing liberty of private revenges or any other kind of disobedience, but care in governors not to countenance anything obliquely which they directly forbid. The examples of princes to those who see them are and always have been more potent to govern their actions than the laws themselves. Though it is our duty to do what they say and not what they do, that duty will never be performed until it pleases God to give men an extraordinary and supernatural grace to follow that precept.

Again, if we compare crimes by the mischief of their effects, when the same fact redounds to the damage of many it is greater than when it redounds to the hurt of few. Therefore when a fact hurts not only in the present but also (by example) in the future it is a greater crime than if it hurt only in the present. For the former is a fertile crime and multiplies to the hurt of many. The latter is barren. To maintain doctrines contrary to the religion established in the commonwealth is a greater fault in an authorized preacher than in a private person. It is also a greater crime to live profanely, incontinently, or to do any irreligious act. Likewise in a professor of law who maintains any point or does any act that tends to weaken the sovereign power is a greater crime than in another man. Also in a man who has such reputation for wisdom that his counsels are followed or his actions are imitated by many, his fact against the law is a greater crime than the fact in another. For such men not only commit crime but teach it for law to all other men. Generally all crimes are greater by the scandal they give—that is to say, by becoming stumbling blocks to the weak who look not so much upon the way they go in as upon the light that other men carry before them.

Acts of hostility against the present state of the commonwealth are greater crimes than the same acts done to private men. For the damage extends itself to all. Examples are betraying the strengths or revealing the secrets of the commonwealth to an enemy, all attempts upon the representative of the commonwealth (monarch or assembly) and all endeavors by word or deed to diminish the authority of the same either now or in succession . . . and consist in design or act contrary to a fundamental law.

Likewise, those crimes which render judgments of no effect are greater crimes than injuries done to one or a few persons, such as to receive money to give false judgment or testimony is a greater crime than otherwise to deceive a man of the like or a greater sum. This is true because not only he who was wronged falls by such judgments but all judgments are rendered useless and lead to force and private revenges.

Robbery and depeculation of the public treasure or revenues is a greater crime than robbing or defrauding a private man because to rob the public is to rob many at once. Also, the counterfeit usurpation of public ministry, counterfeiting public seals or public coin is a greater crime than counterfeiting a private man's person or his seal because the fraud extends to the damage of many.

Of facts against the law done to private men, the greater crime is that where the damage in the common opinion of men is most sensible. And therefore, to kill against the law is a greater crime than any other injury, life preserved. To kill with torment is greater than simply to kill. Mutilation of a limb is greater than spoiling a man of his goods. Spoiling a man of his goods by terror of death or wounds is greater than by clandestine surreption. Clandestine surreption is greater than by consent fraudulently obtained. Violation of chastity by force is greater than by flattery—and of a married woman than of an unmarried woman.

For all these things are commonly so valued even though some men are more and some less sensible of the same offense. But the law regards the general inclination of mankind, not the particular. Therefore the offense men take from contumely in words or gesture when they produce no other harm than the present grief of the person who is reproached has been neglected in the laws of the Greeks, Romans, and other ancient and modern commonwealths. Supposing the true cause of such grief to consist in the pusillanimity and not the contumely (which takes no hold upon men who are conscious of their own virtue) of him who is offended by it.

Also, a crime against a private man is much aggravated by the person, time, and place. To kill one's parent is a greater crime than to kill another for the parent ought to have the honor of a sovereign (though he has surrendered his power to the civil law) because he had it originally by nature. And to rob a poor man is a greater crime than to rob a rich man because it is to the poor a more sensible damage. A crime committed in the time or place appointed for devotion is greater than if committed at another time or place for it proceeds from greater contempt of the law. Many other cases of aggravation and extenuation might be added, but by these I have set down it is obvious to every man to take the attitude of any other crime proposed.

Lastly, in almost all crimes there is injury done not only to some private man but also to the commonwealth. The same crime is called public crime when the accusation is in the name of the commonwealth and it is a private crime when in the name of a private man. And pleas according to it called public, *judicia publica*, pleas of the crown or private pleas. As in an accusation of murder if the accuser is a private man the plea is a private plea. If the accuser is the sovereign, the plea is a public plea.

Chapter XXVIII. Of Punishments, and Rewards

For those who are responsible for the commission of crime, Hobbes provides specifications and clarifications concerning punishment. He also discusses rewards to a person for meritorious action. It is Hobbes' position that the law of nature prohibits the infliction of punishment for any reason but the correction of the offender or the instruction of the public. To inflict punishment out of hostility violates laws of nature. In this chapter, Hobbes also makes a distinction between subjects of a state and its enemies, clarifying his position that hostile action against an enemy is not punishment.

"A punishment is an evil inflicted by public authority on him who has done or omitted that which is judged by the same authority to be a transgression of the law to the end that the will of men may thereby be better disposed to obedience." Before I infer anything from this definition, there is a very important question to be answered. It is this. By what door the right or authority of punishing in any case came in. For by that which has been said before, no man is supposed bound by covenant not to resist violence and consequently it cannot be intended that he gave any right to another to lay violent hands upon his person. In making a commonwealth, every man gives away the right of defending another but not the right of defending himself. In addition, he obliges himself to assist him who has the sovereignty in punishing another. But of himself, this is not the case. To covenant to assist the sovereign in doing hurt to another is not to give him a right to punish unless he who so covenants has a right to do it himself. It is clear therefore that the right which the commonwealth (that is, he or they who represent it) has to punish is not grounded on any concession or gift of the subjects. But I have also shown formerly that before the institution of commonwealth, every man had a right to everything and to do whatever he thought necessary for his own preservation and subduing, hurting, or killing any many in order to do so. This is the foundation of that right of punishing which is exercised in every commonwealth. For the subjects did not give the sovereign that right, but only in laying down theirs they strengthened him to use his own as he should think fit for the preservation of all. So that it was not given but left to him and to him only and (excepting the limits set by natural law) as entire as in the condition of mere nature and of war of everyone against his neighbor.

From the definition of punishment I infer, first, that neither private revenges nor injuries of private men can properly be styled punishment because they do not proceed from public authority. Second, that to be neglected and unpreferred by the public favor is not a punishment because no new evil is thereby inflicted on any man. He is only left in the estate in which he existed before. Third, that the evil inflicted by public authority, without precedent public condemnation, is not to be styled by the name of punishment but of a hostile act because the fact for which a man is punished ought first to be judged by public authority to be a transgression of the law. Fourth, that the evil inflicted by usurped power and judges without authority from the sovereign is not punishment but is an act of hostility because acts of power usurped do not have the person condemned as their author and therefore are not acts of public authority. Fifth, that all evil which is inflicted without intention or possibility of disposing the delinquent or (by his example) other men to obey the laws is not punishment but an act of hostility. This is true because without such an end, no hurt done is contained under that name.

Sixth, to certain actions there are annexed by nature diverse hurtful consequences such as when a man in assaulting another is himself slain or wounded or when he falls into sickness by doing some unlawful act. Such hurt may be said to be inflicted and therefore a divine punishment in respect of God who is the author of nature. Yet it is not contained in the name of punishment in respect of men because it is not inflicted by the authority of man. Seventh, if the harm inflicted is less than the benefit or contentment that naturally follows the crime, the harm is not within the definition and is instead the price or redemption rather than the punishment of a crime. Because it is of the nature of punishment to have for its end disposing men to obey the law and if the end is not attained and if it is less than the benefit of the transgression, it works a contrary effect. Eighth, if a punishment is determined and prescribed in the law itself and after the crime is committed there is greater punishment inflicted, the excess is not punishment but an act of hostility. Seeing the aim of punishment is not revenge but terror and the terror of a great unknown punishment is taken away by the declaration of a lesser punishment, the unexpected addition is not part of the punishment. But where there is no punishment at all determined by the law, there whatever is inflicted has the nature of punishment. For he who goes about the violation of a law where no penalty is determined expects an indeterminate, i.e., an arbitrary punishment. Ninth, harm inflicted for a fact done before there was a law forbidding it is not punishment but an act of hostility. Before the law there is no transgression of the law. But punishment supposes a fact judged to have been a transgression of the law. Therefore, harm inflicted before the law made is not punishment but an act of hostility. Tenth, hurt inflicted on the representative of the commonwealth is not punishment but an act of hostility because it is of the nature of punishment to be inflicted by public authority, which is the authority of the representative itself.

Last, harm inflicted upon one who is a declared enemy does not fall under the name of punishment. Seeing they were either never subject to the law and therefore cannot transgress it or having been subject to it and professing no longer to be so, they consequently deny they can transgress it, all harms that can be done to them must be taken as acts of hostility. But in declared hostility all infliction of evil is lawful. From this it follows that if a subject shall by fact or word deliberately and wittingly deny the authority of the representative of the commonwealth (whatever penalty has been formerly ordained for treason) he may be lawfully made to suffer whatever the representative will. For in denying subjection he denies such punishment as has been ordained by the law and therefore suffers as an enemy of the commonwealth, i.e., according to the will of the representative. For the punishments set down in the law are for subjects not for enemies, such as they who have been by their own acts subjects deny the sovereign power by deliberately revolting.

The first and most general distribution of punishments is into divine and human. Of the former I shall have occasion to speak in a more convenient place hereafter.[54] Human punishments are those inflicted by the commandment of man and are either corporal or pecuniary, or ignominy or imprisonment, or exile or a mix of these.

Corporal punishment is that which is inflicted on the body directly and according to the intention of him who inflicts it. Examples are stripes or wounds or deprivation of such pleasures of the body that were lawfully enjoyed before. Of these punishments, some are capital and some less than capital. Capital is the infliction of death and that either simply or with torment. Less than capital punishment are stripes, wounds, chains, and any other corporal pain that is not in its own nature mortal. For if upon the infliction of a punishment death follows but it is not in the intention of the person who inflicts it, the punishment is not to be esteemed capital even though the harm proves to be mortal by an accident not to be foreseen. In this case, death is not inflicted but hastened.

Pecuniary punishment is that which consists not only in the deprivation of a sum of money but also of lands or any other goods which are usually bought and sold for money. In case the law that ordains such punishment is made with design to gather money from those who transgress, it is not properly a punishment but the price and privilege and exemption from the law which does not absolutely forbid the fact but only to those who are not able to pay the money. This is true except where the law is natural or part of religion, because in that case it is not an exemption from the law but a transgression of it. As where a law exacts a pecuniary mulct of those who take the name of God in vain, the payment of the mulct is not the price of a dispensation to swear but the punishment of the transgression of an indispensable law. In like manner if the law imposes a sum of money to be paid to him who has been injured, this is a satisfaction for the hurt done to him and extinguishes the accusation of the injured party, but not the crime of the offender.

Ignominy is the infliction of such evil as is made dishonorable for the deprivation of such good as is made honorable by the commonwealth. There are some things that are honorable by nature, such as effects of courage, magnanimity, strength, wisdom, and other abilities of body and mind. Others are made honorable by the commonwealth such as badges, titles, offices, or any other singular mark of the sovereign's favor. The former (though they may fail by nature or accident) cannot be taken away by law. Therefore the loss of them is not punishment. But the latter may be taken away by the public authority that made them honorable, and they are properly punishments. Such are degrading condemned men of their badges, titles, and offices or declaring them incapable of the like in time to come.

---

54. Part III.

Imprisonment is when a man is deprived of liberty by public authority and it may happen from two diverse ends. One is the safe custody of an accused man. The other is inflicting pain on a condemned man. The former is not punishment because no man is supposed to be punished before he is judicially heard and declared guilty. And therefore whatever hurt a man is made to suffer by bonds or restraint before his cause is heard that is over and above that which is necessary to assure his custody is against the law of nature. But the latter is punishment because it is evil and inflicted by public authority for something that has by the same authority been judged a transgression of the law. Under the word "imprisonment" I comprehend all restraint of motion caused by an external obstacle, be it a house (which is called by the general name of a prison or an island, as when men are said to be confined to it or a place where men are set to work as in old time men have been condemned to quarries and in these times to galleys) or be it a chain or any other such impediment.

Exile (banishment) is when a man is condemned to depart out of the dominion of the commonwealth or out of a certain part of it and during a fixed time or forever not to return to it. This seems without other circumstances not to be a punishment but rather an escape or public commandment to avoid punishment by flight. . . . For if a banished man is nevertheless permitted to enjoy his goods and revenue of his lands, the mere change of air is not punishment nor does it tend to the benefit of the commonwealth for which all punishments are ordained (that is to say, to forming men's wills to observation of the law) but many times to the damage of the commonwealth. A banished man is a lawful enemy of the commonwealth that banished him as being no more a member of it. But if he is deprived of his lands or goods, then the punishment is not in exile but is to be reckoned among pecuniary punishments.

All punishments of innocent subjects (whether great or little punishments) are against the law of nature because punishment is only of transgression of the law and therefore there can be no punishment of the innocent. It is therefore a violation, first, of the law of nature that forbids all men in their revenges to look at anything but some future good. No good can come to the commonwealth by punishing the innocent. Second, it is a violation of the law which forbids ingratitude. For seeing all sovereign power is originally given by consent of every one of the subjects to the end of being protected they should be obedient, the punishment of the innocent is rendering evil for good. Third, punishing the innocent is violation of the law that commands equity, that is to say an equal distribution of justice.[55]

---

55. While the sovereign is answerable to none of her or his subjects, it does not mean that the sovereign is not bound (1) by the laws of nature or (2) to God since the laws of nature are both rational as well as divine in Hobbes' view. So while the sovereign can do anything, it is not reasonable for the sovereign to act in ways that are contrary to the laws of nature. Because this is the case, the sovereign who acts against the laws of nature, just like the individual human being in the state of nature who acts against the laws of nature, creates a condition of war with all others. There is, therefore, a sense in which a sovereign who violates the laws of nature is acting in a way that may precipitate revolution even if revolution is legally not permitted.

But the infliction of whatever evil on an innocent man who is not a subject, if it is for the benefit of the commonwealth and without violation of any former covenant, is not a breach of the law of nature. For all men who are not subjects are either enemies or they have ceased being so by some preceding covenants. But against enemies judged by the commonwealth capable of doing hurt, it is lawful by the right of nature to make war wherein the sword does not judge nor does the victor make the distinction of nocent and innocent. . . . Upon this ground it also is that in subjects who deliberately deny the authority of the established commonwealth vengeance is lawfully extended not only to the fathers but also to the third and fourth generation not yet existing and consequently innocent of the fact for which they are afflicted. This is true because the nature of this offense consists in renouncing subjection, which is a relapse into the condition of war commonly called rebellion, and they who so offend suffer not as subjects but as enemies because rebellion is nothing but war renewed.

Reward is either a gift or by contract. When it is by contract it is called salary and wages which are benefit due for services performed or promised. When a gift it is benefit proceeding from the grace of those who bestow it to encourage or enable men to do them service. Therefore when the sovereign of a commonwealth appoints a salary to any public office, he who receives it is bound in justice to perform his office. Otherwise, he is bound only in honor to acknowledgment and endeavor of requital. For though men have no lawful remedy when they are commanded to quit their private business to serve the public without reward or salary, they are not bound to it by the law of nature nor by the institution of commonwealth unless the service cannot otherwise be done. This is because it is supposed that the sovereign may make use of all their means insomuch as a common soldier may demand the wages of his warfare as a debt.

The benefits which a sovereign bestows on a subject for fear of some power and ability he has to do hurt to the commonwealth are not properly rewards or salaries because in this case there is no contract supposed when every man is obliged already not to do disservice to the commonwealth. Nor are they graces because they are extorted by fear which ought not to be incident to the sovereign power but are rather sacrifices which the sovereign (considered in his natural person and not in the person of the commonwealth) makes for appeasing the discontent of the person he thinks more potent than himself and does not encourage obedience, but on the contrary the continuance and increase of further extortion.

Some salaries are certain and proceed from the public treasure and others are uncertain and casual, proceeding from the execution of the office for which the salary is ordained. The latter is in some cases hurtful to the commonwealth as in the case of judicature. For where the benefit of the judges and ministers of a court of justice arises for the multitude of causes that are brought to their cognizance, there must follow two inconveniences. One is nourishing suit for the more suits the greater benefit. Another that depends on it which is contention about jurisdiction, each court drawing to itself as many causes as it can. In offices of execution there are not those inconveniences because their enjoyment cannot be increased by any endeavor of their own. This much shall suffice for the nature of punishment and reward which are, as it were, the nerves and tendons that move the limbs and joints of a commonwealth.

Previously I have set forth the nature of man (whose pride and other passions have compelled him to submit himself to government) together with the great powers of his governor, whom I compared to Leviathan, taking that comparison out of the last two verses of the one and fortieth of Job. There, God set forth the great power of Leviathan, called him king of the Proud. "There is nothing," said he, "on Earth to be compared with him. He is made so as not to be afraid. He sees every high thing below him and is king of all the children of pride." But because he is mortal and subject to decay as all other earthly creatures and because there is in Heaven (though not on Earth) that of which he should stand in fear and whose laws he ought to obey, I shall next speak of his diseases and the causes of his mortality and of what laws of nature he is bound to obey.

Chapter XXIX. Of Those Things That Weaken or Tend to the Dissolution of a Commonwealth

No matter how carefully the laws are promulgated and enforced, no matter that the majority of subjects have consented to the laws of the sovereign, and no matter the honesty and knowledge of counselors to the sovereign to try to ensure the smooth running of the commonwealth, there are still problems that loom in the political state that require attention. These are the subject matter of Chapter XXIX, regarding things that tend to weaken or dissolve the commonwealth.

Hobbes' intent in writing Leviathan *for the instruction of subjects and sovereigns in the creation of a well-functioning political state included the intent, in principle, to create a "mortal God" to ensure peace and protection from the danger of early, violent death at the hands of others. But for all this, Hobbes was aware of the contingencies of human action and of the world of experience and reminds us that nothing created by mankind will last forever. But he has tried to provide instruction such that if people use their reason properly, commonwealths will be protected against "internal diseases." Such "infirmities of commonwealth" are, Hobbes states, the imperfect institution of commonwealth (that is, not founding government on proper principles); the existence of seditious doctrines that lead people to dispute and act against sovereign commands; and the problem of subjects believing that their consciences trump the commands of the sovereign, in which case subjects become judges of good and evil (just as they had been in the natural condition). For subjects to believe that their conscience and faith, attained by inspiration and infusion from God, is to supplant the rule of the sovereign is dangerous because, if this belief is accepted, it would mean that any individual could claim to be a prophet and anyone could decide to ignore or violate the laws of his country. It is because of people with these beliefs that great care in the administration of the commonwealth must be taken because there are those who believe they are inspired in some supernatural way, and such belief can lead to the dissolution of the commonwealth. Other problematic beliefs of subjects are that the sovereign is subject to civil laws, that subjects have absolute right to property, and that the right of the sovereign to rule is lost when vanquished in war.*

Though nothing can be immortal that is made by mortals, if men had the use of reason to which they pretend, their commonwealths might be secured at least from perishing by internal diseases. For by the nature of their institution they are designed to live as long as mankind or as long as the laws of nature or justice itself, which gives them life. Therefore, when they come to be dissolved by intestine disorder and not by external violence, the fault is not in men as they are the matter, but as they are the makers and orderers of them. They become at last weary of irregular jostling and hewing one another and desire with all their hearts to conform themselves into one firm and lasting edifice. So for lacking both the art of making fit laws by which to square their actions and also of humility and patience to suffer the rude and cumbersome points of their present greatness to be taken off, they cannot without the help of a very able architect be compiled into anything other than a crazy building such as hardly lasting out their own time must assuredly fall upon the heads of their posterity.

Therefore, among the infirmities of a commonwealth I reckon in the first place those arising from an imperfect institution and resembling the diseases of a natural body that proceed from defective procreation. One of these is "that a man to obtain a kingdom is sometimes content with less power than to the peace and defense of a commonwealth is necessarily required." From this it comes to pass that when the exercise of the power laid by is to be resumed for the public safety, it has the resemblance of an unjust act which disposes great numbers of men (when the occasion is presented) to rebel. [It is like] bodies of children that are gotten by diseased parents are subject either to untimely death or to purge the ill quality that is derived from their vicious conception by breaking out into boils and scabs. When kings deny themselves some necessary power it is not always (though sometimes) out of ignorance of what is necessary to the office they undertake. But many times it is out of a hope to recover the same again at their pleasure. In this they do not reason well because such as will hold them to their promises shall be maintained against them by foreign commonwealths, who in order to the good of their own subjects let slip few occasions to weaken the estate of their neighbors. . . .[56]

Second, I observe the diseases of a commonwealth that proceed from the poison of seditious doctrines. One is "That every private man is judge of good and evil actions." This is true in the condition of mere nature where there are no civil laws and also under civil government in such cases that are not determined by the law. But otherwise it is manifest that the measure of good and evil actions is the civil law and the judge the legislator who is always representative of the commonwealth. From this false doctrine men are disposed to debate with themselves and dispute the commands of the commonwealth and afterward to obey or disobey them in private judgments they shall think fit, whereby the commonwealth is distracted and weakened.

Another doctrine repugnant to civil society is that "Whatever a man does against his conscience is a sin," and it depends on the presumption of making himself a judge of good and evil. For a man's conscience and his judgment is the same thing and as the judgment, so also the conscience may be erroneous. Therefore, though he who is subject to no civil law sins in all he does against his conscience because he has no other rule to follow but his own reason, it is not so within the commonwealth because the law is the public conscience by which he has already undertaken to be guided. Otherwise in such diversity as there is of private consciences

---

56. In the original, Hobbes added several historical examples concerning previous English monarchies and states in ancient Greece and Rome to support his point.

which are private opinions, the commonwealth will be distracted and no man dare to obey the sovereign power farther than shall seem good in his own eyes.

It has also been commonly taught "that faith and sanctity are not to be attained by study and reason but by natural inspiration or infusion." If this is granted, I do not see why any man should render a reason of his faith or why every Christian should not also be a prophet, or why any man should take the law of his country rather than his own inspiration for the rule of his action.[57] Thus we fall again into the fault of taking upon us to judge of good and evil or to make judges of it such private men who pretend to be supernaturally inspired to the dissolution of all civil government. Faith comes by hearing and hearing by those accidents which guide us into the presence of those who speak to us, which are accidents all contrived by God Almighty, and yet are not supernatural but only for the greater number of them who concur to every effect, unobservable. Faith and sanctity are indeed not very frequent but they are not miracles. They are brought to pass by education, discipline, correction, and other natural ways by which God works them in his elect at such time he thinks fit. And these three opinions that are pernicious to peace and government proceed chiefly from the tongues and pens of unlearned divines who join the words of Holy Scripture together in ways other than agreeable to reason and do what they can to make men think that sanctity and natural reason cannot stand together.[58]

A fourth opinion repugnant to the nature of commonwealth is this, "that he who has sovereign power is subject to the civil laws." It is true that sovereigns are all subject to the laws of nature because they are divine and cannot be abrogated by any man or commonwealth. But the laws which the sovereign himself—that is, the commonwealth—makes, the sovereign is not subject. For to be subject to laws is to be subject to the commonwealth—that is, to the sovereign representative, and that is to himself—is not subjection but freedom from the laws. This error sets the laws above the sovereign which sets a judge above him and a power to punish him, and this is to make a new sovereign and again for the same reason a third to punish the second, and so continually without end to the confusion and dissolution of the commonwealth.[59]

---

57. There were contemporaries of Hobbes, such as the Quakers, who held the opinion that all members of a congregation had equal authority and heard from God.

58. Hobbes makes it clear in Part III why the sovereign must be the sovereign both of the state and over religious doctrines. Religious doctrines are, for Hobbes, the most pernicious doctrines and common reasons for internal discord in political states.

59. Hobbes' argument regarding the need for multiplication of sovereigns in a case in which the sovereign is subject to his own laws is the analog to the rejection of an infinite regress of causes with respect to arguments for the existence of God. If there is an infinite regress of causes, it is impossible to reach a first cause. If it is impossible to reach a first cause, there can be nothing now because there is nothing to begin the series of causes. In the same way, if the sovereign is subject to laws, the sovereign is subject to a lawgiver, who is then subject to another, and so on to infinity. This, for Hobbes and those he follows in this reasoning, creates absurdity. Hobbes applies the absurdity of believing in an infinite regress of causes to the reason for the absolute power of the political sovereign.

A fifth doctrine tending to the dissolution of a commonwealth is "that every private man has absolute propriety in his goods such as excludes the right of the sovereign." Every man indeed has propriety that excludes the right of every other subject. And he has it only from the sovereign power without the protection whereof every other man should have equal right to the same. But if the right of the sovereign is also excluded, he cannot perform the office into which they have put him, which is to defend them both from foreign enemies and from the injuries of one another and consequently there is no longer a commonwealth. . . .

There is a sixth doctrine that is plainly and directly against the essence of a commonwealth. It is this, "that the sovereign power may be divided." For what is it to divide the power of a commonwealth but to dissolve it? For powers divided mutually destroy each other. For these doctrines men are chiefly beholding to some of those who, making profession of the laws, endeavor to make them depend on their own learning and not upon the legislative power.

Often the example of a different government in a neighboring nation disposes men to alteration of the form already settled. So the people of the Jews were stirred up to reject God and to call upon the prophet Samuel for a king after the manner of the nations. So also the lesser cities of Greece were continually disturbed with the seditions of aristocratic and democratic factions, one part almost of every commonwealth desiring to imitate the Lacedemonians and the other the Athenians. I do not doubt that many men have been contented to see the late troubles in England out of an imitation of the low countries, supposing there needed no more to grow rich than to change their form of government, as they had done. For the constitution of man's nature is of itself subject to desire novelty. When therefore they are provoked to the same by the neighborhood also of those who have been enriched by it, it is almost impossible for them not to be content with those who solicit them to change and love the first beginnings though they are grieved with the continuance of disorder. . . .

As to rebellion in particular against monarchy, one of the most frequent causes of it is reading books of policy and histories of the ancient Greeks and Romans. Young men and all others who are not provided with the antidote of solid reason receive a strong and delightful impression of the great exploits of war achieved by the conductors of their armies and receive a pleasing idea of all they have done besides and imagine their great prosperity not to have proceeded from the emulation of particular men but from the virtue of their popular form of government. They do not consider the frequent seditions and civil wars produced by the imperfection of their policy. From reading such books, in my opinion, men have undertaken to kill their kings because the Greek and Latin writers in their books and discourses of policy make it lawful and laudable for any man to do so provided he calls him a tyrant before he does it. They do not say that regicide is killing the king, but tyrannicide—that is, killing a tyrant—is lawful. From the same books they who live under a monarch conceive an opinion that the subjects in a popular commonwealth enjoy liberty but that in a monarchy they are slaves. I say they who live under a monarchy conceive such an opinion, not that they live under a popular government, for they find no such matter. In sum, I cannot imagine how anything can be more prejudicial to monarchy than allowing such books to be publicly read without applying such correctives of discrete masters as are fit to take away their venom. I will not doubt to compare that venom to the biting of a mad dog. . . . For as he who is so bitten has a continual torment of thirst and yet abhors water and is in such an estate as if the poison endeavored to convert him into a dog. So when a monarchy is once bitten to the quick by those democratic writers who continually snarl at that estate, it wants nothing more than a strong monarchy, which neverthe-less out of a certain tyrannophobia or fear of being strongly governed, when they have him they abhor.

Just as there have been Doctors[60] who hold that there are three souls in a man, so there are also those who think there may be more souls (that is, more sovereigns) than one in a commonwealth and set up supremacy against sovereignty canons and laws and ghostly authority against the civil laws, working on men's minds with words and distinctions that of themselves signify nothing but betray (by their obscurity) that there walks (as some think invisibly) another kingdom (as it were a kingdom of fairies) in the dark. It is manifest that the civil power and the power of the commonwealth is the same thing and that supremacy and the power of mak-ing canons and granting faculties implies a commonwealth. It follows that where one is sovereign, another supreme where one can make laws and another can make canons, there must be two commonwealths of one and the same subjects, which is a kingdom divided against itself and cannot stand. Notwithstanding the insignificant distinction of temporal and ghostly, they are still two kingdoms and every subject is subject to two masters. For seeing the ghostly power challenges the right to declare what is sin, it challenges by consequence to declare what is law (sin being nothing but transgression of the law) and again, the civil power challenging to declare what is law, every subject must obey two masters who will both have their commands observed as law, which is impossible. Or, if it is one kingdom either the civil law which is the power of the commonwealth must be subordinate to the ghostly, or the ghostly must be subordinate to the temporal and then there is no supremacy but the temporal. When therefore these two powers oppose each other, the com-monwealth cannot help but be in danger of civil war and dissolution. The civil authority that is more visible and standing in the clearer light of natural reason can-not choose but to draw to it in all times a very considerable part of the people. And the spiritual, though it stand in the darkness of school distinctions and hard words, because the fear of darkness and ghosts is greater than other fears it cannot lack a party sufficient to trouble and sometimes destroy a commonwealth. This is a disease which not unfitly may be compared to epilepsy or falling sickness . . . in the natu-ral body. For as in this disease there is an unnatural spirit or wind in the head that obstructs the roots of the nerves and moving them violently takes away the natural motion they should have from the power of the soul in the brain and thereby causes violent and irregular motions (convulsions) in the parts. Insomuch as he who is seized falls down sometimes into the water and sometimes into the fire as a man deprived of his senses, so also in the political body when the spiritual power moves

---

60. That is, "Doctors" of the Church such as St. Thomas Aquinas and other "divines."

the members of the commonwealth by the terror of punishments and the hope of rewards (which are the nerves of it) otherwise than by the civil power (which is the soul of the commonwealth) by which they ought to be moved, strange and hard words suffocate the people and either overwhelms the commonwealth with oppression or casts it into the fire of a civil war.

Sometimes also in merely civil government there is more than one soul such as when the power of levying money (the nutritive faculty) has depended on a general assembly, the power of conduct and command (the motive faculty) on one man, and the power of making laws (the rational faculty) on the accidental consent of those two and a third. This endangers the commonwealth sometimes for lack of consent to good laws but most often for lack of such nourishment as is necessary to life and motion. For although few perceive that such government is not government but division of the commonwealth into three factions and call it mixed monarchy. Yet the truth is that it is not one independent commonwealth but three independent factions. It is not one representative person, but three.

In the Kingdom of God there may be three persons independent without breach of unity in God who reigns, but where men reign that is subject to diversity of opinions it cannot be so. Therefore if the king bears the person of the people and the general assembly also bears the person of the people and another assembly bears the person of a part of the people, they are not one person nor one sovereign, but three persons and three sovereigns. I do not know to what disease of the natural body of man to compare this irregularity of a commonwealth. But I have seen a man who had another man growing out of his side with a head, arms, breast, and stomach of his own.[61] If he had another man growing out of his other side, the comparison might then have been exact.

I have previously named such diseases of commonwealth that are of the greatest and most present danger. There are others that are not so great which nevertheless are not unfit to be observed. First is the difficulty of raising money for the necessary uses of the commonwealth, especially in the approach of war. The difficulty arises from the opinion that every subject has a propriety in his lands and goods exclusive of the sovereign's right to the use of them. From this it comes to pass that the sovereign power which foresees the necessities and dangers of the commonwealth (finding the passage of money to the public treasure obstructed by the tenacity of the people) whereas it ought to extend itself to encounter and prevent such dangers in their beginnings, contracts itself as long as it can and when it cannot any longer it struggles with the people by stratagems of law to obtain little sums that are not sufficient, he violently opens the way for present supply or perish. And being put often to these extremes, it at last reduces the people to their due temper or the commonwealth must perish. Insomuch as we may compare this distemper very aptly to an ague, wherein the fleshy parts being congealed or obstructed by venomous matter . . . it breaks at last to the contumacy of the obstructed parts and dissipates the sweat, or if nature is too weak the patient dies.

---

61. Conjoined twins.

Again, there is sometimes a disease in a commonwealth that resembles pleurisy and that is when the treasure of a commonwealth that flows out of its due course is gathered in too much abundance in one or a few private men by monopolies or by farms of the public revenues in the same manner as blood in pleurisy gets into the membrane of the breast and breeds an inflammation accompanied by fever and painful stitches.

In addition, the popularity of a potent subject (unless the commonwealth has a very good caution of his fidelity) is a dangerous disease because the people (which should receive their motion from the authority of the sovereign) by flattery and reputation of an ambitious man are drawn away from their obedience to the laws to follow a man of whose virtues and designs they have no knowledge. This is commonly of more danger in a popular government than in a monarchy as it may easily be made believe that they are the people. By this means it was that Julius Caesar who was set up by the people against the senate and won the affections of his army made himself master of both senate and the people. And this proceeding of popular and ambitious men is plain rebellion and may be compared to the effects of witchcraft.

Another infirmity of a commonwealth is the immoderate greatness of a town when it is able to furnish out of its own circuit the number and expense of a great army. As also the great number of corporations are as it were many lesser commonwealths in the bowels of a greater commonwealth and are like worms in the entrails of a natural man.

To this may be added the liberty of disputing by pretenders to political prudence against absolute power. This is bred for the most part in the lees of the people but animated by false doctrines perpetually meddling with the fundamental laws to the molestation of the commonwealth like little worms that physicians call ascarides. We may further add the insatiable appetite or bulimia of enlarging dominion with the incurable wounds thereby many times received from the enemy. And the wens of disunited conquests, which are many times a burden and with less danger lost than kept, as also the lethargy of ease and consumption of riot and vain expense.

Last, when in a war (foreign or intestine) the enemies got a final victory so as (the forces of the commonwealth keeping the field no longer) there is no further protection of subjects in their loyalty, then the commonwealth is dissolved and every man is at liberty to protect himself by such courses as his own discretion shall suggest to him. The sovereign is the public soul that gives life and motion to the commonwealth. When it expires, the members are no longer governed by it any more than the carcass of a man by his departed (though immortal) soul. For though the right of a sovereign monarch cannot be extinguished by the act of another, the obligation of the members may. For he who wants protection may seek it anywhere and when he has it, he is obliged (without fraudulent pretense of having submitted himself out of fear) to protect his protection as long as he is able. But when the power of an assembly is once suppressed, the right of the same perishes utterly because the assembly itself is extinct and consequently there is no possibility for the sovereignty to reenter.

Chapter XXX. Of the Office of the Sovereign Representative

The function of the sovereign is to preserve the lives of subjects, but it is in this chapter that Hobbes adds clearly that more than mere survival is required. It is also to ensure "other contentments of life" that the people might obtain for themselves. To provide for the safety and lives of the people involves other conditions or requirements of sovereignty, including the sovereign's obligation never to renounce sovereignty, to clarify subjects' duties and to educate them properly, to treat the subjects equally, and to provide for subjects who are unable to care for themselves.

The office of the sovereign (whether monarch or assembly) consists in the end for which he was trusted with the sovereign power, namely the procuration of the safety of the people to which he is obliged by the law of nature and to render an account to God who is the author of that law and to none but him. But by safety here is not meant bare preservation, but also all other contentments of life which every man by lawful industry without danger or hurt to the commonwealth shall acquire to himself.

This is intended to be done not by care applied to individuals further than their protection from injuries when they complain, but by general Providence contained in public instruction both of doctrine and example and in making and executing good laws to which individual persons may apply their own cases.

Because, if the essential rights of sovereignty (specified in the Chapter XVIII) are taken away, the commonwealth is thereby dissolved and every man returns to the condition and calamity of war with every other man (which is the greatest evil that can happen in this life), it is, first, the office of the sovereign to maintain all those rights and it is consequently against his duty to transfer to another or to set aside any of them. He who deserts the means deserts the ends and he deserts the means who, being sovereign, acknowledges himself subject to civil laws and renounces the power of supreme judicature or making war or peace by his own authority or judging the necessities of the commonwealth, or levying money and soldiers when and as much as in his own conscience he judges necessary of making officers and ministers of war and peace or of appointing teachers and examining which doctrines are conformable or contrary to the defense, peace, and good of the people. Second, it is against his duty to let the people be ignorant or misinformed of the grounds and reasons of his essential rights because thereby men are easily seduced and drawn to resist him when the commonwealth requires their use and exercise.

The grounds of these rights need to be diligently and truly taught because they cannot be maintained by any civil law or terror of legal punishment. For a civil law that forbids rebellion (and such is all resistance to the essential rights of sovereignty) is not (as civil law) any obligation but by virtue only of the law of nature that forbids violation of faith which subjects cannot know the right of any law the sovereign makes if they do not know the natural obligation. They take punishment as an act of hostility which when they think they have strength enough they will by acts of hostility try to avoid.

As I have heard some say that justice is just a word without substance and that whatever a man can acquire to himself by force or art (not only in a condition of war but also in a commonwealth) is his own I have already shown to be false. So there are also those who claim that there are no grounds or principles of reason to sustain those essential rights which make sovereignty absolute. If there were they would have been found out in some place or other. Whereas we see there has not before been any commonwealth where those rights have been acknowledged or challenged. They argue badly as if the savage people of America should deny there were any grounds or principles of reason to build a house to last as long as the materials because they never saw any so well built. Time and industry produce new knowledge every day. As the art of well building is derived from principles of reason observed by industrious men who had long studied the nature of materials and the diverse effects of figure and proportion long after mankind began (though poorly) to build. So, long after men have begun to constitute imperfect commonwealths that are apt to relapse into disorder there may be principles of reason found out by industrious meditation to make use of them or be neglected by them or not. . . . But supposing that these of mine are not such principles of reason, I am sure they are principles from the authority of Scripture as I shall make it appear when I come to speak of the Kingdom of God (administered by Moses) over the Jews who are his people by covenant.

But they say again that though the principles are taught, common people are not capable of understanding them. I should be glad that the rich and potent subjects of a kingdom are those who are accounted the most learned were no less capable than they. But all men know that the obstructions to the kind of doctrine proceed not so much from the difficulty of the matter as from the interest of those who are to learn. Potent men hardly digest anything that sets up a power to bridle their affections, and learned men anything that discovers their errors and thereby lessens their authority. Whereas the minds of the common people are like clean paper fit to receive whatever by public authority shall be imprinted in them unless they are tainted with dependence on the potent or scribbled over with the opinions of their Doctors. Shall whole nations be brought to acquiesce in the great mysteries of Christian religion, which are above reason, and millions of men made to believe that the same body may be in innumerable places at one and the same time, which is against reason. And shall not men be able by their teaching and preaching, protected by law, to make that received which is so consonant to reason that any unprejudiced man needs no more to learn it than to hear it. I conclude that in the instruction of the people in the essential rights (which are the natural and fundamental laws) of sovereignty, there is no difficulty (while a sovereign has his whole power) but what proceeds from his own fault or those whom he trusts in the administration of the commonwealth. Consequently, it is his duty to cause them to be instructed not only in his duty but also his benefit and security against the danger that may arrive to himself in his natural person from rebellion.

To descend to particulars, the people are to be taught, first, that they ought not to be in love with any form of government they see in their neighbor nations more than with their own, nor (whatever present prosperity they behold of nations governed differently) to desire change. For the prosperity of a people ruled by an aristocratic or democratic assembly does not come from the aristocracy or the democracy, but from obedience and concord of the subjects. Nor do the people flourish in a monarchy because one man has the right to rule them, but because they obey him. Take away obedience (and consequently the concord of the people) in any kind of state and they shall not only not flourish, but in short time they will be dissolved. They who go about by disobedience to do no more than reform the commonwealth shall find that they thereby destroy it like the foolish daughters of Peleus (in the fable) who desired to renew the youth of their father and by the counsel of Medea cut him in pieces and boiled him together with strange herbs but did not make a new man of him. The desire of change is like the breach of the first of God's commandments. For there God says . . . thou shall not have the gods of other nations and in another place concerning kings, they are gods.

Second, they are to be taught that they ought not to be led with admiration of the virtue of any of their fellow subjects no matter how high they stand or how conspicuously he shines in the commonwealth. Nor of any assembly (except the sovereign assembly) so as to defer to them any obedience or honor appropriate only to the sovereign whom (in their particular stations) they represent, nor to receive any influence from them but such as is conveyed by them from their sovereign authority. For that sovereign cannot be imagined to love his people as he ought who is not jealous of them but suffers them by the flattery of popular men to be seduced from their loyalty . . . which may be fitly compared to the violation of the second commandment.[62]

Third, in consequence, they ought to be informed how great a fault it is to speak evil of the sovereign representative (whether one man or an assembly) or to argue and dispute his power or in any way to use his name irreverently whereby he may be brought into contempt with his people and their obedience (in which the safety of the commonwealth consists) slackened. The third commandment by resemblance points to this.

Fourth, seeing people cannot be taught this, nor when it is taught remember it, nor after one generation past so much as knows in whom the sovereign power is placed without setting a part from their ordinary labor some certain times in which they may attend those that are appointed to instruct them. It is necessary that some such times be determined wherein they may assemble together and (after prayers

---

62. The commandments to which Hobbes refers in the following series are found in Exod. 20.2–17.

and praises given to God, the sovereign of sovereigns) hear their duties told to them and the positive laws that generally concern them all read and expounded and be put in mind of the authority that makes them laws. To this end the Jews had every seventh day a Sabbath in which the law was read and expounded and in solemnity of it they were put in mind that their king was God. . . . So that the first table of the commandments is spent in setting down the sum of God's absolute power not only as God but as king by pact (in peculiar) of the Jews and may therefore give light to those who have the sovereign power conferred on them by the consent of men to see what doctrine they ought to teach their subjects.

Because the first instruction of children depends on the care of their parents, it is necessary that they should be obedient to them while they are under their tuition and not only then but afterward (as gratitude requires) acknowledge the benefit of their education by external signs of honor. To this end they are taught that originally the father of every man was also his sovereign lord with power over him of life and death and that the fathers of families, when instituting a commonwealth, resigned that absolute power, yet it was never intended they should lose the honor due to them for their education. To relinquish such right was not necessary to the institution of sovereign power nor would there be any reason why any man should desire to have children or to take the care to nourish and instruct them if they were afterward to have no other benefit from them than from other men. This accords with the fifth commandment.

Again, every sovereign ought to cause justice to be taught which (consisting in taking from no man what is his) is as much as to say to cause men to be taught not to deprive their neighbor by violence or fraud anything which is theirs by the sovereign authority. Of things held in propriety those who are dearest to a man are his own life and limbs. In the next degree (in most men) those that concern conjugal affection and after them riches and means of living. Therefore the people are to be taught to abstain from violence to one another's person by private revenges, from violation of conjugal honor, and from forcible rape and fraudulent surreption of one another's goods. For this purpose it is also necessary they be shown the evil consequences of false judgment by corruption of judges or witnesses whereby the distinction of propriety is taken away and justice becomes of no effect. All these things are intimated in the sixth, seventh, eighth, and ninth commandments.

Last, they are to be taught that not only the unjust acts but the designs and intentions to do them (though by accident hindered) are injustice. Injustice consists in the pravity of the will as well as in the irregularity of the act. This is the intention of the tenth commandment and the sum of the second table which is reduced to this one commandment of mutual charity. "Thou shall love thy neighbor as thyself" as the sum of the first table is reduced to "the love of God" whom they had then newly received as their king.

Concerning the sources of instruction of the people, we are to search by what means so many opinions contrary to peace have been so deeply rooted in them upon weak and false principles. I mean those which I have in the preceding chapter specified, such that men shall judge of what is lawful and unlawful not by the law itself but by their private judgments, such as:

- That men shall judge of what is lawful and unlawful not by the law itself but by their own private judgments.
- That subjects sin in obeying the commands of the commonwealth unless they themselves have first judged them to be lawful.
- That their propriety in their riches is such as to exclude the dominion which the commonwealth has over the same.
- That it is lawful for subjects to kill such as they call tyrants.
- That the sovereign power may be divided, and the like, which come to be instilled in the people by this means.
- They whom necessity or covetousness keeps attention on their trades and labor, and they on the other side whom superfluity or sloth carries after their sensual pleasures (which two sorts of men take up the greatest part of mankind) diverted from the deep meditation which learning truth not only in the matter of natural justice but also of all other sciences necessarily requires. They receive the notions of their duty chiefly from the divines in the pulpit and partly from neighbors or familiar acquaintance who, having the faculty of discoursing readily and plausibly seem wiser and better learned in case of law and conscience than themselves.
- And the divines and others who make a show of learning derive their knowledge from the universities, from the schools of law, or from the books which by men eminent in those schools and universities have been published.

It is therefore manifest that instruction of the people depends wholly on right teaching of youth in the universities. But are not (may some men say) the universities of England learned enough already to do that? Or is it you who will undertake to teach the universities? These are hard questions. Yet to the first question I doubt not to answer that until toward the later end of the Henry the Eighth, the power of the pope was always upheld principally by the universities against the power of the commonwealth. And doctrines maintained by so many preachers against the sovereign power of the king and by so many lawyers and others who had their education there is sufficient argument that though universities were not authors of those false doctrines, they did not know how to plant the true ones. For in such a contradiction of opinions, it is most certain that they have not been sufficiently instructed and it is no wonder if they retain a relish of that subtle liquor by which they were first seasoned against the civil authority. But to the latter question, it is not fit or needful for me to say anything, for any man who sees what I am doing may easily perceive what I think.[63]

The safety of the people requires no further from him or them who have sovereign power than justice be equally administered to all degrees of the people—that is, that as well as the right and mighty, as poor and obscure persons may be righted of the injuries done to them so as the great may have no greater hope of impunity when they do violence, dishonor, or any injury to the meaner sort than when one

---

63. Hobbes, apparently, thought he was the person to teach the universities what to teach and how to teach it.

of these does the like to one of them. For in this consists equity to which a sovereign is as much subject as any of the meanest of his people because it is a precept of the law of nature. All breaches of the law are offenses against the commonwealth, but there may be some who are also against private persons. Those concerning the commonwealth only may be pardoned without breach of equity for every man may pardon what is done against himself according to his own discretion. But an offense against a private man cannot in equity be pardoned without the consent of him who is injured or without reasonable satisfaction.

The inequality of subjects proceeds from the acts of sovereign power and therefore has no more place in the presence of the sovereign—that is to say, in a court of justice—than the inequality between kings and their subjects in the presence of the king of kings. The honor of great persons is to be valued for the beneficence and the aids they give to men of inferior rank or not at all. The violent acts, oppressions, or injuries they do are not extenuated but aggravated by the greatness of their persons because they have least need to commit them. The consequences of this, particularly toward the great, proceed in this manner. Impunity makes insolence, insolence makes hatred, and hatred makes an endeavor to pull down all oppressing and contumelious greatness, though with the ruin of the commonwealth.

To equal justice appertains also the equal imposition of taxes, the equality of which does not depend on the equality of riches but on the equality of the debt that every man owes to the commonwealth for his defense. It is not enough for a man to labor for the maintenance of his life but also to fight (if need be) for securing his labor. They must either do as the Jews did after their return from captivity in reedifying the temple and build with one hand and hold the sword in the other, or they must hire others to fight for them. For the impositions that are laid on the people by the sovereign are nothing but the wages due to them who hold the public sword to defend private men in the exercise of trades and callings. Seeing then the benefit that everyone receives from it is the enjoyment of life which is equally dear to poor and rich. The debt which a poor man owes to those who defend his life is the same which a rich man owes for defense of his except that the rich, who have the service of the poor, may be debtors not only for their own persons but for many more. When considering this, the equality of imposition consists rather in the equality of that which is consumed than the riches of the persons who consume the same.[64] For what reason is there that he who labors much and spares the fruits of his labor and consumes little should be charged more than he who lives idly, gets little, and spends all he gets, seeing that the one has no more protection from the commonwealth than the other? But when the impositions are laid upon those things which men consume, every man pays equally for what he uses. Nor is the commonwealth defrauded by the luxurious waste of private men.

---

64. Hobbes is arguing in this section for a tax levied on all for defense of the commonwealth generally through use and luxury taxes rather than mere income taxes. Hobbes' position is that it is unfair to tax a person who saves his money the same as one who wastes it ("luxurious waste of private men"), so Hobbes here agrees either with a flat tax percentage for all or for tax to be levied based on what is spent, not on what is earned.

Whereas many men by inevitable accident become unable to maintain themselves by their labor, they ought not to be left to the charity of private persons but to be provided for (as far forth as the necessities of nature require) by the laws of the commonwealth. As it is uncharitableness in any man to neglect the impotent, so it is uncharitableness in the sovereign of a commonwealth to expose them to the hazard of such uncertain charity.[65]

For those who have strong bodies the case is otherwise. They are to be forced to work and to avoid the excuse of not finding employment. There ought to be such laws as may encourage all manner of arts such as navigation, architecture, fishing, and all manner of manufacture that requires labor. The multitude of poor and yet strong people still increasing, they are to be transplanted to countries not sufficiently inhabited where nevertheless they are not to exterminate those they find there but constrain them to inhabit closer together and to range a great deal of ground to snatch what they find, but to court each little plot with art and labor to give them their sustenance in due season. When all the world is overcharged with inhabitants, the last remedy of all is war which provides for every man by victory or death.[66]

It is left to the care of the sovereign to make good laws. But what is a good law? By a good law I mean not a just law, for no law can be unjust. The law is made by the sovereign power, and all that is done by such power is warranted and owned by every one of the people, and that which every man will have so no man can say is unjust. It is in the laws of a commonwealth as in the laws of gaming, whatever all gamesters agree on is injustice to none of them. A good law is that which is needful for the good of the people and completely perspicuous.

For the use of laws (which are but authorized rules) is not to bind the people from all voluntary actions but to direct and keep them in such motion as not to hurt themselves by their own impetuous desires, rashness, or indiscretion, as hedges are not set to stop travelers but to keep them on their way. Therefore a law that is not needful is not having the true end of a law, and is not good. A law may be conceived to be good when it is for the benefit of the sovereign though it is not necessary for the people. But it is not so. For the good of the sovereign and the good of the people cannot be separated. It is a weak sovereign who has weak subjects and a weak people whose sovereign lacks power to rule them at his will. Unnecessary

---

65. Hobbes indicated previously that it is not the responsibility of private citizens to take care of others, nor should anyone expect them to do so. While charity is a virtue, virtues cannot be commanded. The sovereign, however, exhibits the virtue of charitableness in providing for the sick, the disabled, and the elderly.

66. Thomas Malthus, in *An Essay on the Principle of Population*, ed. Philip Appleman (New York: W. W. Norton, 2003), argued in 1798 that increases in population would be controlled by famine and disease. Hobbes goes a bit further, arguing that population will be controlled by war. For Hobbes, the extension makes perfectly good sense since famine and disease will likely lead to civil unrest and then to the war of everyone against everyone. Regardless, this is a rather nasty position to take, even for Hobbes, especially if the phrase "the last remedy of all is war which provides for every man by victory or death" is meant prescriptively rather than descriptively.

laws are not good laws but they are traps for money which, where the right of sovereign power is acknowledged, are superfluous. And where it is not acknowledged, it is insufficient to defend the people.

Perspicuity consists not so much in the words of the law itself as in a declaration of the causes and motives for which it was made. What shows us the meaning of the legislator and the meaning of the legislator known, the law is more easily understood by few rather than many words. All words are subject to ambiguity and therefore multiplication of words in the body of the law is multiplication of ambiguity. Besides, it seems to imply (by too much diligence) that whoever can evade the words is without the compass of the law. This is a cause of many unnecessary processes. For when I consider how short were the laws of the penners and pleaders of the law, the former seeking to circumscribe the later and the latter to evade their circumscriptions, and the pleaders have got the victory. It belongs therefore to the office of a legislator (and as in all commonwealths the supreme representative, whether one man or an assembly) to make the reason the law was made perspicuous and the body of the law itself as short but in as proper and significant terms as may be.

It also belongs to the office of the sovereign to make right application of punishments and rewards. Seeing the end of punishing is not revenge and discharge of choler but correction either of the offender or of others by his example, the most severe punishments are to be inflicted for those crimes that are of most danger to the public. Examples are those which proceed from malice to the established government, those that spring from contempt of justice, those that provoke indignation in the multitude, and those which are unpunished and seem authorized, such as when they are committed by sons, servants, or favorites of men in authority. For indignation carries men not only against the actors and authors of injustice but against all power that is likely to protect them. . . . But crimes of infirmity, such as are those proceeding from great provocation, from great fear, great need, or from ignorance whether the fact is a great crime or not, there is place many times for leniency without prejudice to the commonwealth. And lenience, when there is such place for it, is required by the law of nature. The punishment of the leaders and teachers in a commotion, not the poor seduced people when they are punished, can profit the commonwealth by their example. To be severe to the people is to punish that ignorance which may in great part be imputed to the sovereign whose fault it was they were not better instructed.

In like manner it belongs to the office and duty of the sovereign to apply rewards always so there may arise from them benefit to the commonwealth that consists of their use and end. It is then done when they who have well served the commonwealth are so well recompensed with as little expense to the commonwealth as possible that others may thereby be encouraged both to serve as faithfully as they can and to study the arts by which they may be enabled to do it better. To buy with money or preferment from a popular ambitious subject to be quiet and desist from making ill impressions in the minds of the people has nothing of the nature of reward (which is ordained for past service not for disservice) nor a public sign of gratitude, but of fear. Nor does it tend to the benefit but to the damage of the public. It is a contention with ambition like that of Hercules with the monster, Hydra, that had many heads and for every one that was vanquished three grew in their place. In like manner when stubbornness of one popular man is overcome with reward, there arise many more (by example) who do the same mischief in hope of like benefit and as all sorts of manufacture so also malice increases by being vendible. Though sometimes a civil war may be deferred by such ways as that, the danger grows still greater and the public ruin is more assured. It is therefore against the duty of the sovereign to whom the public safety is committed to reward those who aspire to greatness by disturbing the peace of their country and not rather to oppose the beginnings of such men with a little danger than after a long time with greater danger.

Another business of the sovereign is to choose good counselors. I mean those whose advice he is to take in the government of the commonwealth. For this word "counsel" . . . is a larger signification and comprehends all assemblies of men who sit together not only to deliberate what is to be done hereafter, but also to judge of past facts and of law for the present. I take it here in the first sense only. In this sense there is no choice of counsel either in a democracy or an aristocracy because the persons counseling are members of the person counseled. The choice of counselors therefore is in monarchy in which the sovereign who endeavors not to make choice of those who in every kind are the most able does not discharge his office as he ought to do. The most able counselors are they who have least hope of benefit by giving evil counsel and most knowledge of those things that conduce to the peace and defense of the commonwealth. It is a hard matter to know who expects benefit from public troubles, but the signs that guide to a just suspicion is the soothing of the people in their unreasonable or irremediable grievances by men whose estates are not sufficient to discharge their accustomed expenses and may be easily observed by anyone whom it concerns to know it. But to know who has most knowledge of public affairs is even harder and they who know them need them a great deal less. For to know who knows the rules of almost any art is a great degree of the knowledge of the same art because no man can be assured of the truth of another's rules except he who is first taught to understand them. But the best signs of knowledge of any art are much conversing in it and constant good effects of it. Good counsel does not come by lot or by inheritance and therefore there is no more reason to expect good advice from the rich or noble in matters of state than in delineating the dimensions of a fortress unless we think there needs no method in the study of politics (as there does in the study of geometry) but only to be onlookers, which is not so. For politics is the harder study of the two. Whereas in these parts of Europe it has been taken for a right of certain persons to have a place in the highest council of state by inheritance, it is derived from the conquests of the ancient Germans in which many absolute lords joined together to conquer other nations would not enter into the confederacy without such privileges that might be marks of a difference in time following between their posterity and the posterity of their subjects. Such privileges are inconsistent with the sovereign power by the favor of the sovereign they may seem to keep, but contending for them as their right they must by degrees let them go and have at last no further honor than what adheres naturally to their abilities.

No matter how able the counselors in any affair, the benefit of their counsel is greater when they can give everyone his advice and reasons of it apart than when they do it in an assembly by way of orations and when they have premeditated than when they speak on the sudden. This is true both because they have more time to survey the consequences of action and are less subject to be carried away to contradiction through envy, emulation, or other passions arising from difference of opinion.

The best counsel in things that do not concern other nations but only the ease and benefit the subject may enjoy by laws that look only inward is to be taken from the general information and complaints of the people of each province who are best acquainted with their own wants. They ought, therefore, to be diligently taken notice of when they demand nothing in derogation of the essential rights of sovereignty. For without those essential rights (as I have often said before) the commonwealth cannot at all subsist.

If a commander of an army in chief is not popular, he shall not be beloved nor feared as he ought to be by his army and consequently he cannot perform that office with good success. He must therefore be industrious, valiant, affable, liberal and fortunate that he may gain an opinion both of sufficiency and of loving his soldiers. This is popularity and breeds in the soldiers both desire and courage to recommend themselves to his favor and protects the severity of the general in punishing (when need be) the mutinous or negligent soldiers. But this love of soldiers (if caution is not given of the commander's fidelity) is a dangerous thing to sovereign power especially when it is in the hands of an assembly that is not popular. It belongs therefore to the safety of the people both that they be good conductors and faithful subjects to whom the sovereign commits his armies.

But when the sovereign himself is popular—that is, reverenced and beloved by his people—there is no danger at all from the popularity of a subject. For soldiers are never so generally unjust as to side with their captain though they love him against their sovereign when they love not only his person but also his cause. And therefore those who by violence have at any time suppressed the power of their lawful sovereign before they could settle themselves in his place have always been put to the trouble of contriving their titles to save the people from the shame of receiving them. To have a known right to sovereign power is so popular a quality as he who has it needs no more for his own part to turn the hearts of his subjects to him but that they see him able absolutely to govern his own family. Nor on the part of his enemies but a disbanding of their armies. For the greatest and most active part of mankind has never before been well contented with the present.

Concerning the offices of one sovereign to another, which are comprehended in that law which is commonly called the law of nations, I need not say anything in this place because the law of nations and the law of nature are the same thing. Every sovereign has the same right in procuring the safety of his people that any particular man can have in procuring the safety of his own body. The same law that dictates to men who have no civil government what they ought to do and what to avoid in regard to one another dictates the same to commonwealths—that is, to the consciences of sovereign princes and sovereign assemblies—there being no court of natural justice but in the conscience only where not man but God reigns and whose laws (such as those that oblige all mankind) in respect of God as he is the author of nature are natural and in respect of the same God as he is the king of kings are laws. But to the Kingdom of God as king of kings, and as king also of a particular people, I shall speak in the rest of this discourse.

Chapter XXXI. Of the Kingdom of God by Nature

In Chapter XXXI, Hobbes sums up Part II of Leviathan *in his commentary on the Kingdom of God by nature, reiterating that the subjects "owe to sovereigns simple obedience in all things wherein their obedience is not repugnant to the laws of God." Being that the commonwealth itself is one person, it can have only one worship exhibited toward God. There is therefore no freedom of religious practice in Hobbes' political thought, but it remains the case that a person can believe whatever he wants (at his own personal risk) so long as externally he worships and confesses as prescribed by the sovereign.*

The scope of the following chapters is that the condition of mere nature—that is to say, of absolute liberty—such as theirs who are neither sovereigns nor subjects is anarchy and the condition of war. It is that the precepts by which men are governed to avoid that condition are the laws of nature. A commonwealth without a sovereign power is but a word without substance and cannot stand. I have sufficiently proved in what I have already written that subjects owe to sovereigns simple obedience in all things wherein their obedience is not repugnant to the laws of God. There wants only for the entire knowledge of civil duty to know what are the laws of God. For without that, a man does not know when he is commanded by anything by the civil power whether it is contrary to the law of God or not, and so either by too much civil obedience offends the divine majesty or through fear of offending God transgresses the commandments of the commonwealth.[67] To avoid both these rocks, it is necessary to know the divine laws. Seeing the knowledge of all law depends on knowledge of sovereign power, I shall say something in what follows of the Kingdom of God.

"God is king, let the Earth rejoice," said the psalmist. And again, "God is king though the nations are angry, and he who sits on the Cherubins, though the Earth be moved." Whether men will or not, they must be subject always to divine power. By denying the existence or Providence of God men may shake off their ease but not their yoke. But to call this power of God which extends itself not only to man

---

67. Hobbes has already indicated that the laws of nature are divine laws and that no other laws are needed for the proper conduct of people in a commonwealth. Some commentators therefore hold that the position that Parts III and IV of *Leviathan* are actually not necessary to Hobbes' political theory and that, perhaps, he wrote Parts III and IV simply because he could also show in them, at least to his own satisfaction, that his reading of Scripture supports his design for political existence. It is probably more to the purpose to show that religion is to be subordinate to political society since he has already indicated that there are no more pernicious doctrines that lead to war than those arising through interpretations of Scripture.

but also to beasts and plants and inanimate bodies by the name of kingdom is but a metaphorical use of the word. For he only is properly said to reign who governs his subjects by his word and by promise of rewards to those who obey it and by threatening them with punishment who do not obey it. Therefore, subjects in the Kingdom of God are not inanimate bodies nor irrational creatures because they understand no precepts as his. Nor are atheists subjects in the Kingdom of God, nor they who do not believe God has any care of the actions of mankind because they acknowledge no word for his nor have hope of his rewards or fear of his threats.[68] They therefore who believe there is a God who governs the world and has given precepts and propounded rewards and punishments to mankind are subjects. All the rest are to be understood as enemies.

To rule by words requires that such words be manifestly made known or they are not laws. For to the nature of laws belongs a sufficient and clear promulgation such as may take away the excuse of ignorance which in the laws of men is of only one kind which is proclamation or promulgation by the voice of man. But God declares his laws three ways: by the dictates of natural reason, by revelation, and by the voice of some man to whom the operation of miracles he procures credit with the rest. From this there arises a triple Word of God—rational, sensible, and prophetic, to which corresponds a triple hearing—right reason, supernatural sense, and faith. There have not been any universal laws given for supernatural sense which consists in revelation or inspiration because God does not speak in that manner except to particular persons and to diverse men diverse things.

From the difference between the other two kinds of God's word—rational and prophetic—there may be attributed to God a twofold kingdom, natural and prophetic. Natural is that in which he governs as many of mankind as acknowledge his Providence by natural dictates of right reason. Prophetic is where having chosen out of one particular nation (the Jews) for his subjects, he governed them and none but them, not only by natural reason but by positive laws which he gave them by the mouths of his holy prophets. I intend to speak of the natural Kingdom of God in this chapter.

The right of nature whereby God reigns over men and punishes those who break his laws is to be derived from his irresistible power, not from his creating them as if he required obedience as of gratitude for his benefits. I have formerly shown how the sovereign right arises from pact. To show how the same right may arise from nature requires no more but to show in what case it is never taken away. Seeing all men by nature had a right to all things, each one had right to reign over all the rest. But because this right could not be obtained by force, it concerned the safety of everyone, laying by that right to set up men (with sovereign authority) by common consent to rule and defend them. Whereas if there had been any man of irresistible power there had been no reason why he should not by that power be ruled and defended both of himself and them according to his own discretion.

---

68. In the seventeenth century, the definition of "atheist" was much broader (and the term was often used polemically against one's theological and philosophical opponents) than the contemporary usage, that there is no divinity.

Therefore, to those whose power is irresistible, the dominion of all men adheres naturally by their excellence of power. Consequently it is from that power that the kingdom of men and the rights of afflicting men at his pleasure belongs naturally to God Almighty as omnipotent, not as creator and gracious. Though punishment is due for sin only because by that word is understood affliction for sin, the right of afflicting is not always derived from men's sin but from God's power.

The question, "why evil men often prosper and good men suffer adversity," has been much disputed by the ancients and is the same as ours, "By what right God dispenses the prosperities and adversities of this life," and is of that difficulty as it has shaken the faith not only of the vulgar but of philosophers.[69] And which is more, of the saints concerning divine Providence. "How good," said David, "is the God of Israel to those who are upright in heart and yet my feet were almost gone, my treadings had well-nigh slipped, for I was grieved at the wicked when I saw the ungodly in such prosperity."[70] And Job, how earnestly does he expostulate with God for the many afflictions he suffered, notwithstanding his righteousness? This question in the case of Job is decided by God himself, not by arguments derived from Job's sin, but his own power. For whereas the friends of Job drew their arguments for his affliction to his sin and he defended himself by the conscience of his innocence, God himself takes up the matter and having justified the affliction by arguments from his power. Examples are "Where were you when I laid the foundations of the Earth,"[71] and the like, both approved Job's innocence and reproved the erroneous doctrine of his friends. Conformable to this doctrine is the sentence of our Savior concerning the man who was born blind in these words, "Neither has this man sinned, nor his fathers, but that the works of God might be made manifest in him." And though it is said "that death entered into the world by sin" (by which is meant that if Adam had never sinned he had never died, that is, never suffered any separation of his soul from his body) it does not follow that God could not have justly afflicted him though he had not sinned as well as he afflicts other living creatures that cannot sin.

Having spoken of the rights of God's sovereignty as grounded only on nature, we are to consider next what are the divine laws or dictates of natural reason, which laws concern either the natural duties of one man to another or the honor naturally

---

69. Hobbes is referring here to the "Problem of Evil," one of the oldest and most discussed questions in the philosophy of religion. It is discussed by the medieval philosophers such as Augustine in *Confessions* VII (*Confessions*, trans. Maria Boulding [New York: New City Press, 2001]) and moderns such as Leibniz and Spinoza (see *The Problem of Evil in Early Modern Philosophy*, ed. Elmar J. Kremer and Michael J. Latzer [Toronto: University of Toronto Press, 2001]), critically appraised by Voltaire in *Candide* (*Candide; or, Optimism: A New Translation, Backgrounds, Criticism*, ed. and trans. Robert M. Adams [New York: W. W. Norton, 1991]), and continues to this day. For an accessible discussion of the Problem of Evil, see Michael Tooley, "The Problem of Evil," *Stanford Encyclopedia of Philosophy*, http://plato.stanford.edu/entries/evil/ and an anthology edited by William L. Rowe, *God and the Problem of Evil* (Malden, MA: Blackwell, 2001).

70. Pss. 73.1–3.

71. Job 38.4.

due to our divine sovereign. The first are the same laws of nature of which I have spoken already in Chapters XIV and XV of this treatise. They are, namely, equity, justice, mercy, humility, and the rest of the moral virtues. It remains therefore that we consider what precepts are dictated to men only by their natural reason without other Word of God, touching the honor and worship of the divine majesty.

Honor consists in the inward thought and opinion of the power and goodness of another, and therefore to honor God is to think as highly of his power and goodness as possible. Of the opinion that the external signs appearing in the words and actions of men are called worship is one part of that which the Latins understand by the word *cultus*. For *cultus* signifies properly and constantly the labor which a man bestows on anything with a purpose to make benefit by it. Now, those things of which we make benefit are either subject to us and the profit they yield follows the labor we bestow upon them as a natural effect or they are not subject to us but answer our labor according to their own wills. In the first sense the labor bestowed on the Earth is called culture, and the education of children a culture of their minds. In the second sense, where men's wills are to be wrought to our purpose by complaisance and not by force, it signifies as much as courting, that is, a winning of favor by good offices as by praises, by acknowledging their power, and whatever is pleasing to them from whom we look for any benefit. This is properly worship in which sense *publicola* is understood for a worshipper of the people and *cultus dei* for the worship of God.

From internal honor consisting in the opinion of power and goodness arises three passions: love, which has reference to goodness, and hope and fear that relate to power. And three parts of external worship: praise, magnifying, and blessing. The subject of praise is goodness, the subject of magnifying and blessing are power, and the effect of them is felicity. Praise and magnifying are significant both by words and actions. It is by words when we say a man is good or great. It is by actions when we thank him for his bounty and obey his power. The opinion of the happiness of another can only be expressed by words.

There are some signs of honor (both in attributes and actions) that are naturally so such as attributes of good, just, liberal and the like and actions such as prayers, thanks, and obedience. Others are so by institution or custom of men and in some times and places are honorable, in others dishonorable, and in others indifferent such as are the gestures in salutation, prayer and thanksgiving in different times and places differently used. The former is natural and the latter is arbitrary worship.

There are two differences in arbitrary worship. Sometimes it is a command and sometimes voluntary worship. It is commanded when it is such as he requires who is worshipped. It is free when it is such as the worshipper thinks fit. When it is commanded, not the words and gestures but the obedience is worship. But when free, the worship consists in the opinion of the beholders. For if to them the words or actions by which we intend honor seem ridiculous and tending to contumely, they are not worship because a sign is not a sign to him who gives it but to him to whom it is made, that is, to the spectator.

Again, there is public and private worship. Public is worship that a commonwealth performs as one person. Private is that which a private person exhibits.

Public in respect of the whole commonwealth is free. In respect of particular men it is not free. Private is in secret free but in the sight of the multitude it is never without some restraint either from laws or from the opinion of men which is contrary to the nature of liberty.

The end of worship among men is power. For where a man sees another worshipped he supposes him powerful and is more ready to obey him which makes his power greater. But God has no ends. The worship we do him proceeds from our duty and is directed according to our capacity by those rules of honor that reason dictates to be done by the weak toward the more potent men in hope of benefit for fear of damage or in thankfulness for good already received from them.

That we may know what worship of God is taught us by the light of nature, I will begin with his attributes. Where, first, it is manifest we ought to attribute to him existence. For no man can have the will to honor that which he thinks not to exist. Second, those philosophers who said the world or the soul of the world was God spoke unworthily of him and denied his existence.[72] For by God is understood to be the cause of the world and to say the world is God is to say there is no cause of it, that is, no God. Third, to say the world was not created but eternal (seeing that which is eternal has no cause) is to deny there is a God.[73] Fourth, they who attribute (as they think) ease to God take from him the care of mankind. They take from him his honor for it takes away men's love and fear of him which is the root of honor.[74] Fifth, in those things that signify greatness and power, to say he is finite is not to honor him for it is not a sign of the will to honor God to attribute to him less than we can. And finite is less than we can because to finite it is easy to add more.

Therefore, to attribute figure to him is not to honor for all figure is finite. Nor to say we conceive and imagine or have an idea of him in our mind for whatever we conceive is finite. Nor to attribute to him parts or totality which are the attributes only of things finite. Nor to say he is this or that place for whatever is in place is bounded and finite. Nor that he is moved or rests for these attributes ascribe to him place. Nor that there are more gods than one because it implies them all finite, for there cannot be more than one infinite. Nor to ascribe to him (unless metaphorically, meaning not the passion but the effect) passions that partake of grief as repentance, anger, mercy, or want as of appetite, hope, desire, or any passive faculty. For passion is power limited by something else.

Therefore when we ascribe a will to God it is not be understood as that of man for a rational appetite but as the power by which he effects everything. Likewise, when we attribute to him sight and other acts of sense as also knowledge and understanding, which is in us nothing but a tumult of the mind raised by external

---

72. The Stoics, for instance.

73. Hobbes agrees with Aristotle in contending that saying "the world is God" or that "the world is eternal" is to say that there is no God.

74. Aristotle's position is again critically assessed by Hobbes at this point. Aristotle's position in his *Metaphysics* is that God is the Unmoved Mover, the Uncaused Cause that has no personal connection to human beings whatsoever and is simply that which "is."

things that press the organic parts of a man's body. For there is no such thing in God and being things that depend on natural causes cannot be attributed to him.

He who will attribute to God nothing but what is warranted by natural reason must either use negative attributes such as finite, eternal, incomprehensible, and superlatives such as most high, most great, and the like, or indefinite such as good, just, holy, creator, and in such sense as if he did not meant to declare what he is (for that would be to circumscribe him within the limits of our fancy) but how much we admire him and how ready we would be to obey him, which is a sign of humility and a will to honor him as much as we can. For there is but one name to signify our conception of his nature—that is, I AM—and one name of his relation to us and that is God in which is contained Father, King, and Lord.

It is a most general precept of reason concerning the actions of divine worship that they are signs of the intention to honor God such as are, first, prayers because it is not the carvers when they made images who were thought to make them gods but the people who prayed to them. Second, thanksgiving, which differs from prayer in divine worship only in that prayers precede and thanks succeed the benefit the end both of the one and the other being to acknowledge God for author of all benefits as well past as future. Third, gifts—that is to say, sacrifices and oblations (if they are of the best)—are signs of honor for they are thanksgivings. Fourth, not to swear by any but God is naturally a sign of honor for it is a confession that God only knows the heart and that no man's wit or strength can protect a man against God's vengeance on the perjured.

Fifth, it is a part of rational worship to speak considerately of God for it argues a fear of him and fear is a confession of his power. It follows that the name of God is not to be used rashly and to no purpose for that is as much as in vain and it is to no purpose unless it is by way of oath and by order of the commonwealth to make judgments certain or between commonwealths to avoid war. And that disputing God's nature is contrary to his honor. For it is supposed that in this natural Kingdom of God there is no other way to know anything but by natural reason, that is, from the principles of natural science which are so far from teaching us anything of God's nature as they cannot teach us our own nature or the nature of the smallest living creature. And therefore when men dispute the attributes of God out of the principles of natural reason, they dishonor him. For in the attributes we give to God, we are not to consider the signification of philosophical truth but the signification of pious intention to do him the greatest honor we are able. From the want of which consideration have proceeded the volumes of disputation about the nature of God that do not tend to his honor but of our own wits and learning and are nothing but inconsiderate and vain abuses of his sacred name.

Sixth, in prayers, thanksgivings, offerings, and sacrifices it is a dictate of natural reason that they are everyone in his kind the best and most significant of honor. As for example that prayers and thanksgiving be made in words and phrases not sudden nor light nor plebeian, but beautiful and well composed. For otherwise we do not honor God as much as we can. Therefore the heathens absurdly worshipped images for gods. But their doing it in verse and with music, both voice and instruments, was reasonable. Also, the beasts they offered in sacrifice and the gifts they offered and their actions in worshipping were full of submission and commemorative of benefits received and were according to reason as proceeding from intention to honor him. Seventh, reason directs not only to worship God in secret but also and especially in public and in sight of men. For without that (that which in honor is most acceptable) procuring others to honor him is lost.

Last, obedience to his laws (that is, in this case to the laws of nature) is the greatest worship of all. For as obedience is more acceptable to God than sacrifice, so also to set light by his commandments is the greatest of all contumelies. And these are the laws of that divine worship which natural reason dictates to private men.

Seeing a commonwealth is only one person it ought also to exhibit to God one worship which, when it does, when it commands it to be exhibited by private men, publicly. This is public worship the property whereof is to be uniform. For those actions that are done differently by different men cannot be said to be a public worship. Therefore where many sorts of worship are allowed, proceeding from different religions of private men, it cannot be said there is any public worship nor that of commonwealth is of any religion at all.

Because words (and consequently the attributes of God) have their signification by agreement and constitution of men, those attributes are to be held significative of honor that men shall intend to be and whatever may be done by the wills of particular men where there is no law but reason may be done by the will of the commonwealth by the civil laws. Because a commonwealth has no will nor makes no laws but those that are made by the will of him or them who have sovereign power, it follows that those attributes which the sovereign ordains in worship of God for signs of honor ought to be taken and used for it by private men in their public worship.

Because not all actions are signs by constitutions but some are naturally signs of honor, and others contumely, the latter (which are those that men are ashamed to do in the sight of them they reverence) cannot be made by human power a part of divine worship. Nor can the former (such as are decent, modest, humble behavior) ever be separated from it. But whereas there is an infinite number of actions and gestures of an indifferent nature, such of them as the commonwealth ordain to be publicly and universally in use as signs of honor and parts of God's worship are to be taken and used for it by the subjects. That which is said in Scripture, "It is better to obey God than men," has place in the Kingdom of God by pact and not by nature.

Having thus briefly spoken of the natural Kingdom of God and his natural laws I will add only to this chapter a short declaration of his natural punishments. There is no action of a man in this life that is not the beginning of so long a chain of consequences as no human Providence is high enough to give a man prospect to the end. In this chain there are linked together both pleasing and unpleasing events in such manner as he who will do anything for his pleasure must engage himself to suffer all the pains annexed to it and these pains are the natural punishments of those actions which are the beginning of more harm than good. Hereby it comes to pass that intemperance is naturally punished with diseases, rashness with mischances, injustice with the violence of enemies, pride with ruin, cowardice with oppression, negligent government of princes with rebellion, and rebellion with slaughter. For seeing punishments are consequent to the breach of laws, natural punishments must be naturally consequent to the breach of the laws of nature and therefore follow them as their natural (not arbitrary) effects.

And thus far concerning the constitution, nature, and right of sovereigns and concerning the duty of subjects derived from the principles of natural reason. And now, considering how different this doctrine is from the practice of the greatest part of the world (especially these western parts) that have received their moral learning from Rome and Athens and how much depth of moral philosophy is required in them who have the administration of sovereign power, I am at the point of believing my labor as useless as the commonwealth of Plato. For he also is of the opinion that it is impossible for the disorders of state and change of governments by civil war ever to be taken away until sovereigns are philosophers.[75] But when I consider again that the science of natural justice is the only science necessary for sovereigns and their principal ministers and that they need not be charged with the mathematical sciences (as they are by Plato) further than by good laws to encouragement to the study of them. I also consider that neither Plato nor any other philosopher hitherto has put into order and sufficiently or probably proved all the theorems of moral doctrine that men may learn thereby how to govern and how to obey. I recover some hope that one time or other this writing of mine may fall into the hands of a sovereign who will consider it himself (for it is short, and I think clear) without the help of any interested or envious interpreter and by the exercise of the entire sovereignty in protecting the public teaching of it convert this truth of speculation into the utility of practice.

---

75. Plato argued in *The Republic* that the best state is one ruled by philosopher-kings. See Plato, *Republic*, trans. G. M. A. Grube, revised by C. D. C. Reeve, 2nd ed. (Indianapolis, IN: Hackett, 1992).

PART III. OF A CHRISTIAN COMMONWEALTH

Chapter XXXII. Of the Principles of Christian Politics

Hobbes begins a slow dissection of traditionally accepted religious views, accounting for them in terms of his materialist philosophical system. God cannot be an immaterial substance since the term "immaterial substance" is a contradiction. This is important for Hobbes to explain how one may "hear" from God, and to do so he introduces the office of the sovereign as prophet.

I have derived the rights of sovereign power and the duty of subjects up to this time from the principles of nature only such as experience has found true or consent (concerning the use of words) has made so—that is to say from the nature of men known to us by experience and from definitions (of such words as are essential to all political reasoning) universally agreed on. But in what I am next to handle, which is the nature and rights of a Christian commonwealth of which there is much dependence upon supernatural revelations of the will of God, the ground of my discourse must be not only the natural Word of God but also the prophetical.

Nevertheless, we are not to renounce our senses and experience. Nor (that which is the undoubted Word of God) our natural reason. For they are the talents which he has put into our hands to negotiate until the coming again of our Blessed Savior and therefore not to be folded up in the napkin[1] of an implicit faith but employed in the purchase of justice, peace, and true religion. Though there may be many things in God's word that are above reason—that is to say, which cannot be

---

1. This is a reference to a parable found in Luke 19.11–27, in which a nobleman gave his servants money to invest while he was away. One servant wrapped what was given to him in a cloth and hid it out of fear of losing what he was given. Rather than investing the money, he stored it away. As a result, while the other servants invested theirs and turned a profit, the servant who hid his money did not. Upon the return of the master, this servant received his wrath. In an alternative account of this parable (Matt. 25.14–30), the author refers to the currency as "talents" though the servant in this narrative buried the currency to hide it rather than wrapping and hiding it.

either demonstrated or confuted by natural reason—there is nothing contrary to it. But when it seems so, the fault is either in our unskillful interpretation or erroneous ratiocination.[2]

Therefore, when anything therein written is too hard for our examination, we are bidden to captivate our understanding to the words and not to labor in sifting out a philosophical truth by logic of mysteries that are not comprehensible or do not fall under any rule of natural science. For it is with the mysteries of our religion, as with wholesome pills for the sick, which if swallowed whole have the virtue to cure but if chewed are for the most part cast up again without effect.

By captivity of our understanding is meant the will to obedience where obedience is due and not submission of the intellectual faculty to the opinion of any other man. For sense, memory, understanding, reason, and opinion are not in our power to change but always and necessarily such as the things we see, hear, and consider suggest to us. And therefore they are not the effects of our will but our will of them. We then captivate our understanding and reason when we forbear contradiction, when we speak as (by lawful authority) we are commanded, and when we live accordingly. This is, in sum, trust and faith reposed in him who speaks though the mind is capable of any notion at all from the words spoken.

When God speaks to man it must be either immediately or by mediation of another man to whom he had formerly spoken by himself immediately. How God speaks to a man immediately may be understood by those well enough to whom he has so spoken. But how the same should be understood by another is hard if not impossible to know. For if a man pretends to me that God has spoken to him supernaturally and immediately and I doubt it, I cannot easily perceive what argument he can produce to oblige me to believe it. It is true that if he is my sovereign he may oblige me to obedience so I do not by act or word declare that I do not believe him, but not to think any other way than my reason persuades me. But if one who does not have such authority over me pretends the same, there is nothing that exacts either belief or obedience.

For to say that God has spoken to him in the Holy Scripture is not to say that God has spoken to him immediately but instead by mediation of the prophets or of the apostles or of the Church in such manner as he speaks to all other Christian men. To say he has spoken to him in a dream is no more than to say that he dreamed God spoke to him which is not of force to win belief from any man who knows that dreams are for the most part natural and may proceed from former thoughts and such dreams as those from self-conceit and foolish arrogance as well as false opinion of a man's own godliness or any other virtue which he thinks has merited

---

2. Hobbes will not, even for supernatural revelation, let go of natural reason as the one and only source of verification of the truth of claims. This is an indication of Hobbes' disagreement with many who claim that the Word of God is ineffable and therefore also sometimes incomprehensible. Hobbes shares with many Deists (such as Thomas Paine in the *Age of Reason*, http://www.ushistory.org/paine/reason/singlehtml.htm, to give a prominent example from the Enlightenment period of modern thought in the eighteenth century) the notion that there is nothing in God's words or actions that is contrary to reason.

the favor of extraordinary revelation. To say he has seen a vision or heard a voice is to say that he has dreamed between sleeping and waking. For in this manner a man many times naturally takes his dream for a vision since he has not well observed his own slumbering. To say he speaks by supernatural inspiration is to say he finds an ardent desire to speak or some strong opinion of himself for which he can allege no natural and sufficient reason. God Almighty can speak to a man by dreams, visions, voice, and inspiration but he obliges no man to believe he has done so to he who pretends it because he is a man and may err, and (which is more) he may lie.

How then can he to whom God has never revealed his will immediately (except by the way of natural reason) know when he is to obey or not to obey his word that is delivered by a person who claims to be a prophet? . . . If one prophet deceives another, what certainty is there of knowing the will of God except by reason? I answer: Out of the Holy Scripture that there are two marks which together a true prophet is to be known. One is doing miracles and the other is not teaching any other religion than that which is already established. Separately, neither of these is sufficient. [Deut. 13.1–5 indicate that if a prophet claims to do a miracle and subsequently he says to follow strange gods that are unknown, the prophet is to be put to death for speaking to you to revolt from the Lord your God.] In these words two things are to be observed. First, that God will not have miracles alone serve for arguments to approve the prophet's calling but for an experiment of the constancy of our adherence to himself.[3] . . . Second, no matter how great a miracle may be, if it tends to stir up revolt against the king or the person who governs by the king's authority, he who does such miracle is to be considered as sent to make a trial of their allegiance. For these words, "revolt from the Lord your God" are in this place equivalent to "revolt from your king." [Christ also warned of the danger of miracles (Matt. 24.24)] by which it appears that false prophets may have the power of miracles but we are not to take their doctrine for God's word. . . .

Just as miracles without preaching God's established doctrine is an insufficient argument of immediate revelation, so is preaching true doctrine without doing miracles. If a man who does not teach false doctrine pretends to be a prophet without showing any miracle, he is not to be regarded for his pretense. This is evident by Deut. 18.21–22 [in which the Lord claims that we should not fear the prophet who speaks in the name of the Lord of things that shall not come to pass because he has spoken it out of the pride of his own heart]. A man may here again ask "When the prophet has foretold a thing, how shall we know whether it will come to pass or not? For he may foretell it as a thing to arrive after a certain long time, longer than the time of a man's life or indefinitely that it will come to pass one time or other. In this case the mark of a prophet is not useful." Therefore the miracles that oblige us to believe a prophet ought to be confirmed by an immediate and not a long deferred event.[4] It is clear that teaching the religion which God

---

3. Hobbes here gives a scriptural example of pagan sorcerers who exercised magic to perform miracles.
4. It is worth noting that in Part I, Chapter III, Hobbes has already established that prophetic prediction is merely a matter of prudence: a prophet is the best guesser.

has established and showing a present miracle, joined together, were the only marks whereby Scripture would have a true prophet—that is to say immediate revelation to be acknowledged—neither of them being singly sufficient to oblige any other man to regard what he says.

Seeing miracles now cease we have no sign left by which to acknowledge the pretended revelations or inspirations of private men. Nor are we obliged to hear any doctrine farther than conformable to Holy Scriptures since they supply since the time of our Savior the lack of all other prophecy from which, by wise and careful ratiocination, all rules and precepts necessary to knowledge of our duty both to God and man—without enthusiasm or supernatural inspiration—may easily be deduced. It is Scripture out of which I am to take the principles of my own discourse concerning the rights of those who are the supreme governors on Earth of Christian commonwealths and of the duty of Christian subjects toward their sovereigns. To that end, I shall speak in the next chapter of the books, writers, scope, and authority of the Bible.

Chapter XXXIII. Of the Number, Antiquity, Scope, Authority, and Interpreters of the Books of Holy Scriptures

In this chapter, Hobbes undertakes the task of biblical criticism, including questioning the canonical nature of Scriptures as well as their authorship, and offers his own new definitions of theological terms such as "angel" and "Spirit." Hobbes treats metaphorically some terms that have been taken literally, and others that have been taken metaphorically, Hobbes treats literally.

Further, Hobbes notes that God speaks to people either immediately or by mediation of another person. And even though a sovereign might command a subject to believe that God has spoken to him, Hobbes contends that there is no one who can make a subject believe anything other than what reason persuades him to believe.

The Books of Holy Scripture are those which ought to be the canon—that is to say—the rules of Christian life. Because all rules of life which men are bound to observe in conscience are laws, the question of the Scripture is the question of what is natural and civil law throughout all Christendom. Though it is not determined in Scripture what laws every Christian king shall constitute in his own dominions, it is determined what laws he shall not constitute. Seeing therefore that I have already proved that sovereigns in their own dominions are the sole legislators, those books only are canonical—that is, law—in every nation that are established to be so by sovereign authority. It is true that God is sovereign of all sovereigns and therefore when he speaks to any subject he ought to be obeyed, whatever any earthly potentate commands to the contrary. But the question is not of obedience to God but of when and what God has said. This, to subjects who have no supernatural revelation cannot be known except by natural reason that guided them to obtain peace and justice to obey the authority of their several commonwealths—that is, to obey their lawful sovereigns. According to this obligation, I can acknowledge no other books of the Old Testament to be Holy Scripture except those which have been commanded to be acknowledged to be so by the authority of the Church of England.[5] What books these are is sufficiently known without a catalog of them here. . . . The books of the New Testament are equally acknowledged as canon by all Christian Churches and by all sects of Christians who admit any books at all to be canonical.

---

5. There is dispute, highlighted during the Protestant Reformation, as to which books belong in the Christian Bible. The Roman Catholic Bible followed the Latin Vulgate and included writings that the Protestants rejected, calling them Apocrypha.

It has not been made evident by any sufficient testimony of other history (which is the only proof of matter of fact) nor can there be any arguments of natural reason (for reason serves only to convince of the truth of consequence and not of fact) who were the original writers of the several Books of Holy Scripture. The light therefore that must guide us in this question must be that which is held out to us from the books themselves. . . .

Although these books were written by diverse men, it is manifest the writers were all indued with one and the same spirit in that they conspire to one and the same end, which is setting forth the rights of the Kingdom of God, the Father, Son, and Holy Ghost. . . . The histories and prophecies of the Old Testament and the Gospels and epistles of the New Testament have had one and the same scope, to convert men to the obedience of God. . . .

From what source the Scriptures derive their authority is a question much disputed between the diverse sects of Christian religion. The question is also stated in these terms such as how we know them to be the Word of God or why we believe them to be so. The difficulty of resolving it arises chiefly from the improperness of the words in which the question itself is couched. For it is believed on all hands that the first and original author of them is God and consequently the question disputed is not that. It is clear that none can know they are God's word (though all true Christians believe it) but those to whom God himself has revealed it supernaturally. And therefore the question is not rightly moved of our knowledge of it. Last, when the question is propounded for our belief some for one and others for other reasons there can be rendered no one general answer for them all. The question truly stated is: By what authority are they made law.

As far as they do not differ from the laws of nature there is no doubt that they are the law of God and carry their authority with them, legible to all men who have the use of natural reason. But this is no authority than that of all other moral doctrine consonant to reason. The dictates whereof are eternal laws, not made. If they are made law by God himself they are of the nature of written law which are laws only to those to whom God has sufficiently published them so that no man can excuse himself saying he did not know they were his.

Therefore, he to whom God has not supernaturally revealed that they are his nor that those who published them were sent by him is not obliged to obey them by any authority but his whose commands already have the force of laws, that is to say by any other authority than that of the commonwealth residing in the sovereign who alone has legislative power. Again, if it is not the legislative authority of the commonwealth that gives them the force of laws it must be some other authority derived from God, either public or private. If private, it obliges only him to whom in particular God has been pleased to reveal it. If every man should be obliged to take for God's law what particular men on pretense of private inspiration or revelation should obtrude upon him and out of pride and ignorance, take their own dreams and extravagant fancies, and their madness, for testimonies of God's spirit— or out of ambition, they pretend to such divine testimonies falsely and contrary to their own consciences—it would be impossible that any divine law should be acknowledged. If public, it is the authority of the commonwealth or of the Church.

But the Church, if it is one person, is the same thing with a commonwealth of Christians, called a commonwealth because it consists of men united in one person who is their sovereign. And a church, because it consists in Christian men united in one Christian sovereign. But if the Church is not one person, then it has no authority at all. It can neither command nor do any action at all, nor is it capable of having any power or right to anything. Nor has it any will, reason, or voice, for all these qualities are personal. If the whole number of Christians is not contained in one commonwealth, they are not one person. Nor is there a universal church that has any authority over them. Therefore the Scriptures are not made laws by the universal church. Or if it is one commonwealth, then all Christian monarchs and states are private persons and subject to be judged, deposed and punished by a universal sovereign of all Christendom. So that the question of the authority of the Scripture is reduced to this: "Whether Christian Kings and the sovereign assemblies in Christian commonwealths are absolute in their own territories immediately under God or subject to one vicar of Christ constituted over the universal church to be judged, condemned, deposed, and put to death as he shall think expedient or necessary for the common good."

This question cannot be resolved without a more particular consideration of the Kingdom of God from which also we are to judge of the authority of interpretation of Scripture. Whoever has a lawful power over any writing to make it law has the power also to approve or disapprove of the interpretation of it.

Chapter XXXIV. Of the Signification of Spirit, Angel, and Inspiration in the Books of Holy Scriptures

Hobbes accounts for parts of Scripture that (under traditional interpretation) are contrary to his materialism. Examples are "spirit," "angel," and what it means for Scripture to be "inspired." Hobbes' position is that we use terms such as "spirit" and "angel" to denote things that we fail to understand, and we simply have to be satisfied that this is the case and accept that we use the terms with the intent to honor God.

Seeing that the true foundation of all ratiocination is the constant signification of words which, in the following doctrine, does not depend (as in natural science) on the will of the writer nor (as in common conversation) on vulgar use, but on the sense they carry in the Scripture, it is necessary before I proceed any further to determine out of the Bible the meaning of ambiguous words. The ambiguity of the words may render what I am to infer upon them obscure or disputable. I will begin with the words "body" and "spirit" which, in the language of the Schools are termed corporeal and incorporeal substances.

The word "body" in the most general acceptation signifies that which fills or occupies some certain room or imagined place and does not depend on the imagination but is a real part of what we call the Universe. For the Universe, being the aggregate of all bodies, there is no real part of it that is not also body nor anything properly a body that is not also a part of (that aggregate of all bodies) the Universe. Because bodies are subject to change—that is to say, to variety of appearance to the sense of living creatures—they are called substance, that is to say, subject to various accidents as sometimes to be moved, sometimes to stand still and to seem to our senses sometimes hot, sometimes cold, sometimes of one color, smell, taste, or sound, and sometimes of another. The diversity of seeming (produced by the diversity of the operation of bodies on the organs of our sense) we attribute to alterations of the bodies that operate and call them accidents of those bodies. According to this acceptation of the word, substance and body signify the same thing. Therefore incorporeal substance are words, when joined together, destroy one another, as if a man should say, an "incorporeal body."

But in the sense of the common people not all the Universe is called a body, but only such parts of it as they can discern by the sense of feeling to resist their force or by the sense of their eyes to hinder them from a farther prospect. Therefore in the common language of men, air and aerial substances used not to be taken for bodies but (as often as men are sensible of their effects) are called wind or breath or . . . spirits as when they call that aerial substance in the body of any creature that gives it life and motion vital and animal spirits. But for those idols of the brain that represent bodies to us, where they are not as in a looking glass in a dream or to a distempered brain waking, they are . . . nothing. Nothing at all, I say, there where they seem to be and in the brain itself nothing but tumult proceeding either from the action of the objects or from the disorderly agitation of the organs of our sense. And men who are otherwise employed then search into their causes, not known of themselves what to call them and may therefore easily be persuaded by those whose knowledge they revere much, some to call them bodies and think them made of air compacted by a supernatural power because the sight judges them corporal. And some call them spirits because the sense of touch discerns nothing in the place where they appear to resist their fingers. So the proper signification of spirit in common speech is either a subtle fluid and invisible body or a ghost or other idol or phantasm of the imagination. But there may be many metaphorical significations. For sometimes it is taken for a disposition or inclination of the mind. . . .

Other significations of "spirit" I find nowhere and where none of these can satisfy the sense of that word in Scripture, the place does not fall under human understanding and our faith therein does not consist in our opinion but in our submission as in all places where God is said to be a spirit or where by the Spirit of God is meant God himself. For the nature of God is incomprehensible, that is to say, we understand nothing of what he is but only that he is and therefore the attributes we give him are not to tell one another what he is nor to signify our opinion of his nature, but our desire to honor him with names we conceive most honorable among ourselves.

In Genesis, "The Spirit of God moved upon the face of the waters." Here, if by Spirit of God is meant God himself, then motion is attributed to God and consequently place, which are intelligible only of bodies and not of incorporeal substances. And so the place is above our understanding that can conceive nothing moved that does not change place or that has no dimension. And whatever has dimension is body. But the meaning of those words is best understood also in Genesis where when the Earth was covered with waters—as in the beginning— God intending to abate them and again to discover dry land used words like: "I will bring my spirit upon the Earth and the waters shall be diminished," in which place by spirit is understood a wind (that is, an air or spirit moved) which might be called (as in the former place) the Spirit of God because it was God's work. . . . In like manner, by the Spirit of God that came upon Saul when he was among the prophets who praised God in songs and music is to be understood an unexpected and sudden zeal to join with them in their own devotion, not a ghost. . . .[6]

---

6. Hobbes gives a number of additional examples from Scripture at this point on different meanings of the word "spirit" in various biblical contexts. He is showing that it is not an immaterial person or substance and should be understood in other ways that fit within his materialist project. Hobbes' position is that such things are to be understood as "thin" substances that are invisible but have the same dimensions as other bodies.

The name "angel" generally signifies a messenger and most often a messenger of God. By messenger of God is signified anything that makes known his extraordinary presence, that is to say, the extraordinary manifestation of his power especially by a dream or vision. Concerning the creation of angels, there is nothing delivered in the Scriptures. It is often repeated that they are spirits but by the name of spirit is signified in Scripture and vulgarly among the Jews and Gentiles sometimes thin bodies such as the air, the wind, and vital and animal spirits of living creatures, and sometimes the images that rise in the fancy in dreams and visions which are not real substances but accidents of the brain. Yet when God raises them supernaturally to signify his will, they are not improperly termed God's messengers, that is to say, his angels.

The Gentiles vulgarly conceived the imagery of the brain for things really subsistent without them and not dependent on the fancy and framed their opinions of good and evil demons out of them. Because they seemed really to subsist they called them substances. Because they could not feel them with their hands, they called them incorporeal. So also the Jews on the same ground . . . had generally an opinion . . . that those apparitions (which it pleased God sometimes to produce in the fancy of men for his own service and therefore called them his angels) were substances and not dependent on the fancy but permanent creatures of God. The ones they thought were good to them they esteemed the angels of God and those they thought would hurt them they called evil angels or evil spirits. . . . such were . . . the spirits of madmen, of lunatics, and epileptics: for they considered those troubled with such diseases to be demoniacs.

But if we consider the places of the Old Testament where angels are mentioned we shall find that in most of them there can be nothing else understood by the word "angel" but some image raised (supernaturally) in the fancy to signify the presence of God in the execution of some supernatural work. And therefore in the rest where their nature is not expressed it may be understood in the same manner. . . .

To men who understand the signification of these words, "Substance" and "Incorporeal," they imply a contradiction who take "incorporeal" for "not-body" and not for a subtle body, as to say an angel or spirit is (in that sense) an incorporeal substance is to say in effect that there is no angel or spirit at all. Therefore, considering the signification of the word "angel" in the Old Testament and the nature of dreams and visions that happen to men in the ordinary way of nature, I was inclined to the opinion that angels were nothing but supernatural apparitions of the fancy raised by special and extraordinary operation of God to make his presence and commandments known to mankind and chiefly to his own people. But the many places of the New Testament and our Savior's own words and in such texts where there no suspicion of corruption of the Scripture have extorted from my feeble reason an acknowledgment and belief that there may also be substantial and permanent angels. But to believe they are in no place, that is to say, nowhere, that is to say, nothing, as they (though indirectly) say that will have them be incorporeal, cannot be evinced by Scripture.

Inspiration depends on the signification of the word "spirit," which must either be taken properly and then it is nothing but blowing into a man some thin and subtle air or wind in the manner as a man fills a bladder with his breath. Or if spirits are not corporeal but have their existence only in the fancy it is nothing but blowing in of a phantasm. This is improper to say and impossible, for phantasms do not exist but only seem to be something. That word therefore is only used in the Scriptures metaphorically, such as in Genesis where it is said that God inspired into man the breath of life. No more is meant than that God gave him vital motion. . . .

In the same manner, to take inspiration in the proper sense or to say that Good Spirits entered into men to make them prophecy or evil spirits into those who became frenetic, lunatic, or epileptic is not to take the word in the sense of the Scripture for the spirit there is taken for the power of God working by causes unknown to us. . . .

Chapter XXXV. Of the Signification in Scripture of Kingdom of God, of Holy, Sacred, and Sacrament

Hobbes continues to redefine theological terms in this chapter. One of the terms, "Kingdom of God," is of great significance due to its entirely different meaning from its common use. By "Kingdom of God," Hobbes does not mean some ethereal location outside this world. Instead, he means a civil government in which the political sovereign is God's prophet or spokesperson. In addition, Hobbes discusses sacraments: baptism and the "Lord's Supper." The discussion of sacraments is important for the implications of baptism regarding Church membership and state citizenship.

The Kingdom of God in the writings of divines and especially in sermons and treatises of devotion is taken most commonly for eternal felicity after this life in the highest Heaven, which they also call the kingdom of glory and sometimes for . . . sanctification which they term the kingdom of grace. But never for the monarchy, that is to say, the sovereign power of God over any subjects acquired by their own consent which is the proper signification of kingdom.

To the contrary, I find the Kingdom of God to signify in most places of Scripture a kingdom properly so named and constituted by the votes of the people of Israel in the peculiar manner where they chose God for their king by covenant made with him upon God's promising them possession of the land of Canaan. It is seldom meant metaphorically, and then it is taken for dominion over sin (and only in the New Testament) because such a dominion as that every subject shall have in the Kingdom of God and without prejudice to the sovereign.

From the very creation, God not only reigned over all men naturally by his might but also had peculiar subjects whom he commanded by a voice as one man speaks to another. In this manner he reigned over Adam and gave him commandment to abstain from the tree of knowledge of Good and evil. When he did not obey and tasted of it, he took upon him to be as God judging between good and evil by his own sense and not by his creator's commandment. His punishment was privation of the estate of eternal life wherein God had at first created him. And afterward God punished all but eight persons of his posterity with a universal deluge.[7] And in these eight consisted the Kingdom of God at that time. . . .

---

7. This is the deluge or the Great Flood told of in Gen. 6–9. In this account, there were eight survivors in the world: Noah and his wife along with their three sons and daughters-in-law.

The Kingdom of God is a civil kingdom which consisted, first, in the obligation of the people of Israel to those laws which Moses should bring unto them from Mount Sinai. . . . If the Kingdom of God (also called the kingdom of Heaven from the gloriousness and admirable height of that throne) were not a kingdom which God by his lieutenant or vicars who deliver his commandments to the people exercised on Earth, there would not have been so much contention and war about who it is by whom God speaks to us. Neither would many priests have troubled themselves with spiritual jurisdiction nor any king have denied it to them.

Out of this literal interpretation of the Kingdom of God arises also the true interpretation of the word "holy." For it is a word that in God's kingdom answers to that which men in their kingdoms used to call public, or the king's.

The king of any country is the public person or representative of all his own subjects. And God the king of Israel was the Holy One of Israel. The nation which is subject to one earthly sovereign is the nation of that sovereign, that is, of the public person. So the Jews, who were God's nation, were called "a holy nation" in Exodus. For by "holy" is always understood either God himself or that which is God's in propriety as by "public" is always meant either the person of the commonwealth itself or something that is of the commonwealth as no private person can claim any propriety in it.

Therefore, the Sabbath (God's day) is a holy day. The temple (God's house) is a holy house. Sacrifices, tithes, and offerings (God's tribute) are holy duties. Priests, prophets and anointed kings under Christ (God's ministers) are holy men. The celestial ministering spirits (God's messengers) are holy angels, and the like, and wherever the word "holy" is taken properly, there is still something signified of propriety gotten by consent. In saying "hallowed be thy name," we pray to God for grace to keep the first commandment of "having no other Gods but him." Mankind is God's nation in propriety. But only the Jews were a holy nation. This is because they became his propriety by covenant.

The word "profane" is usually taken in the Scripture to mean the same as "common" and consequently their contraries, "holy" and "proper" in the Kingdom of God must be the same also. But figuratively, those men are also called holy who led such godly lives as if they had forsaken all worldly designs and wholly devoted and given themselves to God. In the proper sense, that which is made holy by God's appropriating and separating it to his own use is said to be sanctified by God as the seventh day in the fourth commandment and as the elect in the New Testament were said to be sanctified when they were endued with the spirit of godliness. And that which is made holy by the dedication of men and given to God to be used only in his public service is also called sacred and said to be consecrated such as temples and other houses of public prayer and their utensils, priests, and ministers, victims, offerings, and all external matter of sacraments.

There are degrees of holiness for of those things that are set apart for the service of God there may be some set apart again for a nearer and more special service. The whole nation of Israelites were a people holy to God, yet the tribe of Levi was among the Israelites a holy tribe and among the Levites the priests were yet more holy. And among the priests, the high priest was the most holy. So the land of Judea was the holy land but the Holy City in which God was to be worshipped was more holy. And again, the temples are more holy than the city and the sanctum sanctorum more holy than the rest of the Temple.

A sacrament is a separation of some visible thing from common use and a consecration of it to God's service for a sign either of our admission into the Kingdom of God to be of the number of his peculiar people or for a commemoration of the same. In the Old Testament the sign of admission was circumcision. In the New Testament it was baptism. The commemoration of it in the Old Testament was eating (at a certain time, which was anniversary) of the lamb by which they were put in mind of the night in which they were delivered out of their bondage in Egypt and in the New Testament, celebrating the Lord's Supper, by which we are put in mind of our deliverance from the bondage of sin by our Blessed Savior's death upon the cross. The sacraments of admission are but once used because there needs but one admission. But because we have need of being often put in mind of our deliverance and our allegiance, the sacraments of commemoration have need to be reiterated. And these are the principal sacraments and, as it were, the solemn oaths we make of our allegiance. There are also other consecrations that may be called sacraments as the word implies only consecration to God's service. But as it implies an oath or promise of allegiance to God there were no other in the Old Testament but circumcision and the Passover, nor are there any other in the New Testament but Baptism and the Lord's Supper.

Chapter XXXVI. Of the Word
of God, and of Prophets

In his efforts to mitigate threats from religious enthusiasm, Hobbes addresses the qualities of true prophecy and the marks of a true prophet. For Hobbes, teaching true religion denotes a genuine prophet, and true religion is established by the political sovereign. Therefore, the only true prophet is either aligned with the sovereign (as a subordinate prophet), and writes in support of or in praise of the true religion as established, or is the sovereign himself as supreme prophet.

When there is mention of the Word of God or of man, it does not signify a part of speech such as grammarians call a noun or a verb or any simple voice without a context with other words to make it significative, but it is a perfect speech or discourse whereby the speaker affirms, denies, commands, promises, threatens, wishes, or interrogates. In this sense it is not vocabulum that signifies a word but . . . some speech, discourse, or saying. Again, if we say the "Word of God" or of man, it may be understood sometimes of the speaker (as the words that God has spoken or that a man has spoken), in which sense, when we say, the Gospel of St. Matthew we understand St. Matthew to be the writer of it and sometimes of the subject. . . .

Considering these two significations of the Word of God as it is taken in Scripture, it is manifest in the latter sense (where it is taken for the doctrine of the Christian religion) that the whole Scripture is the Word of God. But in the former sense it is not so. . . . The Word of God as it is taken for that which he has spoken is sometimes understood properly and sometimes metaphorically. Properly is as the words he has spoken to his prophets. Metaphorically is for his wisdom, power, and eternal decree in making the world in which sense those fiats, "Let there be light," "Let there be a firmament," "Let us Make Man," etc. (Gen. 1) are the Word of God. . . .

Second, for the effect of his Word, that is to say for the thing itself, by which his word is affirmed, commanded, threatened or promised . . . it is meant the thing itself was to come to pass. . . .[8]

There are also places in the Scripture where the Word of God signifies such words as are consonant to reason and equity, though spoken sometimes neither by a

---

8. With this second sense, Hobbes describes instances where the "Word of God" is confirmed by coming to pass: what God says will happen, will happen. He gives several examples in the original text, including a scriptural account in which Joseph is kept in an Egyptian prison until God's word has come to pass. That is, the event itself occurred (Gen. 40.13; Pss. 105.19).

prophet nor by a holy man. An example is the Pharaoh Necho who was an idolater. His words to the good King Josiah in which he advised him by messengers not to oppose him in his march against Carchemish, are said to have proceeded from the mouth of God. . . . [9] The Word of God is then also to be taken for the dictates of reason and equity when the same is said in the Scripture to be written in man's heart. . . .

The name "Prophet" sometimes signifies in Scripture prolocutor, that is, he who speaks from God to man or from man to God and sometimes predictor, as a fore-teller of things to come. And sometimes one who speaks incoherently as men who are distracted. It is most frequently used in the sense of speaking from God to the people. So Moses, Samuel, Elijah, Isaiah, Jeremiah, and others were proph-ets. . . . Also those who in Christian congregations taught the people are said to prophesy (1 Cor. 14.3). . . . For prophesy, in [other places in Scripture], signifies no more but praising God in psalms and holy songs . . . The poets of the heathen who composed hymns and other sorts of poems in honor of their gods were called *Vates* (prophets) . . . and it is evident (Titus 1.12) where St. Paul said of the Cretans that a prophet of their own said they were liars. It is not that St. Paul held their poets to be prophets, but acknowledged that the word "prophet" was commonly used to signify those who celebrated the honor of God in verse.

By "prophecy" is sometimes meant "prediction" or foretelling of future contin-gents, not only they who were prophets who were God's spokesmen and foretold those things to others which God had foretold to them, but also all the impostors who pretend by the help of familiar spirits or superstitious divination of past events from false causes to foretell the like events in the future. Of this (as I have declared already in Chapter XII of this discourse) there are many kinds who gain in the opinion of the most common men a greater reputation by prophecy by one casual event that may be wrested to their purpose than can be lost again by never so many failings. Prophecy is not an art nor (when it is taken for prediction) a constant vocation but an extraordinary and temporary employment from God most often of good men but sometimes also of the wicked . . . . Incoherent speech was among the Gentiles taken for one sort of prophecy because the prophets of their oracles who were intoxicated with a spirit or vapor of the cave of the Pythian Oracle at Delphi were for the time really made and spoke like madmen of whose loose words a sense might be made to fit any event in such sort as all bodies are said to be made of prime matter. In the Scripture I also find it so taken (1 Sam. 18.10) in the words "And the evil spirit came upon Saul, and he prophesied in the midst of the house."

Although there are not so many significations in Scripture of the word "prophet," yet it is the most frequent in which it is taken for him to whom God speaks imme-diately that which the prophet is to say from him to some other man or to the people. Hereupon a question may be asked in what manner God speaks to such a prophet. Can it (may some say) be properly said that God has voice and language when it cannot be properly said he has a tongue or other organs as a man? The prophet David argues thus: "Shall he who made the eye not see? Or he who made

9. Hobbes is referencing 2 Chron. 3.21–23.

the ear not hear?" But this may be spoken to signify our intention to honor him and not (as usually) to signify God's nature. For to see and hear are honorable attributes and may be given to God to declare (as far as our capacity can conceive) his Almighty power. If it were to be taken in the strict and proper sense, one might argue from his making all parts of a man's body that he also had the same use of them which we have which would be many of them so uncomely as it would be the greatest contumely in the world to ascribe them to him. Therefore, we are to interpret God speaking to men immediately for that way (whatever it is) by which God makes them understand his will. And the ways by which he does this are many and to be sought only in the Holy Scripture where, though many times it is said that God spoke to this or that person without declaring in what manner, yet there are again many places that deliver also the signs by which they were to acknowledge his presence and commandment. By these may be understood how he spoke to many of the rest.[10]

In what manner God spoke to Adam, Eve, Cain and Noah is not expressed nor how he spoke to Abraham until the time he came out of his own country to Sichem in the land of Canaan and then God is said to have appeared to him. So there is one way by which God made his presence clear and that is by an apparition or vision. . . . And "Your sons and your daughters shall prophesy, your old men shall dream dreams, and your young men shall see visions." (Joel 2.28) where again the word "prophesy" is expounded by dream and vision.

To say God spoke or appeared as he is in his own nature is to deny his infiniteness, invisibility, and incomprehensibility. To say he spoke by inspiration or infusion of the Holy Spirit as the Holy Spirit signifies the Deity is to make Moses equal with Christ in whom only the Godhead dwells bodily. . . . To say he spoke by the Holy Spirit as it signifies the graces or gifts of the Holy Spirit is to attribute nothing supernatural to him. For God disposes men to piety, justice, mercy, truth, faith and all manner of virtue, both moral and intellectual, by doctrine, example, and by several natural and ordinary occasions. . . . In what manner God spoke to those sovereign prophets of the Old Testament whose office it was to enquire of him is not intelligible. In the time of the New Testament there was no sovereign prophet except our Savior who was both God who spoke and the prophet to whom he spoke. . . . There is no good inclination that is not the operation of God. But these operations are not always supernatural. When, therefore, a prophet is said to speak in the spirit or by the spirit we are to understand no more but that he speaks according to God's will declared by the supreme prophet. For the most common acceptation of the word "spirit" is the signification of a man's intention, mind, or disposition.

In the time of Moses, there were seventy men besides himself who prophesied in the camp of the Israelites. In what manner God spoke to them is declared, "The Lord came down in a cloud, and spake unto Moses, and took of the spirit that

---

10. Some read Hobbes rhetorically on points such as this. The reason is that though Hobbes says God speaks to man in whatever way the Scriptures say, he also just spent many pages deconstructing what the Scriptures actually say about hearing from God.

was upon him, and gave it to the seventy elders. And it came to pass, when the spirit rested upon them, they prophesied and did not cease."[11] By which it is clear, first, that their prophesying to the people was subservient and subordinate to the prophesying of Moses for that God took of the spirit of Moses to put upon them so that they prophesied, as Moses would have them. Otherwise, they would not have suffered to prophesy at all. . . . Second, that the Spirit of God in that place signifies nothing but the mind and disposition to obey and assist Moses in the administration of the government. For if it were meant they had the substantial Spirit of God—that is, the divine nature—inspired into them, then they had it in no less manner than Christ himself, in whom only the Spirit of God dwelt bodily. It is meant, therefore, of the gift and grace of God that guided them to cooperate with Moses from whom their spirit was derived. . . . We are [also] told that Moses . . . did appoint judges and officers over the people . . . and of these were those seventy, whom God, by putting upon them Moses' spirit, inclined to aid Moses in the administration of the kingdom. . . . So that by the spirit is meant inclination to God's service and not any supernatural revelation. . . .

All prophecy supposes vision or dream (when they are natural they are the same) or some special gift of God rarely observed in mankind to be admired where observed. Gifts such as the most extraordinary dreams and visions may proceed from God by his supernatural and immediate as well as his natural operation and by mediation of second causes. Therefore, there is need of reason and judgment to discern between natural and supernatural gifts and between natural and supernatural visions or dreams. Consequently, men need to be very circumspect and wary in obeying the voice of a man pretending to be a prophet who requires us to obey God in that way he tells us in God's name to be the way to happiness. For he who pretends to teach men the way of so great felicity pretends to govern them—that is to say, to rule and reign over them—which is a thing that all men naturally desire and therefore worthy to be suspected of ambition and imposture. Consequently, it ought to be examined and tried by every man before he yields them obedience unless he has yielded it to them already in the institution of commonwealth such as when the prophet is the civil sovereign or is authorized by the civil sovereign. If this examination of prophets and spirits was not allowed to every one of the people it would be to no purpose to set out the marks by which every man might be able to distinguish between those whom they ought and ought not to follow. . . .

Every man was then [in the time of the Old Testament] and is now bound to make use of his natural reason to apply all prophecy to those rules God has given us to discern the true from the false. One of those rules in the Old Testament was conformable to the doctrine that Moses the Sovereign had taught them and another is the miraculous power of foretelling what God would bring to pass. . . .

The rule is perfect on both sides. He is a true prophet who preaches the Messiah has already come in the person of Jesus. And he is a false one who denies that he has come and looks for him in some future impostor who shall take upon him that honor falsely and whom the Apostle properly called Anti-Christ. Every man

---

11. Num. 11.25.

therefore ought to consider who is the sovereign prophet—that is to say, who is God's viceregent on Earth and has next under God the authority of governing Christian men and to observe for a rule that doctrine which he in the name of God commanded to be taught and thereby to examine and try out the truth of those doctrines which pretended prophets with or without miracles shall at any time advance. If they find it contrary to that rule to do as they did that came to Moses and complained that there were some who prophesied in the camp whose authority so to do they doubted and leave to the sovereign as they did to Moses to uphold or to forbid them as he should see cause. And if he disavows them then they are no more to obey their voice or if he approves them then to obey them as men to whom God has given part of the spirit of their sovereign. For when Christian men do not take their Christian sovereign for God's prophet they must either take their own dreams for the prophecy by which they mean to be governed and the tumor of their own hearts for the Spirit of God or they must suffer themselves to be led by some strange prince or by some of their fellow subjects who can bewitch them by slander of government into rebellion without any other miracle to confirm their calling than an occasional extraordinary success and impunity. By this means all laws both divine and human are destroyed and all order, government, and society reduced to the first chaos of violence and civil war.

Chapter XXXVII. Of Miracles and Their Use

For Hobbes, there is no good reason to believe in miracles. We think of things that are strange or uncommon as admirable or objects of wonder, but that does not mean that miracles exist. Events cease to be considered miraculous when natural causes and explanations are found for them, and what is a miracle to one person does not seem miraculous to another. If there are miracles, Hobbes contends, they are designed by God to create belief in the elect. Any person who claims to be able to perform a miracle is simply a deceiver.

Miracles signify the admirable works of God and therefore they are also called wonders. Because they are for the most part done for a signification of his commandment in such occasions as without them men are apt to doubt (following their private natural reasoning) what he has commanded and what not, they are commonly called signs in Holy Scripture . . . for showing and fore-signifying that which the Almighty is about to bring to pass.

To understand what is a miracle we must first understand what works they are which men wonder at and call admirable. There are but two things which make men wonder at any event. One is, if it is strange . . . such as the like of it has never or very rarely been produced. The other is when it is produced we cannot imagine it to have been done by natural means but only by the immediate hand of God. But when we see some possible, natural cause of it, no matter how rarely the like has been done—or if the like has not been done often no matter how impossible it is to imagine a natural means of it—we wonder no more nor esteem it for a miracle.

Therefore, if a horse or cow should speak it would be a miracle because it is the case that the thing is strange and the natural cause is difficult to imagine. It would be like this to see a strange deviation of nature in the production of some new shape of a living creature. But when a man or other animal engenders his like, though we know no more how this is done than the other, yet because it is usual it is not a miracle. Similarly, if a man is metamorphosed into a stone or into a pillar it is a miracle because it is strange. But if a piece of wood is so changed, because we see it often it is not a miracle. And yet we know no more by what operation of God the one is brought to pass than the other.

The first rainbow that was seen in the world was a miracle because it was the first and consequently it was strange and served for a sign from God placed in Heaven to assure his people there would be no more universal destruction of the world by water. But at this day, because they are frequent they are not miracles either to those who know their natural causes or to those who do not know them. Again, there are many rare works produced by the art of man, but when we know they are done because we also know the means by which they are done, we do not count them for miracles because they are not wrought by the hand of God but by mediation of human industry.

Furthermore, seeing admiration and wonder are consequent to knowledge and experience by which some men are endued more and some less, it follows that the same thing may be a miracle to one and not to another. Then, ignorant and superstitious men make great wonders of those works which other men, knowing they proceed from nature (which is not the immediate but the ordinary work of God) do not admire at all. Examples are when an eclipse of the Sun and moon have been taken for supernatural works by the common people when, nevertheless, there were others who could from their natural causes have foretold the very hour they should arrive. Or when a man by confederacy and secret intelligence gets knowledge of the private actions of an ignorant and unwary man and thereby tells him what he has done in a former time it seems to him a miraculous thing. . . .

It belongs to the nature of a miracle that it be wrought for procuring credit to God's messengers, ministers and prophets that thereby men may know that they are called, sent, and employed by God and thereby are better inclined to obey them. Therefore, though all the creation of the world and after that the destruction of all living creatures in the universal deluge were admirable works. But because they were not done to procure credit to any prophet or other minister of God they used not to be called miracles. For no matter how admirable a work is, the admiration consists not in that it could be done because men naturally believe the Almighty can do all things, but because he does it at the prayer or word of man. . . .

We may observe in Scripture that the end of miracles was to beget belief not universally in all elect or reprobate men but in the elect only, that is, such as God had determined should become his subjects. For those miraculous plagues of Egypt did not have for their end the conversion of Pharaoh. God had told Moses before that he would harden the heart of Pharaoh that he should not let the people go. And when he let them go at last, miracles did not persuade him but the plagues forced him to it. . . . The end of all the miracles of Moses, of prophets, of our Savior and his apostles was to add men to the Church . . . such as could be saved—that is to say, such as God had elected. Therefore our Savior sent from his Father could not use his power in the conversion of those his Father had rejected. . . .

From what I have here set down of the nature and use of a miracle, we may define it thus: "A miracle is a work of God (besides his operation by the way of nature ordained in the creation) done for making manifest to his elect the mission of an extraordinary minister for tier salvation." From this definition we may infer, first, that in all miracles the work done is not the effect of any virtue in the prophet because it is the effect of the immediate hand of God, that is to say God has done it without the use of the prophet therein as a subordinate cause. Second, that no devil, angel, or other created spirit can do a miracle. For it must either be by virtue of some natural science or by incantation—that is—virtue of words. For if the enchanters do it by their own independent power, there is some power that does not proceed from God which all men deny. And if they do it by power of them, then it is not the work from the immediate hand of God but natural and consequently it is not a miracle.

There seem to be some texts of Scripture that seem to attribute the power of working wonders (equal to some of those immediate miracles wrought by God himself) to certain arts of magic and incantation. . . . Yet there is no place in Scripture that tells us what an enchantment is. If therefore enchantment is not, as many think it to be, working of strange effects by spells and words, but imposture and delusion wrought by ordinary means and they are so far from supernatural as the impostors need not study so much as of natural causes but the ordinary ignorance, stupidity, and superstition of mankind to do them, those texts that seem to countenance the power of magic, witchcraft, and enchantment must have another sense than at first sight they seem to bear.

It is evident enough that words have no effect but on those who understand them and then they have no other but to signify the intentions or passions of those who speak and thereby produce hope, fear, or other passions or conceptions in the hearer. Therefore when a rod seems a serpent or the water blood or any other miracle seems done by enchantment if it is not to the edification of God's people, neither the rod nor water nor any other thing is enchanted, that is to say wrought upon by the words but the spectator. So that all the miracles consist in is that the enchanter has deceived a man which is no miracle but a very easy matter to do.

For such is the ignorance and aptitude to error generally of all men but especially of those who do not have much knowledge of natural causes and of the nature and interests of men as by innumerable and easy tricks to be abused. What opinion of miraculous power before it was known there was a science of the course of stars might a man have gained who should have told the people this hour or day the Sun should be darkened? A juggler by the handling of his goblets and other trinkets if it were not now ordinarily practiced would be thought to do his wonders by the power at least of the Devil. A man who has practiced to speak by drawing in his breath (which kind of men in ancient time were called *Ventriloqui*) and so make the weakness of his voice seem to proceed from the distance of place and not from the weak impulsion of the organs of speech and is able to make very many men believe it is a voice from Heaven, whatever he pleases to tell them. And for a crafty man who has inquired into the secrets and familiar confessions that one man ordinarily makes to another of his actions and past adventures to tell them him again is no hard matter, and yet there are many who by such means obtain the reputation of being conjurers. . . . These do all they do by their own single dexterity. But if we look upon the impostures wrought by confederacy there is nothing no matter how impossible to be done that is impossible to be believed. For two men conspiring, one to seem lame and the other to cure him with a charm, will deceive many. But many conspiring, one to seem lame and another to cure him and all the rest to bear witness, will deceive many more.

In this aptitude of mankind to give too hasty belief to pretended miracles there can be no better nor I think any other caution than that which God has prescribed . . . in the beginning of the thirteenth and end of the eighteenth chapter of Deuteronomy: That we do not take anyone for a prophet who teaches any other religion than that which God's lieutenant (which at that time was Moses) has established nor any (though he teaches the same religion) whose prediction we do not see come to pass. Moses therefore in his time and Aaron and his successors in their times and the sovereign governor of God's people, next under himself—that is to say, the head of the Church in all times—are to be consulted what doctrine he has established before we give credit to a pretended miracle or prophet. And when that is done, the thing they pretend to be a miracle must both be seen done and to use all means possible to consider whether it is really done and not only so but whether it is such as no man can do the like by his natural power but that it requires the immediate hand of God. In this also we must have recourse to God's lieutenant to whom in all doubtful cases we have submitted our private judgments. For example, if a man pretends that after certain words spoken over a piece of bread that presently God has made it not bread but a God or a man or both—and nevertheless it looks still as like bread as it always did—there is no reason for any man to think it really done nor consequently to fear him until he inquires of God, by his vicar or lieutenant whether it is done or not. If he says not, then follow that which Moses said in Deuteronomy that "thou shalt not fear him who has spoken it presumptuously." If he says it is done then he is not to contradict it. So also if we do not see but only hear from someone else of a miracle, we are to consult the lawful church—that is to say, the lawful head thereof—how far we are to give credit to the relaters of it. This is chiefly the case of men who in these days live under Christian sovereigns. For in these times I do not know one man who ever saw any such wondrous work done by the charm or at the word or prayer of a man that a man endued with only a mediocrity of reason would think supernatural. And the question is no more whether what we see done is a miracle whether the miracle we hear or read of was a real work and not the act of a tongue or pen, but in plain terms, whether the report is true or a lie. In this question we are not each to make our own private reason or conscience, but the public reason, that is, the reason of God's supreme lieutenant, judge. And indeed we have made him judge already if we have given him sovereign power to do all that is necessary for our peace and defense. A private man always has the liberty (because thought is free) to believe or not to believe in his heart those acts that have been given for miracles according as he shall see what benefit can accrue by men's belief to those who pretend or countenance them and thereby conjecture whether they are miracles or lies. But when it comes to confession of faith, private reason must submit to the public—that is to say, to God's lieutenant. But who is this lieutenant of God, and head of the Church, shall be considered in its proper place hereafter.

Chapter XXXVIII. Of the Signification in Scripture of Eternal Life, Hell, Salvation, the World to Come, and Redemption

Hobbes extends skepticism about miracles to what is typically considered topics relevant to an afterlife such as eternal life, hell, and salvation. A motivating factor for mutiny, revolution, and civil unrest is the promise of life after death. But for Hobbes, those motivating factors are removed from civil society when we understand the proper meaning of terms. For example, Hobbes explains that hellfire is simply metaphorical, deriving from a story of the Valley of Hinnon, and Satan is nothing more than an enemy of the Church and not some kind of demon in an imaginary netherworld.

The maintenance of civil society depends on justice and justice on the power of life and death and other lesser rewards and punishments and resides in those who have the sovereignty of the commonwealth. It is impossible a commonwealth should stand where any other than the sovereign has power of giving greater rewards than life and of inflicting greater punishments than death. Seeing eternal life is a greater reward than the present life and eternal torment a greater punishment than death of nature, it is a thing worthy to be well considered of all men who desire (by obeying authority) to avoid the calamities of confusion and civil war what is meant in Holy Scripture by eternal life and eternal torment and for what offenses committed against whom men are to be eternally tormented and for what actions they are to obtain eternal life.

First we find that Adam was created in such a condition of life that had he not broken the commandment of God he would have enjoyed it in the paradise of Eden everlastingly. For there was the tree of life of which he was as long allowed to eat as he should forbear to east of the tree of knowledge of good and evil, which was not allowed to him. Therefore as soon as he had eaten of it, God thrust him out of paradise, "lest he should put forth his hand and also take of the tree of life and live forever." By which it seems to me (with submission nevertheless both in this and in all questions of which the determination depends on Scriptures to the interpretation of the Bible authorized by the commonwealth, whose subject I am) that if Adam had not sinned he would have had an eternal life on Earth and that mortality entered upon itself and his posterity by his first sin. It is not that actual death then entered, for Adam then could never have had children, whereas he lived long after and saw numerous posterity before he died. But where it is said, "In the day that you eat thereof, you shall surely die," it must be meant of his morality and certitude of death. Seeing then that eternal life was lost by Adam's forfeiture in committing sin, he who should cancel that forfeiture was to recover by it that life again. Now, Jesus Christ has satisfied for the sins of all who believe in him and therefore recovered to all believers that eternal life which was lost by the sin of Adam. [This is] . . . more perspicuously delivered in these words: "For since by man came death by man came also the resurrection of the dead. For as in Adam all shall die, even so in Christ shall all be made alive."

Concerning the place wherein men shall enjoy eternal life which Christ has obtained for them, the texts [of the Bible] seem to make it on Earth. For if as in Adam all die, that is, have forfeited paradise and eternal life on Earth, even so in Christ all shall be made alive. Then all men shall be made to live on Earth for else the comparison is not proper. The psalmist (133.3) said, "Upon Zion God commanded the blessing, even life for evermore" for Zion is in Jerusalem upon the Earth. Also that of St. John (Rev. 2.7) "To him who overcomes I will give to eat of the tree of life which is in the midst of the paradise of God." This was the tree of Adam's eternal life, but his life was to have been on Earth. The same seems to be confirmed again by St. John. (Rev. 21.2) where he says, "I John saw the Holy City, New Jerusalem, coming down from God out of Heaven, prepared as a bride adorned for her husband," and again v.10. to the same effect as if he should say the new Jerusalem, the paradise of God, at the coming again of Christ should come down to God's people from Heaven and not they go up to it from Earth. . . . Seeing Adam and Eve would have lived on Earth eternally had they not sinned, it is clear they should not continually have procreated their kind. For if immortals should have generated as mankind do now, the Earth in little time would not have been able to afford them a place on which to stand. The Jews who asked our Savior the question whose wife the woman who had married many brothers should be in the resurrection, did not know the consequences of immortality that there shall be no generation and consequently no marriage any more than there is marriage or generation among the angels. The comparison between eternal life which Adam lost and our Savior by his victory over death has recovered and holds also in this: that as Adam lost eternal life by his sin and yet lived after it for a time, so the faithful Christian has recovered eternal life by Christ's passion even though he dies a natural death and remains dead for a long time, namely, until the resurrection. For as death is reckoned from the condemnation of Adam and not from the execution, so life is reckoned from the absolution and not from the resurrection of those who are elected in Christ.

That the place in which men are to live eternally after the resurrection is the Heavens, and meaning by Heaven those parts of the world which are the most remote from Earth as where the stars are, or above them, in another higher Heaven . . . is not easily to be drawn from any text that I can find. By the kingdom of Heaven is meant the kingdom of the king who dwells in Heaven and his kingdom was the people of Israel whom he ruled by the prophets. . . . And when our Savior Christ by the preaching of his minister shall have persuaded the Jews to return and called the Gentiles to his obedience, then there shall be a new kingdom of Heaven because our king shall then be God whose throne is Heaven without any necessity evident in the Scripture that man shall ascend to his happiness any higher than God's footstool the Earth. On the contrary . . . our Savior means that those patriarchs were immortal not by a property consequent to the essence and nature of mankind but by the will of God that was pleased of his mere grace to bestow eternal life upon the faithful. And though at that time the patriarch and many other faithful men were dead, yet as in the text they lived to God—that is, they were written in the Book of Life with them who were absolved of their sins and ordained to eternal life at the resurrection. That the soul of man is in its own nature eternal and a living creature independent of the body, or that any mere man is immortal other than by resurrection in the last day . . . is a doctrine not apparent in Scripture. . . .

Seeing it has already been proved out of diverse evident places of Scripture in Chapter XXXV of this book that the Kingdom of God is a civil commonwealth where God himself is sovereign by virtue first of the Old and since of the New covenant wherein he reigns by his vicar or lieutenant. The same places do therefore also prove that after the coming again of our Savior in his majesty and glory to reign actually and eternally, the Kingdom of God is to be on Earth. But because of this doctrine (even though it is proved in several familiar places in Scripture it will appear to most men a novelty), I suggest the idea that it maintains nothing in this or any other paradox of religion other than attending to the end of the dispute of the sword concerning the authority . . . by which all sorts of doctrines are to be approved or rejected and whose commands, both in speech and writing (whatever are the opinions of private men) must by all men who mean to be protected by their laws, are obeyed. For the points of doctrine concerning the Kingdom of God have so great influence on the kingdom of Man as not to be determined but by them who under God have the sovereign power.

As the Kingdom of God and eternal life so also God's enemies and their torments after judgment appear by the Scripture to have their place on Earth. The name of the place where all men remain until the resurrection that were either buried or swallowed up by the Earth is usually called in Scripture by words that signify underground. The Latins read this generally as *infernus* and *inferni* and the Greeks *Hades*, that is to say, a place where men cannot see and contain the grave as any other deeper place. The place of the damned after the resurrection is not determined either in the Old or the New Testament by any note of situation but only by the company as that it shall be where such wicked men were as God . . . had destroyed from off the face of the Earth. As for example that they are in Inferno in Tartarus or in the bottomless pit because Corah, Dathan, and Abiram were swallowed up alive into the Earth. Not that the writers of the Scripture would have us believe there could be in the globe of the Earth a pit without bottom or a hole of infinite depth since it is not only finite but also (compared with the height of the stars) of no considerable magnitude. . . . We should believe them there indefinitely where those men are on whom God inflicted that exemplary punishment.

Again, because those mighty men of the Earth who lived in the time of Noah before the flood (which the Greeks called heroes and the Scripture Giants, and both say were begotten by copulation of the children of God with the children of men) were for their wicked life destroyed by the general deluge, the place of the damned is therefore sometimes also marked out by the company of those deceased giants as in Prov. 21.16, "The man who wanders out of the way of understanding shall remain in the congregation of the Giants," and Job 26.5, "Behold the Giants groan under water and they who dwell with them." Here the place of the damned is under the water. . . .

Because the cities of Sodom and Gomorrah were consumed for their wickedness with fire and brimstone by the extraordinary wrath of God and together with them the country about made a stinking bituminous lake, the place of the damned is sometimes expressed by fire and a fiery lake as in the Apocalypse Rev. 21.8. "But the timorous, incredulous, and abominable, and murderers and whoremongers and sorcerers and idolaters and all liars shall have their part in the lake that burns with fire and brimstone, which is the second death." So it is manifest that Hell fire, which is here expressed by metaphor from the real fire of Sodom does not signify any certain kind or place of torment but is to be taken indefinitely for destruction. . . .

From the plague of darkness inflicted on the Egyptians, it is written in Exod. (10.23) "That they did not see one another, nor did any man rise from his place for three days, but all the children of Israel had light in their dwellings," the place of the wicked after judgment is called utter darkness. . . .

Last, there was a place near Jerusalem called the Valley of the Children of Hinnon and in a part of it called Tophet the Jews committed the most grievous idolatry sacrificing their children to the idol Moloch. God also had afflicted his enemies with most grievous punishments there where Josias had burned the priests of Moloch upon their own altars and appears in 2 Kings 23 and the place served afterward to receive the filth and garbage which was carried there out of the city. There used to be fires made there from time to time to purify the air and take away the stench of carrion. From this abominable place, the Jews used ever after to call the place of the damned by the name of Gehenna or Valley of Hinnon. Gehenna is the word which is usually now translated as "Hell" and from the first from time to time burning there we have the notion of everlasting and unquenchable fire.

Seeing now [there are various interpretations of Scripture] so that after the day of Judgment the wicked are eternally to be punished in the Valley of Hinnon or they shall rise again as to be ever underground or under water, or that after the resurrection they shall not see each other nor stir from one place to another, it follows, I think, very necessarily that what is thus said concerning Hell fire is spoken metaphorically. Therefore there is a proper sense to be enquired after (for of all metaphors there is some real ground that may be expressed in proper words) both of the place of Hell and the nature of Hellish torment and of tormentors.

First, for the tormentors, we have their nature and properties exactly and properly delivered by the names of the enemy or Satan, the Accuser, or Diabolus, the Destroyer or Abbadon. The significant names, "Satan," "Devil," "Abbadon," do not set forth to us any individual person as proper names do, but only an office or quality and are therefore appellatives which ought not to have been left untranslated as they are in Latin and modern Bibles because thereby they seem to be the proper names of demons. And men are more easily seduced to believe the doctrine of devils which at that time was the religion of the Gentiles and contrary to that of Moses and of Christ. Because the enemy, the accuser, and destroyer is meant the enemy of those who shall be in the Kingdom of God, if the Kingdom of God after the resurrection is on the Earth (as in the former chapter I have shown by Scripture it seems to be) the enemy and his kingdom must be on Earth, also. For so also was it in the time before the Jews deposed God. For God's kingdom was in Palestine and the nations around it were the kingdoms of the enemy, and consequently by Satan is meant any earthly enemy of the Church.

The torments of Hell are expressed sometimes by "weeping and gnashing of teeth," sometimes by "the worm of conscience," and sometimes by fire. . . . Sometimes it is indicated by "shame and contempt" as in Dan. 12.2. "And many of them who sleep in the dust of the Earth shall awake, some to everlasting life and some to shame and everlasting contempt." All these places design metaphorically a grief and discontent of mind from the sight of the eternal felicity in others which they themselves through their own incredulity and disobedience have lost. Because such felicity in others is not sensible except by comparison with their own actual miseries, it follows that they are to suffer such bodily pains and calamities as are incident to those who not only live under evil and cruel governors but have also for the enemy the eternal king of the saints, God Almighty. Among these bodily pains is to be reckoned also to every one of the wicked a second death. For though the Scripture is clear for a universal resurrection we do not read that to any of the reprobate is promised an eternal life. . . . Glory and power cannot be applied to the bodies of the wicked, nor can the name of second death be applied to the bodies of the wicked. Nor can the name of second death be applied to those who can never die but once. Though in metaphorical speech a calamitous everlasting life may be called an everlasting death, it cannot well be understood of a second death. The fire prepared for the wicked is an everlasting fire, that is to say, the estate in which no man can be without torture both of body and mind after the resurrection shall endure forever. And in that sense the fire shall be unquenchable and the torments everlasting, but it cannot from this be inferred that he who shall be cast into that fire or be tormented with those torments shall endure and resist them so as to be eternally burned and tortured and yet never be destroyed or die. Though there are many places that affirm everlasting fire and torments (into which men may be cast successively one after another forever) yet I find none that affirm there shall be eternal life therein of any individual person but on the contrary, an everlasting death, which is second death (Rev. 20.13–14). "For after death and the grave shall have delivered up the dead which were in them and every man is judged according to his works. Death and the grave shall also be cast into the lake of fire. This is the second death." Whereby it is evident that there is to be a second death of everyone who is condemned at the day of Judgment, after which he shall die no more.

The joys of eternal life are all comprehended in Scripture under the name of salvation or being saved. To be saved is to be secured either respectively against special evils or absolutely against all evil, which comprehends want, sickness, and death itself. Because man was created in an immortal condition not subject to corruption and consequently to nothing that tends to the dissolution of his nature and fell from happiness by the sin of Adam, it follows that to be saved from sin is to be saved from all evil and calamities that sin has brought upon us. Therefore in the Holy Scripture, remission of sin and salvation from death and misery is the same thing as it appears by the words of our Savior who cured a sick man of the palsy. He said (Matt. 9.2) "Son be of good cheer, your sins are forgiven," and knowing the Scribes took for blasphemy that a man should pretend to forgive sins, asked them whether it was easier to say, "Thy sins be forgiven thee," or "Arise and walk," signifying in this that it was all one as to the saving of the sick to say "Thy sins are forgiven" and "Arise and walk." He used that form of speech only to show he had the power to forgive sins. It is evident in reason that since death and misery were the punishments of sin, the discharge of sin must also be a discharge of death and misery—that is to say, absolute salvation such as the faithful are to enjoy after the day of Judgment by the power and favor of Jesus Christ, who for that cause is called our Savior. . . .

Because the general salvation must be in the kingdom of Heaven, there is great difficulty concerning the place. On one side, by "kingdom" (which is an estate ordained by men for their perpetual security against enemies and want) it seems that this salvation should be on Earth. For by salvation is set forth unto us a glorious reign of our king by conquest, not a safety by escape, and therefore there where we look for salvation we must look also for triumph. And before triumph for victory, and before victory for battle, which cannot well be supposed shall be in Heaven. But how good this reason may be, I will not trust to it without very evident places of Scripture. The state of salvation is described at large in Isa. 33.20–24. . . .

In those words we have the place from which our salvation is to proceed ("Jerusalem, a quiet habitation"), the eternity of it ("a tabernacle that shall not be taken down," etc.), the Savior of it ("the Lord, their judge, their lawgiver, their king, he will save us"), the salvation ("the Lord shall be to them a broad mote of swift waters," etc.), and the condition of their enemies ("their tacklings are loose, their masts are weak, the lame shall take the spoil of them"). The condition of the saved is "The inhabitants shall not say I am sick." And last, all this is comprehended in forgiveness of sin ("The people who dwell there shall be forgiven their iniquity") by which it is evident that salvation shall be on Earth then, when God shall reign (at the coming again of Christ) in Jerusalem and from Jerusalem shall proceed the salvation of the Gentiles who shall be received into God's kingdom. . . .

On the other side I have not found any text that can be probably drawn to prove any ascension of the saints into Heaven . . . except that it is called the kingdom of Heaven, which name it may have because God who was king of the Jews governed them by his commands sent to Moses by angels from Heaven to reduce them to their obedience and shall send him again to rule both them and all other faithful men from the day of Judgment everlastingly. . . . But that the subjects of God should have any place as high as his throne or higher than his footstool does not seem suitable to the dignity of a king, nor can I find any evident texts for it in Holy Scripture.

From what has been said of the Kingdom of God and of salvation, it is not hard to interpret what is meant by the world to come. There are three worlds mentioned in Scripture: the old world, the present world, and the world to come. . . . The first world was from Adam to the general flood. Of the present world, our Savior [indicates that his kingdom is not of this world] for he came only to teach men the way of salvation and to renew the kingdom of his Father by his doctrine. Of the world to come . . . it is that world wherein Christ comes down from Heaven in the clouds with great power and glory and shall send his angels and gather together his elect from the four winds and from the uttermost parts of the Earth and from that point reign over them (under his Father) everlastingly.

Salvation of a sinner supposes a preceding redemption, for he who is once guilty of sin is obnoxious to the penalty of the same and must pay (or some other must pay for him) such ransom as that he who is offended and has him in his power shall require. Seeing the person offended is Almighty God in whose power are all things, such ransom is to be paid before salvation can be acquired as God has been pleased to require. By this ransom is not intended a satisfaction for sin that is equivalent to the offense. No sinner for himself nor a righteous man can ever be able to make for another. The damage a man does to another may be made amends for by restitution or recompense, but sin cannot be taken away by recompense for that would be to make the liberty to sin something vendible. But sins may be pardoned to the repentant either gratis or upon such penalty as God is pleased to accept. That which God usually accepted in the Old Testament was some sacrifice or oblation. To forgive sin is not an act of injustice, though the punishment has been threatened. Even among men, though the promise of good binds the promiser, threats (that is to say, promises of evil) do not bind them much less shall they bind God who is infinitely more merciful than men. Our Savior Christ therefore, to redeem us, did not satisfy for the sins of men in that sense as that his death of its own virtue could make it unjust in God to punish sinners with eternal death. But it did make that sacrifice and the oblation of himself at his first coming which God was pleased to require for the salvation at his second coming of such men as in the meantime should repent and believe in him. Though this act of our redemption is not always called a sacrifice and oblation in Scripture, but sometimes a price. Yet by price we are not to understand anything the value of could claim right to a pardon for us from his offended Father, but that price which God the Father was pleased in mercy to demand.

Chapter XXXIX. Of the Signification in Scripture of the Word "Church"

The word "Church" is of particular importance for Hobbes' political system. Unlike traditional meanings such as "God's house," Hobbes contends that "Church" is one person having the power to will and command, which means that "Church" is a group of people who profess Christianity and are united in the person of the political sovereign by the sovereign's command. This meaning has important implications regarding the existence of unlawful Churches and the impossibility of a universal Church.

The word "church" (Ecclesia) signifies in the Books of Holy Scripture diverse things. Sometimes (though not often) it is taken for God's house—that is to say, for a temple—in which Christians assemble to perform holy duties publicly. . . .

Church (when not taken for a house) signifies the same that Ecclesia signified in the Grecian commonwealths, that is to say, a congregation or an assembly of citizens called forth to hear the magistrate speak to them. . . .

It is also taken sometimes for the men who have right to be of the congregation, though not actually assembled—that is to say, for the whole multitude of Christian men however far they are dispersed. . . . In this sense Christ is said to be head of the Church. Sometimes it is taken for a certain part of Christians . . . and sometimes also for the elect only . . . and sometimes for a congregation assembled of professors of Christianity whether their profession is true or counterfeit. . . .

In this last sense only is it that the Church can be taken for one person—that is to say, that it can be said to have power to will, pronounce, command, to be obeyed, to make laws, or to do any other action whatsoever. Without authority from a lawful congregation, whatever act is done in a concourse of people it is the particular act of every one of those who were present and gave their aid to the performance of it and not the act of them all in gross as of one body, much less the act of those who were absent or who were present but not willing that it should be done. According to this sense, I define a church to be "A company of men professing Christian religion, united in the person of one sovereign at whose command they ought to assemble and without whose authority they ought not to assemble." And because in all commonwealths that assembly which is without warrant from the civil sovereign is unlawful, also that church which is assembled in any commonwealth that has forbidden them to assemble is an unlawful assembly.

It follows also that there is on Earth no such universal church as all Christians are bound to obey because there is no power on Earth to which all other commonwealths are subject. There are Christians in the dominions of several princes and states, but every one of them is subject to the commonwealth of which he is himself a member and consequently cannot be subject to the commands of any other person. Therefore a church, such as one as is capable to command, judge, absolve, condemn, or do any other act, is the same thing with a civil commonwealth consisting of Christian men and is called a civil state for that the subjects of it are men, and a church for that the subjects of it are Christians. Temporal and spiritual government are but two words brought into the world to make men see double and mistake their lawful sovereign. It is true that the bodies of the faithful after the resurrection shall be not only spiritual but eternal. But in this life they are gross and corruptible. There is therefore no other government in this life, neither of the state nor religion, except temporal. Nor is teaching any doctrine lawful to any subject which the governor both of the state and of the religion forbids to be taught. That governor must be one, or else there needs to follow faction and civil war in the commonwealth between the church and state, between spiritualists and temporalists, between the sword of justice and the shield of faith, and which is more, in every Christian man's own breast between the Christian and the man. The Doctors of the Church are called pastors and so also are civil sovereigns. But if pastors are not subordinate to one another so that there may be one chief pastor, men will be taught contrary doctrines of which both may be, and one must be, false. Who that one chief pastor is, according to the law of nature, has already been shown, namely, that it is the civil sovereign. To whom the Scripture has assigned that office we shall see in the following chapters.

Chapter XL. Of the Rights of the Kingdom of God in Abraham, Moses, High Priests, and the Kings of Judah

Hobbes traces a history of sovereigns who held civil and ecclesiastical power. The Hobbesian sovereign is naturally the next in this lineage of supreme prophets. Justifying this claim is important in establishing the temporal nature of government in this life.

The father of the faithful and first in the Kingdom of God by covenant was Abraham. For with him the covenant was first made in which he obliged himself and his seed after him to acknowledge and obey the commands of God. It was not only such as he could take notice of (as moral laws) by the light of nature but also such as God should in special manner deliver to him by dreams and visions. For as to the moral law, they were already obliged and did not need to have been contracted by promise of the Land of Canaan. Nor was there any contract that could add to or strengthen the obligation by which both they and all men were bound naturally to obey God Almighty. And therefore the covenant which Abraham made with God was to take for the commandment of God that which in the name of God was commanded him in a dream or vision and to deliver it to his family and cause them to observe it.

In the contract of God with Abraham we may observe three points of important consequence in the government of God's people. First, that at making this covenant, God spoke only to Abraham and therefore did not contract with any of his family or seed, otherwise than as their wills (which make the essence of all covenants) were before the contract involved in the will of Abraham who was therefore supposed to have had a lawful power to make them perform all that he covenanted for them.... From this may be concluded this first point that they to whom God has not spoken immediately are to receive positive commandments of God from their sovereign as the family and seed of Abraham did from Abraham their father and lord and civil sovereign. Consequently in every commonwealth they who have no supernatural revelation to the contrary ought to obey the laws of their own sovereign in the external acts and profession of religion. As for inward thought and belief of men of which human governors can take no notice (for God only knows the heart) they are not voluntary nor the effect of the laws, but of the unrevealed will and power of God and consequently do not fall under obligation.

From this proceeds another point that it was not unlawful for Abraham to punish them when any of his subjects should pretend to private vision or spirit or other revelation from God to countenance any doctrine Abraham forbid or when they followed or adhered to any such pretender. Consequently, it is lawful now for the sovereign to punish any man who shall oppose his private spirit against the laws. For he has the same place in the commonwealth that Abraham had in his own family.

There arises from the same a third point that as none but Abraham in his family, so none but the sovereign in a Christian commonwealth can take notice of what is or what is not the Word of God. For God spoke only to Abraham and it was he only who was able to know what God said and to interpret it to his family. Therefore also they who have the place of Abraham in a commonwealth are the only interpreters of what God has spoken.

The same covenant was renewed with Isaac and afterward with Jacob, but afterward no more until the Israelites were freed from the Egyptians and arrived at the foot of Mount Sinai, and then it was renewed by Moses (as I have said before in Chapter XXXV) in such manner as they became from that time forward the peculiar Kingdom of God whose lieutenant was Moses for his own time and the succession to that office was settled upon Aaron and his heirs after him to be to God a sacerdotal kingdom forever.

By this constitution a kingdom is acquired to God. Seeing Moses had no authority to govern the Israelites as a successor to the right of Abraham because he could not claim it by inheritance. It appears not as yet that the people were obliged to take him for God's lieutenant longer than they believed that God spoke unto him. Therefore his authority (notwithstanding the covenant they made with God) depended merely upon the opinion they had of his sanctity and of the reality of his conferences with God and the verity of his miracles. . . . We are therefore to consider what other ground there was of their obligation to obey him. For it could not be the commandment of God that could oblige them because God did not speak to them immediately but by the mediation of Moses himself. . . . Therefore his authority, as the authority of all other princes, must be grounded on the consent of the people and their promise to obey him. So it was (in Exod. 20.18) "the people when they saw the thunderings and lightnings and the noise of the trumpet and the smoking mountain removed and stood far off. And they said unto Moses, speak with us and we will hear, but let not God speak with us lest we die." Here was their promise of obedience and by this it was they obliged themselves to obey whatever he should deliver unto them for the commandment of God.

Notwithstanding the covenant constituted a sacerdotal kingdom—that is to say, a kingdom hereditary to Aaron—yet that is to be understood to the succession after Moses was dead. For whoever orders and establishes the policy as the first founder of a commonwealth (whether a monarchy, aristocracy, or democracy) must have sovereign power over the people all the while he is doing it. That Moses had the power all his own time is evidently affirmed in the Scripture. . . . It is plain that Moses was alone called up to God (and not Aaron, nor the other priests, nor the seventy elders, nor the people who were forbidden to come up) was alone he who represented to the Israelites the person of God, that is to say, was their sole sovereign under God.

. . . Moses alone had next under God sovereignty over the Israelites and that not only in causes of civil policy but also of religion. For Moses only spoke with God and therefore only could tell the people what God required at their hands. . . . Out of this we may conclude that whoever in a Christian commonwealth holds the place of Moses is the sole messenger of God and interpreter of his commandments. According to this, no man ought in the interpretation of Scripture to proceed further than the bounds which are set by their several sovereigns. For the Scriptures since God now speaks in them are the Mount Sinai, the bounds of which are the laws of those who represent God's person on Earth. To look upon them and in them to behold the wondrous works of God and to learn to fear him is allowed. But to interpret them, that is, to pry into what God said to him whom he appointed to govern under him and make themselves judges whether he governs as God commanded him or not is to transgress the bounds God has set us and to gaze upon God irreverently.

There was no prophet in the time of Moses nor was there a pretender to the Spirit of God except such as Moses had approved and authorized. There were in his time but seventy men who are said to prophesy by the Spirit of God and these were all of Moses' election. . . . But as I have shown before (Chapter XXXVI) by spirit is understood the mind so that the sense of the place is no other than that God endued them with a mind conformable and subordinate to that of Moses so that they might prophesy, that is, to speak to the people in God's name in such manner to set forward (as ministers of Moses and by his authority) such doctrine that was agreeable to Moses' doctrine. For they were but ministers. When two of them prophesied in the camp it was thought a new and unlawful thing and . . . they were accused of it, and Joshua advised Moses to forbid them as not knowing that it was by Moses his spirit that they prophesied. By which it is manifest that no subject ought to pretend to prophesy or to the spirit in opposition to the doctrine established by him whom God has set in the place of Moses.

After Aaron and Moses had died, the kingdom, being a sacerdotal kingdom, descended by virtue of the covenant to Aaron's son, Eleazar the High Priest. God declared him (next under himself) for sovereign at the same time that he appointed Joshua for the general of their army. [God said expressly in Num. 27.21 concerning Joshua that] "He shall stand before Eleazar the Priest who shall ask counsel for him before the Lord, at his word they shall go out and at his word they shall come in, both he and all the children of Israel with him." Therefore, the supreme power of making war and peace was in the priest. The supreme power of judicature also belonged to the high priest. For the book of the law was in their keeping and the priests and Levites only were the subordinate judges in civil causes. . . . For the manner of God's worship, there was never doubt made but that the high priest until the time of Saul had supreme authority. Therefore, the civil and ecclesiastic power were both joined together in one and the same person, the high priest, and ought to be so in whoever governs by divine right, that is, by authority immediately from God.

After the death of Joshua until the time of Saul [there was no king in Israel] and sometimes [in the Book of Judges] it was added that "every man did that which was right in his own eyes." By this is to be understood that where it is said there was no king is meant there was no sovereign power in Israel. . . . But . . . the right of governing, the sovereign power was still in the high priest. Whatever obedience was yielded to any of the judges (who were men chosen by God extraordinarily to save his rebellious subjects out of the hands of the enemy) it cannot be drawn into argument against the right the high priest had to the sovereign power in all matters both of policy and religion. Neither the judges nor Samuel himself had an ordinary, but instead an extraordinary calling to the government and were obeyed by the Israelites out of reverence to their favor with God not out of duty, appearing in their wisdom, courage, or felicity. From this point the right of regulating both policy and religion were inseparable.

To the judges succeeded kings and whereas before all authority both in religion and policy was in the high priest, so now it was all in the king. For the sovereignty over the people which was before, not only by virtue of the divine power but also by a particular pact of the Israelites in God and next under him in the high priest as his viceregent on Earth was cast off by the people with the consent of God himself. When they said to Samuel (1 Sam. 8.5) "make us a king to judge us like all the nations," they signified they would no longer be governed by the commands that should be laid upon them by the priest in the name of God but by one who should command them in the same manner that all other nations were commanded. Consequently in deposing the high priest of royal authority they deposed that peculiar government of God. And yet God consented to it. . . . Having therefore rejected God in whose right the priests governed, there was no authority left to the priests but what the king was pleased to allow them, which was more or less according as the kings were good or evil. For the government of civil affairs it is manifest that it was all in the hands of the king. . . . They say they will be like all the nations that their king shall be their judge and go before them and fight their battles. That is, he shall have the whole authority both in peace and war. In this is contained also the ordering of religion. For there was no other Word of God in that time by which to regulate religion but the Law of Moses, which was their civil law. . . . He therefore had authority over the high priest as over any other subject, which is a great mark of supremacy in religion. . . . From the first institution of God's kingdom to the captivity, the supremacy of religion was in the same hand with that of the civil sovereignty and the priest's office after the election of Saul was not magisterial but ministerial.

Notwithstanding the government both in policy and religion were joined first in the high priests and afterward in the kings as far forth as concerned the right, it appears by the same holy history that the people did not understand it but there were among them a great part—and probably the greatest part—that no longer than they saw miracles or (which is equivalent to a miracle) great abilities or great felicity in the enterprises of their governors gave sufficient credit either to the frame of Moses or to the colloquies between God and the priests. They took occasion as often as their governors displeased them by sometimes blaming the policy, sometimes, the religion, to change government or revolt from their obedience at their pleasure. From this proceeded from time to time the civil troubles, divisions, and calamities of the nation. As, for example, after the death of Eleazar and Joshua, the next generation that had not seen the wonders of God but where left to their own weak reason, did not know they were obliged by the covenant of a sacerdotal kingdom and no longer regarded the commandment of the priest or the Law of Moses but every man did what was right in his own eyes and obeyed in civil affairs such men as from time to time they thought able to deliver them from neighbors that oppressed them. They did not consult with God (as they ought to do) but with such men or women as they guessed to be prophets by their predictions of things to come. . . .

Afterward, when they demanded a king after the manner of other nations, it was not with a design to depart from the worship of God their king. Instead, despairing of the justice of the sons of Samuel, they would have a king to judge them in civil actions. But not that they would allow their king to change the religion which they thought was recommended to them by Moses. So they always kept in store a pretext either of justice or religion to discharge themselves of their obedience whenever they had hope to prevail. . . . It appears that though the power both of state and religion was in kings, none of them were uncontrolled in the use of it but such as were gracious for their own natural abilities or felicities. So from the practice of those times there can be no argument drawn that the right of supremacy in religion was not in the kings. . . .

During the captivity, the Jews had no commonwealth at all. After their return, even though they renewed their covenant with God, there was no promise made of their obedience [to anyone] and presently after they became subjects to the Greeks (from whose customs and demonology, and from the doctrine of the Cabalists, their religion became much corrupted). In such sort as nothing can be gathered from their confusion both in state and religion concerning the supremacy in either. And therefore so far forth as does concerns the Old Testament, we may conclude that whoever had the sovereignty of the commonwealth among the Jews also had the supreme authority in matter of God's external worship and represented God's person, that is, the person of God the Father until such time as he sent his Son Jesus Christ into the world to redeem mankind from their sins and bring them into his everlasting kingdom to be saved forever. Of this we are to speak in the next chapter.

Chapter XLI. Of the Office of Our Blessed Savior

Chapter XLI contains one of Hobbes' more contentious claims: that the Trinity is Moses, Jesus, and the prophets, and not God the Father, God the Son, and God the Holy Spirit.

In Holy Scripture we find three parts of the office of the Messiah. The first is of a redeemer or Savior. The second is of a pastor, counselor, or teacher, that is, of a prophet sent from God to convert those God has elected to salvation. The third is of a king, and eternal king but under his Father as Moses and the High Priests were in their several times. And to these three parts correspond three times. For our redemption he wrought at his first coming by the sacrifice in which he offered up himself for our sins upon the cross. He wrought our conversion partly then in his own person and works partly now by his ministers and will continue to work until his coming again. And after his coming again shall begin his glorious reign over his elect which is to last eternally.

It appertains to the office of a redeemer (that is, of one who paid the ransom of sin, which ransom is death) that he was sacrificed and thereby bare upon his own head and carried away from us our iniquities in such was as God required. Not that the death of one man—though without sin—can satisfy for the offenses of all men in the rigor of justice but in the mercy of God who ordained such sacrifices for sin as he was pleased in his mercy to accept. In the old law (as we may read in Lev. 16) the Lord required that there should be once a year an atonement made for the sins of all Israel, both of priests and others. For doing this Aaron alone was to sacrifice for himself and the priests a young bull and for the rest of the people he was to receive from them two young goats of which he was to sacrifice one. The other, which was the Scape Goat, he was to lay hands on the head of it and by confession of the iniquities of the people to lay them all on that head and then by some opportune man cause the goat to be led into the wilderness and to escape and carry away with him the iniquities of the people. As the sacrifice of one goat was a sufficient price for the ransom of all Israel (because it was acceptable), so the death of the Messiah is a sufficient price for the sins of all mankind because there was no more required. . . . The lamb of God is equivalent to both of those goats. One sacrificed in that he died and in escaping in his resurrection being raised opportunely by his Father and removed from the habitation of men in his ascension.

Since he who redeems has no title to the thing redeemed before the redemption and the ransom paid (and is ransom was the death of the redeemer) it is manifest that our Savior (as a man) was not king of those he redeemed before he suffered death. That is, during the time he conversed bodily on Earth, I say, he was not then king in present, by virtue of the pact which the faithful make with him in baptism. Nevertheless, by renewing their pact with God in baptism, they are obliged to obey him for king (under his Father) whenever he should be pleased to take the kingdom upon him. According to this, our Savior himself expressly said in John 18.36 that "My kingdom is not of this world." Now, seeing the Scripture makes mention of two worlds—the one now and shall remain to the day of Judgment (which is therefore also called the last day) and that which shall be a new Heaven and a new Earth, the kingdom of Christ is not to begin until the general resurrection. . . . To reward every man according to his works is to execute the office of a king and this is not to be until he comes in the glory of his Father with his angels. When our Savior said in Matt. 23.2 "The Scribes and Pharisees sit in Moses' seat. All therefore whatever they bid you to do, observe and do," he declared plainly that he ascribed kingly power for that time not to himself but to them. And so he has also where he said "Who made me a judge or divider over you?" in Luke 12.14 and in John 12.47, "I came not to judge the world but to save the world." Yet our Savior came into this world so that he might be a king and a judge in the world to come. . . . This is spoken of the present world [and so it is not repugnant to the notion that Jesus did not come to judge the world].

If then Christ had no kingdom in this world while he was on Earth, to what end was his first coming? It was to restore unto God by a new covenant the kingdom which, being his by the old covenant, had been cut off by the rebellion of the Israelites in the election of Saul. . . . There are two parts of our Savior's office during his abode upon the Earth. One is to proclaim himself the Christ and another by teaching and by working miracles to persuade and prepare men to live so as to be worthy of the immortality believers were to enjoy at such time as he should come in majesty to take possession of his Father's kingdom. Therefore it is that the time of his preaching is often by himself called the regeneration which is not properly a kingdom and thereby a warrant to deny obedience to the magistrates who then were . . . but only an earnest of the Kingdom of God that was to come to those God had given the grace to be his disciples and believe in him. For this, the godly are said already to be in the kingdom of grace as naturalized in that heavenly kingdom.

Before this time there is nothing done or taught by Christ that tended to the diminution of the civil rights of the Jews or of Caesar. For as touching the commonwealth which then was among the Jews, both they who bear rule among them that they were governed all expected the Messiah and Kingdom of God which they could not have done if their laws had forbidden him (when he came) to manifest and declare himself. Seeing therefore he did nothing but by preaching and miracles go about to prove himself to be the Messiah he did nothing therein against their laws. The kingdom he claimed was to be in another world. He taught all men to obey in the meantime those who sat in Moses' seat. He allowed them to give Caesar his tribute and refused to take upon himself to be a judge. How then could his words or actions be seditious or tend to the overthrow of their then civil government? God, having determined his sacrifice for the reduction of his elect to their former covenanted obedience for the means by which he would bring the same to effect made use of their malice and ingratitude. Nor was it contrary to the laws of Caesar. For though Pilate himself (to gratify the Jews) delivered him to be crucified, yet before he did so he pronounced openly that he found no fault in him and put for title of his condemnation simply that he was king of the Jews and not, as the Jews required, "that he pretended to be king" and regardless of their clamor he refused to alter it saying, "What I have written, I have written."

I have already shown for the third part of his office which was to be king that his kingdom was not to begin until the resurrection. But then he shall be king not only as God in which sense he is king already and always shall be of all the Earth in virtue of his omnipotence but also specifically of his own elect by virtue of the pact they make with him in their baptism. Therefore it is that our Savior said in Matt. (19.28) that his apostles should sit upon twelve thrones judging the twelve tribes of Israel "When the son of man shall sit in the throne of his glory," whereby he signified that he should reign in his human nature. . . . By this it is manifest that the kingdom of Christ appointed to him by his Father is not to be before the son of man shall come in glory and make his apostles judges of the twelve tribes of Israel. But a man may here ask, seeing there is no marriage in the kingdom of Heaven, whether men shall then eat and drink and what by eating is meant in this place? This is expounded by our Savior where he said in John (6.27) "Labor not for the meat which perishes but for that meat which endures unto everlasting life which the son of man shall give you." So that by eating at Christ's table is meant eating of the Tree of Life—that is to say, enjoying immortality in the kingdom of the son of man. By this and many more places it is evident that our Savior's kingdom is to be exercised by him in his human nature.

Again, he is to be king, then, no otherwise than as subordinate or viceregent of God the Father, as Moses was in the wilderness and as the high priests were before the reign of Saul and as the kings were after it. . . . Again, our Savior resembled Moses in the institutions of sacraments both of admission into the Kingdom of God and of commemoration of his deliverance of his elect from their miserable condition. . . . Seeing the authority of Moses was subordinate and he but a lieutenant to God it follows that Christ, whose authority as man was to be like that of Moses, was no more but subordinate to the authority of his Father. . . .

Our Savior therefore both in teaching and reigning represents (as Moses did) the person of God which God from that time forward, but not before, is called the Father and being still one and the same substance is one person as represented by Moses and another person as represented by his Son the Christ. For "person" being a relative to a "representer," it is consequent to a plurality of representers that there is a plurality of persons though of one and the same substance.

Chapter XLII. Of Ecclesiastical Power

Ecclesiastical power concerns the various offices and gifts within the Church. Christ's ministers are to make people believe and have faith, but it is also the case that faith cannot be commanded, so the ministers of Christ have no power to punish anyone for not believing. On the other hand, such ministers may punish violation of the laws, and since punishment belongs only to the sovereign, it must be only the sovereign who is the true minister of Christ. Martyrdom and excommunication are also prominent topics in this chapter, and both have important political implications. Hobbes denies that martyrdom is praiseworthy and he also denies that any authority, religious or otherwise, has the right to excommunicate the sovereign.

For understanding ecclesiastical power and in what and in whom it is we are to distinguish the time from the ascension of our Savior into two parts. One is before the conversion of kings and men endued with sovereign civil power and the other after their conversion. For it was long after the ascension before any king or civil sovereign embraced and publicly allowed teaching of Christian religion.

It is manifest for the time between that the ecclesiastical power was in the apostles and after them in such as were by them ordained to preach the Gospel and to convert men to Christianity and to direct them who were converted in the way of salvation. And after these the power was delivered again to others ordained by these and this was done by imposition of hands upon such as were ordained . . . to advance his kingdom. That imposition of hands was nothing more than the seal of their commission to preach Christ and to teach his doctrine. The giving of the Holy Ghost by . . . imposition of hands was an imitation of that which Moses did. Moses used the same ceremony to his minister Joshua. As we read, "And Joshua . . . was full of the spirit of wisdom; for Moses had laid his hands upon him." (Deut. 34.9) Our Savior, therefore, between his resurrection and ascension, gave his spirit to the apostles. First, by breathing on them, saying, "Receive ye the Holy Spirit," (John 20.22) and after his ascension by sending down upon them "a mighty wind, and cloven tongues of fire" (Acts 2.2–3) and not by imposition of hands. Likewise, God did not lay his hands on Moses. But afterward his apostles transmitted the same spirit by imposition of hands, as Moses did to Joshua. So that as a result it is manifest in whom the ecclesiastical power continually remained in those times where there was not any Christian commonwealth—namely, in them who received the same from the apostles by successive laying on of hands. . . .

Here we have the person of God now born the third time. For as Moses and the high priests were God's representative in the Old Testament and our Savior himself as men during his abode on Earth, so the Holy Ghost—that is to say, the apostles and their successors in the office of preaching and teaching that had received the Holy Spirit—have represented him ever since. But a person (as I have shown before in Chapter XVI) is he who is represented as often as he is properly enough to be said to be three persons, though neither the word "person" nor "trinity" is ascribed to him in the Bible. St. John indeed said in Epistles 1, 5.7 "There are three that bear witness in Heaven, the Father, the Word, and the Holy Spirit, and these three are one." But this does not disagree but accords fitly with three persons in the proper signification of persons which is that which is represented by another. For so God the Father as represented by Moses is one person. As represented by his Son another person, and as represented by the apostles and by the Doctors who taught by authority derived from them is a third person and yet every person here is the person of one and the same God. . . . In the Trinity on Earth the unity is not of the thing for the spirit, the water and the blood are not the same substance though they give the same testimony. But in the Trinity of Heaven the persons are the persons of one and the same God though represented in three different times and occasions. To conclude, the doctrine of the Trinity, as far as can be gathered directly from Scripture, is in substance this: That God who is always one and the same was the person represented by Moses, the person represented by his Son incarnate, and the person represented by the apostles. As represented by the apostles, the Holy Spirit by which they spoke is God. As represented by his Son (that was God and man) the Son is that God. As represented by Moses and the high priests, the Father . . . of our Lord Jesus Christ is that God. From this we may gather the reason why those names "Father," "Son," and "Holy Spirit" in the signification of the Godhead are never used in the Old Testament because they are persons, that is, they have their names from representing. This could not be until diverse men had represented God's person in ruling or in directing under him.

Thus we see how the ecclesiastical power was left by our Savior to the apostles and how they were (to the end they might better exercise that power) endued with the Holy Spirit which is therefore sometimes called in the New Testament *paracletus* which signifies an assister or one called to for help though it is commonly translated a "comforter." Let us now consider the power itself, what it was, and over whom.

In his third general controversy, Cardinal Bellarmine has handled a great many questions concerning the ecclesiastical power of the pope of Rome and begins with this: Whether it ought to be monarchical, aristocratical, or democratical. All these sorts of power are sovereign and coercive. If it should not appear that there is no coercive power left them by our Savior but only a power to proclaim the kingdom of Christ and to persuade men to submit themselves to it and by precepts and good counsel to teach them who have submitted what they are to do so they may be received into the Kingdom of God when it comes and that the apostles and other ministers of the Gospel are our schoolmasters and not our commanders, and their precepts are not laws but wholesome counsels then were all that dispute in vain.

I have shown already (in the last chapter) that the kingdom of Christ is not of this world. Therefore neither can his ministers (unless they are kings) require obedience in his name. For if the supreme king does not have his regal power in this world, by what authority can obedience be required to his officers? As my Father sent me (so said our Savior) I send you. But our Savior was sent to persuade the Jews to return to and to invite the Gentiles to receive the kingdom of his Father and not to reign in majesty . . . as his Father's lieutenant until the day of Judgment.

The time between the ascension and the general resurrection is called a regeneration, not a reigning, that is, a preparation of men for the second and glorious coming of Christ at the day of Judgment. . . . It is compared by our Savior to fishing, that is, to winning men to obedience by persuasion and not by coercion and punishing. Therefore he said to his apostles he would make them fishers of men not so many Nimrods, Hunters of Men. It is compared also to leaven, to sowing of seed, and to the multiplication of a grain of mustard seed, by all which compulsion is excluded and consequently there can be in that time no actual reigning. The work of Christ's ministers is evangelization, that is, a proclamation of Christ and a preparation for his second coming as the evangelization of John Baptist was preparation to his first coming.

Again, the office of Christ's ministers in this world is to make men believe and have faith in Christ. But faith has no relation to nor dependence at all upon compulsion or commandment, but only upon certainty or probability of arguments drawn from reason or from something men believe already. Therefore the ministers of Christ in this world have no power by that title to punish any man for not believing or for contradicting what they say. I say they have no power by the title of Christ's ministers to punish such, but if they have sovereign civil power by political institution, then they may indeed lawfully punish any contradiction to their laws whatsoever. St. Paul said of himself and other preachers of the Gospel in express words in 2 Cor. (1.24) "We have no dominion over your faith but are helpers of your joy."

Another argument may be drawn from the lawful authority which Christ left to all princes as well Christians as infidels that the ministers of Christ in this world have no right of commanding. St. Paul said in Col. (3.20) "Children obey your parents in all things, for this is well pleasing to the Lord," and verse 22, "Servants obey in all things your masters according to the flesh not with eye service as men pleasers, but in singleness of heart as fearing the Lord." This is spoken to them whose masters were infidels and yet they are bidden to obey them in all things. . . . Princes and powers of which St. Peter and St. Paul speak (in Titus 3.1) were all infidels. Much more therefore are we to obey those Christians whom God has ordained to have sovereign power over us. How then can we be obliged to do anything contrary to the command of the king or other sovereign representant of the commonwealth of which we are members and by whom we look to be protected? It is manifest that Christ has not left to his ministers in this world unless they are also endued with civil authority any authority to command other men.

But what (some may object) if a king or a senate or other sovereign person forbids us to believe in Christ? To this I answer that such forbidding is of no effect because belief and unbelief never follow men's commands. Faith is a gift of God which man can neither give nor take away by promise of rewards or menaces of torture. If it be further asked, what if we are commanded by our lawful prince to say with our tongue that we do not believe, must we obey such command? Profession with the tongue is only an external thing and no more than any other gesture by which we signify our obedience. And in what respect a Christian who holds firmly in his heart the faith of Christ has the same liberty which the prophet Elisha allowed to Naaman the Syrian. Naaman was converted in his heart to the God of Israel . . . Naaman believed in his heart but by bowing before the idol Rimmon he denied the true God in effect as much as if he had done it with his lips. But then what shall we answer to our Savior's saying, "Whosoever denies me before men I will deny him before my Father which is in Heaven?" This we may say that whatever a subject, as Naaman was, is compelled to do in obedience to his sovereign and does not do it in order to his own mind but in order to the laws of his country, that action is not his but his sovereign's. Nor is it he who in this case denies Christ before men, but his governor and the laws of his country. If any man shall accuse this doctrine as repugnant to true and unfeigned Christianity, I ask him in case there should be a subject in any Christian commonwealth who should be inwardly in his heart of the Mahometan religion whether if his sovereign command him to be present at the divine service of the Christian Church and that on pain of death he thinks that Mahometan obliged in conscience to suffer death for that cause rather than to obey the command of his lawful prince. If he says he ought rather to suffer death, then he authorizes all private men to disobey their princes in maintenance of their religion, true or false. If he says he ought to be obedient, then he allows to himself that which he denies to another, contrary to the words of our Savior, "Whatsoever you would that men should do unto you, that do you unto them," and contrary to the law of nature (which is the indubitable everlasting law of God) "Do not to another that which you would not he should do unto you."

But what then shall we say of all those martyrs we read of in the history of the Church who have needlessly cast away their lives? For an answer, we are to distinguish the persons who have been for that cause put to death. Some have received a calling to preach and profess the kingdom of Christ openly. Others have had no such calling nor more has been required of them than their own faith. If the former sort have been put to death for bearing witness to this point that Jesus Christ is risen from the dead were true martyrs. For a martyr is (to give the true definition of the word) a witness to the resurrection of Jesus the Messiah, which none can be but those who conversed with him on Earth and saw after he was risen. For a witness must have seen what he testifies or else his testimony is not good. . . . He who is to be a witness of the truth of the resurrection of Christ—that is to say, of the truth of this fundamental article of Christian religion—that Jesus was the Christ must be some disciple who conversed with him and saw him before and after his resurrection and consequently must be one of his original disciples. Whereas they who were not so can witness no more but that their ancestors said and are therefore only witnesses of other men's testimony and are but second martyrs or martyrs of Christ's witnesses.

He who opposes the laws and authority of the civil state to maintain every doctrine which he himself draws out of the history of our Savior's life and of the acts or epistles of the apostles of which he believes upon the authority of a private men is very far from being a martyr of Christ or a martyr of his martyrs. It is one article only which to die for merits so honorable a name, and that article is that Jesus is the Christ, that is to say, he who has redeemed us and shall come again to give us salvation and eternal life in his glorious kingdom. To die for every tenet that serves the ambition or profit of the clergy is not required, nor is it the death of the witness but the testimony itself that makes the martyr, for the word signifies nothing else but the man who bears witness, whether he is put to death for his testimony or not.

Also, he who is not sent to preach this fundamental article but takes it upon himself of his private authority, though he is a witness and consequently a martyr either primary of Christ or secondarily of his apostles, disciples, or their successors, yet he is not obliged to suffer death for that cause because not being called to it, it is not required at his hands, nor ought he to complain if he loses the reward he expects from those who never set him on work. None therefore can be a martyr, either of the first or second degree, who do not have a warrant to preach Christ come in the flesh. That is to say, none but such as are sent to the conversion of infidels. For no man is a witness to him who already believes and therefore needs no witness, but to them who deny or doubt or have not heard it. Christ sent his apostles and his seventy disciples with authority to preach. He did not send all who believed. And he sent them to unbelievers . . . not as sheep to other sheep.

Last, the points of their commission as they are expressly set down in the Gospel do not contain any authority over the congregation.

[The twelve apostles were sent and commanded to preach] that the Kingdom of God was at hand. Preaching in the original is the act which a crier or herald or other officer uses to do publicly in proclaiming of a king. But a crier does not have a right to command any man. . . . Preachers [however] have not magisterial but ministerial power. . . . [12]

Another point of their commission is to teach all nations. . . . Teaching and preaching is therefore the same thing for they who proclaim the coming of a king must make known by what right he comes if they mean shall submit themselves to him. . . . But to teach out of the Old Testament that Jesus was Christ (that is to say, King) and risen from the dead is not to say that men are bound after they believe it to obey those who tell them so against the laws and commands of their sovereigns, but that they shall do wisely to expect the coming of Christ hereafter in patience and faith with obedience to their present magistrates.

Another point of their commission is to baptize. . . . What is baptism? Dipping into water. But what is it to dip a man into the water in the name of anything? The meaning of the words of baptism is that he is baptized or dipped or washed as a sign of becoming a new man and a loyal subject to . . . God . . . and to acknowledge the doctrine of the apostles who assisted by the spirit of the Father and of the Son were left for guides to bring us into that kingdom to be the only assured way to

---

12. In the original text, Hobbes offers a lengthy argument to defend this point using biblical passages. Since those are not included in this edition, the word "therefore" has been replaced with "however" to retain contextual clarity.

do it. . . . We do not in baptism constitute over us another authority by which our external actions are to be governed in this life but promise to take the doctrine of the apostles for our direction to eternal life.

The power of remission and retention of sins, also called the power of loosing and binding and sometimes the keys of the kingdom of Heaven, is a consequence of the authority to baptize or to refuse to baptize. For baptism is the sacrament of allegiance of those who are to be received into the Kingdom of God, that is to say, into eternal life, that is to say, to remission of sin. For as eternal life was lost by committing, so it is recovered by remitting of men's sins. The end of baptism is remission of sins and therefore St. Peter asked what they were to do when those who were converted by his sermon on the day of Pentecost, advised them to "repent and be baptized in the name of Jesus for the remission of sins." Therefore, seeing to baptize is to declare the reception of men into God's kingdom and to refuse to baptize is to declare their exclusion, it follows that the power to declare them cast out or retained in it was given to the same apostles and their substitutes and successors. . . . Words do not grant an authority to give or retain sins simply and absolutely as God forgives or retains them because he knows the heart of man and truth of his penitence and conversion. But it is conditionally to the penitent. This forgiveness or absolution in case the absolved has only a feigned repentance is thereby without other act or sentence of the absolvent made void and has no effect at all to salvation but on the contrary to the aggravation of his sin. The apostles and their successors are to follow the outward marks of repentance. When they appear, they have no authority to deny absolution, and if they do not appear they have no authority to absolve. The same is also observed in baptism for to a converted Jew or Gentile the apostles did not have the power to deny baptism nor to grant it to the unpenitent. Seeing man is able to discern the truth of another man's repentance further than by external marks taken from his words and actions which are subject to hypocrisy, another question will arise. Who is it who is constituted judge of those marks? This question is decided by our Savior himself. . . . Judgment concerning the truth of repentance does not belong to any one man but to the Church, that is, to the assembly of the faithful or to those who have authority to be their representative. . . .

The part of the power of the keys by which men were thrust out from the Kingdom of God is that which is called excommunication. To excommunicate is . . . to cast out of the synagogue, that is, out of the place of divine service. It is a word drawn from the custom of the Jews to cast out of their synagogues such as they thought in manners or doctrine to be contagious as lepers were by the Law of Moses separated from the congregation of Israel until such time as they should be pronounced clean by the priest.

The use and effect of excommunication when it was not strengthened with civil power was no more than that they who were not excommunicated were to avoid the company of those who were. It was not enough to repute them as heathen that had never been Christians for with such they might eat and drink and which with excommunicate persons they might not do. . . . They had no power to keep them out of their synagogues or other places of assembly but that of the owner of the place whether he were Christian or heathen. Because all places are by right in the dominion of the commonwealth as well he who was excommunicated as he who never was baptized might enter into them by commission from the civil magistrate as Paul before his conversion entered into their synagogues at Damascus (Acts 9.2) to apprehend Christian men and women and to carry them bound to Jerusalem by commission from the high priest.

By this it appears that upon a Christian who should become an apostate in place where the civil power did not persecute or not assist the Church, the effect of excommunication had nothing in it of damage in this world or of terror. Not of terror because of their unbelief nor of damage because they returned thereby into the favor of the world and in the world to come were to be in no worse estate than they who never believed. The damage redounded rather to the Church by provocation of those they cast out, to a freer execution of their malice.

Excommunication therefore had its effect only upon those who believed that Jesus Christ was to come again in glory to reign over and to judge both the quick and the dead and should therefore refuse entrance into his kingdom to those whose sins were retained, that is, to those who were excommunicated by the Church. Thence it is that St. Paul calls excommunication a delivery of the excommunicate person to Satan. For without the kingdom of Christ, all other kingdoms after judgment are comprehended in the kingdom of Satan. This is what the faithful stood in fear of as long as they stood excommunicate—that is to say, in an estate in which their sins were not forgiven. By this we may understand that excommunication in the time that Christian religion was not authorized by the civil power was used only for a correction of manners, not of errors in opinion. For it is a punishment of which none could be sensible but such who believed and expected the coming again of our Savior to judge the world and they who so believed needed no other opinion but only uprightness of life to be saved.

There exists excommunication for injustice . . . and for scandalous life. . . . But to excommunicate a man who held the foundation that Jesus was the Christ for difference of opinion in other points by which that foundation was not destroyed, there appears no authority in the Scripture nor example in the apostles. . . .

A heretic is he, who being a member of the Church, teaches nevertheless some private opinion forbidden by the Church. . . . But to reject (in this place) is not to excommunicate the man but to give over admonishing him, to let him alone, to set by disputing with him, as one who is to be convinced only by himself. . . .

There are many conditions requisite that a man be liable to excommunication. First, that he is a member of some commonalty, that is, of some lawful assembly— that is, of some Christian Church—that has the power to judge of the cause for which he is to be excommunicated. For where there is no community there can be no excommunication, nor where there is no power to judge can there be any power to give sentence. From this it follows that one Church cannot be excommunicated by another. For either they have equal power to excommunicate each other, in which case excommunication is not discipline nor an act of authority but schism and dissolution of charity. Or one is so subordinate to the other as that they both have but one voice and then they are but one Church and the part excommunicated is no longer a church but a dissolute member of individual persons.

Because the sentence of excommunication imports and advises not to keep company nor so much as to eat with he who is excommunicated, if a sovereign prince or assembly is excommunicated, the sentence is of no effect. For all subjects are bound to be in the company and presence of their own sovereign (when he requires it) by the law of nature, nor can they lawfully either expel him from any place of his own dominion, whether profane or holy, nor go out of his dominion without his leave, much less (if he calls them to that honor) to refuse to eat with him. As to other princes and states, because they are not parts of one and the same congregation, they do not need any other sentence to keep them from keeping company with the excommunicated state. For the very institution as it unites many men into one community, so it dissociates one community from another, so that excommunication is not needed for keeping kings and states asunder nor has any further effect than is in the nature of policy itself unless it is to instigate princes to war upon one another.

Nor is the excommunication of a Christian subject who obeys the laws of his own sovereign (whether Christian or heathen) of any effect. For if he believes (1 John 4.15) that [Jesus is Christ, then he has the Spirit of God]. But he who has the Spirit of God, he who dwells in God, and he in whom God dwells can receive no harm by the excommunication of men. Therefore, he who believes that Jesus is the Christ is free from all the dangers threatened to persons excommunicated. He who does not believe it is not a Christian. Therefore, a true and unfeigned Christian is not liable to excommunication nor he who is a professed Christian until his hypocrisy appears in his manners—that is, until his behavior is contrary to the law of his sovereign, which is the rule of manners and which Christ and his apostles have commanded us to be subject to. For the Church cannot judge of manners except by external actions, and actions can never be unlawful except when they are against the law of the commonwealth.

If a man's father or mother or master is excommunicated, the children are not forbidden to keep them company nor to eat with them because that would be for the most part to oblige them not to eat at all for want of means to get food and to authorize them to disobey their parents and masters, contrary to the precept of the apostles.[13]

In sum, the power of excommunication cannot be extended further than to the end for which the apostles and pastors of the Church have their commission from our Savior, which is not to rule by command and coaction, but by teaching and direction of men in the way of salvation in the world to come. And as a master in any science may abandon his scholar when he obstinately neglects the practice of his rules, he may not accuse him of any injustice because he was never bound to obey him. So a teacher of Christian doctrine may abandon his disciples who obstinately continue in an unchristian life, but he cannot say they do him wrong because they are not obliged to obey him. . . . Therefore when excommunication

---

13. A tension exists here, as Hobbes says in Chapter XX that the father is like the sovereign of the family. In this case, the parents are not acting in accordance with the sovereign, but the children should obey these disobedient parents.

wants the assistance of civil power as it does when a Christian state or prince is excommunicated by a foreign authority, it is without effect and consequently ought to be without terror. . . .

There are two senses in which a writing may be said to be canonical. For canon signifies a rule and a rule is a precept by which a man is guided and directed to any action whatsoever. Such precepts, though given by a teacher to his disciple or a counselor to his friend without power to compel him to observe them are nevertheless canons because they are rules. But when they are given by one whom the receiver of them is bound to obey, then they are canons, not only rules but laws. The question therefore here is of the power to make the Scriptures (which are the rules of Christian faith) laws.

The part of the Scripture which was the first law was the Ten Commandments . . . delivered by God himself to Moses. Moses made them known to the people. Before that time there was no written law of God, who as yet having not chosen any people to be his peculiar kingdom had given no law to men but the law of nature—that is to say, the precepts of natural reason written in every man's own heart. Of the two Tables [on which the commandments were written], the first contains the law of sovereignty: (1) That they should not obey nor honor the gods of other nations in these words, . . . "thou shalt not have for Gods the Gods that other nations worship, but only me" whereby they were forbidden to obey or honor as their king and governor any other God than he who spoke unto them by Moses and afterward by the high priest. (2) That they "should not make any image to represent him," that is to say, they were not to choose to themselves either in Heaven or in Earth any representative of their own fancying but obey Moses and Aaron whom he had appointed to that office. (3) That "they should not take the name of God in vain," that is they should not speak rashly of their king nor dispute his right nor the commissions of Moses and Aaron, his lieutenants. (4) That "they should every seventh day abstain from their ordinary labor" and employ that time in doing him public honor. The second table contains the duty of one man toward another, as to honor parents; not to kill; not to commit adultery; not to steal; not to corrupt judgment by false witness, and finally, not so much as to design in their heart doing any injury to one another. The question now is who it was who gave to these written tables the obligatory force of laws. There is no doubt that they were made laws by God himself. But because a law does not oblige nor is law to any but to them who acknowledge it to be the act of the sovereign, how could the people of Israel who were forbidden to approach the mountain to hear what God said to Moses be obliged to obedience all those laws which Moses propounded to them? Some of them were indeed the laws of nature as all in the second table, and therefore acknowledged to be God's laws to all people, not to the Israelites alone. But of those that were peculiar to the Israelites, as those of the first table, the question remains except that they had obliged themselves . . . to obey Moses in these words in Exod. 20.19: "Speak them thou to us and we will hear thee. But let not God speak to us lest we die." It was therefore only Moses then, and after him the high priest whom (by Moses) God declared should administer this his peculiar kingdom that had on Earth the power to make this short Scripture of the Decalogue to be law in the commonwealth of Israel. But Moses and Aaron and the succeeding high priests were civil sovereigns. Therefore from then on the canonizing or making law of the Scripture belonged to civil sovereigns. . . .

The judicial law—that is to say, the laws that God prescribed to the magistrates of Israel for the rule of their administration of justice—and the sentences or judgments they should pronounce . . . were all delivered to them by Moses only and therefore also became laws by virtue of the same promise of obedience to Moses. . . . They were all positive laws and equivalent to Holy Scripture, and made canonical by Moses the civil sovereign. . . .[14]

Of ecclesiastical officers in the time of the apostles, some were magisterial and some ministerial. Magisterial were the offices of preaching . . . , administering sacraments, divine service, and teaching the rules of faith and manners to those that were converted. Ministerial was the office of the deacons, that is, those that were appointed to the administration of the secular necessities of the Church, such as the time when they lived upon a common stock of money raised out of the voluntary contributions of the faithful.[15]

We are to remember that the right of judging what doctrines are fit for peace and to be taught the subjects in all commonwealths is in all commonwealths inseparably annexed (as has been proved in Chapter XVIII) to the sovereign civil power, whether it is one man or one assembly of men. For it is evident to the meanest capacity that men's actions are derived from the opinions they have of the good or evil that redound to themselves from those actions and consequently men who are once possessed of an opinion that their obedience to the sovereign power will be more hurtful to them than their disobedience will disobey the laws and thereby overthrow the commonwealth and introduce confusion and civil war. All civil government was ordained to avoid civil war. Therefore in all commonwealths of the heathen, sovereigns have had the name of pastors of the people because there was no subject that could lawfully teach the people but by their permission and authority.

---

14. Here a considerable section of the original text is omitted. Briefly, his topic of discussion is ecclesiastical law and its relation to civil authority. Hobbes recounts that the Law of Moses was lost for many years and then rediscovered by Israel's King Josiah. Hobbes notes that both Moses (who wrote the law) and Josiah (who recovered the law) were civil sovereigns. The laws in the Old Testament only became laws, then, when a sovereign established them as law. He offers similar arguments for New Testament laws. When Christianity was still considered a deviant Jewish sect by many, its followers embraced doctrines not as law but personal conviction. At this point, though the early Christians believed these doctrines, they were neither law nor canon but personal beliefs and invitations for others to join them. The apostles of Jesus, then, were not establishing law in their teaching, for only the sovereign can do this. He also dismisses any church council not established by a civil sovereign on these grounds; if the council of Jesus' apostles did not establish law or canon, surely no lesser counsel could do so.
15. After this, Hobbes discusses the twelve apostles or disciples and how they fit into his magisterial/ministerial distinction. He also considers the offices of bishops (including the pope), ministers, deacons, the priesthood, and pastors as well as the gifts of evangelists and prophets.

The right of the heathen kings cannot be thought taken from them by their conversion to the faith of Christ who never ordained that kings should be deposed for believing in him, that is, subjected to any but himself or (which is all one) be deprived of the power necessary for the conservation of the peace among their subjects and for their defense against foreign enemies. Therefore Christian kings are still the supreme pastors of their people and have the power to ordain what pastors they please to teach the Church—that is—to teach the people committed to their charge.

Let the right of choosing them be (as before the conversion of kings) in the Church for so it was in the time of the apostles themselves . . . , even so also the right will be in the Christian civil sovereign. For in that he is a Christian, he allows the teaching and in that he is the sovereign (which is as much as to say, the Church by representation) the teachers he elects are elected by the Church. And when an assembly of Christians chooses their pastor in a Christian commonwealth, it is the sovereign who elects him because it is done by his authority. In the same manner, as when a town chooses their mayor, it is the act of him who has the sovereign power. For every act done is the act of him without whose consent it is invalid. Therefore whatsoever examples may be drawn out of history concerning the election of pastors by the people or by the clergy, they are not arguments against the right of any civil sovereign because they who elected them did it by his authority.

Seeing then in every Christian commonwealth the civil sovereign is the supreme pastor to whose charge the whole flock of his subjects is committed and consequently that it is by his authority that all other pastors are made and have the power to teach and perform all other pastoral offices, it follows also that it is from the civil sovereign that all other pastors derive their right of teaching, preaching, and all other functions pertaining to that office. . . . Let it be supposed that a Christian king commit the authority of ordaining pastors in his dominions to another king (as diverse Christian kings allow that power to the pope), he does not thereby constitute a pastor over himself nor a sovereign pastor over his people, for that would be to deprive himself of the civil power. . . . Christian Doctors are our schoolmasters to Christianity, but kings are the fathers of families and may receive schoolmasters for their subjects from the recommendation of a stranger but not from the command, especially when the ill teaching them shall redound to the great and manifest profit of him that recommends them, nor can they be obliged to retain them longer than is for the public good. . . .

If a man should ask a pastor in the execution of his office . . . by what authority he does things and who gave the authority, he can make no other just answer but that he does it by the authority of the commonwealth, given him by the king or the assembly that represents it. All pastors, except the supreme, execute their charges in the right, that is by the authority of the civil sovereign, that is *jure civili*. But the king and every other sovereign executes his office of supreme pastor by immediate authority from God, that is to say, in God's right, or *jure divino*. . . .

If every Christian sovereign is supreme pastor of his own subjects, it seems that he also has the authority not only to preach (which perhaps no man will deny) but also to baptize and to administer the sacrament of the Lord's Supper, and to consecrate both temples and pastors to God's service, which most men deny partly because they are not used to it and partly because the administration of sacraments and the consecration of person and places to holy uses requires the imposition of men's hands ... ordained to the like ministry. For proof therefore that Christian kings have the power to baptize and to consecrate I am to render a reason why they used not to do it and how, without the ordinary ceremony of imposition of hands, they are made capable of doing it when they will.

There is no doubt but any king might by the same right of his office read lectures of the sciences if he were skillful in them by which he authorizes others to read them in the universities. Nevertheless, because the care of the sum and happiness of the commonwealth takes up his whole time, it is not convenient for him to apply himself in person to that particular. A king may also, if he please, sit in judgment to hear and determine all manner of causes as well as give others authority to do it in his name. But the charge that lies upon him of command and government constrain him to be continually at the helm and to commit ministerial offices to others under him. In like manner our Savior (who surely had power to baptize) baptized none himself but sent his apostles and disciples to baptize.... Whereby it is manifest that the greater charge (such as the government of the Church) is a dispensation for the less. Therefore the reason why kings used not to baptize is evident and the same for which at this day there are few baptized by bishops and by the pope, fewer....[16]

From the consolidation of the political right and ecclesiastic in Christian sovereigns it is evident that they have all manner of power over their subjects that can be given to man for the government of men's external actions both in policy and religion and may make such laws as they shall judge fittest for the government of their own subjects both as they are the commonwealth and as they are the Church. For both state and church are the same men.

Therefore, if they please they may (as many Christian kings now do) commit the government of their subjects in matters of religion to the pope. But then the pope is in that point subordinate to them and exercises that charge in another's dominion *jure civili*, in the right of the civil sovereign and not *jure divino*, in God's right, and may therefore be discharged of that office when the sovereign, for the good of his subjects, shall think necessary.... It is the civil sovereign that is to appoint judges and interpreters of the canonical scriptures, for it is he who makes them laws. It is he also who gives strength to excommunications, which but for such laws and

---

16. Hobbes revisits the imposition of hands again here in the original text. Imposition of hands is receiving ecclesiastical authority that derives from another's authority, by means of the one dispensing authority placing his hands upon the body of the recipient accompanied with prayer. Hobbes uses this as an argument for the succession of ecclesiastical authority, which mirrors the succession of civil authority in Part II.

punishments as may humble obstinate libertines and reduce them to the union with the rest of the Church would be contemned. In sum, he has the supreme power in all ecclesiastical and civil causes as far as concerns the actions and words, for these only are known and may be accused . . . and these rights are incident to all sovereigns, whether monarchs or assemblies, for they that are the representatives of a Christian people are representatives of the Church, for a church and a commonwealth of Christian people are the same thing. . . .[17]

---

17. What follows here is Hobbes' exploration of topics such as the authority of popes and bishops in a lengthy tirade against a Roman Catholic cardinal, Bellarmine.

Chapter XLIII. Of What Is Necessary for a Man's Reception into the Kingdom of Heaven

Chapter XLIII includes practical matters regarding the relationship between believing Jesus is the Christ and one's intention to follow the laws to the best of one's ability. Part of that intention is to accept that Jesus is the Christ and to know that this is the entirety of the question of salvation. With respect to the question of various interpretations of Scripture and questioning the accuracy of one's beliefs, Hobbes provides a solution: it is the sovereign, and only the sovereign, who is appropriate to determine the Word of God.

The most frequent pretext of sedition and civil war in Christian commonwealths has a long time proceeded from a difficulty that is not yet sufficiently resolved of obeying at once both God and man when their commandments are one contrary to the other. It is manifest enough that when a man receives two contrary commands and knows that one of them is God's he ought to obey that and not the other even if it is the command of his lawful sovereign . . . or the command of his Father. The difficulty consists in this, that men who are commanded in the name of God do not know in different cases whether the command is from God or whether he who commands does but abuse God's name for some private ends of his own. . . . There have been in all times in the Church of Christ false teachers who seek reputation with the people by fantastical and false doctrines and by such reputation (as is the nature of ambition) to govern them for their private benefit.

All that is necessary to salvation is contained in two virtues: faith in Christ and obedience to laws. If the latter of these were perfect it would be enough to us. But because we are all guilty of disobedience to God's law not only originally in Adam but also actually by our own transgressions, there is required at our hands now for a remission of sins from the past and obedience for the rest of our time. Remission is the reward for our faith in Christ. That nothing else is necessarily required for salvation is clear from this, that the kingdom of Heaven is shut to none but sinners, that is to say, the disobedient or transgressors of the law, nor to them in case they repent and believe all the articles of Christian faith necessary to salvation. . . .

But what commandments are those that God has given us? Are all those laws which were given to the Jews by the hand of Moses, the commandments of God? If they are, why are Christians not taught to obey them?[18] If they are not, what others

---

18. This refers to the Pentateuch, the first five books of the Hebrew Bible. It is often called the Law of Moses and contains many commandments that are not practiced or recognized by Christian Churches as binding: forbidding tattoos and the rounding of hair on one's temples

are besides the law of nature? For our Savior Christ has not given us new laws, but counsel to observe those we are subject to—that is to say, the laws of nature and the laws of the sovereigns. Nor did he make any new law to the Jews in his sermon on the Mount, but only expounded on the Law of Moses to which they were subject before.[19] The laws of God therefore are none but the laws of nature, of which the principle is that we should not violate our faith—that is, a commandment to obey our civil sovereigns which we constituted over us by mutual pact with one another. This law of God that commands obedience to the civil law commands by consequence obedience to all the precepts of the Bible, which as I have proved in the previous chapter is only law when the civil sovereign makes it so and otherwise only counsel which a man may, at his own peril, refuse to obey without injustice.

Having shown what is necessary to salvation, it is not hard to reconcile our obedience to the civil sovereign who is either Christian or infidel. If he is a Christian he allows the belief of this article that Jesus is the Christ and of all the articles that are contained in or are evident consequences deduced from it. This is all the faith necessary to salvation. Because he is a sovereign he requires obedience to all his own, that is, to all the civil laws in which are also contained all the laws of nature and the laws of the Church which are part of the civil law (for the Church that can make laws is the commonwealth), there are no other divine laws. Whoever therefore obeys his Christian sovereign is not thereby hindered from believing nor from obeying God. But suppose a Christian king should from this foundation, Jesus is the Christ, draw some false consequences. . . . Seeing St. Paul says he shall be saved, much more shall he be saved who teaches them by his command and much more yet he who does not teach but only believes his lawful teacher. In case a subject is forbidden by the civil sovereign to profess some of his opinions, on what grounds can he disobey? Christian kings may err in deducing a consequence, but who shall judge? Shall a private man judge when the question is of his own obedience? Or shall any man judge but he who is appointed thereto by the Church, that is, by the civil sovereign who represents it? Or if the pope or an apostle judge, may he not err in deducing a consequence? Did not one of the two, St. Peter or St. Paul, err in a superstructure when St. Paul withstood St. Peter to his face? There can therefore be no contradiction between the laws of God and the laws of a Christian commonwealth.

When the civil sovereign is an infidel, every one of his subjects who resists him sins against the laws of God (for such are the laws of nature) and rejects the counsel of the apostles that admonishes all Christians to obey their princes and all children and servants to obey their parents and masters in all things. Their faith is internal and invisible. They have the license that Naaman had and need not put themselves into danger for it.[20] But if they do, they ought to expect their reward in Heaven and

---

(Lev. 19.27–28), stoning those who curse God (Lev. 24.13–16), prohibiting consumption of finless, scaleless seafood (Deut. 14.10), and so forth.

19. Matt. 5.17.

20. Naaman was commander of the army of the king of Aram. Naaman was cured of leprosy by washing in the Jordan River seven times. See 2 Kings 5.

not complain of their lawful sovereign much less make war upon him. For he who is not glad of any just occasion of martyrdom does not have the faith he professes but pretends it only. . . . But what infidel king is so unreasonable as knowing he has a subject that waits for the second coming of Christ after the present world shall be burned and intends then to obey him (which is the intent of believing that Jesus is the Christ) and in the meantime thinks himself bound to obey the laws of that infidel king (which all Christians are obliged in conscience to do) to put to death or to persecute such a subject?

Thus much shall suffice concerning the Kingdom of God and ecclesiastical policy. I pretend not to advance any position of my own but only to show what are the consequences that seem to me deducible from the principles of Christian politics (which are the Holy Scriptures) in confirmation of the power of civil sovereigns and the duty of their subjects. In the allegation of Scripture I have endeavored to avoid such texts as are of obscure or controverted interpretation and to allege none but is such sense as is most plain and agreeable to the harmony and scope of the whole Bible which was written for the reestablishment of the Kingdom of God in Christ.[21] For it is not the bare words but the scope of the writer that gives the true light by which any writing is to be interpreted and they who insist upon single texts without considering the main design can derive nothing from them clearly but rather by casting atoms of Scripture and dust before men's eyes, make everything more obscure than it is, an ordinary artifice of those who do not seek the truth but their own advantage.

21. Since in this volume many scriptural texts have been omitted, among them may be some that support or refute this point. It is therefore worth noting that Hobbes is likely adding rhetorical flourish, as he frequently makes reference to obscure biblical passes to make a point.

PART IV: OF THE KINGDOM OF DARKNESS

Chapter XLIV. Of Spiritual Darkness from Misinterpretation of Scripture

Hobbes returns to biblical interpretation with a focus on the kingdom of darkness. Threats to the commonwealth arise from ignorance of Scripture and introducing fantasies such as demons and ghosts. For Hobbes, the solution to ignorance of Scripture is that only one person or assembly (the sovereign) is responsible for giving law to all Christians and that the sovereign is the head of state, not the pope. Hobbes clarifies the origins and implications of mistaken theological views on civil stability, including the meaning of the Eucharist and eternal life and death by means of an immortal soul.

Besides these divine and human sovereign powers of which I have previously discoursed, there is mention in Scripture of another power, namely, that of "the rulers of the darkness of this world," "the kingdom of Satan" and "the principality of Beelzebub over demons" that is to say, over phantasms that appear in the air....[1] They who are under his dominion in opposition to the faithful (who are the children of the light) are called the children of darkness....The kingdom of darkness [is set forth in several places of Scripture] is nothing else but a "confederacy of deceivers, that to obtain dominion over men in this present world endeavor by dark and erroneous doctrines to extinguish them in the light of nature and the light of the Gospel and so disprepare them for the Kingdom of God to come."

As men who are utterly deprived of the natural sensation of light have no idea at all of any such light, and no man conceives in his imagination any greater light than he has at some time or other perceived by his outward senses, so also is it of the light of the Gospel and the light of the understanding that no man can conceive there is any greater degree of it than that which he has already attained. From this it comes to pass that men have no other means to acknowledge their own darkness but only by reasoning from the unforeseen mischances that befall them in their ways. The darkest part of the kingdom of Satan is that which is without

---

1. Eph. 6.12; Matt. 11.26; Matt. 9.34.

the Church of God, that is to say, among them who do not believe in Jesus Christ. But we cannot say that therefore the Church enjoys ... all the light which to the performance of the work enjoined us by God is necessary. . . . Where does it come from if in Christendom there has been, almost from the time of the apostles such a jostling of one another out of their places by both foreign and civil war—such a stumbling at every little asperity of their own fortune, and every little eminence of that of other men—such diversity of ways in running to the same mark of felicity? Where does it come from if there is not night among us, or at least a mist? We are therefore yet in the dark.

The enemy has been here in the night of our natural ignorance and sown the tares of spiritual errors. First, [the enemy has done this] by abusing and putting out the light of the Scriptures, for we err not knowing the Scriptures. Second, by introducing the demonology of the heathen poets, that is to say, their fabulous doctrine concerning demons which are but idols or phantasms of the brain without any real nature of their own distinct from human fancy. Examples are dead men's ghosts and fairies and other matter of old wives' tales. Third, by mixing diverse relics of the religion with Scripture and much of the vain and erroneous philosophy of the Greeks, especially that of Aristotle. Fourth, by mingling with both these false or uncertain traditions and feigned or uncertain history. . . . Concerning the first of these, which is seducing men by abuse of Scripture, I intend to speak briefly in this chapter.

The greatest and main abuse of Scripture and to which almost all the rest are either consequent or subservient in the wresting of it to prove that the Kingdom of God . . . is the present Church or multitude of Christian men now living or that being dead are to rise again at the last day. Whereas the Kingdom of God was first instituted by the ministry of Moses over the Jews only, who were therefore called his peculiar people. . . .

Consequent to the error that the present Church is Christ's kingdom, there ought to be some one man or assembly by whose mouth our Savior (now in Heaven) speaks, gives law, and which represents his person to all Christians or diverse men or diverse assemblies that do the same to diverse parts of Christendom. This regal power under Christ, being challenged universally by that pope and in particular commonwealths by assemblies of the pastors of the place (when the Scripture gives it to none but to civil sovereigns) comes to be so passionately disputed that it puts out the light of nature and causes so great a darkness in men's understanding that they do not see who it is to whom they have engaged their obedience.

Consequent to the claim of the pope to Vicar General of Christ in the present Church . . . is the doctrine that it is necessary for a Christian king to receive his crown by a bishop as if it were from that ceremony that he derives the clause of *Dei Gratia* in his title, and that then only he is made king by the favor of God when he is crowned by the authority of God's universal viceregent on Earth, and that every bishop whosoever is his sovereign taken at his consecration an oath of absolute obedience to the pope. . . . By heresies are understood all opinions which the Church of Rome has forbidden to be maintained. By this means they are made to fight one against another without discerning their enemies from their friends under the conduct of another man's ambition. . . .

From the same opinion that the present Church is the Kingdom of God it proceeds that pastors and deacons and all other ministers of the Church take the name to themselves of clergy and give to other Christians the name of Laity, that is, simply "people." Clergy signifies those whose maintenance is the revenue which God has reserved to himself during his reign over the Israelites. . . . The people everywhere were obliged to a double tribute—one to the state, another to the clergy. . . .

From the same mistaking of the present Church for the Kingdom of God came in the distinction between civil and canon laws. The civil law is the acts of sovereigns in their own dominions and the canon law is the acts of the pope in the same dominions. . . .

It is this window [of false beliefs from misinterpreting Scripture] that gives entrance to the dark doctrine, first, of eternal torments and afterward of Purgatory, and consequently . . . the ghosts of deceased men. Thereby also the pretenses of exorcism, conjuring phantasms, and also the invocation of the dead. . . . For men being generally possessed . . . by contagion of the demonology of the Greek [philosophies] an opinion that the souls of men were substances distinct from their bodies and therefore that when the body was dead the soul of every man . . . must subsist somewhere. . . .

The immortality of man's soul is not proved by Scripture to be [an immortality] of nature but of grace. There are diverse places which at first sight seem to prove that the soul separated from the body, lives eternally . . . to the faithful as well to the reprobates . . . but seem to me much more subject to diverse interpretation. . . .[2] We are therefore to consider what the meaning is of *everlasting fire* and other like phrases of Scripture. . . .

---

2. Hobbes gives several pages of biblical examples here, suggesting that traditional arguments for the immortality of the soul and those places where it would reside (heaven, purgatory, or hell) are misinterpretations. He denies the immortality of the soul and, thus, any place where it might reside, as it would require an immaterial substance, a contradiction, and thus an impossibility.

Chapter XLV. Of Demonology, and Other Relics of the Religion of the Gentiles

Hobbes is careful to combat beliefs that may incite fear and provide motiva-tion to disobey the sovereign. Belief in demons (whether good or evil) was used by "heathens" to control the population, but it is more efficient and reasonable to understand and adopt true religion that does not depend upon such fabrications.

The impression made on the organs of sight by lucid bodies, either in one direct line or in many lines reflected from opaque or refracted in the passage through diaphanous bodies, produces in living creatures in whom God has placed such organs an imagination of the object from which the impression proceeds. This imagination is called sight and seems not to be merely imagination but the body itself outside us. In the same manner, when a man violently presses his eye there appears to him a light without and before him which no man perceives but him-self because there is indeed no such thing without him but only a motion in the interior organs pressing by resistance outward that makes him think so. The motion made by this pressure, continuing after the object which caused it is removed, is what we call imagination and memory and in sleep (and sometimes in great dis-temper of the organs by sickness or violence) a dream. I have already spoken of these things briefly in Chapters II and III.

The nature of sight having never been discovered by the ancient pretenders to natural knowledge, it was hard for men to conceive of those images in the fancy and in the sense otherwise than of things really without us which some, because they vanish away and they do not know where nor how, [were said to be] absolutely incorporeal—that is to say, immaterial or forms without matter, color, and figure—without any colored or figured body. Also that they can put on airy bodies, as a gar-ment to make them visible when they will to our bodily eyes. Others say they are bodies and living creatures but made of air or other more subtle and ethereal matter which is then, when they will to be seen, condensed. Both of them agree on one general appellation of them, demons, as if the dead of whom they dreamed were not inhabitants of their own brain but of the air, or of Heaven or Hell; not phan-tasms, but ghosts. With just as much reason as if one should say he saw his own ghost in a looking glass or the ghosts of the stars in a river or call the ordinary apparition of the Sun . . . the demon or ghost of that great Sun that enlightens the whole vis-ible world. By that means people have feared them as things of an unknown or lim-ited power to do them good or harm. Consequently, this has given occasion to the governors of the heathen commonwealths to regulate this their fear by establishing demonology . . . to the public peace and to the obedience of subjects necessary to maintain this peace. Making some good demons and others evil, the one as a spur to observing laws, the other as reins to withhold them from violation.

. . . The worship we exhibit to those we esteem to be but men, as to kings and men in authority, is civil worship. But the worship we exhibit to that which we think to be God, whatsoever the words, ceremonies, gestures, or other actions are, is divine worship. To fall prostrate before a king in him who thinks him but a man is but civil worship. And he who but puts off his hat in the Church because he thinks it the house of God worships with divine worship. They who seek the distinction between divine and civil worship . . . deceive themselves. For whereas there are two sorts of servants—that sort which is of those who are absolutely in the power of their masters, as slaves taken in war and their issue whose bodies are not in their own power (their lives depending on the will of their masters in such manner as to forfeit them upon the least disobedience) and that are bought and sold as beasts were called . . . slaves. . . . The other, which is of those who serve (for hire or in hope of benefit from their masters) voluntarily are called . . . domestic servants, to whose service the masters have no further right than is contained in the covenants between them. These two kinds of servants have in common to them both that their labor is appointed to them by another whether as a slave or a voluntary servant. . . . In all kinds of service is contained not only obedience but worship, that is, such actions, gestures, and words that signify honor. . . .

Chapter XLVI. Of Darkness from Vain Philosophy and Fabulous Traditions

Hobbes' criticism of ancient philosophy, especially that of Aristotle, is scathing. Hobbes contends that Aristotle's work is "not properly philosophy (the nature of which is not dependent on authors) but Aristotelity." Such philosophies are very dangerous because they frighten men away from obeying laws, and they instead expect a Spirit of God to blow obedience into them.

By "philosophy" is understood "the knowledge acquired by reasoning from the manner of the generation of anything to the properties or from the properties to some possible way of generation of the same to the end to be able to produce, as far as matter and human force permit, such effects as human life requires." So the geometrician from the construction of figures finds out many properties thereof and from the properties, new ways of their construction by reasoning to the end to be able to measure land and water and for infinite other uses. So the astronomer, from the rising, setting, and moving of the Sun,[3] and stars, in diverse parts of the Heavens finds out the causes of day and night and of the different seasons of the year by which he keeps an account of time, and the like of other sciences.

By this definition it is evident that we are not to account as any part thereof that original knowledge called experience in which consists prudence. Because it is not attained by reasoning but is found as well in brute beasts as in man and is but a memory of successions of events in times past, wherein the omission of every little circumstance altering the effect frustrates the expectation of the most prudent. Whereas nothing is produced by reasoning aright but general, eternal, and immutable truth.

Nor are we therefore to give that name to any false conclusions. For he who reasons right in words he understands can never conclude an error. Nor that which any man knows by supernatural revelation because it is not acquired by reasoning. Nor that which is gotten by reasoning from authority of books because it is not by reasoning from the cause to the effect nor from the effect to the cause, and is not knowledge but faith.

---

3. Just eighteen years before Hobbes published *Leviathan*, Galileo was condemned for writing that the Earth might move. Even if Hobbes believed in a heliocentric solar system, it was certainly pragmatically rational for him not to say so. Later in this chapter, Hobbes explicitly addressed this, writing, "And every day it appears more and more that years and days are determined by motions of the Earth. Nevertheless, men who have in their writings supposed such doctrine as an occasion to lay open the reasons for and against it have been punished for it by ecclesiastical authority."

The faculty of reasoning being consequent to the use of speech, it was not possible but that there should have been some general truths found out by reasoning as ancient almost as language itself. The savages of America are not without some good moral sentences. Also they have a little arithmetic to add and divide in but they are not therefore philosophers . . . . There have been diverse true, general, and profitable speculations from the beginning as being the natural plants of human reason. But they were at first few in number. Men lived upon gross experience. There was no method, that is to say, no sowing nor planting of knowledge itself apart from the weeds and common plants of error and conjecture. The cause of it was the want of leisure from procuring the necessities of life and defending themselves against their neighbors, it was impossible until erecting great commonwealths that it should be otherwise. Leisure is the mother of philosophy and commonwealth is the mother of peace and leisure. Where first were great and flourishing cities was first the study of philosophy. . . .

After the Athenians by the overthrow of Persian armies had gotten the dominion of the sea and thereby of all the islands and maritime cities of the archipelago as well as of Asia and Europe and were grown wealthy, they who had no employment at home nor abroad had little else to employ themselves but either "in telling and hearing news" or in discoursing of philosophy publicly to the youth of the city. Every master took some place for that purpose, Plato in certain public walks called academia . . . and Aristotle in the walk of the temple of Pan, called Lyceum. Others in the Stoa or covered walk wherein the merchant's goods were brought to land. Others in other places where they spent the time of their leisure in teaching or in disputing their opinions and some in any place where they could get the city together to hear them talk. . . .

From this it was that the place where any of them taught and disputed was called *schola*, which in their tongue signified leisure and their disputations, *diatribae*, that is to say, passing of the time. Also the philosophers themselves had the name of their sects, some of them from their schools. For they who followed Plato's doctrine were called *academiques*, the followers of Aristotle, *peripatetics*, from the walk in which he taught, and those that Zeno taught, Stoics from the Stoa, as if we should denominate men from More-fields, from Paul's Church, and from the exchange because they meet here often to prate and loiter.

Nevertheless, men were so much taken with this custom that in time it spread itself over all Europe and the best part of Africa so that there were schools publicly erected and maintained for lectures and disputations in almost every commonwealth.

There were also schools anciently both before and after the time of our Savior among the Jews, but they were schools of their law. . . .

But what has been the utility of those schools? What science is there at this day acquired by their readings and disputings? We are not indebted for geometry, the mother of all natural science, to the schools. Plato who was the best philosopher of the Greeks forbade entrance into his school to all who were not already in some measure geometricians. There were many who studied that science to the great advantage of mankind, but there is no mention of their schools nor was there any sect of geometricians, nor did they then pass under the name of philosophers. The natural philosophy of those schools was rather a dream than science and set forth in senseless and insignificant language which cannot be avoided by those who will teach philosophy without having first attained great knowledge in geometry. For nature works by motion, the ways and degrees of cannot be known without knowledge of the proportions and properties of lines and figures. Their moral philosophy is but a description of their own passions. For the rule of manners without civil government is the law of nature and in it the civil law that determines what is honest and dishonest, what is just and unjust, and generally what is good and evil. Whereas they make the rules of good and bad by their own liking and disliking. By which means in so great diversity of taste there is nothing generally agreed on but everyone does (as far as he dares) whatever seems good in his own eyes to the subversion of commonwealth. Their logic, which should be the method of reasoning, is nothing but captions of words and inventions how to puzzle such as should go about to pose them. To conclude, there is nothing so absurd that the old philosophers (as Cicero said, who was one of them) have not some of them maintained. And I believe that scarcely anything can be more absurdly said in natural philosophy than that which now is called Aristotle's *Metaphysics*, nor more repugnant to government than much of what he has said in his *Politics*, nor more ignorantly than a great part of his *Ethics*.

The school of the Jews was originally a school of the Law of Moses, who commanded that at the end of every seventh year at the feast of the tabernacles it should be read to all the people that they might hear and learn it. Therefore the reading of the law . . . every Sabbath day ought to have had no other end but acquainting the people with the commandments they were to obey and to expound unto them the writings of the prophets. But it is manifest by the many reprehensions of them by our Savior that they corrupted the text of the law with false commentaries and vain traditions and so little understood the prophets that they neither acknowledged Christ nor the works he did for which the prophets prophesied. By their lectures and disputations in synagogues they turned the doctrine of their law into a fantastical kind of philosophy concerning the incomprehensible nature of God and of spirits which they compounded of the vain philosophy and theology of the Greeks, mingled with their own fancies drawn from the more obscure places of the Scripture and which might most easily be wrested to their purpose and from fabulous traditions of their ancestors.

That which is now called a university is a joining together and an incorporation under one government of many public schools in one and the same town or city in which the principal schools were ordained for the three professions . . . of the Roman religion, of the Roman law, and of the art of medicine. For the study of philosophy it has no other place than as a handmaid to Roman religion. Since the authority of Aristotle is only current there, that study is not properly philosophy (the nature of which is not dependent on authors) but Aristotelity. And for geometry, until of very late times it had no place at all being subservient to nothing but rigid truth. If any man by the ingenuity of his own nature had attained to any degree of perfection in it, he was commonly though a magician and his art diabolical.

Now, to descend to the particular tenets of vain philosophy derived to the universities and then into the Church, partly from Aristotle and partly from blindness of understanding, I shall first consider their principles. There is a certain *philosophia prima* on which all other philosophy ought to depend and consists principally in right limiting of the significations of such appellations or names as are of all others the most universal. These limitations serve to avoid ambiguity and equivocation in reasoning and are commonly called definitions, such as are the definitions of "body," "time," "place," "matter," "form," "essence," "subject," "substance," "accident," "power," "act," "finite," "infinite," "quantity," "quality," "motion," "action," "passion," and diverse others necessary to explain man's conceptions concerning the nature and generation of bodies. The explication (that is, settling the meaning) of which and the like terms is commonly in the Schools called metaphysics. As being a part of the philosophy of Aristotle, which has that for its title, but it is in another sense for there it signifies as much as "Books written or placed after his natural philosophy." But the Schools take them for Books of Supernatural Philosophy, for the word "metaphysics" will bear both these sense. And indeed that which is there written is for the most part so far from the possibility of being understood and so repugnant to natural reason that anyone who thinks there is anything to be understood by it must think it supernatural.

From these metaphysics which are mingled with the Scripture to make School divinity, we are told there are in the world certain essences separated from bodies, which they call abstract essences and substantial forms. To interpreting this jargon, there is need of something more than ordinary attention in this place. Also, I ask pardon of those who are not used to this kind of discourse, for applying myself to those who are. The world (I do not mean the Earth only, that denominates the lovers of it worldly men, but the Universe, that is, the whole mass of all things that are) is corporeal, that is to say, body. And it has the dimensions of magnitude, namely length, breadth, and depth. Also every part of body is likewise body and has the like dimensions and consequently every part of the Universe is body and that which is not-body is no part of the Universe. Because the Universe is all, that which is not part of it is nothing and consequently nowhere. Nor does it follow from this that Spirits are nothing, for they have dimensions and are therefore real bodies, though that name in common speech is given to such bodies only as are visible or palpable, that is, that have some degree of opacity. But for spirits they call them incorporeal, which is a name of more honor and may therefore with more piety be attributed to God himself in whom we do not consider what attributes express best his nature, which is incomprehensible, but what best expresses our desire to honor him.

To know now upon what grounds they say there are abstract essences or substantial forms, we are to consider what those words properly signify. The use of words is to register ourselves and make manifest to others the thoughts and consequences of our minds. Some words are the names of things conceived as the names of all sorts of bodies that work upon the senses and leave an impression in the imagination. Others are the names of the imaginations themselves, that is to say, of those ideas or mental images we have of all things we see or remember. And others again are names of names or different sorts of speech as universal, plural, singular, negation, true, false, syllogism, interrogation, promise, covenant, and are the names of certain forms of speech. Others serve to show the consequence or repugnance of one name to another, as when one says "A man is a body" he intends that the name of body is necessarily consequent to the name of man, as being but several names of the same thing, Man, which consequence is signified by coupling them together with the word "is." And as we use the verb "is," so the Latins use their verb, *est* and the Greeks their *esti* through all its declinations. Whether all other nations of the world have in their several languages a word that answers to it or not, I cannot tell. But I am sure they do not have need of it. For placing two names in order may serve to signify their consequence, if it were the custom (for custom is it that gives words their force) as well as the words "is" or "be" or "are," and the like.

If there was a language without a verb answerable to *est* or "is" or "be," the men who used it would not be a jot less capable of inferring, concluding and all kind of reasoning than were the Greeks and Latins. But what then would become of these terms: "entity," "essence," "essential," "essentially" that are derived from it and many more that depend on these, applied as most commonly they are? They are therefore not names of things but signs by which we make known that we conceive the consequence of one name or attribute to another as when we say, "A man is a living body," we do not mean that the man is one thing and the living body another, and the "is" or "being" a third, but that the man and the living body is the same thing. Because the consequence, "If he is a man, he is a living body" is a true consequence, signified by the word "is." Therefore, to be a body, to walk, to speak, to live, to see, and the like infinitives and also corporeity, walking, speaking, life, sight and the like that signify the same are the names of nothing as I have elsewhere more amply expressed.

But to what purpose (some man may say) is such subtlety in a work of this nature where I pretend to nothing but what is necessary to the doctrine of government and obedience? It is to this purpose: that men may no longer suffer themselves to be abused by those who by this doctrine of separated essences, built on the vain philosophy of Aristotle, would frighten them from obeying the laws of their country with empty names as men fright birds from the corn with an empty doublet, a hat, and a crooked stick. For it is upon this ground that when a man is dead and buried, they say his soul (that is, his life) can walk separated from his body and is seen by night among the graves. Upon the same ground they say that the figure, color, and taste of a piece of bread has a being there where they say there is no bread. And upon the same ground they say that faith and wisdom and other virtues are sometimes powered into a man, sometimes blown into him from Heaven as if the virtuous and their virtues could be asunder and a great many other things that serve to lessen the dependence of subjects on the sovereign power of their country. For who will endeavor to obey the laws if he expects obedience to be powered or blown into him? Who will not obey a priest who can make God rather than the sovereign, nay than God himself? Or who will not bear great respect to those who can make the holy water that drives the ghosts he fears from him? This shall suffice for an example of the errors which are brought into the Church from the entities and essences of Aristotle, which it may be he knew to be false philosophy but wrote it as a thing consonant to and corroborative of their religion and fearing the fate of Socrates.

Once fallen into this error of separated essences, they are thereby necessarily involved in many other absurdities that follow it. Seeing that they will have these forms to be real, they are obliged to assign them some place. Because they hold them to be incorporeal without all dimension of quantity and all men know that place is dimension and not to be filled except by that which is corporeal, they are driven to uphold their credit with a distinction that they are not indeed anywhere circumscriptive but definitive these terms are mere words and in this occasion insignificant, pass only in Latin that the vanity of them may be concealed. For the circumscription of a thing is nothing else but the determination or defining of its place. So both the terms of the distinction are the same. In particular, they affirm the essence of man which (they say) is his soul and all of it is in his little finger and all of it in every other part (no matter how small) of his body and yet no more soul in the whole body than in any one of those parts. Can any man think that God is served with such absurdities? And yet all this is necessary to believe—to those who will believe—the existence of an incorporeal soul separated from the body.

When they come to give account of how an incorporeal substance can be capable of pain and be tormented in the fire of Hell or Purgatory, they have no answer but that it cannot be known how fire can burn souls. Whereas motion is change of place and incorporeal substances are not capable of place, they are troubled to make it seem possible how a soul can go somewhere without the body to Heaven, Hell, or Purgatory and how the ghosts of men (and I may add of their clothes in which they appear) can walk by night in churches, churchyards, and other places of sepulture. To which I do not know what they can answer unless they will say they walk definitively not circumscriptively or spiritually and not temporally. Such egregious distinctions are equally applicable to any difficulty whatsoever.

They will not have the meaning of eternity be an endless succession of time for then they should not be able to render a reason how God's will and preordaining things to come should not be before his prescience of the same as with the efficient cause before the effect or the agent before the action or of many other of their bold opinions concerning the incomprehensible nature of God. But they will teach us that eternity is standing still of present time, a *Nunc-stans* (as the Schools call it) which neither they nor anyone else understands more than they would a *Hic-stans* for an infinite greatness of place.

Whereas men divide a body in their thought by numbering parts of it and in numbering those parts they also number the parts of the place it filled, it cannot be but in making many parts we also make many places of those parts whereby there cannot be conceived in the mind of any man more or fewer parts than there are places for. Yet they will have us believe that by the Almighty power of God one body may be at one and the same time in many places and many bodies at one and the same time in one place, as if it were an acknowledgment of the divine power to say that which is, is not or that which has been, has not been. These are but a small part of the incongruities they are forced to from their philosophical disputes instead of admiring and adoring the divine and incomprehensible nature whose attributes we cannot signify what he is but ought to signify our design to honor him with the best appellations on which we can think. But they who venture to reason of his nature from these attributes of honor, lose their understanding in the very first attempt and fall from one inconvenience to another without end and without number in the same manner as when a man who is ignorant of the ceremonies of court comes into the presence of a greater person than he is used to speak to and stumbles at his entrance to save himself from falling and lets his cloak slip. To recover his cloak, he lets his hat fall, and with one disorder after another discovers his astonishment and rusticity.

Then, for physics (that is, the knowledge of the subordinate and secondary causes of natural events) they render none at all but empty words. If you desire to know why some kinds of bodies sink naturally downward toward the Earth and others go naturally from it, the Schools will tell you out of Aristotle that the bodies that sink downward are heavy and this heaviness causes them to descend. But if you ask them what they mean by heaviness, they will define it to be an endeavor to go to the center of the Earth so that the cause of things sinking downward is an endeavor to be below. This is as much as to say that bodies descend or ascend because they do. Or they will tell you the center of the Earth is a place of rest and conservation for heavy things. Therefore they endeavor to be there as if stones and metals had a desire or could discern the place where they would be as man does, or loved rest as a man does not, or that a piece of glass was less safe in a window than falling into the street.

If we would know why the same body seems greater (without adding to it) one time than another, they say when it seems less it is condensed, when greater, rarefied. What is that condensed and rarefied? Condensed is when there is in the very same matter, less quantity than before and rarefied when more. As if there could be matter that did not have some determined quantity, when quantity is nothing else but the determination of matter, that is to say, of body, by which we say one body is greater or lesser than another by thus or thus much. Or as if a body were made without any quantity at all and that afterward more or less was put into it according as it is intended the body should be more or less dense.

They say that the cause of the soul of man is that "it is created by powering it in" and "powered in by creation." For the cause of sense, a ubiquity of species—that is, of the shows or apparitions of objects, which when they are apparitions to the eye is sight, when to the ear is hearing, to the palate is taste, to the nostril is smelling, and to the rest of the body is feeling.

For cause of the will to do any particular action which is called volition, they assign the faculty—that is to say, the capacity—in general that men have to will sometimes one thing and sometimes another, which is . . . making the power the cause of the act, as if one should assign for the cause of good or evil acts of men their ability to do them.

On many occasions they put for cause of natural events their own ignorance, but disguised in other words such as when they say that fortune is the cause of contingent things, that is, of things of which they know no cause, and as when they attribute many effects to occult qualities, that is, qualities not known to them, and therefore also (as they think) to no other man. To sympathy, antipathy, antiperistasis, specific qualities, and other terms which signify neither the agent that produces them nor the operation by which they are produced. If such metaphysics and physics as this are not vain philosophy, there never was any nor need of St. Paul to give us warning to avoid it.[4]

Their moral and civil philosophy has the same or greater absurdities. If a man does an action of injustice, that is to say, an action contrary to the law, they say God is the prime cause of the law and also the prime cause of that and all other actions, but not the cause of injustice, which is the inconformity of the action to the law. This is vain philosophy. A man might well say that one man makes both a straight line and a crooked line and another makes their incongruity. Such is the philosophy of all men who resolve their conclusions before they know their premises, pretending to comprehend that which is incomprehensible and of attributes of honor to make attributes of nature as this distinction was made to maintain the doctrine of free-will, that is, of a will of man not subject to the will of God.

Aristotle and the other heathen philosophers define good and evil by the appetite of men and well enough as long as we consider every one of them governed by his own law. For in the condition of men who have no other law but their own appetites, there can be no general rule of good and evil actions. But in a commonwealth this measure is false. It is not the appetite of private men but the law which is the will and appetite of the state is the measure. And yet this doctrine is still practiced and men judge the goodness and wickedness of their own and other men's actions, and of the actions of the commonwealth itself by their own passions. No man calls good or evil but that which is so in his own eyes without any regard at all to the public laws (except only monks and friars who are bound by vow to simple obedience to their superior) to which every subject ought to think himself bound by the law of nature to the civil sovereign. This private measure of good is a doctrine not only vain but also pernicious to the public state.[5]

It is also vain and false philosophy to say the work of marriage is repugnant to chastity or continence and by consequence to make them moral vices as they do who pretend chastity and continence are the ground of denying marriage to the clergy. For they confess it is no more but a constitution of the Church that require in those holy orders that continually attend the altar and administration of the Eucharist a continual abstinence from women under the name of continual chastity, continence, and purity. Therefore they call the lawful use of wives a want of chastity and continence and so make marriage a sin or at least a thing so impure and unclean as to render a man unfit for the altar. If the law were made because the use of wives is incontinence and contrary to chastity, then all marriage is vice.

---

4. Hobbes is referring to Col. 2.8, a letter in which the Colossian Churches are encouraged to avoid philosophy and vain deceit that follows human tradition, not Christ.

5. Hobbes' reasoning regarding private measures of good is discussed early in *Leviathan* as one of the major causes of war. The political sovereign, therefore, is not only the ultimate political authority but also the ultimate authority in matters of morals and religion. See esp. Chapters XVI, XVIII, and XXXVI.

If because a thing is too impure and unclean for a man consecrated to God, much more should other natural, necessary, and daily works which men do render men unworthy to be priests because they are more unclean.[6]

But the secret foundation of this prohibition of marriage of priests is not likely to have been laid so slightly as upon such errors in moral philosophy, nor yet upon the preference of a single life to the estate of matrimony, which proceeded from the wisdom of St. Paul who perceived how inconvenient it was for those who in those times of persecution were preachers of the Gospel and forced to fly from one country to another to be clogged with the care of wife and children, but upon the design of the popes and priests of later times to make themselves the clergy, that is to say, sole heirs of the Kingdom of God in this world. It was necessary to take from them the use of marriage because our Savior said that at the coming of his kingdom the children of God shall "neither marry nor be given in marriage but shall be as angels in Heaven," that is to say, spiritual. Seeing then they had taken on them the name of spiritual, to have allowed themselves (when there was no need) the propriety of wives would be an incongruity.

From Aristotle's civil philosophy they have learned to call all manner of commonwealths except the popular (such as was at that time the state of Athens) tyranny. They called all kings tyrants and the aristocracy of the thirty governors set up there by the Lacedemonians that subdued them the thirty tyrants. They called liberty the condition of the people under the democracy. A tyrant originally signified no more simply but a monarch. But when afterward in most parts of Greece that kind of government was abolished, the name began to signify not only the thing it did before but with it the hatred which the poplar states bore toward it. As the name of the king became odious after deposing the kings in Rome as being a thing natural to all men to conceive some great fault to be signified in any attribute that is given despite and to a great enemy. And when the same men shall be pleased with those who have the administration of democracy or aristocracy, they are not to seek for disgraceful names in which to express their anger but call readily the one anarchy and the other oligarchy or the tyranny of a few. And that which offends the people is no other thing but that they are governed not as every one of them would himself but as the public representative, be it one man or an assembly of men thinks fit, that is, by an arbitrary government for which they give evil names to their superiors never knowing (until perhaps a little after a civil war) that without such arbitrary government, such war must be perpetual and that it is men and arms, not words and promises, that make the force and power of the laws.

Therefore this is another error of Aristotle's politics that in a well ordered commonwealth, men should not govern, but the laws. What man who has his natural senses even though he can neither write nor read does not find himself governed by those he fears and believes can kill or hurt him when he does not obey? Or who believes the law can hurt him, that is, words and paper, without the hands and swords of men? And this is of the number of pernicious errors for they induce men

---

6. This must be a reference to ordinary natural processes, of which sex is one, as well as bodily fluid and solid elimination.

as often as they do not like their governors to adhere to those who call them tyrants and to think it lawful to raise war against them. Yet they are many times cherished from the pulpit by the clergy.

There is another error in their civil philosophy (which they never learned from Aristotle, Cicero, or any of the other heathens) to extend the power of the law, which is the rule of actions only, to the very thoughts and consciences of men by examination and inquisition of what they hold regardless of the conformity of their speech and actions. By this, men are either punished for answering the truth of their thoughts or constrained to answer an untruth for fear of punishment. It is true that the civil magistrate, intending to employ a minister in charge of teaching, may inquire of him if he is content to preach such and such doctrines and in case of refusal may deny him employment. But to force him to accuse himself of opinions when his actions are not forbidden by law is against the law of nature and especially in them who teach that a man shall be damned to eternal and extreme torments if he dies in a false opinion concerning an article of the Christian faith. For who is there who knows there is so great danger in an error when the natural care of himself does not compel him to hazard his soul upon his own judgment rather than that of any other man who is unconcerned in his damnation?

It is another error in politics for a private man without the authority of the commonwealth, that is to say, without permission from the representative of it, to interpret the law by his own spirit. This is not drawn from Aristotle nor from any other of the heathen philosophers. For none of them deny that the power of explaining laws when there is need is in the power of making laws. Are not the Scriptures, in all places where they are law, made by authority of the commonwealth and consequently a part of the civil law?

Of the same kind it is also when any but the sovereign restrains in any man the power which the commonwealth has not restrained as they do who preach the Gospel inappropriate to one certain order of men where the laws have left it free. If the state gives me leave to preach or teach, that is, if it does not forbid me, no man can forbid me. If I find myself among the idolaters of America, shall I who am a Christian, though not under order, think it a sin to preach Jesus Christ until I have received orders from Rome? Or when I have preached, shall I not answer their doubts and expound the Scriptures to them? That is, shall I not teach? But for this some may say as also for administering to them the sacraments, the necessity shall be esteemed for a sufficient mission, which is true. But it is also true that for whatsoever a dispensation is due for the necessity, for the same there needs no dispensation when there is no law that forbids it. Therefore, to deny these functions to those to whom the civil sovereign has not denied them is taking away a lawful liberty, which is contrary to the doctrine of civil government.

More examples of vain philosophy brought into religion by the Doctors of School divinity might be produced, but other men may if they please observe them for themselves. I shall only add this, that the writings of School divines are nothing else for the most part but insignificant trains of strange and barbarous words, or words otherwise used than in the common use of the Latin tongue such as would pose Cicero and Varro and all the grammarians of ancient Rome. If any man would see proved, let him (as I have said once before) see whether he can translate any School divine into any of the modern tongues as French, English, or any other copious language. For that which cannot in most of these be made intelligible, is not intelligible in Latin. This insignificance of language, though I cannot note it for false philosophy, yet it has a quality not only to hide the truth but to make men think they have it and desist from further search.

Last, for the errors brought in from false or uncertain history, what is all the legend of fictitious miracles in the lives of the saints and all the histories of apparitions and ghosts alleged by the Doctors of the Roman Church to make good their doctrines of Hell and Purgatory, the power of exorcism, and other doctrines that have no warrant either in reason or in Scripture. And also all those traditions which they call the unwritten Word of God but old wives fables? Of these, though they find dispersed somewhat in the writings of the ancient Fathers, yet those Fathers were men who might too easily believe false reports and produce their opinions for testimony of the truth of what they believed had no other force with them (according to the counsel of 1 John 4.1) examine spirits that in all things that concern the power of the Roman Church (the abuse of which either they did not suspect or had benefit by it) to discredit their testimony in respect of too rash belief of reports. The most sincere men, without great knowledge of natural causes (such as the Fathers were) are commonly the most subject to. For naturally the best men are the least suspicious of fraudulent purposes. Gregory to the pope and St. Bernard have somewhat of apparitions of ghosts who said they were in Purgatory and so has our Beda, but nowhere, I believe, but by report from others. If they or any other relate any such stores of their own knowledge, they shall not thereby confirm the more such vain reports but discover their own infirmity or fraud.

With the introduction of the false philosophy, we may join also the suppression of true philosophy by such men, neither by lawful authority nor sufficient study, are competent judges of the truth. Our own navigations make manifest and all men learned in human sciences now acknowledge there are antipodes. And every day it appears more and more that years and days are determined by motions of the Earth. Nevertheless, men who have in their writings supposed such doctrine as an occasion to lay open the reasons for and against it have been punished for it by ecclesiastical authority. But what reason is there for it? Is it because such opinions are contrary to true religion? That cannot be, if they are true. Let therefore the truth be first examined by competent judges or confuted by those who pretend to know the contrary. Is it because they are contrary to established religion? Let them be silenced by the laws of those to whom the teachers of them are subject, that is, by the civil laws. For disobedience may lawfully be punished in those who teaching even true philosophy against the laws. Is it because they tend to disorder in government as countenancing rebellion or sedition? Then let them be silenced and the teachers punished by virtue of his power to whom the care of the public quiet is committed, which is the civil authority. For whatever power ecclesiastics take upon themselves (in any place where they are subject to the state) in their own right, though they call it God's right, it is usurpation.

Chapter XLVII. Of the Benefit That Proceeds from Such Darkness, and to Whom It Accrues

Hobbes continues to criticize religious doctrines grounded upon ancient philosophy, discussing who benefits most from its falsehoods. The beneficiaries are popes and Presbyters. Hobbes compares the Papacy with a fictional kingdom of fairies, ridiculing the Roman Church and accusing Catholicism of being as fantastic and equally absurd as the doctrine of fairies.

Cicero makes honorable mention of one of the Cassii, a severe judge among the Romans for a custom he had in criminal causes (when the testimony of the witnesses was not sufficient) to ask the accusers what profit, honor, or other contentment the accused obtained or expected by the fact (this is called *cui bono*). For among presumptions, there is none that so evidently declare the author as does the benefit of the action. By the same rule I intend in this place to examine who they may be who have possessed the people so long in this part of Christendom with these doctrines that are contrary to the peaceable societies of mankind.

And first to this error that the present Church now militant on Earth is the Kingdom of God (that is, the kingdom of glory, or the land of promise, not the kingdom of grace, which is but a promise of the land) are annexed to these worldly benefits. First, that the pastors and teachers of the Church are entitled thereby as God's public ministers to a right of governing the Church and consequently (because the Church and commonwealth are the same person) to be rectors and governors of the commonwealth. By this title it is that the pope prevailed with the subjects of all Christian princes to believe that to disobey him was to disobey Christ himself and in all differences between him and other princes (charmed with the word "spiritual power") to abandon their lawful sovereigns. This is in effect a universal monarchy over all Christendom. For though they were first invested in the right of being supreme teachers of Christian doctrine by and under Christian emperors within the limits of the Roman Empire (as is acknowledged by themselves) by the title of Pontifex Maximus, who was an officer subject to the civil state, yet after the empire was divided and dissolved it was not hard to obtrude upon the people already subject to them another title, namely the Right of St. Peter, not only to save their entire pretended power but also to extend the same over the same Christian provinces though no longer united in the Empire of Rome. This benefit of a universal monarchy (considering the desire of men to bear rule) is a sufficient presumption that the popes who pretended to it and for a long time enjoyed it were the authors of the doctrine by which it was obtained, namely, that the Church now on Earth is the kingdom of Christ. For that granted, it must be understood that Christ has some lieutenant among us by whom we are to be told what are his commandments.

After that certain Churches had renounced this universal power of the pope, one would expect in reason that the civil sovereigns in all those Churches should have recovered so much of it as (before they had unadvisedly let go) was their own right and in their own hands. And in England it was so in effect except that they by whom the kings administered the government of religion by maintaining their employment to be in God's right seemed to usurp an independency on the civil power if not a supremacy. And they but seemed to usurp it inasmuch as they acknowledged a right in the king to deprive them of the exercise of their functions at his pleasure.

But in those places where the Presbytery took that office, even though many other doctrines of the Church of Rome were forbidden to be taught, yet this doctrine that the kingdom of Christ is already come and that it began at the resurrection of our Savior was still retained. . . . What profit did they expect from it? The same which the popes expected: to have a sovereign power over the people. For what is it for men to excommunicate their lawful king but to keep him from all places of God's public service in his own kingdom? And with force to resist him, when he with force endeavors to correct them? Or what is it without authority from the civil sovereign to excommunicate any person but to take from him his lawful liberty, that is, to usurp an unlawful power over their brethren? Therefore the authors of this darkness in religion are the Roman and the Presbyterian clergy.[7]

To this head I also refer all those doctrines that serve them to keep possession of this spiritual sovereignty after it is gotten. At first, that the pope in his public capacity cannot err. For who is there, believing this to be true, who will not readily obey him in whatever he commands?

Second, that all other bishops in whatever commonwealth, do not have their right either immediately from God nor mediately from their civil sovereigns but from the pope is a doctrine by which there comes to be in every Christian commonwealth many potent men (for so are bishops) who have their dependence on the pope and owe obedience to him though he is a foreign prince. By which means he is able (as he has done many times) to raise a civil war against the state that does not submit itself to be governed according to his pleasure and interest.

Third, the exemption of these and of all other priests and monks and friars from the power of the civil laws. For by this means there is a great part of every commonwealth that enjoys the benefit of the laws and are protected by the power of the civil state which nevertheless pays no part of the public expense. Nor are they liable to the penalties, as other subjects, due to their crimes and consequently do not stand in fear of any man but the pope and adhere to him only to uphold his universal monarchy.

Fourth, giving to their priests (which is no more in the New Testament but Presbyters, that is, Elders) the name of *Sacerdotes*, that is, sacrificers, which was the title of the civil sovereign and his public ministers among the Jews while God was

---

7. The Presbyterians condemned Hobbes' *Leviathan* as heretical.

their king. Also, making the Lord's Supper a sacrifice serves to make the people believe the pope has the same power over all Christians that Moses and Aaron had over the Jews, that is to say, all civil and ecclesiastical power as the high priest then had.

Fifth, teaching that matrimony is a sacrament gives to the clergy judging of the lawfulness of marriages and thereby of what children are legitimate, and consequently of the right of succession to hereditary kingdoms.

Sixth, denial of marriage to priests serves to assure this power of the pope over kings. For if a king is a priest he cannot marry and transmit his kingdom to his posterity. If he is not a priest then the pope pretends this ecclesiastical authority over him and his people.

Seventh, from auricular confession they obtain for the assurance of their power better intelligence of the designs of princes and great persons in the civil state than these can have of the designs of the ecclesiastical state.

Eighth, by the canonization of saints and declaring who are martyrs they assure their power in that they induce simple men into an obstinacy against the laws and commands of their civil sovereigns, even to death, if by the pope's communication they are declared heretics or enemies to the Church, that is (as they interpret it) to the pope.

Ninth, they assure the same by the power they ascribe to every priest of making Christ and by the power of ordaining penance and of remitting or retaining sins.

Tenth, by the doctrine of Purgatory, of justification by external words, and indulgences, the clergy is enriched.

Eleventh, by their demonology and the use of exorcism and other things appertaining thereto, they keep (or think they keep) the people more in awe of their power.

Last, the metaphysics, ethics, and politics of Aristotle, the frivolous distinctions, barbarous terms, and obscure language of the Schoolmen that is taught in the universities (which have all been erected and regulated by the pope's authority) serve them to keep these errors from being detected and to make men mistake the *Ignis Fatuus* of vain philosophy for the light of the Gospel.

To these, if they are not sufficient, might be added other of their dark doctrines, the profit of which redounds manifestly to setting up an unlawful power over the lawful sovereigns of the Christian people or for sustaining the same when it is set up, or to the worldly riches, honor, and authority of those who sustain it. Therefore by the aforesaid rule of *cui bono* we may justly pronounce for the authors of all this spiritual darkness, the pope and Roman clergy and all those besides that endeavor to settle in the minds of men this erroneous doctrine that the Church now on Earth is that Kingdom of God mentioned in the Old and New Testament.

But the emperors and other Christian sovereigns under whose government these errors and the like encroachments of ecclesiastics upon their office at first crept in to the disturbance of their possessions and of the tranquility of their subjects, though they suffered the same for want of foresight of the sequel and of insight into the designs of their teachers may nevertheless be esteemed accessories to their own and the public damage. For without their authority there could at first been no seditious doctrines publicly preached. I say they might have hindered the same in the beginning. But when the people were once possessed by those spiritual men, there was no human remedy to be applied that any man could invent. For the remedies that God should provide, who never fails in his good time to destroy all the machinations of men against the truth, we are to attend his good pleasure who suffers many times the prosperity of his enemies together with their ambition to grow to such a height as the violence of it opened their eyes which the wariness of their predecessors had before sealed up. It makes men by too much grasping let go all, as Peter's net was broken, by the struggling of too great a multitude of fish, whereas the impatience of those who strive to resist such encroachment before their subjects' eyes were opened increased the power they resisted.[8] I do not therefore blame the emperor Frederick for holding the stirrup to our countryman, Pope Adrian, for such was the disposition of his subjects than as if he had not done it, he was not likely to have succeeded in the empire. But I blame those who in the beginning when their power was entire by suffering such doctrines to be forged in the universities of their own dominion have held the stirrup to all the succeeding popes while they mounted into the thrones of all Christian sovereigns to ride and tire both them and their people at their pleasure.

As the inventions of men are woven, so also are they raveled out. The way is the same, but the order is inverted. The web begins at the first elements of power which are wisdom, humility, sincerity, and other virtues of the apostles whom the people converted, obeyed, out of reverence not by obligation. Their consciences were free and their words and actions subject to none but the civil power. Afterward the Presbyters (as the flocks of Christ increased) assembled to consider what they should teach and thereby obliged themselves to teach nothing against the decrees of their assemblies, made it to be thought the people were thereby obliged to follow their doctrine. When they refused, they refused to keep them company (that was then called excommunication) not as being infidels but as being disobedient. This was the first knot upon their liberty. And the number of Presbyters increasing, the Presbyters of the chief city or province got themselves an authority over the parochial Presbyters and appropriated to themselves the names of bishops. This was the second knot on Christian liberty. Last, the bishop of Rome in regard of the imperial city took upon him an authority (partly by the wills of the emperors themselves and by the title of *Pontifex Maximus* and at last when the emperors were grown weak by the privileges of St. Peter) over all other bishops of the empire. This was the third and last knot and the whole synthesis and construction of the Pontifical power.

---

8. This refers to a biblical miracle in which Jesus tells Peter, who has fished unsuccessfully overnight, to recast his net on the opposite side of the boat. Peter's nets are then filled with so many fish when he does this that the nets begin to break and he requires assistance from other boats to pull the fish in. In both accounts, Peter abandons his trade and becomes one of Jesus' disciples (Luke 5; John 21).

Therefore the analysis or resolution is by the same way, but beginning with the knot that was tied last as we may see in the dissolution of the praeterpolitical Church government in England.

First, the power of popes was dissolved totally by Queen Elizabeth and the bishops, who before exercised their functions in right of the pope, afterward exercised the same right of the queen and her successors, though by retaining the phrase of *jure divino*, they were thought to demand it by immediate right from God. And so the first knot was untied. After this, the Presbyterians lately in England obtained putting down Episcopacy. And so the second knot was dissolved. At almost the same time, the power was also taken from the Presbyterians. So we are reduced to the independency of primitive Christians to follow Paul or Cephas or Apollos, every man as he likes best which, it if is without contention and without measuring the doctrine of Christ by our affection to the person of the minister (the fault which the apostle reprehended in the Corinthians) is perhaps the best. First, because there ought to be no power over the consciences of men but of the world itself, working faith in everyone, not always according to the purpose of those who plant and water but of God himself who gives the increase. Second, because it is unreasonable in them who teach there is such danger in every little error to require of a man endued with reason of his own to follow the reason of any other man or the most voices of many other men. This is little better than to venture his salvation at cross and pile. Nor ought those teachers to be displeased with the loss of their ancient authority. For there is no one who should know better than they that power is preserved by the same virtues by which it is acquired, that is to say by wisdom, humility, clearness of doctrine, and sincerity of conversation and not by suppression of the natural sciences and the morality of natural reason, nor by obscure language, nor by arrogating to themselves more knowledge than they make appear, nor by pious frauds, nor by such other faults as in the pastors of God's Church are not only faults but also scandals apt to make men stumble one time or other upon the suppression of their authority.

After this doctrine, "that the Church now militant is the Kingdom of God spoken of in the Old and New Testament," was received in the world, the ambition and canvassing for the office that belong to it and especially for that great office of being Christ's lieutenant and the pomp of those who obtained in it the principal public charges became by degrees so evident that they lost the inward reverence due to the pastoral function. Insomuch as the wisest men of them that had any power in the civil state needed nothing but the authority of their princes to deny them any further obedience. For from the time that the bishop of Rome had gotten to be acknowledged for Universal Bishop by pretense of succession to St. Peter, their whole hierarchy or kingdom of darkness may be compared not unfitly to the kingdom of fairies, that is, to the old wives' fables in England concerning ghosts and spirits and the feats they play in the night. And if a man considers the origin of this great ecclesiastical dominion, he will easily perceive that the Papacy is no other than the ghost of the deceased Roman Empire sitting crowned upon its grave. For so did the Papacy start up on a sudden out of the ruins of that heathen power.

The language they use both in the Churches and in their public acts is Latin, which is not commonly used by any nation now in the world and it is but the ghost of the old Roman language.

The fairies in what nation soever they converse have but one universal king which some poets of ours call King Oberon, but the Scripture calls Beelzebub, Prince of demons. The ecclesiastics likewise in whatever dominions they are found acknowledge only one universal king, the pope.

The ecclesiastics are spiritual men and ghostly fathers. The fairies are spirits and ghosts. Fairies and ghosts inhabit darkness, solitudes, and graves. The ecclesiastics walk in obscurity of doctrine in monasteries, churches, and churchyards.

The ecclesiastics have their cathedral churches which, in whatever town they are erected by virtue of holy water and certain charms called exorcisms, have the power to make those towns into cities, that is to say, seats of empire. The fairies also have their enchanted castles and certain gigantic ghosts that domineer over the regions around them. The fairies are not to be seized on and brought to answer for the hurt they do. So also the ecclesiastics vanish away from the tribunals of civil justice.

The ecclesiastics take from young men the use of reason by certain charms compounded from metaphysics and miracles and traditions and abused Scripture, whereby they are good for nothing else but to execute what they are commanded. The fairies likewise are said to take young children out of their cradles and to change them into natural fools which common people therefore call elves and are apt to mischief.

The old wives have not determined in what shop or operatory the fairies make their enchantment. But the operatories of the clergy are well enough known to be the universities that received their discipline from Pontifical authority.

When the fairies are displeased with anybody, they are said to send their elves to pinch them. The ecclesiastics, when they are displeased with any civil state, also make their elves, that is, superstitious, enchanted subjects, to pinch their princes by preaching sedition or one prince enchanted with promises to pinch another.

The fairies do not marry but there are among them *incubi* who copulate with flesh and blood. The priests also may not marry. The ecclesiastics take the cream of the land by donations of ignorant men who stand in awe of them and by tithes. So also it is in the fable of fairies that they enter into dairies and feast upon the cream which they skim from the milk.

What kind of money is current in the kingdom of fairies is not recorded in the story. But the ecclesiastics in their receipts accept the same money we do, though when they are to make any payment it is in canonizations, indulgences, and masses.

To this and such resemblances between the Papacy and the kingdom of fairies may be added this, that as the fairies have no existence except in the fancies of ignorant people rising from the traditions of old wives or old poets, so the spiritual power of the pope (without the bounds of his own civil dominion) consists only in the fear in which seduced people stand of their excommunication upon hearing of false miracles, false traditions, and false interpretations of Scripture.

It was not therefore a very difficult matter for Henry VIII by his exorcism nor for Queen Elizabeth by hers to cast them out. But who knows that this spirit of

Rome, now gone out and walking by missions through the dry places of China, Japan, and the Indies that yield them little fruit may not return—or rather an assembly of spirits worse than he—enter and inhabit this clean swept house and make the end of it worse than the beginning? For it is not the Roman clergy only that pretends the Kingdom of God to be of this world and thereby to have a power therein distinct from that of the civil state. And this is all I had a design to say concerning the doctrine of the politics, which when I have reviewed I shall willingly expose it to the censure of my country.

A Review, and Conclusion

The final section of Leviathan *is an overview of the significance of Hobbes' work. Hobbes allows that there are clearly some difficulties with respect to whether human beings will be ruled by reason or passion and that human life is always attended with competition for power. But these problems are not insurmountable. They are surmountable through education and discipline. Hobbes contends that there are great benefits in the adoption of his work by the universities, the most important of which are peace and stability.*

From the contrariety of some of the natural faculties of the mind one to another and also of one passion to another, and from their reference to conversation, there has been an argument taken to infer an impossibility that any one man should be sufficiently disposed to all sorts of civil duty. The severity of judgment, they say, makes men censorious and unapt to pardon the errors and infirmities of other men. And on the other side, celerity of fancy makes the thoughts less steady than is necessary to discern exactly between right and wrong. Again, in all deliberations and in all pleadings, the faculty of solid reasoning is necessary. For without it, the resolutions of men are rash and their sentences unjust. And yet if there is not powerful eloquence which procures attention and consent, the effect of reason will be little. But these are contrary faculties, the former being grounded on principles of truth and the other upon opinions already received, whether they are true or false, and upon the passions and interests of men, which are different and mutable.

Among the passions, courage (by which I mean the contempt of wounds and violent death) inclines men to private revenges and sometimes to endeavor unsettling the public peace. And timorousness many times disposes to the desertion of the public defense. Both these they say cannot stand together in the same person.

To consider the contrariety of men's opinions and manner in general, it is they say impossible to entertain a constant civil amity with all those with whom the business of the world constrains us to converse. This business consists almost in nothing else but a perpetual contention for honor, riches, and authority.

To which I answer, that these are indeed great difficulties but not impossibilities. For by education and discipline they may be and are sometimes reconciled. Judgment and fancy may have place in the same man but by turns as the end at which he aims requires. As the Israelites in Egypt were sometimes fastened to their labor of making bricks and other times were ranging abroad to gather straw, so also may the judgment sometimes be fixed upon one certain consideration and the fancy at another time wanders about in the world. So also reason and eloquence (though not perhaps in the natural sciences, yet in the moral) may stand very well together.

For wherever there is a place for adorning and preferring error, there is much more place for adorning and preferring truth if they have it to adorn. Nor is there any repugnancy between fearing the laws and not fearing a public enemy nor between abstaining from injury and pardoning it in others. There is therefore no such inconsistency of human nature with civil duties as some think. I have known clearness of judgment and largeness of fancy, strength of reason and graceful elocution, a courage for war and a fear for the laws, and all eminently in one man, and that was my most noble and honored friend, Mr. Sidney Godolphin, who hating no man nor hated by any was unfortunately slain in the beginning of the late civil war in the public quarrel by an undiscerned and an undiscerning hand.

To the laws of nature declared in Chapter XV, I would have this added, "That every man is bound by nature as much as in him lies to protect in war the authority by which he is himself protected in time of peace." For he who pretends a right of nature to preserve his own body cannot pretend a right of nature to destroy him by whose strength he is preserved. It is a manifest contradiction of himself. And though this law may be drawn by consequence from some of those who are there already mentioned, yet the times require to have it inculcated and remembered.

Because I find by diverse English books printed lately that the civil wars have not yet sufficiently taught men in what point of time it is that a subject becomes obliged to the conqueror, nor what is conquest, nor how it comes about, that it obliges men to obey his laws. Therefore for the further satisfaction of men under a new authority, I say that the point of time wherein having liberty to submit to the conqueror, men consent either by express words or by other sufficient sign to be his subject. When it is that a man has liberty to submit, I have shown before in the end of Chapter XXI, namely, that for him who has no obligation to his former sovereign but that of an ordinary subject, it is then when the means of his life is within the guards and garrisons of the enemy. For it is then that he no longer has protection from him but is protected by the adverse party for his contribution. Seeing therefore such contribution is everywhere as a thing inevitable (notwithstanding it is an assistance to the enemy), esteemed lawful as total submission, which is but an assistance to the enemy, cannot be esteemed unlawful. Besides, if a man considers that they who submit assist the enemy but with part of their estates, whereas they who refuse assist him with the whole, there is no reason to call their submission or composition an assistance, but rather a detriment to the enemy. But if a man, besides the obligation of a subject, has taken upon him a new obligation of soldier, then he does not have the liberty to submit to a new power as long as the old one keeps the field and gives him means of subsistence either in arms or in garrisons. For in this case he cannot complain of lack of protection and means to live as a soldier. But when that also fails, a soldier may also seek his protection wherever he has the most hope to have it and may lawfully submit himself to his new master. And so much for the time when he may do it lawfully, if he will. If therefore he does it, he is undoubtedly bound to be a true subject. For a contract lawfully made cannot lawfully be broken.

By this also a man may understand when it is that men may be said to be conquered, and in what the nature of conquest and the right of a conqueror consists.

For this submission in itself implied them all. Conquest is not the victory itself but the acquisition by victory of a right over the persons of men. He therefore who is slain is overcome but not conquered. He who is taken and put into prison or chains is not conquered though overcome, for he is still an enemy and may save himself if he can. But he who upon promise of obedience has his life and liberty allowed to him is then conquered, and a subject, and not before. The Romans used to say that their general had pacified such a province, that is to say, in English, conquered it and that the country was pacified by victory when the people of it had promised to do what the Roman people commanded them. This was to be conquered. But this promise may be either express or tacit: express is by promise in words and tacit is by other signs. As for example a man who has not been called to make such an express promise (because he is one whose power is perhaps not considerable), yet if he lives under the protection openly, he is understood to submit himself to the government. But if he lives there secretly, he is liable to anything that may be done to a spy and enemy of the state. I do not say he does any injustice (for acts of open hostility do not bear that name) but that he may justly be put to death. Likewise, when his country is conquered if a man is out of it he is not conquered nor subject. But if at his return he submits to the government, he is bound to obey it. So that conquest (to define it) is acquiring the right of sovereignty by victory. Which right is acquired in the people's submission by which they contract with the victor, promising obedience for life and liberty.

In Chapter XXIX I have set down for one of the causes of the dissolutions of commonwealth their imperfect generation consisting in the lack of an absolute and arbitrary legislative power, for lack whereof the civil sovereign is fain to handle the sword of justice inconstantly and as if it were too hot for him to hold. One reason for this (which I have not there mentioned) is this, that they will all justify the war by which their power was at first gotten and whereon (as they think) their right depends and not on the possession. As if, for example, the right of the kings of England did depend on the goodness of the cause of William the Conqueror and upon their lineal and direct descent from him by which means there would perhaps be no tie of the subjects' obedience to their sovereign at this day in all the world. Wherein while they needlessly think to justify themselves, they justify all the successful rebellions that ambition shall at any time raise against them and their successors. Therefore, I put down for one of the most effective seeds of the death of any state that the conquerors require not only a submission of men's actions to them for the future, but also an approbation of all their past actions when there is scarcely a commonwealth in the world whose beginnings can in conscience be justified.

Because the name of tyranny—signifying nothing more nor less than the name of sovereignty, whether in one or many men saying that they who use the former word are understood to be angry with them they call tyrants—I think the toleration of a professed hatred of tyranny is a toleration of hatred to commonwealth in general and another evil seed not differing much from the former. For to the justification of the cause of a conqueror, the reproach of the cause of the conquered is for the most part necessary. But neither of them is necessary for the obligation of the conquered. And this much I have thought fit to say upon the review of the first and second parts of this discourse.

In Chapter XXXV, I have sufficiently declared out of the Scripture that in the commonwealth of the Jews, God himself was made the sovereign by pact with the people, who were therefore called his peculiar people to distinguish them from the rest of the world over whom God reigned not by their consent but by his own power. And that in this kingdom Moses was God's lieutenant on Earth, and that it was he who told them what laws God appointed to do, especially in capital punishments not then thinking it a matter of so necessary consideration as I find it since. We know that generally in all commonwealths, the execution of corporal punishments was either put upon the guards or other soldiers of the sovereign power or given to those in whom want of means, contempt of honor, and hardness of heart concurred to make them sue for such an office. But among the Israelites it was a positive law of God their sovereign that he was convicted of a capital crime, should be stoned to death by the people, and that the witnesses should cast the first stone and after the witnesses, then the rest of the people. This was a law that designed who were to be the executioners, but not that anyone should throw a stone at him before conviction and sentence where the congregation was judge. The witnesses were nevertheless to be heard before they proceeded to execution unless the fact was committed in the presence of the congregation itself, or in sight of the lawful judges. For then there needed no other witnesses but the judges themselves. Nevertheless, this manner of proceeding is not thoroughly understood and has given occasion to a dangerous opinion that any man may kill another is some cases by a right of zeal as if the executions done upon offenders in the Kingdom of God in old time proceeded from the authority of private zeal and not from the sovereign command, which if we consider the texts that seem to favor it, is quite contrary.

First, where the Levites fell upon the people who had made and worshipped the golden calf and slew three thousand of them, it was by the commandment of Moses by the mouth of God. . . .[1] And when the son of a woman of Israel had blasphemed God, they who heard it did not kill him but brought him before Moses who put him under custody until God should give sentence against him. . . .[2] Presumption of a future ratification is sometimes necessary to the safety of a commonwealth as in a sudden rebellion any man can suppress it by his own power in the country where it begins may lawfully do it and provide to have it ratified or pardon while it is in doing or after it is done. . . .

In Chapter XXXVI I have said that it is not declared in what manner God spoke supernaturally to Moses. Not that he spoke to him sometimes by dreams and visions and by a supernatural voice as to other prophets. For the manner how he spoke to him from the mercy seat is expressly set down in Num. 7.89. . . . But it is not declared in what consisted the preeminence of the manner of God's speaking to Moses above that of his speaking to other prophets as to Samuel and Abraham, to whom he also spoke by a voice (that is, by vision) unless the difference consists in

---

1. Exod. 32.27.
2. Lev. 24.11–12.

the clearness of the vision. For face to face and mouth to mouth cannot be literally understood of the infiniteness and incomprehensibility of the divine nature.

As to the whole doctrine, I do not see it yet but the principles of it are true and proper and the ratiocination is solid. For I ground the civil rights of sovereigns and both the duty and liberty of subjects upon the known natural inclinations of mankind and upon the articles of the law of nature of which no man who pretends but reason enough to govern his private family ought to be ignorant. And for ecclesiastical power of the same sovereigns, I ground it on such texts as are both evident in themselves and consonant to the scope of the whole Scripture. Therefore I am persuaded that he who shall read it with a purpose only to be informed shall be informed by it. But for those that by writing or public discourse or by their eminent actions have already engaged themselves to maintaining contrary opinions, they will not be so easily satisfied. For in such cases it is natural for men at one and the same time both to proceed in reading and to lose their attention in the search for objections to what they had read before. Of which, in a time in which the interests of men are changed (seeing much of that doctrine which serves to establish a new government must be contrary to that which conduced to the dissolution of the old) there cannot choose but be very many.

In that part which treats of a Christian commonwealth, there are some new doctrines which it may be in a state where the contrary were already fully determined were a fault for a subject to leave to divulge as being a usurpation of the place of a teacher. But in this time that men call not only for peace but also for truth, to offer such doctrines as I think true and that manifestly tend to peace and loyalty to the consideration of those that are yet in deliberation is no more but to offer new wine to be put into new cask that both may be preserved together. And I suppose that then when novelty can breed no trouble nor disorder in a state, men are not generally so much inclined to reverence of antiquity as to prefer ancient errors before new and well proved truth.

There is nothing I distrust more than my elocution, which nevertheless I am confident (excepting mischances of the presses) is not obscure. That I have neglected the ornament of quoting ancient poets, orators, and philosophers contrary to the custom of late time (whether I have done it well or ill) proceeds from my judgment grounded on many reasons. For first, all truth of doctrine depends either upon reason or upon Scripture, both of which give credit to many but never receive it from any writer. Second, the matters in question are not of fact but of right, in which there is no place for witnesses. Third, there are very few of the old writers who do not contradict both themselves and others, which makes their testimonies insufficient. Fourth, such opinions taken only upon credit of antiquity are not intrinsically the judgment of those who cite them but words that pass (like gaping) from mouth to mouth. Fifth, it is many times with a fraudulent design that men stick their corrupt doctrine with the cloves of other men's wit. Sixth, I do not find that the ancients they cite took it for an ornament to do the like with those who wrote before them. Seventh, it is an argument of indigestion when Greek and Latin sentences unchewed come up again, as they used to do, unchanged. Last, though I revere those men of ancient time who either have written truth perspicuously or set us in a better way to find it ourselves, yet to the antiquity itself I think nothing is due. For if we will revere the age, the present is the oldest. If the antiquity of the writer, I am not sure, that generally they to whom such honor is given were more ancient when they wrote than I am that am writing. But if it is well considered, the praise of ancient authors proceeds from the competition and mutual envy of the living, not from reverence of the dead.

To conclude, there is nothing in this whole discourse nor in that I wrote before of the same subject in Latin[3] as far as I can perceive that is contrary either to the Word of God or to good manners, or to the disturbance of the public tranquility. Therefore, I think it may be profitably printed and more profitably taught in the universities in case they also think so to whom the judgment of the same belongs. For seeing the universities are the fountains of civil and moral doctrine from which preachers and the gentry, drawing such water as they find, use to sprinkle the same (both from the pulpit and in their conversation) upon the people, there ought certainly to be great care taken to have it pure both from the venom of heathen politicians and from the incantation of deceiving spirits. And by that means the most men, knowing their duties, will be the less subject to serve the ambition of a few discontented persons in their purposes against the state and be the less grieved with the contributions necessary for their peace and defense. And the governors themselves have the less cause to maintain at the common charge any greater army than is necessary to make good the public liberty against the invasions and encroachments of foreign enemies.

Thus I have brought to an end my discourse of civil and ecclesiastical government, occasioned by the disorders of the present time without partiality, without application, and without other design than to set before men's eyes the mutual relation between protection and obedience of which the condition of human nature and the divine laws (both natural and positive) require an inviolable observation. And though in the revolution of states there can be no very good constellation for truths of this nature under which to be born (as having an angry aspect from the dissolvers of an old government and seeing but the backs of them who erect a new) yet I cannot think it will be condemned at this time either by the public judge of doctrine or by any who desire the continuance of public peace. In this hope I return to my interrupted speculation of natural bodies wherein (if God gives me health to finish it) I hope the novelty will as much please as in the doctrine of this artificial body it uses to offend. For such truth that opposes no man's profit or pleasure is to all men welcome.

---

3. See *De Cive* in *Man and Citizen (De Homine and De Cive)*, ed. Bernard Gert (Indianapolis, IN: Hackett, 1991).

GLOSSARY

The terms included in this glossary are those used primarily in specialized senses overall or particularly specialized senses for Hobbes. Also included are some terms that Hobbes sometimes uses in different senses at various points in *Leviathan*. There are many terms that Hobbes used in the original English version of *Leviathan* that may not be familiar to contemporary readers, but those that are not specifically pertinent to the development of his philosophical position are not included since their meanings are clear from the context or quickly found in good dictionaries either of the traditional kind or online. For more detailed discussion, definition, and contextual placement of these and many more terms associated with Hobbes' work, see Martinich.[1]

Absurdity: a characteristic of terms, assertions, or statements that are in logical conflict with each other. An absurd term identified by Hobbes, for example, is "immaterial substance." Since Hobbes was a materialist (see also *Materialism, Mechanistic*) and since "substance" must be matter, the term "immaterial substance" makes no sense, or is absurd. The same is to be said with respect to statements that are meaningless because the words used in them are meaningless or because the claims made in or between statements are ambiguous.

Aristocracy: a form of government in which rulers are members of an elite group, usually of very few people. Hobbes does not make a distinction between aristocracy and oligarchy, the latter of which, he claims, is nothing more than what citizens call an aristocracy when they do not like it.

Atheism: the belief, generally, that there is no God. In Hobbes' time, the term "atheist" applied also to those who did not believe the doctrines of the Church or religious sect to which they were purportedly or actually members.

Authorization, Political: the moment at which human beings in the Hobbesian state of nature transfer their right to all things, by agreement with each other, to a/the political sovereign. Hobbes therefore makes a distinction between "author" and "person" (see also *Person*), where the author of an action, process, or creation "authorizes" (approves and verifies) the action(s) of an actor who is, by authorization, an "artificial person."

Command: a statement made by a person who has power over another sufficient to require performance of an action required by the statement. Hobbes is careful to distinguish between command and counsel, since command is by right ultimately of the political sovereign and cannot rightfully be disregarded, while counsel takes the form of suggestions that another person is not required to heed.

---

1. A. P. Martinich, *A Hobbes Dictionary* (Cambridge: Blackwell, 1995).

Commonwealth: the political structure created by the act of authorization of a sovereign power by the human beings who agree with each other to transfer their natural right to the sovereign. The term is as its components imply: a political structure created for the common good.

Compatibilism: a metaphysical position related generally to the doctrine of the will and human responsibility. Broadly construed, compatibilism is a form of causal determinism in which both freedom and determinism are compatible both with each other and with moral responsibility. As expressed in Hobbes' work, a person is "free" when he is not hindered in acting as he wishes to act; that is, a person is free when he is not physically constrained from doing what he wills to do. See also *Determinism*.

Contempt: related to one of the Hobbesian causes of war (glory), in which a person is considered contemptible or to be contemned when that person is thought to be "inconsiderable," of no danger, irrelevant, or to be described in some other way indicating lesser status or importance than others. Outside the context of human beings, a thing is contemptible if it is not considered dangerous, important, or relevant to one's concerns.

Contract: an agreement between individuals or groups composed of individuals in which some benefit is to be gained by each party and in which each party promises the other that they will perform their part of the agreement.

Cosmological Argument: one of several forms of an argument used to demonstrate God's existence by demonstrating that the Universe (cosmos) depends upon a first cause or mover, God; it is an a posteriori argument, meaning it is one that is formulated upon past observations and experiences.

Counsel: to be compared with "command," counsel is constituted by suggestions made to another person, whether natural or artificial, regarding the good of the person who is counseled as well as the counselor.

Covenant: essentially the same as a contract, except that the parties to the contract are situated such that both parties to an agreement make a promise to the other to live up to their part of the agreement, but one party performs prior to the performance of the other, in which case the second party is trusted to live up to her, his, or their part of the agreement.

Deliberation: the last act in the process of decision making when a person or other animal acts freely. Deliberation only occurs and applies to those actions that are possible. So deliberation does not and cannot occur regarding the past or regarding things or actions that are absurd or impossible.

Democracy: a form of government in which all or most of the subjects or citizens are involved as rulers. Hobbes claims that a democracy is called "anarchy" when the citizens do not like this form of government.

Deism: a religious outlook primarily of the Enlightenment period (seventeenth and eighteenth centuries) in which the nature of God and creation are understood on the model of clockwork. Deists generally contend that God is the creator of the world and the Universe but that God does not meddle in the daily or earthly affairs of human beings. Some commentators think of Hobbes as a Deist or at least as having tendencies toward this manifestation of theistic belief.

Determinism: a metaphysical theory of causation in which there is no action that happens by chance or by the free-will of moral agents. It is a doctrine affirming that there is no such thing as "free" will. Contrast with *Compatibilism.*

Diffidence: for Hobbes, diffidence has two distinct meanings. In some contexts, it is like a feeling or emotion that comes over a person when she or he feels a need for self-defense. It is a defensive stance. In other contexts (very few), it means self-doubt or insecurity in one's abilities.

Dominion: power over another person, persons, or thing.

Dualism: a metaphysical position that reality, especially with respect to human beings, is composed of two substances, mind and body. The issue is complicated in that it may also apply to the notion that there are some substances in the Universe that are spiritual and some that are material. Thomas Hobbes was not a dualist but was instead a materialist. See also *Materialism.*

Ecclesiastic/al: pertaining to the Christian Church; ecclesiastical refers to the Church itself while ecclesiastics are the clergy (e.g., bishops and priests).

Egoism, Ethical: a normative (i.e., prescriptive) ethical position stipulating that human beings ought to look out only for and seek their own best interests. It is possible to be an ethical egoist and not be a psychological egoist. See also *Egoism, Psychological.*

Egoism, Psychological: the psychological description of human beings regarding the purported fact that they act normally or always with respect only to their own best interest. Hobbes is often characterized as a psychological egoist by his commentators, but it is not clear that the term fits the complicated and detailed account of human nature and behavior that Hobbes provides in *Leviathan* and other political works. One of the most accessible and straightforward discussions of Hobbesian egoism is found in Bernard Gert.[2]

Empiricism: an epistemological (theory of knowledge) position taken primarily but not solely by British philosophers of the early modern period (seventeenth and eighteenth centuries). It is the position that all ideas arise through sense experience and that there are no innate ideas. See also *Rationalism.*

Empiricist Thesis: the claim made by empiricist philosophers that ideas arise only through sense experience.

---

2. Bernard Gert, *Hobbes: Prince of Peace* (Malden, MA: Polity Press, 2010).

Enthusiasm, Religious: a broad term used to describe any one of a number of Christian sects that were particularly concerned with personal piety and ascetic living. Among them were the Quietists, Moravians, Quakers, and Jansenists.

Evil, Problem of: the question of why evil and suffering exist in the world if it is true that God is omnipotent (all powerful), omniscient (all knowing), and omnibenevolent (all good).

Faction (or Paction): a group of people banded together for a particular interest inside an existent political society. Hobbes was very suspicious of factions since, according to him, they have a tendency to engage in actions that threaten civil peace. For example, a league of citizens who band together for a particular purpose, such as defense of a specific geographic region, become dangerous to the commonwealth because their numbers and strength cannot be trusted not to test or to attempt to violate the power and authority of the state and its sovereign.

Fancy/Fancies: objects of thought; ideas derived through sense experience that are part of the memory or imagination.

Freedom, Negative: the liberty to act or speak that is ensured by the obligation of others not to interfere in the performance of another person's actions or speech. Negative freedom is constituted by the right of noninterference. It includes, therefore, the obligations of others not to hinder a person in the performance of what that person wills to do.

Freedom, Positive: the liberty to act or speak that is to be ensured as a right by the state or by other individuals. Positive freedom indicates the obligation of others or the state to ensure that a person is able to exercise a right.

Freedom, see *Liberty*.

Generalissimo: the supreme commander of a commonwealth's army or other armed forces or protective groups.

Idealism: a metaphysical position that reality is composed only of ideas and minds, not of material things. Hobbes did not address idealism specifically in *Leviathan*, but he rejected beliefs and doctrines that are necessary for it such as the belief that there is an immaterial soul, that matter does not exist, and that there are "ghosts" or "spirits."

Immaterialism, see *Idealism*.

Infinity: limitlessness in time, space, dimensions, or other characteristics of a thing. For Hobbes, infinity is not something of which human beings may have any idea except that it is the negation of the finite.

Justice: for Hobbes, justice consists primarily if not solely in "performing covenants." In other words, abiding by the terms and conditions of one's agreements is justice. Not doing so is injustice.

Kingdom of Darkness: those people and institutions that attempt to spread false doctrines (i.e., ones that are harmful to the commonwealth). The Catholic Church and its ecclesiastics were most often accused by Hobbes of being in this kingdom.

Kingdom of God: a civil society ruled by a sovereign insofar as the sovereign also functions as a divine spokesperson, supreme prophet, and intermediator for God.

Law, Civil: obligations of citizens to do or to forbear; they are the commands of a sovereign representative of a commonwealth that are issued in his, her, or their capacity as authorized representatives of the multitude.

Law, Natural: rules discovered by reason. These are, according to Hobbes, the foundations of a true, first, and only science of morals. They are moral rules that are not enforceable outside the commands and threats of punishment for nonperformance.

Law of Nature: a precept discovered by reason regarding human behavior and moral requirements. Hobbes claimed that the science of the laws of nature is the only true science of morality.

Liberty: the capacity possessed by a person or other animate thing to act or not to act according to the will of that person or animate being. Liberty is absence of external impediments to action. See also *Will*.

Materialism: a metaphysical position in which all constituents of reality are material, physical bodies. See also *Materialism, Mechanistic*.

Materialism, Mechanistic: a position held by Hobbes regarding the nature of reality and the manner by which material things operate. According to Hobbes, all material things (which are the sole constituents of reality) are governed by natural laws, and especially the laws of motion and causation. See also *Materialism*.

Metaphor: using words and speech in ways that confound the original and clear meanings, rendering what is said either incomprehensible or unclear. Metaphorical language is essentially using words to express an idea or concept through analogy to something that does not resemble the thing to which it is being compared.

Metaphysics: a branch of philosophical inquiry concerning the nature of reality. Among topics in metaphysics are the nature of God, the immortality or mortality of the soul, the existence of matter, and freedom of the will, among others.

Mind: in Hobbes' materialist philosophy, mind is nothing more than actions of the brain in thinking, desiring, deliberating, and other functions performed in conceiving.

Monarch/y: one of the three forms of government to which Hobbes refers in *Leviathan*. Monarchy is specific in being political rule by one person, the monarch as a king or queen, having absolute power. While not all historical monarchies are government systems with absolute power, Hobbes argues for the absolute power of all forms of government.

Monism: a metaphysical position contrasted with materialism and idealism (or immaterialism) in which an adherent claims that there is one and only one substance or reality. Baruch Spinoza was a monist in arguing that God is the ultimate and only reality in the Universe.

Necessity: with respect to truth, necessity is a characteristic of statements whose contradictions are logically impossible. That is, a necessary truth is true in all conceivable times, places, and cases. With respect to beings, a necessary being is one that has no beginning, has no end, and is infinite. For Hobbes, the only necessary being is God.

Nominalism: rejects that universals exist as more than mere abstractions. A nominalist holds the position that real existence is all and only individual things. Hobbes was a nominalist. See also *Universals*.

Person: distinguished as, as well as from, a natural human being, a person is one whose words or actions are represented by himself or herself or by another. Hobbes therefore makes a distinction between artificial and natural persons. A natural person represents herself. An artificial person represents others. In addition, a natural person may represent another natural person in addition to herself. Also, an artificial person is the creation of natural persons, especially with reference to the sovereign of the political state, who is an artificial person who represents the words and actions of subjects. See also *Representation, Authorization*, and *Sovereign*.

Personation: to personate is to represent the words or actions of another; to be a representative.

Philosophy: for Hobbes, philosophy is more akin to science than to processes of abstract reasoning to which the term has often been applied from the nineteenth century to the present. In Hobbes' time (and it is possible that Hobbes is the last Western philosopher to so use the term), philosophy is inseparably connected to scientific (both experiential as well as geometrical) reasoning about any number or variety of things.

Primary Qualities: primary qualities, in modern philosophy, are the characteristics of a physical object that belong specifically to it and that cannot be separated from it either in fact or in principle. For example, motion, figure, rest, and number are primary qualities. They are the qualities of an object that are not dependent upon the perceptions or condition of the perceptual organs of the perceiver. See also *Secondary Qualities*.

Rationalism: an epistemological (theory of knowledge) position taken primarily but not solely by Continental Rationalists of the early modern period (seventeenth and eighteenth centuries). It is the position that while some ideas arise through experience, there are some that are innate that serve as a foundation for all other knowledge. In addition, a Rationalist holds the position, like the British Empiricists, that knowledge is characterized by mathematical certainty, and anything short of that is not strict knowledge. See also *Empiricism*.

Representation, Political: based on Hobbes' concept of authorization, political representation is characterized by the notion that a sovereign or sovereign body will act on behalf of those who are represented.

Schools, the: the Scholastic philosophers and their philosophical teachings, which built largely upon the authority of Aristotle's writings.

Secondary Qualities: secondary qualities are, generally speaking, the qualities of an object that are not inherent in the object itself but instead perceiver dependent. So, for example, the color or taste of an object is a secondary quality that is caused indirectly by the action of the primary qualities of the object as they impinge on the senses of a perceiver. See also *Primary Qualities*.

Self-Interest: the tendency, according to Hobbes, of human beings to look out first and foremost for their own interests and more specifically for what they believe is good for themselves. In this belief, some commentators hold the position that Hobbes was an egoist (see also *Egoism*) and that in particular he was a psychological egoist (see also *Egoism, Psychological*). This, however, has not been conclusively established, and some commentators believe that, instead, Hobbes' adherence to egoism does not rise to the level usually characterizing the description of psychological egoism.

Sin: failure to adhere to laws, including laws of nature (see also *Law of Nature*) or laws established by a sovereign. Sin is broader than a crime, as the desire or intention to break a law is also a sin, but it does not become a crime until those desires or intentions are acted upon (at which point it is both a sin and crime).

Soul: usually identified as an immaterial substance that is the essence or center of a human being that is separable from the body, Thomas Hobbes held that the soul is a material thing and nothing more than the actions, processes, or motions of the brain. As such, the soul is not immortal and does not continue to exist after a person dies.

Sovereign: a political representative in the person of an individual human being or a group who acts by authorization of subjects. In Hobbes' system of political thought, the sovereign receives by agreement of people in the state of nature all the rights of individuals to use as she, he, or they see fit to promote and ensure civil peace.

Spirit: usually this would be identified with either an immaterial human soul or the third person of the Christian Trinity, the Holy Spirit. For the Holy Spirit, Hobbes rejects the traditional understanding of the Trinity and describes the Spirit in untraditional ways by leaning on other meanings of the word. For example, the word "Spirit" can also mean the mood of a time, as one may say "the Spirit of the Enlightenment."

Stoic(s/ism): a philosophical way of life as well as a theory developed in ancient Greece and Rome in which adherents believe, and act according to the notion, that simplicity and endurance in the face of hardship or difficulty is a means by which to exhibit virtue.

Substance: an individual thing, or that which comprises reality. For Hobbes, all substance is matter. See also *Materialism*.

Summum Bonum: the ultimate good; the object of ultimate desire. For Hobbes, there is no *summum bonum* to which all human beings either ought or do strive.

Summum Malum: the ultimate evil; the object of ultimate aversion. For Hobbes, the *summum malum* is death, which all rational persons avoid or prefer to avoid.

Teleology: the notion that there is a goal or purpose to life, action, or existence on the whole to which all things strive. A teleological principle is one in which the ultimate good is considered to be the reason for all voluntary actions of sentient or rational beings and one that explains the movement of inanimate things toward their completion or perfection.

Universals: properties or essences that apply to all things of a certain type. So the properties of one triangle will apply to all triangles, for example, and justice is something that exists above particular just actions as more than a mere abstraction of these particulars. Hobbes is a nominalist, so he holds the position that universals are only names, and more specifically they are nouns that denote a number of things with similar characteristics. So two people are individuals, but "human" belongs to both of them.

REFERENCES

Aquinas, Thomas. *The Summa Theologiae of Saint Thomas Aquinas: Latin-English Edition. Volume I: Prima Pars, Q. 1–64*. Scotts Valley, CA: CreateSpace, 2008.

Aristotle. *Metaphysics*. Translated by W. D. Ross. Oxford: Clarendon Press, 1924.

—————. *Nicomachean Ethics*. Translated by Terence Irwin. 2nd ed. Indianapolis, IN: Hackett, 1999.

Augustine. *City of God*. Translated by Henry Bettenson. New York: Penguin Classics, 2003.

—————. *Confessions*. Translated by Maria Boulding. New York: New York City Press, 2001.

Berkeley, George. *A Treatise Concerning the Principles of Human Knowledge*. Edited by Kenneth Winkler. Indianapolis, IN: Hackett, 1982.

Calkins, Mary Whiton, ed. *Metaphysical Writings: Thomas Hobbes*. La Salle, IL: Open Court, 1905.

Cicero. *Pro Caecina XXV*. Edited and translated by H. Grose Hodge. Cambridge, MA: Harvard University Press, 1927.

Descartes, Rene. *Meditations on First Philosophy*. Edited by Donald A. Cress. 3rd ed. Indianapolis, IN: Hackett, 1993.

Gert, Bernard. *Hobbes: Prince of Peace*. Malden, MA: Polity Press, 2010.

—————. "Hobbes's Psychology." In *Cambridge Companion to Hobbes*, edited by Tom Sorell, 157–74. New York: Cambridge University Press, 1996.

Hobbes, Thomas. *De Cive*. In *Man and Citizen (De Homine and De Cive)*, edited by Bernard Gert, 87–386. Indianapolis, IN: Hackett, 1991.

—————. *Leviathan*. Edited by Richard E. Flathman and David Johnston. New York: W. W. Norton, 1997.

—————. *Leviathan*. Edited by C. B. Macpherson. New York: Penguin Classics, 1982.

—————. *Leviathan*. Edited by Noel Malcolm. Oxford, UK: Oxford University Press, 2014.

—————. *Leviathan*. Edited by Michael Oakeshott. London: Basil Blackwell, 1950.

—————. *Leviathan. The English Works of Thomas Hobbes, Vol. III*. Edited by William Molesworth. London: John Bohn, 1839–1845.

—————. *Leviathan: With Selected Variants from the Latin Edition of 1668*. Edited by Edwin Curley. Indianapolis, IN: Hackett, 1994.

—————. *Leviathan, or The matter, forme, and power of a common wealth, eccleasiasticall and civil* (Green Dragon at the St. Paul's Church-yard, 1651). Reprinted in The Pelican Classics series, edited by C. B. Macpherson. New York: Penguin, 1968.

—————. "Questions Concerning Liberty, Necessity, and Chance." In *The English Works of Thomas Hobbes, Vol. V*. Edited by William Molesworth. London: John Bohn, 1841.

Kremer, Elmar J., and Michael J. Latzer, eds. *The Problem of Evil in Early Modern Philosophy.* Toronto: University of Toronto Press, 2001.

Leibniz, G. W. F. "Monadology." In *Discourse on Metaphysics and Other Essays.* Translated by Daniel Garber and Roger Ariew, 68–81. 9th ed. Indianapolis, IN: Hackett, 1991.

Leijenhorst, Cees. "Sense and Nonsense about Sense: Hobbes and the Aristotelians on Sense Perception and Imagination." In *Cambridge Companion to Hobbes's Leviathan,* edited by Patricia Springborg, 82–107. Cambridge, MA: Cambridge University Press, 2007.

Locke, John. *Essay Concerning Human Understanding.* Edited by Kenneth P. Winkler. Indianapolis, IN: Hackett, 1996.

_____. *Second Treatise of Government.* Edited by C. B. Macpherson. Indianapolis, IN: Hackett, 1980.

Malthus, Thomas. *An Essay on the Principle of Population.* Edited by Philip Appleman. New York: W. W. Norton, 2003.

Martinich, A. P. *A Hobbes Dictionary.* Cambridge, MA: Blackwell, 1995.

McKeon, Richard, ed. *Introduction to Aristotle.* New York: Modern Library, 1947.

Paine, Thomas. *The Age of Reason, Part I.* New York: Modern Library, 1925.

_____. *The Age of Reason.* http://www.ushistory.org/paine/reason/singlehtml.htm.

_____. "The Rights of Man." In *Common Sense and Other Political Writings,* edited by Nelson F. Adkins, 73–151. Indianapolis, IN: Bobbs-Merrill, 1953.

Plato. *Republic.* Translated by G. M. A. Grube. Revised by C. D. C. Reeve. Indianapolis, IN: Hackett, 1992.

Romano, Carlin. "The Toxic History of Philosophy's Racism." *Chronicle of Higher Education,* September 8, 2014. http://chronicle.com/article/The-Toxic-History-of/148603.

Rowe, William L. *God and the Problem of Evil.* Malden, MA: Blackwell, 2001.

Sommerville, Johann P. *Thomas Hobbes: Political Ideas in Historical Context.* New York: St. Martin's Press, 1992.

Sorell, Tom, ed. *The Cambridge Companion to Hobbes.* Cambridge: Cambridge University Press, 1996.

Spinoza, Baruch. *Ethics.* Edited by Seymour Felman. Translated by Samuel Shirely. Indianapolis, IN: Hackett, 1992.

Tooley, Michael. "The Problem of Evil." *Stanford Encyclopedia of Philosophy.* http://plato.stanford.edu/entries/evil.

Van Inwagen, Peter. "The Powers of Rational Beings: Freedom of the Will." In *Metaphysics.* Boulder, CO: Westview Press, 2014.

Voltaire. *Candide; or Optimism: A New Translation, Backgrounds, Criticism.* Edited and translated by Robert M. Adams. New York: W. W. Norton, 1991.

Zarka, Yves Charles. "First Philosophy and the Foundation of Knowledge." In *The Cambridge Companion to Thomas Hobbes,* edited by Tom Sorell, 62–85. New York: Cambridge University Press, 1996.

INDEX

Abraham, 62, 154, 214, 230, 231, 280
absurdity, 26, 27, 31, 73
accidents, 22, 26–27, 47
actor, 89, 90, 90n68, 92, 109, 161, 186.
  See also author
anarchy, 105, 190, 267. *See also* war,
  condition of
Angel, 207, 210, 218
anger, defined, 33
appetite(s), 23, 31–33, 35, 37, 87, 194, 266
Aquinas, St. Thomas, 8n3, 21, 21n15,
  44n34, 58n38, 119n28, 176n60
aristocracy, 105, 106, 108, 109, 134
Aristotle, 7, 8n3, 21, 21n15, 27n22, 35n28,
  36n30, 54n36, 58n38, 64n41, 65,
  85, 95, 95n1, 105n15, 118n26, 121,
  194n73, 194n74, 255, 260, 261, 262,
  263, 265, 267, 268, 272
assembly, 98–101, 104–5, 107–9, 128–29,
  144, 162, 178, 228, 244, 248
atheists(s), 191, 191n68
author, 90–92, 92n68, 100–101, 109, 115,
  120, 127, 148, 203. *See also* actor
authority, 90, 100, 123, 150, 154
  authority, appeal to, 21n15
  of books, 20, 29, 141, 150n49, 259
authorization, 89–92, 96n2, 118n24, 136
aversion, defined, 31

baptism, 242–43
belief, defined, 11, 38, 64, 154, 157n51, 256
Bellarmine, Cardinal, 239, 250n17
body, defined, 205
  incorporeal, 22, 205–7

Caesar, Julius, 10, 178
capital punishment, 168
Catholicism, distrust of, 11n7
censorship, 101n8
charity, 74, 185, 185n65
Church, 228–29, 204
Church of England, 202

Cicero, 21, 21n15, 27, 89, 121, 136, 136n41,
  144, 261, 268, 270
Civil War, English, xv n10, 14n8
Coke, Edward, 147n45
command, defined, 139
commonwealth (*Leviathan*), 49, 80, 96, 119
  author of, 101
  as artificial man, 3, 119
  by acquisition, 93, 97, 112
  by institution, 93, 97, 98–104, 112
  consequences of, 99–103
  defense of, 122–23
  dissolution of, 172–78
  fundamental law of, 155
  generation of, 96
  infirmities of, 173–75
  injury of, 83, 128, 157n51, 165
  kinds of, 105–6
  leagues between, 128
  liberty of, 120
  origins of, 62, 98–99
  power of, 49
compassion, 34
compatibilism, 72n52, 119n27
competition, 55, 68, 95, 282
conscience, 38, 162, 173, 220
consent, 96, 100
  of children, 113, 113n17, 113n18
contempt, defined, 31
contract, 74
  between sovereigns, 124
  between subject and sovereign, 121n32
  between subjects, 137
Cosmological Argument, 58n38, 61
counsel, defined, 139
counselors, choice of, 187
covenant, 74, 77–78, 80, 99
  voiding/violating, 76, 81, 100, 116,
    122, 157
  with God, 63, 154, 209, 232, 236
  See also contract
crime, 156, 162, 165

293